MW00807846

38° NORTH LATITUDE | GSM

CONNECTIVE TISSUES

Ground Rules and Dialogues of the Kenan Twelve 2001-2016

Catharine Killien
Claire Casstevens

Danielle Alexander
Gwen McGinn

Spencer Haynsworth Woodcock
Lauren Hackney

Jim Richardson
Maria Bninski

Danielle Willkens
Paul Golisz

Polly Smith Finn
Hannah Barefoot

PETER WALDMAN

A Note to Readers

The Word Made Flesh is an operation commenced in *Lessons From The Lawn* in the front and back cover collages deconstructed below framing 28 PLATES as Mirrors for the Moon. Accompanied by the texts of Surveyors, Nomads, and Lunatics they posit the epistemological imperative to permit heuristic narratives to be read as articulated urban stage sets for the play of human artifice and the preconditions of nature.

ELEMENTS: 1-4
1. Surveyor: Thomas Jefferson, Plan of the Dome Room, Rotunda, 1819. Special Collections Library, University of Virginia.
2. Nomad: Caravaggio, Narcissus, 1599. Galleria Nazionale d'Arte Antica, Roma, Italy
3. Lunatic: Eric Osmundson Monacelli, 2001, School of Architecture, University of Virginia. Photo Credit: Ivan Marbri
4. Surveyor, again: Author, Section of Eric Goodwin Passage, 2004.

CONJUNCTIONS: 5-6

Here in *Connective Tissues*, this book continues the same didactic operation of incremental reconstruction of the multi-layered collages derived now from each of the Kenan Fellow essays and recomposed in dialogues by Kenan Professor Peter Waldman.

The Ground Rules sets the tension between the singularity of instrumental digits and the collective aspiration of a primal communal garden, denied again and again ever since Eden. Each responsive connective tissue by the author first sequences elemental components aggregating into one hybrid collage derived from the Kenan Fellow essays. We commence with Catharine Killien "On Two Hands and Ten Digits" (2010) and then in response Claire Casstevens "On the Academical Garden" (2016). Human instrumentality is innate if not primal as we suckle, then playing out in our unique finger-prints in the act of making, onto finger painting, in the sandbox, in molding clay, cooking, counting numbers, making music as in a five-finger exercise and eventually in the higher art of script. Responding to the primacy of our ten digits collectively on our two hands, Jefferson used the ten pavilions in two colonnades to frame the space of the open-ended common ground known as the Lawn.

We juxtapose this beginning ground rule of human instrumentality and singularity of Killien with Casstevens 's "The Academical Garden" which precedes the urban project of the Academical Village. In western culture, specifically Genesis, the precondition of Eden soon evolves into a paradise which has been lost. Thereafter, with knowledge gained by hunters and gatherers, pastoral settings eventually become the dominant paradigms of the city chronicled by the Duc du Berry and the Limbourg Brothers. Born with the instrumentality of human digits, we soon respond to Semper's mandate: "the first architectural act is to break the ground"; by which some believe is meant "to plant a seed" as the agricultural imperative precedes the need for enduring institutions some call architecture.

The following five chapters of paired essays in dialogue yield elemental lessons and hybrid collages grounded on self-reflected vellums after each of the connective tissues, following the implications of The Word Made Flesh.

Chapter One develops the instrumentality and resultant consequences of the Academical Village through Specifications for Construction: "Tools" (2016) by Danielle Alexander and "Remediation of the Grounds: Roots and Routes" (2014) by Gwen McGinn.

Chapter Two on themes of immediacy and estrangement, traces the temporal agenda of construction site first of the Academical Village by Spencer Haynsworth Woodcock (2004). "Inventories" (2010) is didactically followed by Lauren Hackney's essay on "Chandigarh's Field of Constructed Hallucinations", where time is collapsed between memory and amnesia and by topographic and archeological imaginations.

Chapter Three presents a scaler shift from the Garden as on-going Construction site to the enduring City read by two Kenan Fellows when they were also Carlo Pelliccia Visiting Scholars in residence in Rome measuring the consequences for all before and after the Summer Solstice. Jim Richardson, from Pittsburgh and Nag's Head, journeyed East to dwell in the "Chiaroscuro of the Pantheon" (2006) while Maria Bninski from Poland journeyed West to recount the mythical foundation of Rome as a Spatial Tale of Origin revealed at the sill of "One Good Window" (2008), becoming a Table of Contents surveying the Via Montserrat.

Chapter Four develops a collage as a Mirror for the Moon derived from "The Curious Houses and Collections of Jefferson and Soane" (2008) by Danielle Willkens interrogating the contemporary development of two lifetime projects: Monticello and Lincoln Inn Fields, thereafter contrasted by Paul Golisz with Jefferson's final house project of "Poplar Forest as A Table of Contents" (2015) echoing with intensity back to Bninski's Rome.

Chapter Five concludes these collages as hybrids of spatial tales of origin and the necessity of eschatological renewal. Documented by their deconstructed components, first by coming full circle from Killien, Polly Smith Finn's introspective essay on "Collage " posits the prescient utility of origins, her own recounting of adjacencies at the thickened edge of Bachelard's reflections on clear and deep waters. Finally, Hannah Barefoot's essay on "Leaves of Grass" is in dialogue with Walt Whitman which celebrates *Death Made Legible* as a necessary requisite for eschatology, renewal, and resilience for an *Architecture of Continuity* founded in the *AA Files* of Peter Carl and Dalibor Veseley and in Rebecca Solnit's *A Field Guide for Getting Lost*, and found.

The Epilogue serves not so much as a summation, but a catalyst for an extended adventure advocated by Jef7rey Hildner as one of the author's first students at Princeton. Hildner grounds the Jefferson project in the Daedalus project of the labyrinth revealed by Joseph Campbell in *The Hero of a Thousand Faces* and liberates these connective tissues rather as springboards for heroic imaginations.

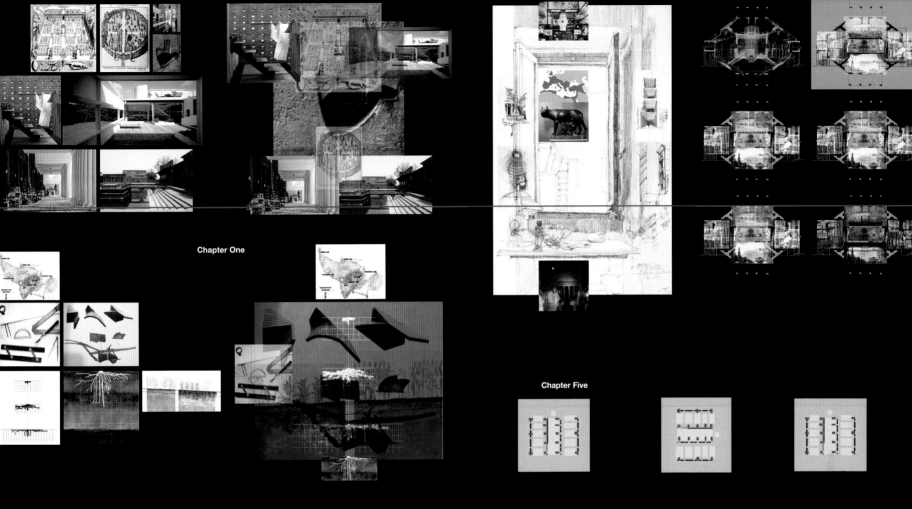

Chapter One

Chapter Five

Chapter Two

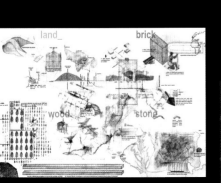

land_

brick

wood

stone

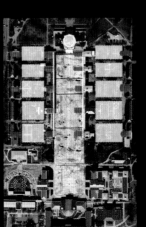

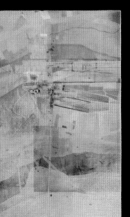

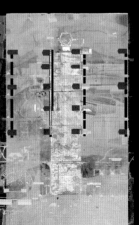

38° NORTH LATITUDE | GSM

solnit   jefferson   cervantes

borges *a garden of walking paths*

daedalus homer   milton   saigyo

CONNECTIVE TISSUES

Ten Essays by University of Virginia Kenan Fellows 2001-2016

PETER WALDMAN

The End and the Beginning
BY WISŁAWA SZYMBORSKA, TRANSLATED BY JOANNA TRZECIAK

After every war
someone has to clean up.
Things won't
straighten themselves up, after all.

Someone has to push the rubble
to the side of the road,
so the corpse-filled wagons
can pass.

Someone has to get mired
in scum and ashes,
sofa springs,
splintered glass,
and bloody rags.

Someone has to drag in a girder
to prop up a wall.
Someone has to glaze a window,
rehang a door.

Photogenic it's not,
and takes years.
All the cameras have left
for another war.

We'll need the bridges back,
and new railway stations.
Sleeves will go ragged
from rolling them up.

Someone, broom in hand,
still recalls the way it was.
Someone else listens
and nods with unsevered head.
But already there are those nearby
starting to mill about
who will find it dull.

From out of the bushes
sometimes someone still unearths
rusted-out arguments
and carries them to the garbage pile.

Those who knew
what was going on here
must make way for
those who know little.
And less than little.
And finally as little as nothing.

In the grass that has overgrown
causes and effects,
someone must be stretched out
blade of grass in his mouth
gazing at the clouds.

Ale Książki (And Yet the Books)
BY CZESŁAW MILOSZ

Ale Książki

Ale książki będą na półkach, prawdziwe istoty,
Które zjawiły się raz, świeże, jeszcze wilgotne,
Niby lśniące kasztany pod drzewem w jesieni,
I dotykane, pieszczone trwać zaczęły
Mimo łun na horyzoncie, zamków wylatujących w powietrze,
Plemion w pochodzie, planet w ruchu.
Jesteśmy - mówiły, nawet kiedy
wydzierano z nich karty
Albo litery zlizywał buzujący płomień,
O ileż trwalsze od nas, których ułomne ciepło
Stygnie razem z pamięcią, rozprasza się, ginie.
Wyobrażam sobie ziemię kiedy mnie nie będzie
I nic, żadnego ubytku, dalej dziwowisko,
Suknie kobiet, mokry jaśmin, pieśń w dolinie.
Ale książki będą na półkach, dobrze urodzone,
Z ludzi, choć też z jasności, wysokości.

And Yet the Books

And yet the books will be there on the shelves, separate beings,
That appeared once, still wet
As shining chestnuts under a tree in autumn,
And, touched, coddled, began to live
In spite of fires on the horizon, castles blown up,
Tribes on the march, planets in motion.
"We are, " they said, even as their pages
Were being torn out, or a buzzing flame
Licked away their letters. So much more durable
Than we are, whose frail warmth
Cools down with memory, disperses, perishes.
I imagine the earth when I am no more:
Nothing happens, no loss, it's still a strange pageant,
Women's dresses, dewy lilacs, a song in the valley.
Yet the books will be there on the shelves, well born,
Derived from people, but also from radiance, heights.

Woda (Water)
BY WISŁAWA SZYMBORSKA

Woda

Kropla deszczu mi spadła na rękę,
utoczona z Gangesu i Nilu,
z wniebowziętego szronu na wąsikach foki,
z wody rozbitych dzbanów w miastach Ys i Tyr.
Na moim wskazującym palcu
Morze Kaspijskie jest morzem otwartym
a Pacyfik potulnie wpływa do Rudawy
tej samej, co fruwała chmurką nad Paryżem
w roku siedemset sześćdziesiątym czwartym
siódmego maja o trzeciej nad ranem.
Nie starczy ust do wymówienia
przelotnych imion twoich, wodo.
Musiałbym cię nazwać we wszystkich językach
wypowiadając naraz wszystkie samogłoski
i jednocześnie milczeć - dla jeziora,
które nie doczekało jakiejkolwiek nazwy
i nie ma go na ziemi - jako i na niebie
gwiazdy odbitej w nim.
Ktoś tonął, ktoś o ciebie wołał umierając.
Było to dawno i było to wczoraj.
Domy gasiłaś, domy porywałaś
jak drzewa, lasy jak miasta.
Byłaś w chrzcielnicach i wannach kurtyzan.
w pocałunkach, całunach.
Gryząc kamienie, karmiąc tęcze.
W pocie i rosie piramid, bzów.
Jakie to lekkie w kropli deszczu.
Jak delikatnie dotyka mnie świat.
Cokolwiek gdziekolwiek kiedykolwiek się działo
spisane jest na wodzie babel.

Water

A raindrop fell on my hand
crafted from the Ganges and the Nile,
from the ascended frost of a seal's whiskers,
from the water in broken pots in the cities of Ys and Tyre.
On my index finger
the Caspian Sea isn't landlocked,
and the Pacific flows meekly into the Rudava;
the one that flew in a cloud over Paris
in seventeen-sixty-four
on the seventh of May at three in the morning.
There are not enough lips to pronounce
your transient names. O water.
I would have to say them in every language
pronouncing all the vowels at once,
at the same time keeping silent – for the sake of a lake
that waited in vain for a name,
and is no longer on earth – as it is in the heavens,
whose stars are no longer reflected in it.
Someone was drowning; someone dying
called out for you. That was long ago and yesterday.
You extinguished houses; you carried them off
like trees, forests like cities.
You were in baptismal fonts and in the bathtubs of courtesans,
in kisses, in shrouds.
Eating away at stones, fueling rainbows.
In the sweat and dew of pyramids and lilacs
How light all this is in a raindrop.
How delicately the world touches me.
Whenever, wherever, whatever has happened
Is written on the water of Babel.

TABLE OF CONTENTS

Catharine Killien is an architect at the Miller Hull Partnership in Seattle, WA where her work has focused on adaptive reuse and educational projects. She received her Master in Architecture from the University of Virginia in 2013 and has a Bachelor of Arts in Architecture from the University of Washington.

Claire Casstevens is a landscape designer at OLIN in Philadelphia. Following studies in art history and anthropology at Vassar College, she received her Master of Landscape Architecture degree from the University of Virginia.

Dani Alexander is a passionate designer working to transform the public realm to be more equitable, resilient, and compelling. She is Founding Principal of Studio AKA, a landscape architecture and urban design practice based in Washington, DC.

Gwendolyn Dora McGinn is an Associate at Studio Outside Landscape Architecture in Dallas, Texas. She graduated from the University of Virginia with a Master Degree in Landscape Architecture and holds a BFA from the Rhode Island School of Design.

Spencer Haynsworth Woodcock is the Director of Marketing and Business Development at Chiang | O'Brien Architects. Spencer holds a bachelor of arts degree from St. John's College in Annapolis, MD and a master of architecture and landscape architecture from the University of Virginia.

Lauren Hackney is Senior Associate at CMG Landscape Architecture in San Francisco. Her design work focuses on cultural landscapes and their dynamic issues of place: community, culture, temporality, and ecology. Lauren received graduate and undergraduate degrees in Landscape Architecture and Architecture from UVA.

Jim Richardson, AIA, LEED AP BD+C is a licensed architect and Senior Associate at VMDO Architects, where he enjoys working on a diverse set of projects that are carefully made and valued in the communities where his work is perceived as perceptive, opportunistic, and inspired.

Maria Bninski was an undergraduate Religious Studies major when she attended Peter Waldman's Lessons of the Lawn course in 2004. She is now an associate at VMDO Architects and lives in Charlottesville, Virginia with her husband and three young daughters.

Dr Danielle S. Willkens is an architectural designer, historian, and educator. She was the 2015 Society of Architectural Historians' H. Allen Brooks Travelling Fellow and her manuscript The Transatlantic Design Network is in development with the University of Virginia Press.

Paul Golisz is a licensed architect practicing in New York City where his professional work focuses on cultural and educational projects. His current research is interested in how architecture relates to, and approaches, the concept of Nature.

Polly Smith Finn is an architect working as a Project Manager at Pursley Dixon Architecture in Charlotte, North Carolina. She received an Masters in Architecture from the University of Virginia. Polly majored in art history and studio art at Washington and Lee University and worked as a development associate at the National Gallery of Art in Washington, DC before pursuing architecture.

Hannah Barefoot is a landscape designer at Surface 678 in Durham, NC. She completed her undergraduate degree in English and Studio Art with a concentration in Printmaking at the University of Virginia. After a year as an Aunspaugh Fellow in the Studio Art Department at UVA she stayed in Charlottesville, receiving her Masters of Landscape Architecture degree from UVA.

Jef7rey Hildner is an award-winning architect, painter, and writer—author of eight books, including VISUAL EF9ECTS: Architecture and the Chess Game of Form & Story. His work appears in JAE and GA Houses. He earned his undergraduate and graduate degrees from Princeton University.

Trouble in Paradise
Robin Dripps

The School of Architecture at the University of Virginia is equally inspired and encumbered by its relation to Thomas Jefferson. As the commanding intellect behind the American experiment with democracy, Jefferson shaped a nation. As an amateur architect he understood more than his contemporaries the powerful potential for spatial organization to support profound social, political and cultural aspirations. Jefferson was also an experimental farmer, plant explorer, and gardener who understood the social as well as the instrumental value of land. The convergence of these multiple framings for constructing the world is a constant reminder of the purpose of architecture, here understood in its most expansive definition: That all of this comes together in his Academical Village is testament to a powerfully synthetic mind. Jefferson set the goals by which we ought to direct our actions and gave a superb example of how this could work. But how is this able to work within our significantly changed contemporary context? There have been many attempts to replicate Jefferson's work. But this misses the point. The Academical Village, as its name ought to suggest, is an idea about how people relate to one another and how this polity engages the natural world. Jefferson's village was as much a political critique as it was template for building the new nation. To extract lessons from the particularity of this place will only prove valuable when the instrumental and historical idiosyncrasies can be absorbed into a more abstract spatial narrative. This is the premise for Peter Waldman's course, "Lessons from the Lawn" where both Waldman's and his students' inventive readings have the potential to reveal hidden opportunities and problematic issues within a place that was thought to be well known.

Andre Gide observed that fiction is history that has yet to happen and history is fiction come true. This would be an appropriate way to understand the methods of Peter Waldman and his Kenan fellows who look closely at this place and invent fictions/histories that have the potential to be even more real- sometimes rivaling or even surpassing the original in terms of how to understand a present that in its intense immediacy is obscured.

The work shown here builds explicitly or implicitly on the phenomenological theories of Bachelard, Heidegger, Eliade and Norberg-Schulz where the structure of the human figure becomes a spatial abstraction capable of positioning and orienting critical human relations to one another and then to a larger political, social, and ecological context. The implicated relations (centrality, edges, frontality, vertically and interiority, etc.) are the basis for students to make substantial propositions about matters of import that might have been obscured by the overabundance of history. At the same time, however, this approach establishes an armature for the particularities of history, the facts that otherwise exist as random events stranded in an apparently chaotic context.

What is not a product of the phenomenology cohort is the constant presence of landscape, nature and garden that runs through so many of these essays. Perhaps this is due to the interwoven presence of a landscape architecture program that has for decades essayed the problematic relations between humans and the natural world. Intense discourse among faculty and students has revealed exciting possibilities for reciprocal relationships between ideas of order within architecture's spatial logics that suggest counter hypotheses about the structure of the land. Operating within these ideas, architecture is seen as something emerging from its natural context. The corollary of landform structure is then recognized as a hypothetical construct between the facts of the ground and the

human's desire for order. Now it is possible to understand Jefferson's Lawn less as a building and more as an inhabited garden: Edenic, wild, productive, and confrontational all at the same time. This aligns well with the writing of Leo Marx in The Machine in the Garden. Marx finds two very different descriptions of the North American continent made by its early European settlers: A bountiful garden of Eden providing all that was ever desired, and a confusing, disorienting and often terrifying wilderness.

The obvious reverence for Jefferson's Academic Village that Professor Waldman has engendered in his students is to be lauded as are their inventive tales. However, it also is worth note how these essays find themselves within a difficult intellectual and environmental context. From our contemporary situation, the heroic ambitions of the enlightenment project can now be seen as a cautionary warning about placing the human so confidently at the metaphorical center of things.

I wonder about the looming presence of the Anthropocene. Is this the end game of the Enlightenment project? Unless we maintain the Enlightenment's hegemony of the human as sole arbiter, the Anthropocene has to be understood as a dismal construct that bears witness to the premature optimism of the Enlightenment.

Perhaps a fictive reread of Jefferson's interventions during the framing of the Constitution, now coming from the perspective of Jefferson the, conscientious farmer, might reveal the possibility of a more inclusive Constitution. Bruno Latour's "Parliament of Things" comes to mind with its much larger cohort of beings, including those pesky animals and other living entities that together with humans would better represent the interests of the planet. This opens up opportunities to re-engage Jefferson in order to find the gaps or fissures where intervention could generate new directions better able to contend with a world that Jefferson could never imagine.

Robin Dripps teaches within the studio design sequence, lectures on architectural theory, and directs a seminar on the relationship between design intent and detail manifestation. The ACSA honored her teaching with its Distinguished Professorship Award in 1992. Educated at Princeton (BA in architecture) and the University of Pennsylvania (M. Arch), she has been writing and lecturing on the structure of myth as a fundamental basis for architectural form.

Pan and Proteus
Michael Lee

"He who cannot attract Pan approaches Proteus in vain." Pico della Mirandola: Conclusiones nongentae (1486)

When the Oxford art historian Edgar Wind paired Pan with Proteus in one of his most widely read essays on Renaissance art, he was seeking among other things to characterize human wisdom's endless quest for the One inherent in the Many. The essays in this volume, distilled from Professor Peter Waldman's long engagement with his "Lessons from the Lawn" project, allow us to sit in on a master class devoted to this perennial endeavor. For these narratives, comprising both word and image, trace a myriad of intersecting themes running riotously across, through, and beneath the core of Thomas Jefferson's Academical Village. Together, they unfold the deceptively serene One of the Lawn's cascading turf panels into the joyfully cacophonous Many of Proteus's individual forms and voices. And once unfolded, they invite the reader to hear this chorus as a deeper, and necessarily more complicated, manifestation of the One—and to catch a glimpse of the elusive Pan who perhaps still animates these spaces. Professor Waldman's Connective Tissues is, therefore, an eminently Orphic pursuit. It is the endeavor of a poet-philosopher and his students to reveal the invisible structures that run through the surficial visible world. One is to charm the animal, vegetative, and human kingdoms alike with the musicality of their wisdom; and the other to insist on recognizing dissonance and silence, the forgotten partners of harmony, as coequal elements in the Lawn's sonic fabric. Positioned at the eminence of the Lawn, Jefferson's Rotunda is the opening statement of these Orphic mysteries, evoking that other distant monument which served a Pantheon for the gods of a now fallen Republic. Originally enclosed on only two sides by its architectonic frame, the Lawn began with this sense of Pan the All in its cultivation of a fully developed humanity, and stepped down toward a vista onto a wider world ruled by a different version of Pan. A wild one. It continued to the horizon as if to revive an ancient yet newly elevated pastoralism beyond all borders, linking this vision with the pursuits of an ideal intellectual community: the cultivation of the true, the good, and the beautiful. The Lawn was thus suspended between two modalities of the One, each directed equally toward a pastoral world. Apollo and Pan: they both taught the shepherds. There is a complementarity to the Orphic gods, such that their attributes support and reinforce one another. Protector of herdsmen and shepherds, Apollo is also the lawgiver who found new towns and institutions (such as universities). Himself a twin, he is a deity especially suited to the Lawn's twin-facing worlds of the pastoral and the urban. Pan is the man-goat who induces panic among the wild groves but also the poet-musician who taught Daphnis to play the pipes. He animates that quiet unease beneath the placidness of the Lawn and serves as a reminder of the unbroken link between our highest aspirations and our embodied animality. By opening the Apollonian world of Jefferson's Pantheon library, a unity enclosed within itself, onto the unruly realm of Pan, the Lawn partakes of this unstable duality. And as it does so, it launches the never-ending project of creating a new Republic to rival and outshine the one that rose and fell in the ancient Mediterranean world. Jefferson's vision for an American Pastoralism is a familiar theme, but Connective Tissues is eloquent testimony that it may not yet be fully exhausted in its implications. As a microcosm of that vision, taking the form of an ideal academic community, the University of Virginia Lawn encapsulates in a single gesture the originary settling of a landscape misunderstood as nature in its "wild" state. As a foundational myth made real, the Lawn embodies the notion that order has been wrested from perceived wilderness. In that respect it bears the imprint of its Enlightenment origins, beginning perhaps with Adorno

and Horkheimer, but aided by many others. We have been made aware of the dark side of an isolated rationality and instrumentality that emerged as an attenuated version of the Enlightenment project. However, the Enlightenment was never simply about rationalism. Its twin went by several names, including sensibility, Empfindsamkeit, and Sturmund Drang, among others, and we owe to Enlightenment thinkers the birth of aesthetics as a disciplined investigation of embodied reason as well as the cultivation of beauty within living communities. Above all, enlightenment (in its broader, lower-case version) was a focused effort to unfetter human freedom toward untested possibilities, but with the discipline of Apollo as its guide and inspiration. As the first academic community in the New World set in a designed landscape, Jefferson's Lawn recalls an ancient version of this more modest form of enlightenment: the school of Epicurus. This philosophical academy, like Jefferson's university, was set in a garden that served as both home and symbol of an intentional community. Located just outside the city, it was a space both within and apart from the world, existing physically and conceptually in parallel with it. From that small distance could emerge a protected and reflective space, one which might operate critically upon the world from which it was slightly removed. The similarly domestic atmosphere of the Lawn belies a more complicated history of unrest, of course, and its gardens were tended at first by enslaved people rather than by students learning object lessons. Nonetheless, the critical space between Apollo and Pan subtended by the Lawn has made possible an education of the Epicurean sort, even if that process has been disappointingly slow at times.

The essays in Connective Tissues are persuasive evidence that Professor Waldman has not only understood but also carried out the form of education the Lawn sets forth as a challenge. In this sense, his "Lessons from the Lawn" echo the words of Mildred Bliss inscribed on the Garden Library at Dumbarton Oaks in Washington, D.C.: "Those responsible for scholarship should remember that the Humanities cannot be fostered by confusing Instruction with Education; that it was my husband and I; as well as it is my wish that the Mediterranean interpretation of the Humanist disciplines shall predominate; that gardens have their place in the Humanist order of life; and that trees are noble elements to be protected by successive generations and are not to be neglected or lightly destroyed."

Much like Goethe, whose immersive Italian journey provided the inspiration to rework the prose of his Iphigenie auf Tauris into lofty iambic pentameter, Connective Tissues captures the peculiar alchemy of the Lawn by which American vernacular has been coaxed to speak Enlightenment classicism. In this sense it is a prolonged meditation on the origins of the Lawn as a New World version of "Mediterranean humanism," the distant echo of a fallen Republic now reborn. But in this new version, with the rigor and freedom of a modern poet, enlightened humanism is no longer confined to the language of the ancients. It is now spoken through multiple voices in the vernacular of the present, mindful of a complicated and layered past, and open to the future. Pan has again been partnered with Proteus.

Michael G. Lee is the Reuben McCorkle Rainey Professor in the History of Landscape Architecture at the University of Virginia. His research explores the intersection of philosophy, literature, and landscape design, with a particular focus on 18th- to 20th-century Germany.

Archeology as Architecture
Shiqiao Li

The perennial geological folds of Appalachia and the depth of Jefferson's intellect have long become Waldman's archaeological sites; an architect with a mind of an archaeologist, Waldman is a tireless custodian of a grand architectural tradition that pays homage to the ground. It is what sustains the primary metaphor of foundation to all aspects of life. Architecture is made of earth's crust: molded, mixed, dried, baked, chiseled and carved out of the ground, cemented together to form spaces and places that hold meanings for long stretches of time, much longer than the duration of a single biological life, so that the existential meanings are recast to be more than it appears to be. Architecture is for eternity, as Christopher Wren sums up for us centuries ago. The materials of architecture have an intriguing similarity to words, which are also long lasting and capable of sustaining longer term meanings. Materials and words are Waldman's favorite digging sites: his hyper-charged synaptic connections light up an infectious imagination that endlessly oscillates between materials and words as they begin to reconstitute architecture. His tool set is unfailingly impressive each time it is deployed. The essays of young scholars assembled here are field notes bearing witness to Waldman's digging at the Lawn. The Grounds of the University of Virginia has a specific meaning in this scheme of things.

Over the past one hundred years, architecture has shifted its principle imagination from one of archaeology to one of climatology. It has been a slow transformation, but looking back now, the difference between the two imaginations is astonishing. Solid architecture has evaporated from the ground into the air, as Karl Marx predicted. We now speak of architecture not as foundations but as flows. First it cracked. Then it floated. Then it reconstituted into blobs, blurs, and clouds. "Atmosphere" is perhaps the best term to capture this new sensibility: temperature, moisture, air movement – both in real and metaphorical terms – are delineated to materialize designs of architecture. Clouds visualize large data sets, usage and movement patterns, shaping the design of architecture distinctively. As a result, structures are painfully engineered away, rather than elegantly engineered in architecture with irregular thin columns and long cantilevers. A parallel development has been a new flatness in architecture, almost willfully framed against the depth of archaeological sites. This is played out in many ways. One is the flatness of architectural drawings through axonometric projections; by removing perspective, one removes distance and depth. Another is surface effects, which can be seen as facade patterns and moving screens; the building envelope seems be necessary and sufficient design layer.

With extraordinary insights and long before flatness reached the current heights, Fredric Jameson described this new flatness, already apparent in Andy Warhol's prints, as a "waning of affect"; here the human psyche works in a very different way: the emotional depth of alienation of modernity gave way to the sensational superficiality of the postmodern burnout. This new aesthetic regime of flows and flatness is precisely what late capitalism embodies: a moving away from depth so that cultures can flow and accumulate, without an apparent purpose, like capital. Circulation and accumulation are the key. The sculptural staircases at Hudson Yard – serving no apparent function yet aestheticizes endless toil without purpose – seems to be one extraordinarily fitting tribute to late capitalism. This late capitalist aesthetic sensibility is appropriately captured by the climatological imagination: the flow and accumulation of moisture, for instance. Thus, we speak of the flood of capital, and the drowning local industries.
Not that this is absolutely unique historically; we have earlier instances of Baroque architecture that had the inclination towards the climatological. Not surprisingly, these were also linked to the flood of money. The rise of commerce in the Medieval European city, the European colonial expansion in the seventeenth century, and the American global capitalism all have their own Baroque moments: the fabulously ornate Gothic church, the unbelievably complex Italian and Spanish Baroque architecture, and the ostentatious ornamentation of the architecture of the American Gilded Age.

This time, with globalization, things are different; we are no longer dealing with just matters of aesthetic delight and tastelessness. The parallel between global capital and the climate is ironic; global capital today is the principle cause of irreversible modifications of the climate that will likely lead to mass extinction of species. Climatology as architecture is the ideology of global capital, seeing architecture and the city not as grounded solidities but as flickering instabilities of business opportunities. Globalization is an enormous production and consumption cycle, hugely profitable because of the unpoliceable negative externalities of human life and the environment resulting from the enormously complicated contracting processes across multiple national legislative frameworks.

Waldman and Virginia is a fortuitous encounter that has an amplified significance in the age of globalization. It is an immense fortune of Virginia that the depth of Jefferson's intellect grasped architecture as a temporal and spatial rootedness for the American idea: the cohesion of a society is, for the first time in human history, through a political ideal rather than through cultural identities. Virginia embodies an architecture that can still serve as the reflexive anchor of life, in an age of flat architecture, and Waldman is a maverick for reaching up to the moon and down into the earth's core, keeping us constantly suspended in disbelief. Of course this an ecologically viable life looks like as architecture, something that the fickle of New York as the world trade city, and the flaunting of Houston as the world oil wealth city gave up too far too quickly.

Waldman shows that we have the wrong globalization: the mind must be global to be both citizens and strangers, and the economy must be local to maintain ecological viability. Not the other way round. For that matter, we have the wrong flatness. Ontology must be flat to augment equality between humans and things, and architecture must be deep to inspire the love of wisdom. Not the other way round. This is perhaps Waldman's principal Lesson of the Lawn: the climatological evaporation of architecture is a cunning ploy of global capital. Only a human race desensitized from paying attention to the ground with all its vibrant and intertwined things can legitimize the practice of using the ground as resource for economic production and for health recuperation. Rather than mining for resources, archaeology digs for knowledge and understanding, giving Waldman his famed fables of origins of architecture at the University of Virginia as The Grounds.

Shiqiao Li is Weedon Professor in Asian Architecture, UVA School of Architecture, where he teaches history and theory, and studios. He was in architectural practice in London and Hong Kong, and published his research in Understanding the Chinese City and Power and Virtue, Architecture and Intellectual Change in England 1650-1730.

Windows in the Forest
Bill Sherman

The many voices in this multi-layered challenge to the constraints of linear narratives and the false clarity of modern reason are products of a unique moment. As a school of architecture broke down the artificial disciplinary structures inscribed on the twentieth century academy, a unique figure, whose fertile imagination inhabits the spaces in between, embarked on the search for a new set of lessons in a hallowed site. With support from the university by way of a scholar of French medieval literature, the Kenan Fellows program enabled a group of students to transgress the traditional boundaries, grounding themselves in both fact and myth. Rediscovering the ground, planting seeds, framing one good window, reveling in spatial complexity and complex singularities, these students of architecture, landscape architecture, and architectural history immersed themselves in the shadowy realms of the forest rather than the familiar vistas of the field.

If we carry forward the latent associations of our names, then Peter Waldman may be understood as the surveyor of the "Wald", exploring a forest of collaged images rather than the perspectival constructions, transparencies and infinite spaces underpinning Western modern architecture. His focus on Serlio's third, satirical scene, frames a world view that revels in the ambiguities of space, time, truth, the animate and inanimate, visible and invisible orders. The first and perhaps only constant is the ground, the marking of which, by bread crumbs or the swing of pickaxe, is the first act of architecture. The enduring sky is known only in fragments by day and night, by reflections and through apertures, beyond the possibility of complete apprehension. The body is the persistent organizing referent, so all that an architect designs, specifies or constructs is imagined to reframe that foundational relationship between body, ground and sky. In this map of the world as an infinitely, irreducibly complex forest of sensory experience, where the literature of imagined mysteries is as meaningful as its tangible reality, the modern divisions of knowledge are wholly inadequate structures.

These explorations unfolded in parallel with a transformation of the culture of the School of Architecture in the first years of the 21st century, with collaborations across the disciplines becoming commonplace, the students pursuing dual degree programs in every possible combination, and even the definition of departmental boundaries in flux. Many of the Kenan Fellows were these student pioneers, firmly grounded in both architecture and landscape architecture, or in combination with architectural history or urban and environmental planning. Their fluid perspectives and robust conversations opened new windows on both the history and present, in a space between design and scholarship, with their distinctive methodologies and sources of legitimation. Each brought a grounding and focus that would be both challenged and enhanced by an immersion in a stew of linguistic, visual and sensory associations. This latent energy is visible in the collage of images, narratives and scholarship in their work, undisciplined in a positive (though possibly dangerous) sense of ideas still in formation, associations suggested, and ephemeral observations captured, but not always verified (or like the mirages in a forest, unverifiable). The work oscillates between Marcel Proust's reflective associations and Paul Valery's sparks of invention, in the mix of dark and light where the imagination is most fertile.

A third character fleshes out the context for the work, the site of the project and subject of the curricular setting, the "Academical Village" and Lawn of the University of Virginia. This work, like its author, is both brilliant and deeply problematic, a masterpiece of Enlightenment reason built on the still unresolved complexities and contradictions of its birth and life. Over the past two hundred years, the modes of description, representation and historical framing reflect more on the times of the telling than any singular enduring truth. If the value of a work can be defined in part by its capacity to support many diverse narratives, then this one contains as many stories and mysteries as an ancient rainforest. No singular interpretation is possible – from the chthonic certainty of its anchoring in the ground, its materiality and construction, to the appropriated histories and fraught allusions, in its afterlife as an inspiration to its offspring around the world, and the many lives it has touched, the imagination embedded in this landscape remains vital to every generation. As an introduction to a curriculum for architecture and as the object of ongoing research, the Lawn provides a profound resource and reference that is then woven into the DNA of all who engage it.

To return to the unfathomable complexity in the original metaphor of the forest, one might imagine the work in this book not as a clearing of the forest, to be replaced by armatures of reason that enable a false conception of an ordered civilization, but as an embrace of the forest itself. The images, texts, designs and constructions here point to the embrace of the mystery, uncertainty and ambiguity as a necessary foundation for the shared understandings upon which covenants, citizenship and cultures are built. The dualities that recur in many of the texts and images are not in dialectical opposition, not black, nor white, nor gray, but are simultaneously all of the above, like a quantum particle/wave. The reality of this world, both inherited and constructed, is not fixed, but contingent on the lens by which it may be understood. This work reflects a lens with a unique capacity to reveal a panoply of insights, with a distinctive combination of precision and speculation, one good window that expands, rather than constrains, understanding.

William Sherman is a practicing architect and the Lawrence Lewis, Jr. Professor of Architecture at the University of Virginia. His academic investigations and design research examine dynamic cultural, institutional and environmental processes through an understanding of the relationship between architectural design and complex systems behavior.

Today
David Turnbull

Today, I am weary of wandering and have decided to stay in Charlottesville, Virginia for the Winter, to read and write. My library here includes books that I read at school, Ovid's "Metamorphoses", Virgil's "Eclogues", and Milton's "Paradise Lost". I had a great teacher, a dissenter, but missed so much. Of course I have read Chatterton's "African Eclogues" from 1769, Wordsworth's "Poems" (1815), and Coleridge's extraordinary "Kubla Khan" that was finally published in 1816, after eighteen years of rumours. Currently, I am reading fragments from the English translation of the "Bhagavad Gita" every day, as I struggle with ideas like duty and liberty. This works as a form of meditation, and has taken the place of the Bible next to my bed. My friends and colleagues are arguing constantly, as is proper, vexed by news from France, but excited by a recent spate of publication, including the young English poet, John Keats' "Ode to Psyche", to a Nightingale, on Melancholy, to Autumn. His magnificent "Ode on a Grecian Urn" has caused some consternation. My imagination is on fire, but some allusions remain opaque.

I need time.

There have been many times, in the past two hundred years, when I have returned to the Lawn, in my dreams — many times when lines of thought passed through this place, that originated in half-remembered essays, in echoes discovered in remote places with Nordic light, in London, Paris, in libraries, in letters and messages from friends.

If Vitruvius' stories make a plausible case. If Laugier's 'Primitive Hut' is exemplary. If Greek masons were really carpenters. Even if, in accord with Claude Perrault's '*Ordonnance des cinq espèces de colonnes*' (1683), it may seem right that '. . . columns do not meet with greater general approval the more they resemble the tree trunks that served as posts in the first huts that men built... .' the column may retain some memory of its ancestral form. Today, the 'Lawn' was, for the first time in the year, a sociable place. There will be many more days like this. I heard the chatter and gossip that I expected to hear on a warm afternoon, but I also heard hammering and the sound of wood being worked. For a moment the atmosphere changed . . . for me. I do not think that anyone else was listening, or cared, but I did. The University disappeared. It was 1818, the first building of the Central College of Virginia was under construction, a Pavilion, a dormitory range, with rooms in pairs, and a covered path, with columns — as illustrated in 'Regola delle cinque ordini d'architettura' by Vignola (1562), and Palladio's "I Quattro Libri dell'Architettura", published eight years later — in the Tuscan Order.

Soon, agreement would be reached that this will be the site on which Thomas Jefferson's Academical Village will be built, but not yet. The columns were made in brick, rendered, but I saw timber, cut from a tree, not any tree. In that moment I saw a mythical past, a quotidian present and agonizingly possible future. I saw springs that were dry, wells that were empty, and I saw the limbs of the tree of life, cut, one by one, a thousand times . . . with every cut, a little death.

Waking early, I read for a while, about the Wilderness . . . about Lakes, Rivers and Mountains, imaginary and real, ancient and modern. Emerson's essay, "Nature" (1836), is engaging, but I am excited by Thoreau, whose words are thrilling. His Buddha speaks more clearly than a Christian God. He reads the Vedas. He practices Yoga. He reads the Quran, and the Bible. He quotes Homer. He listens to Orpheus sing, while he studies Astronomy. I understand . . . and, after the rain,

in intimate moments, I have seen him — in a reservoir of dream-thoughts, fed by the Tigris and Euphrates, the Nile, the Ganges, Brahmaputra, Yangtze and Mississippi — in the Mountains of the Moon. Today is a special day in the lunar calendar, a lunar eclipse and a super-moon, simultaneously. The last time an event of this kind took place was in 1866. I hope that this will be auspicious. I liked the idea that it might be as I drove into Charlottesville . . . the sky, overcast until seven o'clock — too late for the Moon, but still dramatic. I parked between Pavilions IV and VI, and walked up to the Lawn, thinking about the day ahead, imagining the eclipse concealed behind the clouds.

In Buddhism, the Moon is enlightenment and truth. Truth presided over by Veritas or Aletheia, ἀλήθεια - I do not know which, but either way concerned with revelation. The Moon is responsible for the tides. In Roman mythology Veritas is the daughter of Time, Chronos. I am drawn in by the magic of the event that has just moved from the present to the past, to reflect on time and tides, the pull, the lure, the attraction of the moon. I remember Bede (672-735 CE), "On Time" - 'De temporibus', Section XXIX, a chapter devoted to the problem of the tides, their rhythm, timing and duration. For a moment I am utterly convinced by Bede's determination that the tides are caused by the moon breathing. The colour of the sky — the colour of the etheric body, breath, prāṇa, qi — peach blossom, drawn in crayon, shaded, hatched and smudged . . . a new day and a new year . . . sun or moon, I no longer care.

I remember my grandmother brushing her hair. It was early evening. I was ten. She was getting ready to go out. Her hair was long, grey, with strands of silver catching the light as she brushed. I watched. The brush strokes were slow, gentle, meditative. Occasionally she looked at her reflection in a mirror, but not often. She knew her hair. Her breathing matched the movement of the brush. Her eyes seemed sad. I sat next to her, but she did not see me. I had a question but did not ask it.

Today I read a story . . . Cheyenne or Sioux, I am not sure, in "Seven Arrows" (1972) by Hyemeyohsts Storm . . . a story that is told by a grandmother, a teacher, about a journey. The story is full of circles divided according to the four directions. It starts in the south, at sun-rise on the first of four days. On the second day, in the west, a circular clearing is discovered surrounded by trees, the "lodge of all our feelings, thoughts . . . and dreams". In the north, on the third day a lake is 'the mirror of totality', and on the fourth, in the east, the grandmother — teacher prepares a meal, the "food of learning" in the "place of illumination". The day ends as the sun sets, when it becomes clear that the four days are one. After many years my question has been answered.

David Turnbull is a director of ATOPIA design-communication-urbanism (LLC), and a founder of ATOPIA_RESEARCH (inc), He has worked extensively in the UK, Japan, SE Asia, the Middle East, Europe and the USA, and has specific expertise in the area of new lifestyles and the way that individual buildings and new patterns of development take advantage from advances in telecommunications and digital media.

PROJECT ORIGINS

Tracing Subjectivities from **I** onto **WE**

I like to think I have been teaching at the beginning and end of evolving architectural curricula for now fifty years first at Princeton, Cincinnati briefly, Rice substantially, and since 1992 in the Piedmont Condition at the University of Virginia. I teach from both my ongoing research as circumstantial contextuality articulating Spatial Tales of Origin, as well as my practice through Specifications for Construction both contained in my current New York City Studios, on-going Global Thesis Studios and my foundational pedagogic research effort contained in *LESSONS FROM THE LAWN*. For 15 years from 2001-2016, I have worked with 48 Kenan Fellows developing their own voiced theses on re-envisioning the Enlightenment project of Jefferson's Academical Village as relevant, no rather critically contemporary, to a debate on 21st Century cultural landscapes as political postures. We now consider this collaborative teaching effort, voiced as five chapters by pairs of juxtaposed Kenan Fellows, with commentary by me for ORO Editions under the title of *CONNECTIVE TISSUES* as evolving dialogues at Thomas Jefferson's University of Virginia.

There are seminal texts by singular architects who also teach through their own paradigmatic projects and not-so gentle manifestos. This project is not one of them. These dialectical essays are rather speculations though a collaborative set of dialogues of students and educators, who find themselves as Kenan Fellows at Mr. Jefferson's University. This Piedmont setting has always been clearly off the beaten path of American urbanism, somewhere between the permeable membranes of Atlantic flows and the first folds of the Appalachian Mountain Range. None of these voices are from here; rather, we all come from very far away. We find ourselves for distinct tenures as both citizens and strangers here and now, as we learn the lessons of surveyors, nomads and lunatics. And we all take pride in being Pynchon's *Slow Learner* and ask without irony: "What could be more modern than the archaic?" (Kwinter)

This is a collection of tales of being somewhere between Lost & Found through the Lens of the Lawn. As Mason Dixon gave measure to the World from Greenwich, England to Cape Town, South Africa, before they inscribed the Mason-Dixon line between Pennsylvania and Maryland, so Jefferson gave measure to his house on the hill as well as platted the entire Louisiana purchase, before he returned to fallow ground seven miles from his childhood playground to give form to the space of the Academical Village. Architecture as a Covenant with the World, again is the ethical touchstone for meanders and metaphors, which in turn yield national aspiration one step, one heartbeat at a time. This collection of tales, no calls and responses, is perhaps modeled after Homer's *Iliad*, Virgil's *Aeneid*, and Twain's *Huckleberry Finn/Tom Sawyer,* or was it *A Connecticut Yankee in King Arthur's Court*? We will bear witness to the transformation of an Irishman's Sojourn to A Brownfield Site, onto a Centerfold framed by two distinct Himalayan Flood Plains, bounded by both Roman hallucinations and the dream of Indian territories, all traced by an adolescent sensibility for a recurrent Arcadia located somewhere between Eden and Jerusalem and always grounded back home within Virginia's topographic imagination.

This is not another treatise on the heroic nature of the Jeffersonian imagination. Rather, it offers another reading generated by Joseph Campbell's reluctant hero in *The Hero of A Thousand Faces* as offered by Jef7rey Hildner in his prescient Epilogue "Labyrinth R.U.N." It is rather weaving fictions, constructing dialogues, (Rashomon) again and again on Jefferson as boy/man, as adolescent, as dreamer and instrumental explorer of here and there, close at hand and worlds long, long ago and far, far away. This is a collection of meanders, speculations, fog-bound as well as iridescent. Joseph Brodsky, in *Watermark*, would say of such consequential yet circumstantial descriptions (of Venice) that they were visions not based on principles rather were borne from the sensibilities of a very nervous man.

The fact may be that Jefferson was a farmer and politician of significance. But, what we illuminate here was that at thirteen he was an adolescent first. He was orphaned sooner than later as was common at the edge of the Arcadian Wild, as were Romulus and Remus. He was also a custodian of terrains, knowledge, and human energy. He was a Surveyor, Nomad and given his penchant for oculi and mirrors, a certifiable Lunatic.

In recent years generative texts by John Heyduk, *The Education of an Architect* (1989); Robert Venturi, *Complexity and Contradiction in Architecture* (1966), Le Corbusier, *Vers Une Architecture* (1921) have become resources beyond their own educational institutions or national cultures to become benchmarks for the debates within each zeitgeist. These three texts are read as providing generative frictional assumptions inherent in the assumption that architecture serves to advance the debate on the new ways of building within a changing world.

"Both Sides Now", recorded by Judy Collins, was published in the same year of Venturi's "Gentle Manifesto" in the Yale *Perspecta*. This was a time (1967-69) of American cultural upheaval longing for an architecture radically engaged with an enduring sense of time and place in the face of Walter Lippmann's *Preface to Morals*: articulating "America as Barren Ground"; as place and promise of Frampton's appreciation of *Critical Regionalism*, perhaps the cultural idiosyncratic lessons of Aalto's Finnish work to the North and Siza's Portuguese work to the South.

Few architects now seem to build upon cultural landscapes on the edge away from center. But, fewer still remain anchored optimistically, not critically in-between the frictional moment itself, as a lingering infected blister, if not a scar, as an instrumental discourse, never a clean slate.

What makes this collection of essays different is that it is generated from one paradigmatic World Heritage Site, however far from the currency of urban pathways. The Academical Village was conceived at the time of Thoreau's retreat to Walden Pond, of the emergence of American Transcendentalism and Whitman's *Leaves of Grass*. In the current Global yet culturally adrift mindset, this set of essays offers an affinity to Pynchon's "Slow Learner", to find the regenerative spirit within the small project, the village or nomadic oasis rather than envisioning ever more extensive global networks.

This is a book about a pause, about making the most out of materials at hand, keeping the canvas wet, about *pentimento*, mark and erasure, and above all about those who might just imagine the value of Cortezar's *Hopscotch* played with a chalk and a pebble between citizens and strangers. The essential fact is that the setting of an education of an architect might just matter. Heyduk ironically makes a case of New York and Prague through the amnesia of abstraction; Venturi references a scenographic repository in the City of Brotherly Love inscribed with tattoos from Las Vegas and Rome; and Le Corbusier's message has been lost in translation, by Anglo-Saxon offshore re-positionists, abandoning the endurance of Rome on the book's journey from Paris to London. Rome, Paris and the promise of terra incognita are all bound up in this project molded from Virginia red clay, river run sand and endless Arcadian forests of hard and soft woods.

This is a book on American Pragmaticism and self-evident truths in a new culture of Life, Liberty and the Pursuit of Happiness, rooted in the promise of Eden, and the enduring resistance of Jerusalem articulated by William McClung, on the endurance of *The Literary Legacy of An Architecture of Paradise*.

We aligned ourselves with contemporary philosophical debates which posit that, previously called Ancient if not Archaic Belief Systems might hold self-evident truths coincidental with contemporary survival systems of Sustainability, once called common sense, grounded in the recurrent dualities of Architecture. *CONNECTIVE TISSUES* is a philosophical work framed on Epistemological and Ethical questions sustained by Joseph Campbell in *The Hero of a Thousand Faces*. Not only is this a philosophical work, it also seeks to identify the contemporary vitality of American cultural history. If the Lawn is a *tabula rasa* for citizenship, is Monticello the endearing place for the engagement of both the familiar and the strange? Perhaps, the roots of a topographic imagination are found in generative settings. On our way to our collective sense of **WE**, the People, one must remember there was once the **HE**, as in Campbell's singular hero as Jefferson enters from the 38th North Latitude connecting the myth of Daedalus onto the Grounds of Jefferson's own Labyrinth.

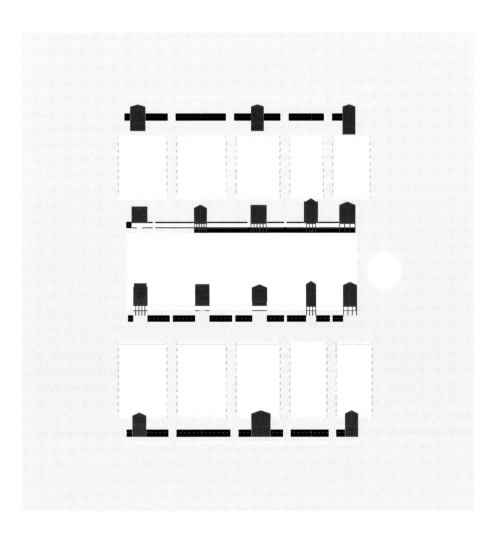

PROJECT ORIGINS

Second Pass: Beyond **I,** the author, now to **HE**, Jefferson, then onto **WE**

When Thomas Jefferson was thirteen, at that moment between boyhood dreams and manhood instrumentalities, his father, Peter Jefferson left him innumerable tracts of land, 365 books, and 256 slaves. The boy/man would retreat alone to Mt. Alto to survey his lands and read a few books, as he looked down onto his beloved playground, Monticello, the place of both fantasy/amusement and the reconstruction of his world, again and again. Four decades before Jefferson commenced the spatial project of The Academical Village, an idealization of inter-generational citizenship for this new Republic in Arcadia, he was to lay the foundation stones for a "good" one room dwelling on an already reconstructed site in Virginia's Piedmont.

The Enlightenment project of encyclopedic knowledge was often tested in the accounts of civilized man's reconstruction of the world, again in the face of the Wilderness. Rousseau's *Noble Savage*, Defoe's *Robinson Crusoe*, and Thoreau's *Walden* all recount the step-by-step acts of dwelling by knowledgeable man in Arcadia. Dwelling is used as a gerund here and will be a pivotal notion of architecture in dialog (process versus accomplishment) as a covenant with the world again. This covenant assumes that architects write specifications for construction implying ethical maintenance by future generations as well as acknowledging the marks, no stains and scars of weathering. This is an archaic, no renaissance, no modern notion, perhaps most important to multiple generations, never singular, finding ourselves in our New World condition.

We will begin the Lessons of the Lawn with the lessons gleaned from this exercise of Jefferson's honeymoon cottage of 1770. As he was leveling the mountain top of his beloved Monticello to terrace orchards, vineyards, a 1,000 foot-long garden and a future house site with extensive and extending dependencies, he made a home in a small shelter at the southwest corner of the future plantation precinct. This "good" one-room house was sited to face east to the rising of the sun, as was the future vestibule of the Monticello, but at the far western corner of a leveled Lawn, with a chimney/hearth to the West to ignite as the sun was setting, flanked by two windows, one to the north and one to the south. Behind and beneath the fireplace there was a stair to the fieldstone basement built into and buttressing the natural slope, where Sally Hemmings tended the hearth and prepared water heated for cooking and bathing. This primal half-excavated basement provided a model for the later Monticello great kitchen, where the cook probably dwelt within or adjacent to that space as well. Above, the one good room was constructed of brick fabricated from the local if not immediately subtracted red clay soil, the framing materials derived from the nearby forests, the roof shakes from trailside red cedar later replaced by local Buckingham slate quarried just across the James River, a stone throw's from the Scottsville Landing which connected Jefferson's extensive terrains to Richmond and eventually the Atlantic and back to the Old World.

Beneath the roof but above the ceiling, there was an accessible dry space, an attic, and a tent like maze of framing where clothing, maps and surveying equipment could be stored in dry sheltered safety. One "good" room with pre-requisite Basement and Attic; these are the elements of Jefferson's later urban project, The Academical Village, down the hill from Jefferson's Olympian dwelling. We begin here with a leveled site to the East and a natural sloped pre-condition always tumbling away to the West, with reliable light to the North and dynamic and long enduring light from the South. It is speculated that Jefferson, even in his youthful marriage, found time to read within the space of a stick laced Windsor chair whose back was adjacent to the indirect light of the North Window, but framing a view to the evolving cultivations to the South. Later, his singular cells for students of his Academical Village would be similar if not recurrent models of juxtaposed dualities, e.g. "good" rooms with one aperture to the East and another to the West. Here the fireplace, a nocturnal window would alternate between the South and the North. All had roofs that were for the gathering of rainwater and served as promenade decking providing different perspectives from distinct points of view. All these varied sequences of student cells sat upon common basements used as latrines, water closets, bathing halls and dwelling space for personal body servants. There was an upstairs—downstairs community of citizens and strangers in this Jefferson version of a new societal contract in Arcadia.

"Author of the Declaration of American Independence, of the Statute of Virginia for Religious Freedom, and Father of the University of Virginia"

—Tombstone Epitaph: July 4, 1826

The Academical Village (1814-26) came late in the life of Jefferson's spatial imagination and can be read as an extension directly from his projects at Monticello (1770-1826) as well as the little evoked pen-ultimate project at Poplar Forest (1808-26). He had one head but two hands, two homes, two libraries and time on his hands as both instruments of the art of the city: politics, as well as agents of a love of knowledge: philosophy. Moreover, his ten digits allowed him to render the world accountable as well. We have five digits on each hand; each of them distinctly jointed variations on a theme. A planter, a harvester, a scripter, a musician, a *homo faber*, all were in dialogue with Defoe's *Robinson Crusoe* and Thoreau and corresponded to Thomas Cole's Hudson River School sequence on *The Course of the Empire*.

Monticello commenced as a one-room dwelling and survives today as a cosmopolitan theater of the enlightenment. Before dawn, for at least eight decades, Thomas Jefferson routinely plunged his two hands with ten digits ritually into a cold basin of water to start his circulation and to take measure of his heart beat to inaugurate his day's work. He then looked up to the two hands of his clock and connected time to place through ten Mirrors for the Moon, by way of France, which faceted eastern light from the interior of the entry hall 180 degrees back to his south-west facing bedroom. He exited 100 paces directly south to his 1,000 foot-long garden where he planted a seed with an indexical finger and covered it over as with the joy of cupping of and then clapping with his hands. Most likely he would repeat this action 10 or 12 times, then scooped up some rich red clay and formed a brick to be fired in the ashes of kilns lining Mulberry Row. Only then and there daily, it is now rumored that he knelt down to wash his two hands and scrubbed his ten digits and then rewarded himself cupping both hands tightly now to relish sweet clear waters from a not-so–secret spring. He was *homo-faber*, man the maker, in syncopation as farmer and scripter being agent and instrument of recurrent dualities of The Word Made Flesh.

Now, on the first day of Lessons, the course, under a full moon **WE** students and faculty first go out to the Lawn to measure with our hands and paces: first the incremental bricks, one hand width, the spacing of the Tuscan colonnades, the meter of one individual's outstretched hands, the measures of the columnar orders in girth and spacing onto the native American trees from the most slender to the vast girth of centennial oaks. Some measures as bricks can be referenced by one digitally extended hand, others such as framing spaces for wood framing require two. The waists of most 18-year-old adolescents approximate the most numerous Tuscan columns; it is rumored there are ancient professors whose girth resembles the measure of the Corinthian columns of the Rotunda's temple front.

Finally, digits/tools/inventories of materials close at hand sum up what it means "to read" architecture. A design primer based on language, the study of linguistics, the discipline of sign and symbol, syntax and semantics, was first explored in "A Primer of Easy Pieces and The Difficult Whole " on my Princeton teaching in JAE 1981. "This Preface from **I** onto **WE**", traces the singularity of a monk's retreat to a final theater of civic congregation in Malta, and paralleled to the first terrace of Jefferson's Rotunda site. This appetite for connection between singularity and the collective was founded on Michael Graves's notion of recurrent dualities, a still useful relevant position of architecture as accountable as well as speculative.

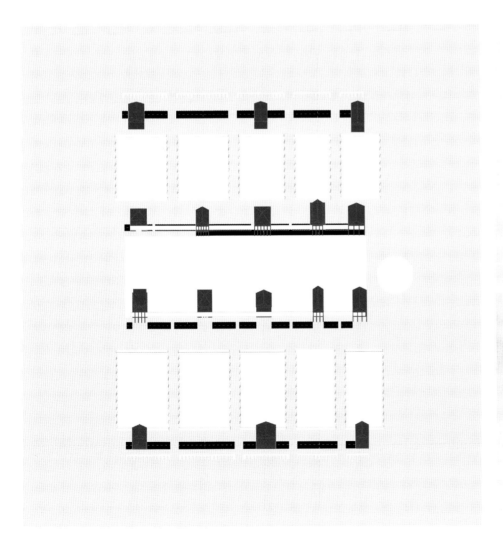

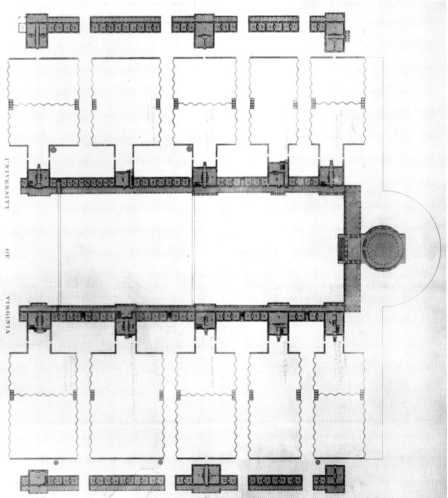

PROJECT ORIGINS

These Voices Then Resonate as Syncopated Echoes in This University

Support from the Kenan Foundation has enabled the publication and dissemination of a catalytic reinterpretation of The Academical Village in the Bicentennial years of the Foundation of the University of Virginia. The approach is unique to the extensive Jeffersonian literature through the heuristic narration of Spatial Tales of Origin grounded in Specifications for Construction by students and faculty in dialogue. *CONNECTIVE TISSUES* is a field guide for getting lost and then found for current citizens and strangers who will encounter Jefferson's University as a covenant with the world. As Kenan Professor since 2001, I have had the charge to advance the significance of The Academical Village in research and pedagogy through the vehicle of Architecture 1010: Lessons of The Lawn. Provosts Peter Low and Barbara Nolan envisioned we work annually as a team, five Kenan Fellows: graduate students in Architecture & Landscape Architecture on research informing lectures for this university-wide humanities elective, now remarkable essays for this project.

The nature of our collaborative research program across generations is to instill a 21st century speculative relevancy to what is assumed to be Jefferson's masterpiece. Richard Guy Wilson, Commonwealth Professor of Architectural History, has revealed that Jefferson's greatest contribution in the academical village was for transformation and change. Jefferson introduced frictional encounters in the ten different Pavilions. These distinct figural references were against a neoclassicism for formulaic resolution, indeed, not a masterpiece, but a work in progress. The program goal here is to infect our university community with an on-going curiosity, if not mannerist irreverence. Jefferson was a Revolutionary figure.

CONNECTIVE TISSUES which has always been conceived as an integral companion text to on-going research efforts of the course Arch 1010: Lessons of the Lawn since 2001. The greatest Lesson is Jefferson's belief in collaboration across generations as the proof of citizenship for this nation founded at the frontiers of Arcadia. At that time, I was granted my chaired Kenan professorship with the stipulation from the Kenan Foundation that I would work on the advancement of a new appreciation of the 19th century project of The Academical Village to be now relevant if not catalytic to the projects of the 21st century. This mandate characterizes our New School, now realized under current academic leadership two decades later. This is the task and hopefully utility of *CONNECTIVE TISSUES*.

The content of this imaginative leap has been seminal for two decades of Kenan Fellows' Research on Master Theses which consistently framed their multiple Nix and Pelliccia Awards and subsequent Rome Prize Fellowships. More than forty graduate students have received substantial grants as research and teaching assistants from 2001-2016 at a total investment of $1,500,000.00 as Kenan Fellows collaborating with me on seminal research in the form of initial lectures and then these selected refined essays herein. *LESSONS*, the first book contains my voice alone, but CONNECTIVE TISSUES employs a chorus of students in dialogue across generations. The research of the Kenan Fellows will encourage the expansion of the heretofore latent imaginations of those who value Jefferson's University only as a project of a past era, the Age of Enlightenment. Rather, it will be advanced to provoke existentially a debate on eschatological renewal, resilience at the edge of Arcadia in the light of the 08/11/2017 initiated Charlottesville Encounters.

These Kenan Fellows through their lectures and now essays herein demonstrated from 2001-2016, and now disseminated hereafter, their creativity, innovation and leadership to inspire undergraduates across Jefferson's University by establishing connective tissues across trans-chronological and trans-cultural case studies establishing recurrent dualities at the scales of cities, buildings and gardens. These connective tissues were based on firm ethical and epistemological beliefs in enduring ground rules of Gravity and Orientation. The inspired work of these graduate students from all four departments of the school have collaborated to inform and inspire students at this University that Jefferson's hobby of his old age, Architecture, was indeed a covenant with the world, again. The collective essays will serve as a textbook for appreciating the foundations of this university as still self-evident truths voiced in dialogues between citizens and strangers. The range of exemplary essays are assembled in part below:

Spencer Haynsworth Woodcock commenced appropriately in 2001 with the geological and cultural pre-conditions of the site which determined the means and methods of construction reinforcing Simon Schama's liberating treatise on the necessity for both topographic and archeological imaginations.

Danielle Willkens' preliminary essay 2008 on the contemporary projects of the un-private houses of Jefferson and Soane, is pivotal to Sanford Kwinter's interrogation of "What can be more Modern than the Archaic?" and has now led ten years later to the University of Virginia Press current publication of Willkens' dissertation from the The Bartlett School, University College, London.

Dani Alexander's essay on "Tools", and Gwen McGinn's on "Roots and Routes" both are in dialogue with the facts and fictions of natural science and the human capacity to break new ground with frictional instruments, to expand boundaries with telescopes and microscopes, curiously just because we can, ethically foreshadowed by JB Jackson's "The Necessity for Ruins", providing the ethical context of failure and fragment as the modern human condition.

As outlined in the Table of Contents, my role has been to select the top ten essays, pavilions, benchmarks of sorts, of the submitted forty, as sets of dialogues between pairs of students from all four of our departmental disciplines, serving as citizens of an emerging School here and now. Beginning with the primordial past, in Ground Rules, these ten essays advance onto the juxtaposed urban projects of Chandigarh and La Villette, as projects framed by Agrest's essay "Memory and Amnesia" and currently Atwood's "Not Interesting." Serving this role is a set of five connective tissues and collages, essays written by me. In the role of the stranger, the other, not from here, I remain dedicated to echoing Raphael's reminder from *The School of Athens* that then and there can serve as mirrors for the moon. The phrase, "here and now" is the inverse of "nowhere," by one simple temporal construct of back and forth. As we all celebrate the growth of Jefferson's University, we will be inspired to re-think this architect's role in envisioning through construction a new continental nation commencing with the East Range representing The Appalachians, framing the Lawn which is read as the great prairie of the Mississippi and Missouri River Basins spawned from The West Range which represents The Rockies. By conceiving of The Academical Village, after Lewis & Clark and the Louisiana Purchase, Jefferson confirmed he had a Continental Imagination to guide our nation's growth.

This proposal is in appreciation for these opportunities to demonstrate how well-funded Kenan Fellows have contributed to both the Bicentennial and Centennial as an exemplary return-on investment for the past two decades of a collaborative faculty and student research project of currency and relevance.

This is a unique project of "call and response" of contemporary citizens of and strangers to Mr. Jefferson's University. There are many scholarly texts on Jefferson's architectural projects, but none set in paired interrogations, responsive dialogues by inquisitive graduate students in the professional programs of Architecture and Landscape Architecture here and now surveying the Academical Village. I have been part of an ongoing debate in the Academy with the following members of the *Frankfurt School of Phenomenology* for fifty years and the student authors reference the following in the case of The Academical Village.

We are never alone even in focused research. However, we are unique to assign a modern interpretative lens to Jefferson's projects heretofore assigned to the Age of Enlightenment. Peter Rowe, former dean at Harvard's GSD, and author of *Design Thinking* (1986) identifies my work in service of heuristic thinking in the company of Peter Carl and Dalibor Veseley, authors of *Architecture and Continuity* and *Architecture in the Age of Divided Representation* of Cambridge, the Architectural Association and University College London, who make a case of Jefferson's recurrent dualities, Emilio Ambasz of Buenos Aires, New York and Bologna, Sanford Kwinter, author of African Genesis, Michael Benedikt of UT Austin, and a few other good story-tellers have been in dialog with me as citizens and strangers for the past fifty years. The collaboration of the Word Made Flesh is the decipherable DNA of my teaching and practice as story-telling. This research is about an inquisitive genre which has never been applied to Jefferson's work as an unfolding dialogue.

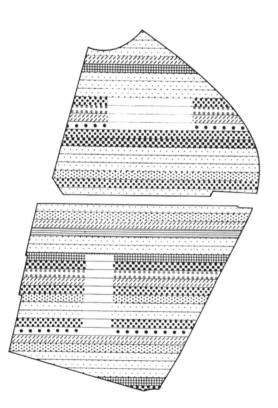

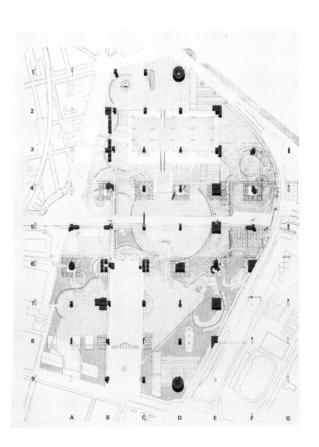

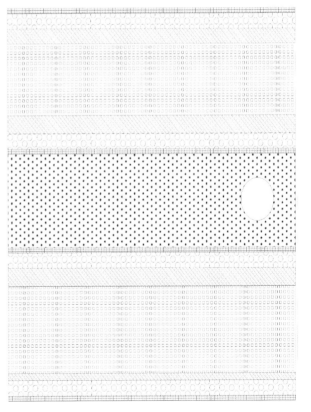

38° NORTH LATITUDE | GSM

Adam came out of the topsoil of Eden in a dirty state indeed. God used his own hands to mold Adam in an image of Himself, and Eve followed shortly thereafter by the same handiwork with the extrapolation of Adam's rib. Dirt and soil can be read as unclean, festering by some, or on the other hand, this eschatological condition can be generative. When the earth is in a fallow state one sees in that rare pause a promise of future resilience.

After capturing the beast of his choice in any stage wanted, the observer then holds it most. As with all capture, at least, it is finally trapped along [...] of the sample problem, with the [...] of [...] light, and we can see from [...] is unknown affected by [...] the [...] and so on, [...] conditions, and is, properly, which, in truth, it is a state of thing which in the case leaves a problem, of being capable.

GROUND RULES

Adam came out of the topsoil of Eden in a dirty state indeed. God used his own hands to mold Adam in an image of Himself, and Eve

followed shortly thereafter by the same handiwork with the extrapolation of Adam's rib. Dirt and soil can be read as unclean, festering by

some, or on the other hand, this eschatological condition can be generative. When the earth is in a fallow state one sees in that rare pause

a promise of future resilience.

ON DIRTY DIGITS & INAUGURAL ACTS
Peter Waldman

Adam came out of the topsoil of Eden in a dirty state indeed. God used his own hands to mold Adam in an image of Himself, and Eve followed shortly thereafter by the same handiwork with the extrapolation of Adam's rib. Dirt and soil can be read as unclean, festering by some, or on the other hand, this eschatological condition can be generative. When the earth is in a fallow state one sees in that rare pause a promise of future resilience.

Killien commences with Two Hands and Ten Digits. Casstevens responds that Jefferson's Academical Village is preceded by Plato's Academical Garden, if not Eden, and that the task of envisioning an Arcadian Nation is to inspire and educate a breed of citizen farmers. Cincinnatus would agree. Ken Frampton in Critical Regionalism reminds us that the bounty of the garden, the art of agriculture, permits the necessity for the art of architecture. Richard Sennett intervenes that Craft plays a role in making by hand and the Cultivation of place handed down through generations to which one might assign the term Cultural Landscapes. Catharine Killien is from Seattle, Washington where she did her undergraduate architectural education at the University of Washington and Master of Architecture at the University of Virginia. Claire Casstevens is from New England and studied Art History at Vassar and received her Master of Landscape Architecture at the University of Virginia.

Catharine Killien commences this joint exercise in Ground Rules by beginning with her own Spatial Tale of Origin in the pre-conditions of the Pacific Northwest Territories. She traces an evolution over several years with two distinct academic studio projects adjacent to one another in Rome and as far as India speculating on Lessons of Making with the aid of telescopes and microscopes. A fearless iterative model maker she traces continuities in sites as far away as the Campo di Fiori in Rome and the Great Courts of Fatehpur Sikri in India revealed again and again in the template of the Academical Village. Just as Jefferson lifted his huge head each morning and stretched out his arms and flexed his five digits on two hands to embrace the world, and shortly thereafter grasp the morning sun which invaded his entry a Cabinet of Curiosities, so Killien offers with digits as well as footnotes a treasury of loose threads which makes her a citizen architect being well with the world.

Claire Casstevens essay On the Academical Garden from Athens to Oxford onto the Piedmont is equally connecting the recurrent dualities of education founded in a sacred grove of olive trees, perhaps a surrogate for Eden, onto medieval Botanical Gardens sharing classification systems with libraries. A garden is not an assemblage of species but an Academical Garden is a device to frame an understanding of the World. She engages Juhani Palassma who invokes The Eyes of the Skin, in dialogue with Killien's digital requisites for making and reading the site. Casstevens reads the Academical Village as Garden as Library as the classification of knowledge in the ten academic disciplines contained collectively in the Rotunda as Library and separately in each Pavilion. There is the collective common ground of the Lawn, but also places of adjacent daily productivity at the microscopic scale of the seminal gardens, backed up by new perspectives revealed on the East and West Ranges of telescopic amusement.

Killien commences with the image of the Open Hand as a concrete relief casting, which later was erected as a kinetic sculpture by Le Corbusier constructed in Chandigarh. It is simultaneously a signal of an open hand and not a fist, saying Namaste for this provincial capital previously torn apart at the time of nationhood. Charles Edouard Jenerette adopted the name Le Corbusier and personified himself as the Raven, a political society who were 17th century Swiss revolutionaries fighting for Swiss Canton independence from the Hapsburg empire. The instrumental hand at Chandigarh, or the spirits of the revolutionary birds, whether Hapsburg eagles or the American Bald Eagle, all join, as leitmotifs, Noah's Dove. They reveal new lands cultivated and constructed by the agency of the hand, hard at work to build a nation from inherited cultures from the ground up. These are connections to be manifested in this prefacing threshold. Perhaps, an archaic dove is a signature of nationhood signaling the art of the city, which comes from imagining a birds-eye-view, a telescopic view from above.

Casstevens commences with two plans of Botanical Gardens from Medieval times Padua and Pisa, The first is round Padua as of a metaphor to read the world of microscopically curved horizons, perhaps the imprint of a digit or better yet a radial fingerprint, the other, Pisa in quadripartite regimen the four corners of the known world: Europe/Asia/Africa and the Americas giving primacy to Cartesian systems leading to the Tyranny of Enlightenment Reason overwhelming the Arc of the Sun and the Phases of the Moon. Guernica by Picasso evokes this battle of fearful and curious digits, discussed in Joseph Campbell's Masks of the Gods citing coincidentally the mythic value of Sun Horse of Apollo and the Moon Bull of the Minitour as spatial tales of origin of reason and fear, one in the sky and the other microscopically hidden deep within the Labyrinth, which is revealed when we plant a simple seed.

I have tried in this inaugural connective tissue on Ground Rules to establish two frames of reference: the telescope to access the sky and the microscope to decipher the DNA of the earth. These themes will be sustained in the next Five Chapters with distinct inflections. I remind myself that in my fictional spatial tale of origin I held a small shard of mica up to the sky to magnify the sun, and then half a life ago found myself under the big sky of Texas working in the shadow of NASA, sustained literally by the fossil fuels emerging from the gumbo clay beneath our feet. And now here Up-East in Virginia we have Jefferson's Rotunda with a certifiable Oculus as well an open-ended Paradise garden he called the Grounds extending to The Blue of Distance of Solnit's west coastal imagination. Memory and Amnesia are coexistent in a world where connective tissues constantly need repair.

When I taught at Rice University (1981-92), I gave a studio brief for A Museum of Texas History for Houston, a city with more future than past. In those early days, I looked at the world objectively, suspecting that Houston gained its speculative quality from the inaugural acts of heroic figures with names. The idea of Houston, thus as aligned with Sam Houston's intention to make a significant settlement in the name of an Anglo leadership, was in contrast to the Mission Cities such as San Antonio determined by the Law of the Indies of New Spain. The topographic imagination had no foothold in that marshy backwater of malarial infections, extensive southern Pine Barrens and occasional coastal Palmetto groves. With the oil and gas discoveries at Spindle Top (1906), Geological Time rushed into the voids of extraction, later to be documented in Fantasia (1939) as the repository of the Jurassic period producing the Halcyon Days of the Fossil Fuel Age, terminating with the limitless future of NASA as Space City. All these timelines and vortices of geological and cultural confrontations yielded a new design agenda for me, Spatial Tales of Origin, inaugurating the expansive prerogative of a World Beyond Arcadia, with an accelerated and heroic sense of Space, Time, and Architecture beyond the accountable. My design work began to be invested in more future than past: The Parasol House (1982), The Hurricane House (1984), Times Square Is A Circle (1984) and the Miami Overton Competitions (1985) all grounded themselves in an archeological assemblage of Archaic Quarries, and an extended sequence of future cities.

It thus came as a shock to my new colleagues when my first studio at the University of Virginia projected an 11th Pavilion, as if the Academical Village had a capacity for growth and change. Our faculty challenged my assumption with this iconic project, even as I read it open ended with bookends of a singular student room at the end of the plan rather than stopping the sequence with the massive Pavilion X to the East and the vulnerable yet supremely modest Pavilion IX to the West. I kept on insisting that the continental minded Jefferson's knew perfectly well that though grounded by the Appalachian Range and the Atlantic to the East that the South tempted one's eye to the Blue of Distance recorded by Lewis & Clark as the endless Prairies and the Rocky Mountain Range to the West dialectically promising growth, expansion, and open-ended-ness; this is another curious phase to be extended in the next five Chapters..

Coming from Texas to the Old Dominion with the posture that there must be more future than past, I posit with my telescope epistemology and eschatology to be set in dialogue with time-shared by citizens and strangers as we are all stained microscopically by clay and grass. The Lessons of the Lawn require that we employ our digits to tend gardens first, then quarry the depths of this earth and finally construct and maintain a dialogue with Celestial soffits above whether we be in Rome or Fatepur Sikri. What could be more Modern than the Archaic? Sanford Kwinter has the last word where Wizlawa Szymrborska had the first in "The End and The Beginning".

On Two Hands and Ten Digits
Catharine Killien

INTRODUCTION

This essay (lecture) concerns the human scale in architecture. By human scale, I do not simply mean that which is the same size as the human body. I refer to that which engages the human experience. Thus, this essay (lecture) explores the complex and intertwined relationship between material, space, and the human body.

All the senses; expand the notion of the human scale beyond the visual alone
The hand is both agent and collaborator with tools in haptic engagements
Digits have touched a wall in Pragpur/ cobblestones in Rome: digits as tools

This thinking requires a re-definition of what we consider to be the human scale.

In a critique of the role of the primacy of the visual Image of Architecture, which you have addressed in the first images of the accountable Pyramid and enigmatic Sphinx, the architectural theorist Juhani Palasma writes:

"It is evident that the architecture of traditional cultures is essentially connected with the tacit wisdom of the body, instead of being visually and conceptually dominated. Construction in traditional cultures is guided by the body in the same way that a bird shapes its nest by movements of its body. Indigenous clay and mud structures seem to be born of the muscular and haptic senses more than the eye."

He continues, saying: "As buildings lose their plasticity and their connection with the language and wisdom of the body, they become isolated in the cool and distant realm of vision. With the loss of tactility and measures and details crafted for the human body – and particularly for the hand – architectural structures become repulsively flat, sharp-edged, immaterial and unreal."

In an attempt to recover the sense of the human hand and body as it relates to the making and experience of architectural space my intention here is to explore works of architecture – both historic and contemporary, near and far, which have maintained a connection to the language and wisdom of the body.

Several of the works I will present to you today are places I visited in India this past summer where I studied and traveled as part of the first UVA India Initiative summer studio. Though materiality and shaping of materials by the human hand have long since been an interest of mine, it was in India that I rediscovered the connection one can have with a work of architecture that engages the human body. I will also present several works from other periods of time in other parts of the world, to show that a sensibility about the human body is present in both contemporary and historic works of architecture, and in societies with and without high-tech (mechanized) construction industries.

A trap one can fall into is becoming nostalgic about architecture built by the human hand. The cost of labor in the United States makes this uneconomic in comparison to the majority of highly skilled laborers with an inheritance of generational craft.

While moments discovered in India of architecture so clearly built by the human hand certainly did delight, my aim here is not only to celebrate these works, but also to understand how such careful attention to the body is possible in a mechanized contemporary culture. It would be easy to critique contemporary "image" architecture as Pallasmaa does in his article. I prefer to argue that sensibility of the human body and hand is still possible even in an architecture driven by the image and highly mechanized construction techniques.

Because there are ten digits, I present ten projects for ten lessons:

1. TECTONICS: Ching Cabin, Maury Island, WA
2. WEATHERING: St. Ignatius: Seattle, WA
3. LAYERING: Mass MOCA, North Adams, MA
4. SCALE: Santa Maria della Pace, Rome, Italy
5. MOVEMENT: Campo de Fiori, Rome, Italy
6. MATERIALITY: Thermal Baths, Vals, Switzerland
7. MAINTENANCE: Ashram Golconde, Pondicherry, India
8. JUXTAPOSITION: Millowner's Association, Ahmedabad, India
9. SECTION: Fatepur Sikri, Agra, India
10. PROCESS: Water Channels, Pragpur, India

I will discuss seemingly disparate works of architecture that are connected throughout by the common thread of their sensitivity to the human body We as students of architecture have a vast knowledge of paradigms we have never visited. I will only discuss works I have visited. Visiting a work of architecture is far different that seeing an image of it (In this regard I will accept Palasmaa's critique). While I am only discussing works that I have visited, these themes run as recurrent dualities across time and context. To visit means to see and to reconfirm by touch in the flesh.

The idea that links all of the above lessons together is an appreciation of linking the parts and whole; the materials and processes that make the architecture. Material constructs and delimits space with our digital hands as maker and feet as we invent the choreography of human scapes; therefore, tracing an architectural promenade which in turn makes the conjunctive experience of well-being with the world.

Materials are used to construct dialectical structure found in caves and tents.; These structures define specific spaces of retreat and engagement; perform to warm and to cool in dialogue with environmental conditions, and create magical transformative atmospheres by engaging the senses specifically through our manipulation of distinct materials by distinct tools as referenced in Dani Alexander's Kenan essay, On Tools.

I will begin to form this connective tissue through a quote by David Pye, from his book Nature and the Art of Workmanship: "In nature, and in all good design, the diversity in scale of the formal elements is such that at any range, in any light, some elements are on or very near the threshold of visibility… as the observer approaches the object, new elements, previously indistinguishable, successively appear and come into play aesthetically."

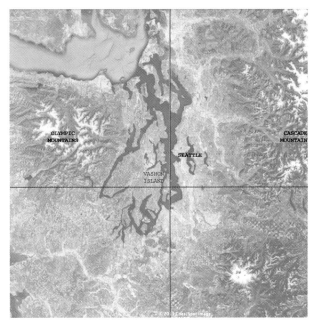

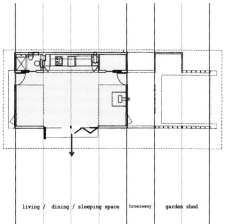

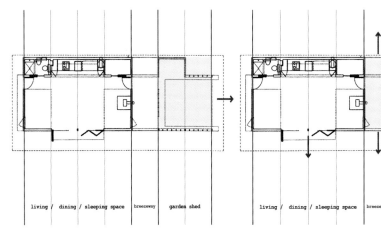

1. TECTONICS
Ching Cabin, Maury Island, WA (Miller Hull Partnership, 1997)

We begin with the simple notion that materials and meters create space.

I will begin with a very modest work, very close to where I grew up, and the smallest I will discuss today. At only 650 square feet, the Ching Cabin, built by the Miller Hull Partnership, is a weekend retreat (for an architect) on Maury Island, Washington, about 15 minutes from Seattle via ferry. The cabin is a simple wood frame built atop a raised concrete slab, with a corrugated metal roof containing carefully selected translucent apertures.

What is spectacular about this seemingly simple work of architecture is both the careful proportioning of the structural system and the way in which the scale of structure is used to create spatial distinctions off large collective spaces and small retreats as well as the in-between. These juxtapositions made to the simple form engage both the movement of the body, the organization of social space, and the relationship of the body to indoor and outdoor space. The changes in level not only allow one to move to the exterior ground plane, but become a place to sit. In a liminal threshold space.

"The tectonic language of architecture, the inner logic of construction itself, expresses gravity and structure, the language of materials as well as processes of construction and details of joining units and materials to one another. In my view, architecture arises from the identification and articulation of the realities of the task in question, rather than from individual fantasy… A great building enhances and articulates our understanding of gravity and materiality, horizontality and verticality, the dimensions of above and below, as well as the eternal enigmas of existence, light and silence." (Pallasmaa 2009)

Construction is the art of making a meaningful whole out of many parts. Buildings are witnesses to the human ability to construct concrete things. I believe that the real core of all architectural work lies in the act of construction. At the point in time when concrete materials are assembled and erected the architecture, we have been looking for, becomes part of the real world. (Zumthor 1999)

Tectonics are the constructive language of architecture – the syntax of structure that determine not only the physical characteristics of the space, but also its experiential qualities. Tectonics govern spatial volume, surface quality, movement through space, structural metering, material laying, light penetration and air flow, the relationship between parts of buildings, floor areas, ceiling heights, and the sense of expansiveness or compression of space. The tectonic language of space is determined primarily by the constructive nature of the materials employed as materials have "innate" properties that forms that they can take.

Count them, ten digital moves: A singular columnar framing element in all its humility defines the threshold on the north south axis. Second, a hearth defines the east west axis and eight requisite bays 16' o.c. complete the requisite count.

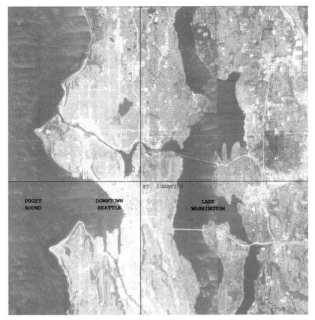

2.

2. WEATHERING
St. Ignatius: Seattle, WA (Steven Holl, 1997)

Nearby, in Seattle, is a more widely recognized work, the St. Ignatius Chapel on the Seattle University Campus, designed by Steven Holl. The project is highly sculptural, using apertures to the sky to manipulate light on the interior. While the project is praised for its sculpting of both natural and artificial lights (as this is what captures one attention immediately upon entering the space), the subtle details of the project to me are the spectacular. These are the details one discovers not at first glance, but upon experiencing the space, time and time again. Concrete plug covers the scale of fingerprints, hand formed bronze door handles upon entry and wall textures within engage our bodies and minds.

Materiality refers to the perceptual and experiential qualities of a material. While material pertains to objective, physical characteristics, materiality is a subjective consideration.

Materiality "reflects our intuition that for something to be real it ought to be [. made of] 'stuff,' material having palpability, a temperature, a weight and inertia, an inherent strength." Materiality lends a building a sense of "presence" when "every material and texture is fully itself and revealed" (Benedikt 1987).

"On Weathering," by David Leatherbarrow and Mohsen Mostafavi explores the ethical implications of materiality and temporarily, defining the idea of weathering as the process that allows materials to reveal their sense of time while heightening the sense of materiality in architecture.

While the Ching Cabin uses a dialectic of tectonics, the singular column at entry and the serial frame in contract to the cave like hearth, it engages us to the memorable horizons of land and water, the St. Ignatius Chapel engages us from the earth as primal cave to the cosmic apertures of the sky. Ten distinctly scaled skylights raise themselves as two hands in prayer as two hands are required to open the entry doors of folded angel wings. Weathering ennobles the constructions of humankind, such as the polychromatic friezes of the Parthenon, by bleaching of the sun and the rain, demanding maintenance of future generations to maintain the works of their ancestors or suffer the isolation of the non-attentive in face of natural conditions stronger than the willful constructions of humankind. Holl commences with a water color of vessels of space, a choreography of luminescences as he then assigns these colors initially on the exterior and interior to transform light from natural and artificial sources. In contrast to the Ching cabin which is elevated above the ground on a clear articulated plinth, set back from the water's edge St. Ignatius sits at the this edge of the reflecting pool doubling itself as narcissus. The Ching cabin blue tone roof alone is reflected in the water beyond perhaps forming in combination two angel wings. On the other hand the roof top skylights of St. Ignatius are a handful of apertures breaking the singularity of a protective roof into the cacophony of spirits, not a singular voice such as an hierarchical dome containing canonical prayer. Multiplicities are the characteristics of circumstantial forces of weathering, leaving, fading/blistering, and scars of forces beyond the intentions of humankind. These two projects juxtapose tectonics, the first (Ching) favors lightness in materials of frames and modular skins, the second project (Holl) of massive heavy pre-cast concrete panels and volumetric containers versus the thin planes of the first.

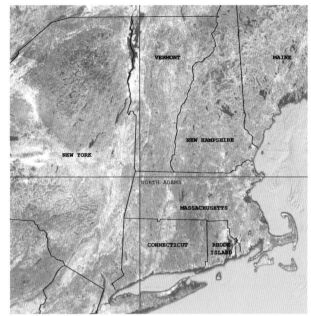

3. LAYERING
MASS MoCA, North Adams, MA (1992)

An abandoned industrial complex of buildings was renovated to provide a new context to appreciate contemporary art for the Massachusetts Museum of Contemporary Art. As the layers of the thematic tectonics of juxtaposed masonry walls and structural steel frames were wedded to the processes of weathering on the interior as well as exterior, a dialectical strategy of multiple layers sensed by the scales of digits and hands is orchestrated in contrast to the vastness of the vacated space to be filled by the imaginations of artists in response to the meters of structure and the palimpsest of mark and erasure.

The existing masonry walls were left exposed in most parts of the building. In contrast to the typical white-washed walls of contemporary art museums, the architects "retained signs of physical weathering and traces left behind by previous inhabitants both inside and outside the buildings," enabling the artists to engage with their context.

The design process was opportunistic and highly dependent on local conditions as the architects "left open room for revelations along the way rather than letting one big idea control project development" as "site conditions and discoveries during the demolition and construction significantly affected the aesthetic outcome. The process of design focused on the experience of making and ultimately inhabiting the space, rather than on creating a preconceived architectural object."

The new museum program required larger floor to ceiling heights that existed in the original building. Large floor areas were subtracted within existing mill buildings. The removal of floors uncovered and intentionally revealed the layers of building construction. We don't just build cabins and cathedrals from scratch. The Tectonics of the Ching Cabin offers us a modular accountable coordination of systems of complementary structure and skin. The Tectonics of St. Ignatius juxtaposed the singular heaviness of concrete jigsaw puzzle panels with the contrasting multitude of light catching apertures of distinct meters. Here in MASS MoCA large structural steel bays are contrasted to the seriality of small steel studs, bar joists are exposed on the ceiling plane, masonry walls thicken as need to be pilasters at the monumental scale of medieval cathedrals, the interior is striped bare to reveal that which is essential. This project does not promote singularity as the first, juxtaposition as in the second, but in celebrating all the scales, meters and materiality to enhance a place of production and the humble dignity of work for those with ditty hands which may be the needed ethical condition of art in this new Millennium.

4.

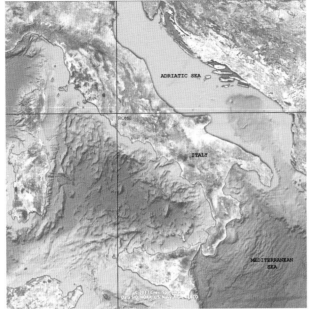

4. CHOREOGRAPHY OF SCALE
SANTA MARIA DELLA PACE, ROME, ITALY

I move now to a project across the Atlantic Ocean built five hundred years before. The cloister of Santa Maria Della Pace, a small church built in Rome is a place one has to discover. There is no clear entrance, no sign marking where tourists ought to go. On my last day in Rome after spending nearly four months in the city, I finally went out to find the place I had heard so many people admire.
One thing the Romans do exceptionally well is that they don't give it all away at the beginning. It is a carefully choreographed sequence, moving between hierarchies. This is something you understand through the body.

One is instructed to go first to the vast spatial landmark of Piazza Navonna, once an ancient chariot race stadium, transformed in the middle ages and Renaissance as the premier location of Palazzi, Churches and in the Baroque period of amazing fountains and statues to mythological figures. The facade of Sant 'Agnese is clearly monumental and one is instructed to find a small via going west to come upon the flank of S.M. della Pace. One encounters a small piazza and a semi-circular porch, Bramante's proto Tempietto of sorts, as one may on rare occasion enter the church when rarely open for masses. Rather, often one meanders around from west to north and finds a small door to enter from the street to the remarkably accountable cloister of two orders of arches below making a cave like enclosure and a syncopated upper cloister for solo mediation above. Here, one is invited to pause to change posture as one sits down alone with a good book to meditate in the enclosure cave-like seats between massive rectangular piers and slender round human scaled columns in between. There is thus a juxtaposition of the cloister spatial type of first caves then tents, in contrast to the singular volumetric cave-like void of the figural church interior itself. Note, that S.M. della Pace references the same language of volumetric skins and juxtaposed frames as MASS MOCA using layering of accountable elements of two scales as a recurrent duality of a series of columns seen previously suggesting a frame-like, tent-like syntax of structure above and below. At his point, we might recall the early projects of first the Ching framed cabin which was followed by Holl's Chapel combining the juxtaposed utility of the tent-like frame, first as a threshold encounter between exterior and interior, followed by Holl's example of a predominately massive enclosed volume. All these projects are in dialogue with one another across time and place, some call, in this course, enduring truths. It is a good place to be engaged with the earth and to reconsider the spirituality of the clearly framed celestial soffit. One pauses here and is invited to take a rest, along with other monks in the study spaces of cave-like if not meditative seats between massive pierces syncopated with slender human-scaled columns. The choreography comes from the architect's communal scale rising in section through this architectural scale of an architectural promenade as a processional group, and then the more solo meditative pause in the study carrels which invite you to humble one's posture and to sit alone. A place to pause is perhaps a requisite consideration as we attempt to read Architecture as a Covenant with the World, Again, as we measure shadows and sunlight and trace their dynamic vitality as we witness them both for a stationary investment in the preciousness of fleeting time.

5.

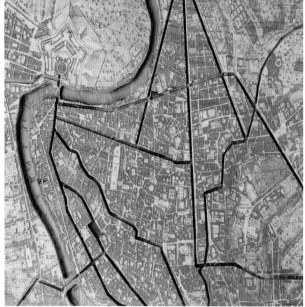

5. CHOREOGRAPHY OF MOVEMENT
Campo di Fiori, Rome, (Paved 1456)

While I visited S.M. della Pace only once in my many travels to Rome, a place I am intimately familiar with is the Campo di Fiori, one of the main public squares within the center of Rome. There one finds the daily routine of people manifested as a manifestation of movement much akin to a sequences of stage-sets documenting a long day's journey into night. This is a civic space, one large outdoor room filled up with people of distinct ages and occupations sustaining the necessities of a market place by day, and the contemporary locus of the magical hallucinations of night-life in contemporary Rome. There is the tactility of fruits and vegetables displayed on small mobile tent-like structures brought in at sun-rise after the streets and campo have been scrubbed by a night crew of bright yellow uniformed sanitation workers. Crowds assemble from all corners and meander through labyrinths of vendors, cafes and then restaurants open in the morning and later afternoon, and the edges become increasingly animated as the fruit and vegetable vendors sell out by high noon; people then move to the edges and several hours are spent demounting the temporal stage sets of the vendor stands. Another crew comes in in the late afternoon to scrub the market square again and for a few minutes at sunset the statue of heretic Giordano Bruno stands alone as the sustaining sun sets and correspondent fires roar for some recalling his moment of heresy, inquisition and burning finality in this very spot.

The sun sets, restaurants are packed first to be followed by the opening of bars and nightclubs. A more youthful crowd arrives and populates this campo with sound and light until the early hours of the next morning. The campo cobblestones are littered with evidence of festive excess and yet another sanitation crew arrives to prepare for the vendors who sustain life of this public space of many characters. But, is this not another lesson derived from the Genesis cycle of regenerative darkness yielding to light, of the earth serially dividing water from land, only to return again and again in Noah's flood of the birth of a garden of Eden for plants and animals and the short term presence of humans and the evil nature of snakes who cast them out, it seems by plagues and conflicts again and again? Thus, the Campo di Fiori may be Tschumi's theater of human events again and again as a Covenant with the World, Again. Where S.M. della Pace is only minutes away tucked behind another impressively large civic space of the Piazza Navonna, this campo is one of the most pivotal and diverse in Rome with a vital 24/7 agenda, where the cloister of S.M. della Pace is peaceful in its enduring accountability and relative silence.

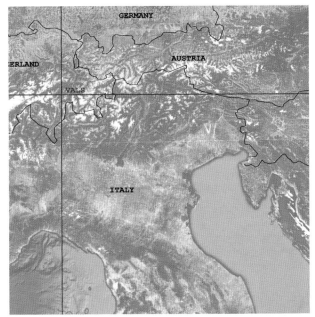

6.

6. MATERIALITY
Thermal Baths, Vals, Switzerland, (Peter Zumthor, 1996)

From Mediterranean Rome, I journeyed north to Switzerland, and rediscovered the power of Le Corbusier's diagram of the mountains and the sea, to contrast the frictional juxtaposition of Swiss cultural landscapes between the Germanic and the Mediterranean. Here, I found myself immersed in the choreography of darkness, in a version of Nordic chiaroscuro now of more shadow than light ,and more in reflective glistening wet surfaces of the spirit of the Grotto than that the sun-bleached panels of Rome. Here in Vals, cut deep into a hill, was inserted a project more derived from the glacial solidity of slopes, of thickened retaining walls, of an institution to immerse the body's skin and bones to the forces of enduring rock transposed as 20th century concrete. I touch the walls to get a new sensibility after being infected by the abstract in sun-bleached Rome.

"I believe that materials can only assume a poetic quality in the context of an architectural object, although only if the architect is able to generate a meaningful situation for them since materials themselves are not poetic. The sense I try to instill into materials is beyond all rules of composition, and their tangibility, smell and their acoustical qualities are elements of the language that we are obliged to use. Sensibilities of materials emerge when I succeed in bringing out the specific marriage of certain materials in my buildings. Resultant meanings can only be perceived in just this specific way in this one building. We must constantly interrogate ourselves what the use of particular materials might mean in a specific architectural context. Good answers to these questions can throw new light on both the way in which the material found and transformed is used and its own found sensuous qualities.(Rock as fact, and concrete as transformed fiction is at the heart of the dialogue sought in this course based on the utility of recurrent dualities.) If we succeed in this contextual dialogue, architecture can be vitalized, generate light and vibrate in meter with our heartbeat." (Zumthor)

Building is about the senses, and I now introduce the idea of phenomenology to this course, a design process where experience of an architectural promenade from deep within the earth to aspirations for the sky are the driving force of material engagement as an ethical Covenant with the World again at the scale of skin and bones. There are sequences of intentional juxtapositions of heavily textured walls, and smooth glistening floors, first a red-hot dry room, and then a cool room which introduces us to darkness and then regenerative water, where we sense the raw direct sense of our bodies. These themes will be readdressed in Pragpur, India as we trace these lessons of diverse cultural landscapes introduced by Bill McClung the lushness of the generative Garden and his case for the endurance of the City of stone represented biblically by Eden and Jerusalem.

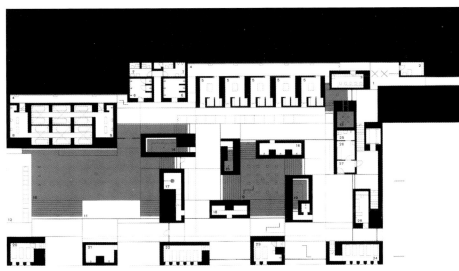

7.

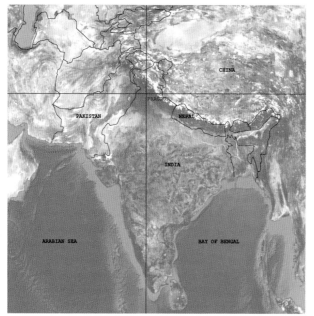

7. FOOTSTEPS AND FINGERPRINTS
Water Channels, Pragpur, India

I move now to a place far away, a context beyond the familiar in India. I find a community's essential appreciation of water as compared with the individual, appropriation, if not self- appreciation of the tactility of moisture registered by our skin and bones often in isolation found in Vals.

We travelled first north of Delhi to Chandigarh by Train for half a day at the speed of 40 miles of hour where we spent several days surveying the vast dimensions of an expansive city at the scale of the newly emergent nation-state of India. India there seemed vast. Finally, we continued on road nested Land Rovers in caravan at about ten miles an hour wading through recently rutted rural roads, through herds of water buffalo, alternating herds of goats and sheep, Getting out often to push these sturdy vehicles up hills until we arrived water-soaked by the monsoon rains to the mountain village of Pragpur for a week of reflection. We were housed as royalty in a prince's former estate surrounded by mango groves and peacock flocks at the edge of a rural and 'preserved" heritage village sustained by a water tank, irrigation canals and two mighty rivers to the east and the west making a fortuitous junction at this point. We each had our own guest apartments in isolation, but a few steps away from one another. Along the way we encountered all manner of abundant life: fallen mangos and gigantic fruit-eating ants. One species sustained the other and life seemed a harmonious yet sweet cycle. Nothing is wasted here. After generous breakfasts and lunches of fish and fruits and what we suspected were Peacock eggs, we ventured forth, following one's own meander to discover the village, its tank breaming with fish, to be encountered in the evening meal, to the bountiful orchards everywhere making shade along the streets, and sacred cows being tended and milked late in the day to make paneer overnight for our morning's breakfast. Everything echoed the modest and consistent meter of our footsteps. We returned as indeed the prince's guests and shared tall tales of this miniature and self-sustainable world with our classmates now distinctly modest souls after absorbing the heady grandeur and monumental expansiveness of Chandigarh. One had to race across the vast dimensions of that megacity's avenues and civic plazas. Everything here in this enduring village was a few steps, a mere meter away, as the social distance of isolation currently known to us; but, then and there, an immediate community was close at hand.

Walking by footsteps we discovered a self-satisfying world, reading this village as an essential urban covenant harmonious with each step at the pace of one's heartbeat. We realized the hand, so important previously as a unit of measure and instrumentality, now possesses five fingertips, the digital was instrumental in peeling a banana, in puncturing a mango to drink its sweet pulp. We encountered villagers in a different light than Mind Craft, but here in paradise the monkeys encountered us and instructed us in the art of their digital world. We had a remarkable week as "guests" in Pragpur, and then learned to slow down, to sense the world in is fecundities, and were beginning to learn the lessons of the enduring village as an alternative to the megacity derived from the canonical lessons emerging from our Jeffersonian Enlightenment, We arrived to Pragpur perhaps infected with an uncritical belief in the advantages of progress. After a week, we were jolted again as we traveled this time by air to the site of India's paradigmatic Golconde Ashram, in the city of Pondicherry on the Bay of Bengal.

8.

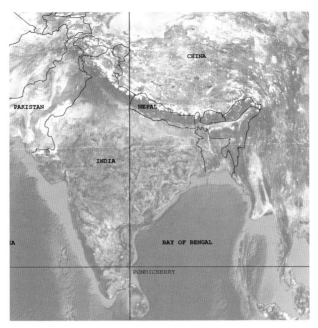

8. MAINTENANCE
Golconde Ashram, Pondicherry, India , (George Nakashima, 1938)

This journey from India's ancient and modern capitals, then transported rut by rut to the heritage mountain village in the north west, ended in Pondicherry a former French colonial city at the edge of the southeast Tamil region of India. It has attracted international free thinkers for millennia as a place of pause and reorientation. An ashram is not a place of retreat from the world, but rather one must manifest here the tenacious imprints of both our two hands and ten digits. Nakashima came to Pondicherry to construct wood formwork for this first reinforced concrete building in India, and stayed to influence the use of the tactility of wood on rails, movable screen louvers and stairs to reach the warmth of the sky. We were in his hands at all scales from the start as we touched and then moved the modest portal gate.

"Each board, each plank can only have one clear use… the woodworker applying a thousand skills must find that clear use and then shape the wood to realize its true potential." (Nakashima, Woodworker and Architect)

This encounter with the Ashram will take us back to where we started in the modest Ching cabin framed by the enduring Forest at the edge of the Water.

Note now, the care taken to wipe down surfaces, during construction and ongoing daily ethical maintenance. Our two hands make us instruments of something between us and others who touch our imprints. How can we be simultaneously citizens and strangers and yet literally touch one another intermittently through a third haptic moment, such as a door handle? Here we learned something we did not ever consider. In this place future residents were asked to bring discarded cooking pots of their grandparents to be melted down to make the door handles used daily to open and close their bedchambers. We in the west, often assume a door handle comes from a hardware store, manufactured in an industrial setting produced by total strangers. Here at the Ashram we learned to sustain the touch of our grandparents' life-sustaining instruments so generously offered in their lifetimes to be sustained as we engage routinely our connection to the world at sunrise and sunset. We watched bricks laid up by men and boys to form garden walls during the heat of the day, while a team of women and girls washed down the efflorescent salts from these surfaces with the tenderness of washing a baby. This maintenance was repeated each morning cleaning the collected slime from the irrigation canals of glistening marbles which laced the gardens of careful fecundity. At the same time another group of more mature residents wash the daily laundry in the sunken areas of coolness below the elevated building plinth. These fortunate souls work in the bountiful shade of the morning, in which soap-laced and sun-warmed waters are then used to cleanse the cooking pots of rice and lentils, spinach and pungent peppers of all possible colors and tastes. This water is then used to refresh the gardens. Peacocks reappear in this alternative vision of paradise. We follow the laundresses as they mount the elegant stairs with their laundry baskets up several flights to the rooftop drying terraces. There we find Nakashima's elegant wooden stair to help these souls, with generous hands, to hang with individually carved clothes pins with their fingers the sheets and shirts of their hands resultant labor performed below. This daily activity took us from sunrise to sunset from the basement to the attic. We retire for the night still literally in touch with the hands of ancestors who have sustained our lives through theirs.

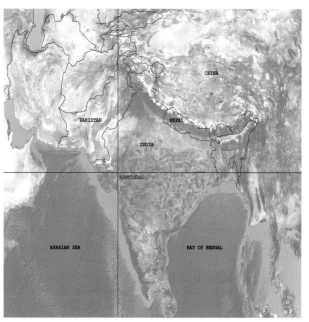

9. MONUMENTALITY AND THE MEASURE OF MAN
Millowner's Association Building, Ahmedabad, India (Le Corbusier, 1957)

From Pondicherry, we journeyed west again to the Arabian Sea to visit the ancient step-wells cut deep into the earth and the Jali screens which tempered life-giving sunlight in a myriad of pixielations offered daily by the sky reminding us of the multiplicities of the cosmos. Here we imagined and then longed for the deep grottos of scientific inquiry below and singular oculus above of Jefferson's Rotunda illuminating his vast collection of an Enlightenment Library.
In Ahmedabad, we saw many of Le Corbusier's monumental projects and permutations on Dwelling. All share a commitment in this extreme climatic condition to Tanazaki's ethical requisite criticism of Western Culture of progress evoked "In Praise of Shadows", published curiously in the same time of Le Corbusier's "Vers Une Architecture".

Le Corbusier had an incredible ability to create in both these monumental and modest structures a primary response to pervasive light and resultant chiaroscuro, but never losing the reference to the scale of the human hand as an instrument and active agent of change. This architect provided a seat outside the entry door of the Millowners's Association at the destination end of the ramp to pause; to change one's posture to look back from where one came. Upon entry, one finds an elongated bench within as a way to pause now as a group before entering the association hall of the association. One journeys up to a second level, by a twenty incremental digit stair to get to the piano nobile where a balcony is projected as a counterpart of the entry ramp to view the larger city extending to the western sea as another leitmotif of the Acropolis. The journey does not stop here but one mounts to the roof terrace with more benches to pause briefly to catch one's breath, and then a vast view is framed to the east where we see the Sarabhai River, however now engineered to become a lake from which this desert oasis springs. Here, we come yet again full circle to encounter the lessons of water at all scales in India from Pragpur the northern heritage village of canals and irrigation canals, to Pondicherry on the East where one sustains the soul within by dedicated daily maintenance, and now onto the 360-degree view from the roof of the Millowners Association. There are then explicit connective tissues in the watermarks that stain these surface and which nourish the genesis of our imaginative capacities. This project reminded us again that though we first sense and then read architecture primarily by hand and our ten digits there, it is also the journey, the promenade step by step at the pace of our heartbeats that takes us on a narrative passage from here to there by means of our two feet and their ten digits as well enabling our derivation from our four- limbed origins. Maybe, we now comprehend the enduring presence in myth and coincidental citizenship with the tribal monkeys of the Indian sub-continent who wisely and optimistically offer us this useful mantra "see no evil, speak no evil, think no evil".

10.

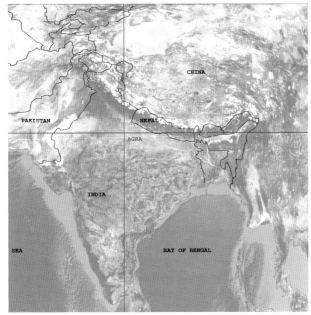

10. IMMENSITY AND PAUSE
Fatepur Sikri, Agra India , (Actors and Witnesses, 1571)

Our last stop took us North and East of Delhi again to Agra and to the constructed city of Fatepur Sikri by Akbar, the visionary Mogul Emperor who provided a vision of connective tissues for the hybridized Indian sub-continent for Hindus and Muslims specifically in distinct political and religious precincts. It is a world of both vast and intimate spaces, of sunlight and shadow, of groups and individuals, pavilions and colonnades, figures and fields, all the lessons seen in our fragmentary journeys touched with our hands and digits in this seven-week odyssey in India, yet infected by the Academical Village in our initial quarantine there. This modern project of hybridity demonstrates the archaic enduring lessons we have appreciated first in Chandigarh, then Pragpur, Pondicherry, onto Ahmedabad and finally Fatepur Sikri.

The vast Lawn of the Academical Village has its counterpart in the political forecourt of Fatepur Sikri where the high court pavilion of Akbar oversees the pavilion of the chess board for human-scapes beyond, surrounded by a water parterre, frontal stability contrasted to a dynamic play of figure and fields. These two pavilions respond to the space of the vast Islamic court where a prismatic shrine serves as an extroverted oculus, a distinct realm of the religious connected to a labyrinth of courts and gardens mediating the political from the religious as the Ranges and Gardens mediate the democratic Lawn of multiple botanical hybridity from the outer world of the America as a new Arcadian republic. Here we overlay our footsteps of correspondent dimensions and take measure of the two similar scales, then retreat as necessary into grottos of shade and the protective edges of the Akbar colonnades. Here we encounter ten steps, recalling the ten digits on our feet which hep us negotiate our humble human scale through architecture to serve as a covenant with the world, again and again. We are curiously at home with the scale of our modest limbs as well as the monumentality of these new world enterprises of Akbar and Jefferson. Against the vastness of the origins of the transposed Indian sub-continent from Africa with the resultant vast Himalaya Mountain range, we have taken measure of the Arabian Sea to the West and the Bay of Bengal to the East, as Jefferson left his project open to the South but placed the Rotunda as head to the North, clearly bounded by the water sources of Arcadia's vast rivers from the Ranges of the Appalachians and the Rockies. It is hoped that William Morrish would be pleased by these geological, archaeological and topographic heuristic narratives.

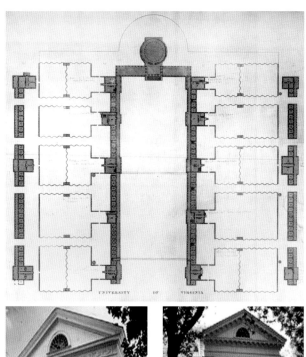

SYNTHESIS
The Academical Village, Charlottesville, Virginia (Thomas Jefferson, 1819-1826)

I return now to a place which is familiar to us all, the Lawn. How might these readings of projects from around the world be interpreted and translated to our reading of the Lawn? How can the Maverick plan be superimposed on the centers and edges of all these diverse projects close at hand and far, far away? What happens to our imaginative capacities if we imprint them true to scale on one another and then true to orientation? Does a human body appear? These works of architecture, through intense material consideration and rigor in craft, generate a greater diversity in scale of formal elements, and in the process more effectively relate to the scales of the human body, from our spine as accountable meter, onto the delicate but instrumental joints of our digits. These are structural, one might say systems within systems, while the weavings of connective tissues we associate with muscles and skins are nourished by our nervous, digestive and circulatory systems, the rivers and canals permitting the magic of our celestial soffits, and sensory aperture.

In each of these projects, the process of making architecture is integral to recovering the smallest scales of design which impact us the most at the modest sensorial oases of our digits by which we sense our world and which identifies our unique fingerprints, our visible ID, hiding our universal DNA of hybridity and connectivity.

Early in our educations, we learn to delight in combinations and permutations. The ten pavilions Jefferson projected on the Lawn is such an exercise in the delight of variations on a theme of caves and tents, the forest edge and the temple front, of the connective spaces of the accountable colonnades, the serpentine walls of Eden's gardens, Each distinct pavilion has a top, a middle and a bottom as if in decorum on the collective front Lawn, but all invest a deep basement if not grotto on their garden back sides, as if other orders of resistance assert themselves as necessary circumstance. The spatial edges of the Ranges encountered the vast topographic pre-conditions of Arcadia close by and familiar to the East, but extensive in Rebecca Solnit's prophecy of "The Blue of Distance" to the West. Look at each Pavilion, and one is not in the Hellenic Agora of serial transaction, but in the Roman Republican frictional Forum of the multiplicities of a she-wolf in dialogue with the enduring embers of the Vestal Virgins. Thomas Cole initiated a heuristic narrative for a New World cultural history; Solnit in her story continues this tale of connective tissues in praise of Lars Lerup's "Building the Incomplete". Here again Sanford Kwinter has the last word "What can be more Modern than the Archaic?"

"A foreigner visiting Oxford or Cambridge for the first time is shown a number of colleges, libraries, playing fields, museums, scientific departments, and administrative offices. He then asks 'But where is the University? I have seen where the members of the Colleges live, where the Registrar works, where the scientists experiment and the rest. But I have not yet seen the University in which reside and work the members of your University.' It has then to be explained to him that the University is not another collateral institution, some ulterior counterpart to the colleges, laboratories and offices which he has seen. The University is the way in which all that he has already seen is organized. When they are seen and when their coordination is understood, the University has been seen."

— Gilbert Ryle in The Concept of the Mind

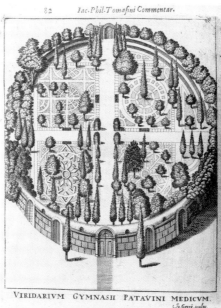

19

On Academical Gardens from Athens to Oxbridge onto The Piedmont
Claire Casstevens

ACADEMICAL GARDENS

Site matters. Architecture is not just about the structures that are built; it's about where they are grounded, too. Good architecture, I would argue, will consider where the sun rises and sets, the foundational geology, the topographic nature of a place, and the natural systems that are at play there. Several of the case studies you have covered through the past few lectures have pointed out the mutual framing that happens between architecture and its site or surrounds. The Miller House and Garden, Villa Savoye, Fallingwater—these are all works of architecture that provide particular thresholds for looking at the landscape. Today, I want to build upon that thread. But, I am going to shift the conversation beyond the house to a larger kind of dwelling: the university. It's a specialized place that educates and houses what might be considered a very large family.

SCHOOL OF ATHENS

In his essay *Academos*, which some of you may have had a chance to skim, Robert Pogue Harrison asks the question, "What does an education have to do with gardens?" He points out that "institutions of higher learning have had a long history of association with the garden." One of these is Plato's Academy in Athens, and that is where I want to begin my talk today. When we think about a modern educational institution, an image like this might come to mind: Raphael's fresco, The School of Athens. We see the acts of teaching and learning taking place within an architectural setting: lofty arches, white marble niches.

ACADEMY OF PLATO

This was not always true. The philosopher Plato had his own school in a place called Akademeia, a suburb about a mile northwest of the center of Athens. The site for his school was a sacred grove of olive trees. It was a place important to Athena, the goddess of wisdom, and it was there beneath the canopy that Plato taught through lectures and seminars. The words "academy" and "academic" are directly related to this place, Akademeia, and so we find the origins of a certain kind of education in none other than the garden. Today, I am going to explore this idea further—what is a university, what is a campus? How might we think of it through the lens of a pedagogical landscape, or an academical garden? Before I launch into this, I want to read to you one quotation from the British philosopher Gilbert Ryle's book, The Concept of the Mind. He writes: "A foreigner visiting Oxford or Cambridge for the first time is shown a number of colleges, libraries, playing fields, museums, scientific departments, and administrative offices. He then asks 'But where is the University? I have seen where the members of the Colleges live, where the Registrar works, where the scientists experiment and the rest. But I have not yet seen the University in which reside and work the members of your University.' It has then to be explained to him that the University is not another collateral institution, some ulterior counterpart to the colleges, laboratories, and offices which he has seen. The University is the way in which all that he has already seen is organized. When they are seen and when their coordination is understood, the University has been seen." Try to carry that with you. There's something more to the identity of a university than a collection of buildings. There are connections within and beyond, a sense of the institution is an interwoven collective rather than just an assemblage. Over the next hour or so, I am going to talk about some of the parts and some of the wholes that contribute to this. And I am going to do this through a landscape lens.

PADUA

A botanical garden is a world in a garden. A managed collection of plants usually organized by plant family; different species within a certain family are planted together in a garden bed. Botanical gardens offer a structured and distilled experience of the natural world.

Botanical gardens have a long history with universities extends back to 1543, when the University in Pisa in northern Italy established the world's first academic botanic garden" (Hough).

COMPARISON: LIBRARY AND GARDEN

In this direct comparison, the library at Leiden is on the left, and the botanical garden is on the right. You could see the garden as a living library, or the library as a garden of the night. These two places share the principle of being organized by some classification system to make the vastness of their contents, the vastness of the world, more understandable.

The library has shelves of topics, such as mathematics and philosophy, while the botanical garden shows plants arranged as individual specimens in rectangular beds grouped according to plant families. The rows of books have just enough space for a person to slip between them. The garden beds are also long and thin with a ground of gravel or grass in between them. This shape allowed all the plants to be directly accessed but also compared to one another. The two spaces both manage to separate information and bring information together at the same time. The big difference is the way you "read" that information. In the library, you read with your eyes and then use your imagination to explore a certain realm of thought; in the garden, you read with all of your senses and then use your imagination to explore a slightly different realm. It's as Pallasmaa writes in his book The Eyes of the Skin: "The senses define the interface between the skin and the world."

WATTS

Watts is an ecologist who, like a nomad, experiences the landscape through movement and through time. She keeps a close eye to her surroundings, carefully observing changes in the land and the plants that populate it. This passage that I am about to read takes place on the side of a road—a place of journeys—in the Great Smoky Mountains. She writes about finding a magnolia flower: "As I stood at the side of the hard modern road by the shiny modern automobile, and cupped the moonlight of the magnolia flower in my two modern prehensile hands, the warm June dusk around me seemed to brighten to a warm dawn—the dawn of flowering on the young earth. I could imagine the plash of broad reptilian feet behind me, and could pretend that I was seeing what no man ever saw: one of Nature's first experiments in producing a showy flower" (2). Watts here has keyed us in to the deep ecological history of this site in the Great Smoky Mountains through a single magnolia flower—a specimen. She has probed beyond superficial layers to traverse not only space but also time. She has imagined a place of origins, where the first flower first blossomed. The complexity of all of this is contained in the small talisman of this magnolia flower, which fits so simply in the palm of a hand. As one might read a book, she reads this flower and calls upon its power of association. She understands its language.

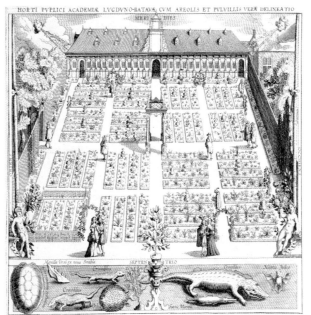

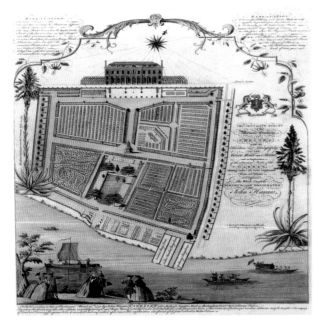

"Sometimes there were small sprays of brown oak leaves on the ground, though there were no trees anywhere within sight and shore was far away. Sometimes sodden crumpled clots of feather and bone that had once been birds sat on the strand. How the leaves arrived, how the birds died, was unfathom-able, that word meaning depths that cannot be plumbed. Be-hind me etched high into the rocks and mountains beyond the Great Salt lake was the waterline of Lake Bonneville, which had been so much bigger, so much deeper, long ago in a wet-ter era on ear th, when redwoods grew in Arizona and Death Valley was likewise a lake. Ten thousand years or more have passed since that lake ceased to exist , but its ring all around the landscape insisted that where I walked was once deep underwater

—*A Field Guide to Getting Lost by Rebecca Solnit*

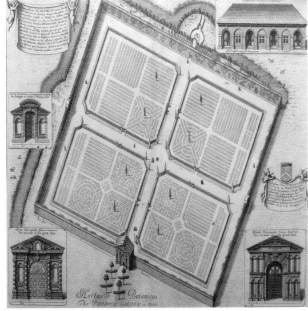

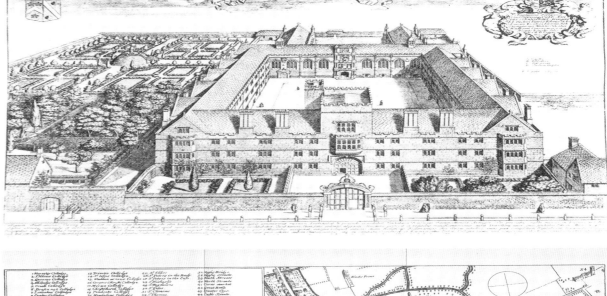

OXFORDE.

22

SOLNIT

Another example of this comes from Rebecca Solnit's A Field Guide to Getting Lost, which you have read. In one of her sections on "The Blue of Distance," she describes how she was able to walk over the floor of the Great Salt Lake in Utah during a year of drought. Like May Watts, Rebecca Solnit migrates through time as she migrates over the topography. She has the nomad's gift for sensing how this place is more than what might first meet the eye.

> Sometimes there were small sprays of brown oak leaves on the ground, though there were no trees anywhere within sight and shore was far away. Sometimes sodden crumpled clots of feather and bone that had once been birds sat on the strand. How the leaves arrived, how the birds died, was unfathomable, that word meaning depths that cannot be plumbed. Behind me etched high into the rocks and mountains beyond the Great Salt Lake was the waterline of Lake Bonneville, which had been so much bigger, so much deeper, long ago in a wetter era on earth, when redwoods grew in Arizona and Death Valley was likewise a lake. Ten thousand years or more have passed since that lake ceased to exist, but its ring all around the landscape insisted that where I walked was once deep underwater.

WINDOWS + FRAMES

So like the library, the botanical garden is a kind of pedagogical landscape that works as a tool for learning about medicine, botany, and horticulture, yes—but also more broadly illustrates how we as people, as societies, as cultures, attempt understand our place in the world through frames and windows, both literal and imagined.

MAP OF OXFORD

I am going to switch gears now and move on to the second part of the talk, which is based on the senior thesis in art history that I wrote as an undergrad at Vassar. This part is going to focus more on the idea of landscape as a setting for learning, and more specifically, the power of the image of a university to convey an idea or impression of what that institution for learning is all about. The focus here is representation—architecture and landscape as a mode of representation. We will be looking at the English universities of Oxford and Cambridge as represented in two sets of books that I studied for my thesis. To set the scene, here is a map of Oxford in the mid-1600s. Pretty much all of this is university land. Think about how you might describe what you see in this map. What spatial patterns emerge? Where do you find what you would call landscape, and what you would call city? How does it compare to some of the American universities that you have visited? For one, you might get a sense of the piecemeal operation of building up the University of Oxford over several centuries. Like botanical gardens, both Oxford and Cambridge are rooted in monastic tradition and functioned first as religious institutions. Before the advent of the modern university as we know it, it was the monastery where you would go to get an education.

Throughout the map, you can see a certain typology of buildings with enclose courtyards. This is the source for the collegiate quadrangle.

WADHAM COLLEGE

Oxford and Cambridge are both sprawling, complex university landscapes with quads as well as many other types of landscape and garden scattered throughout. In this one image, you can see several of them: lawns, enclosed gardens, botanical gardens, groves, maybe even an orchard.

COMPARISON: CHRIST CHURCH KITCHEN AND ALL SOULS LIBRARY

The messiest it gets in these two books is something like this on the left—a plate of Christ Church Kitchen. This is the banal subterranean hell occupied by university employees.

The kitchen is a polluted cavern full of billowing smoke. Despite the tall stacks of windows piercing the walls, the space remains dark and rather claustrophobically packed with seventeen laborers, each of which is consumed by a particular task: washing flatware; chopping vegetables; plating dishes; tending to the giant inferno. It's a scene of productivity, although the productivity here is distinct from the intellectual labor of the students.

The representation of spaces here speaks volumes about what is happening within them. The settings of these scenes could be interpreted as a reflection of the minds of those who inhabit them, for instance. We can easily visualize the difference between the students at work in the Library at All Souls College, where the lofty and dramatically-lit space suggests ultimate mental acuity, and the individuals in Christ Church Kitchen, where the soot of mindless labor suffocates intellect.

COMPARISON: MAGPIE LAND

Again, these books are using architecture, landscape, and space to suggest certain ideas, to portray priorities. Here is another comparison of an image from the Oxford book and an image by Rowlandson. In Pugin's image on the left, we see a vernacular scene: a street hemmed in by modest dwellings and shops. A window has been flung open on a building in the foreground, drawing attention to the effect of time and weather: faded paint exposes cracked brickwork. There's quiet conversation, the selling of goods. But the towering Gothic form of Merton College Chapel rising above the low rooftops is the main attraction of Pugin's work; offset by the billowing foliage next to it, it commands our attention. In the other rendition, Rowlandson has widened the street and the surrounding architecture remains nothing more than a scenic backdrop for a congregation of figures. Vendors, scholars, and a full stagecoach of passengers interrupt the clear path to the tower that is so venerated in Pugin's work. Rowlandson's Oxford is unmistakably one of people; Ackermann's is one of buildings.

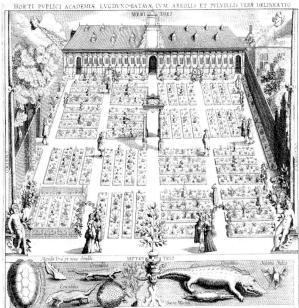

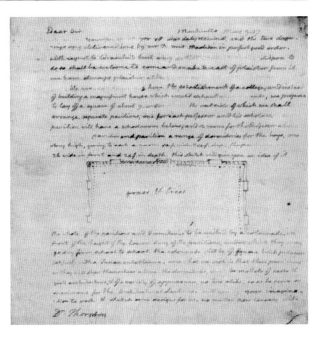

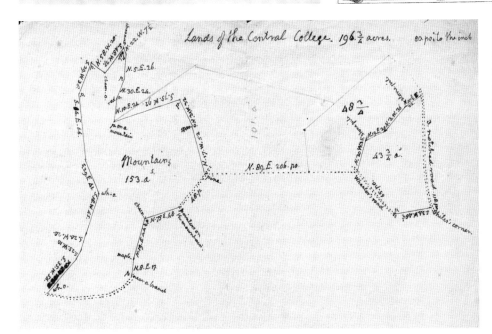

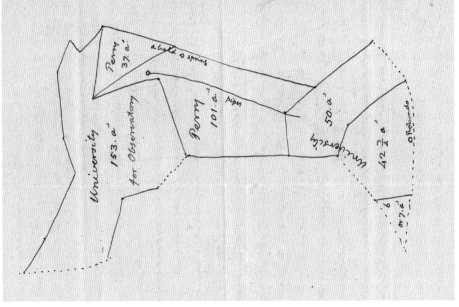

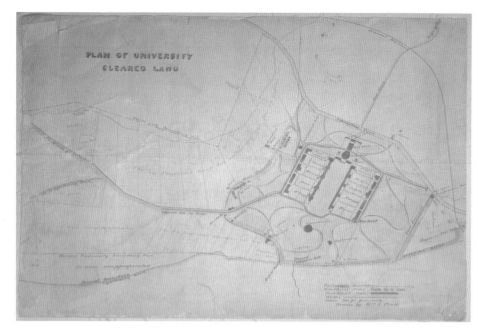

CLOISTERS AT MAGDALEN

In this image of the cloisters at Magdalen College, Pugin reminds us of the constructed nature of this place. We catch a gardener in the act of maintaining the grounds. The university is a place of great appearances, where what can be seen on the surface—the celebrated landscape, the masterful buildings, and even the traditional costumes of its populate—may not be representative of what was truly unfolding within. Thus, illustrations such as this one emphasize the power of the landscapes and architecture at Oxford and Cambridge to lend a beautiful veneer to the campuses and towns, one that suppresses interior worlds rife with institutional chaos near the turn of the 19th century.

MAINTENANCE

And actually, you see images of maintenance permeating these books. That round thing was a barrel usually filled with water that a gardener would roll over a lawn to flatten the grass and the ground beneath.

CLARE HALL

The books underscore the importance of the built and imaged campus landscape and architecture to the public reception of the universities—the idea that the buildings and the spaces between are a strong statement of identity and potential. In reading the text of these books and looking at the representations therein, we are much like the students that actually studied there. We are invited to stroll through this pedagogical space, this large-scale academical garden. We choose our imaginative experience—to be on this side of the river where agricultural fields are worked or the other where one dwells in a city? One celebrates either solid land or one of the boats floating in limbo in between the banks on either side.

BODLEIAN PLATE

What I hope to arrive at is an image of our own place of learning as less a village, and more an Academical Garden. But first, I wanted to share this pairing of a plate showing the College of William and Mary, the school that Jefferson attended, next to the print of the Leiden Botanical Garden that we looked at earlier. Hopefully it is clear that there is some kind of transmission that has happened between Europe and America. There's the importance of gardens as part of educational landscapes, also that specific practice of categorizing and organizing the plants and critters of the natural world as part of an educational agenda.

ORIGINAL SURVEY

This is the original survey. Showing it to you to illustrate that Jefferson's awareness of the importance of landscapes and gardens to his university has been central to the development of UVA. Jefferson actually purchased two plats of land, not one: the first was the land that the Academical Village sits upon, but the second was the top of Observatory Mountain.

SPRING SURVEY

This provided access to a spring, the headwaters of Meadow Creek, which provided the university with a water source. Land is resource.

GRASS AND TREES

His plan for the Academical Village didn't just include buildings but also grass and trees. A later map shows gardens for professors, lakes and water bodies, and even a botanic garden, and of course the Pavilion Gardens. Sensitive to the idea of landscape as a source for inspiration, as a tool and a setting for learning.

BOTANIC GARDEN SITE

But something you might not know about is an unbuilt project that Jefferson originally envisioned as being part of his university. And this was a botanical garden. Jefferson was a man who loved plants. I have found that discussions of Jefferson usually focus on either Jefferson the gardener or Jefferson the founder of the University of Virginia—rarely both.

But to me there is definitely cross-pollination between these two personas. As an avid gardener, Jefferson was well aware of the activities taking place at botanical gardens overseas. This was especially true for the Jardin du Roi in Paris, where the head gardener was a man by the name of Andre Thouin. On our tour at Monticello, the guide for my group said something about international seed exchange being illegal. But this was not at all the case—Thouin and Jefferson sent seeds back and forth to each other all the time. Jefferson even sent seeds collected from the Lewis and Clark expedition to Thouin.

This botanical exchange was really key to the development of Jefferson's gardens at Monticello, and probably influenced his desire to incorporate a botanical garden as part of his university. You might suddenly wonder, do we have a botanical garden today? Unfortunately, we do not. Because even though Jefferson was adamant about construction getting underway, he died before the project was ever started. He had even gotten so far as to pick a site for the garden—about six acres where Memorial Gym and the tennis courts now sit. This was the western edge of the university's landholdings, behind what was then the Anatomical Theatre and just south of Three Notch'd Road. The hillside would be planted with trees, while the base would contain the garden enclosed by a serpentine brick wall. It would have served as a teaching garden for a fledgling School of Botany within the university. In a letter written in 1814, Jefferson wrote that he ranked botany, "with the most valuable sciences, whether we consider its subjects as furnishing the orchards, the adornment of flower-borders, shade and perfume of our groves, materials for our buildings, or medicaments for our bodies… no country gentleman should be without what amuses every step he takes into his fields" (Fox-Brugiere). For Jefferson, then, having a botanical garden, and having plants on Grounds in general, was really important.

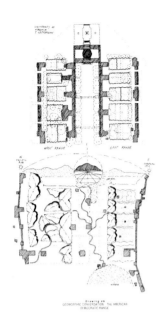

AERIAL

Often described as an architectural textbook—a place where the varying styles of the ten Pavilions help to educate students outside of the formal classroom setting. It enhances learning through observation and comparison of what are essentially living specimens. Given the scale of the space, you might also think of the Academical Village as a garden of people as well: About two hundred feet from one side to the other, the Lawn is small enough so that you can recognize the faces of those who walk on the other side. Similar to a botanical garden, the Academical Village houses a contained collection of students that you get to know very well.

PLATES

As much as Jefferson was aware of Oxford and Cambridge as a model for higher education—he even had this set of plates depicting scenes from the two universities at his home at Poplar Forest—he chose not to emulate them by importing their building styles. The Academical Village is no cloister, no enclosed garden. Instead, it throws open its arms to the mountains beyond and has a strong visual connection to the surrounding landscape. It turns outward to gaze at its natural condition. It is "poised between civilization and wilderness" (Chapman, quoting Goldberger). This is a garden, no?

COLE IMAGES

There was no need for the campus to look inward, when out there was a bountiful, expansive, sublime world. Jefferson was fascinated with what was out there—he was an avid gardener, he was the man who set the Lewis and Clark expedition in motion to explore the American West, he produced his own Notes on the State of Virginia.

Offer three examples of how the lawn connects to regional context.

MORRISH

On a broad scale, imagine the two external arcades of the Academical Village, the ones we call the "East and West Ranges." This refers to the way they are oriented, but it is also a continental diagram in which the ranges refer to the Appalachian Mountain range along the Atlantic and the Rocky Mountain Range along the Pacific. The transformation of this architectural world back into preconditions of the site is literal in this drawing, which comes from the book Civilizing Terrains. Throughout the book, the author William Morrish acknowledges how a region's topography—slope, aspect, geomorphology—might inspire and be reflected in architectural form.

INVENTORIES

Red clay was dug up from Madison Bowl and fired to make bricks. Wood was harvested from Observatory Hill. Sand was collected from the Rivanna River, mixed into a kind of plaster that covers the columns to make them look like they have been carved out of stone. The effect of this is lost when the columns are painted white, but when unpainted, they also truly recall the river because there are small flakes of mica that glisten when the light hits them just right. The presence of trees that provide shade on the Lawn is an acknowledgement of local climate—the hot, humid Virginia summer, where shade is a necessity. These materials—dug, harvested, planted—link the history of a site to the built works that sit upon it and suggest the Academical Village as an Academical Garden. A garden, then, is both connected and set apart.

SERLIO

Like a stage set, it mimics the world out there but is a condensed and reassembled version. The tradition in America, at least, is to go off to college. You confront the world on your own for perhaps the first time. You begin to establish your stance, your worldview, the way you relate and respond. You form a relationship with a place, becoming embedded in both a new society as well as the preconditions of a biophysical world. You learn in the classroom from other students, but also through this process of navigating this microcosm within the larger university.

FRIEDRICH

You may get a little lost in the vast groves of Academe, or in the microcosm of a flower, in a book, one's own imagination, or better yet engaged in conversation with others. But, hopefully when you find yourself again, you have learned something new.

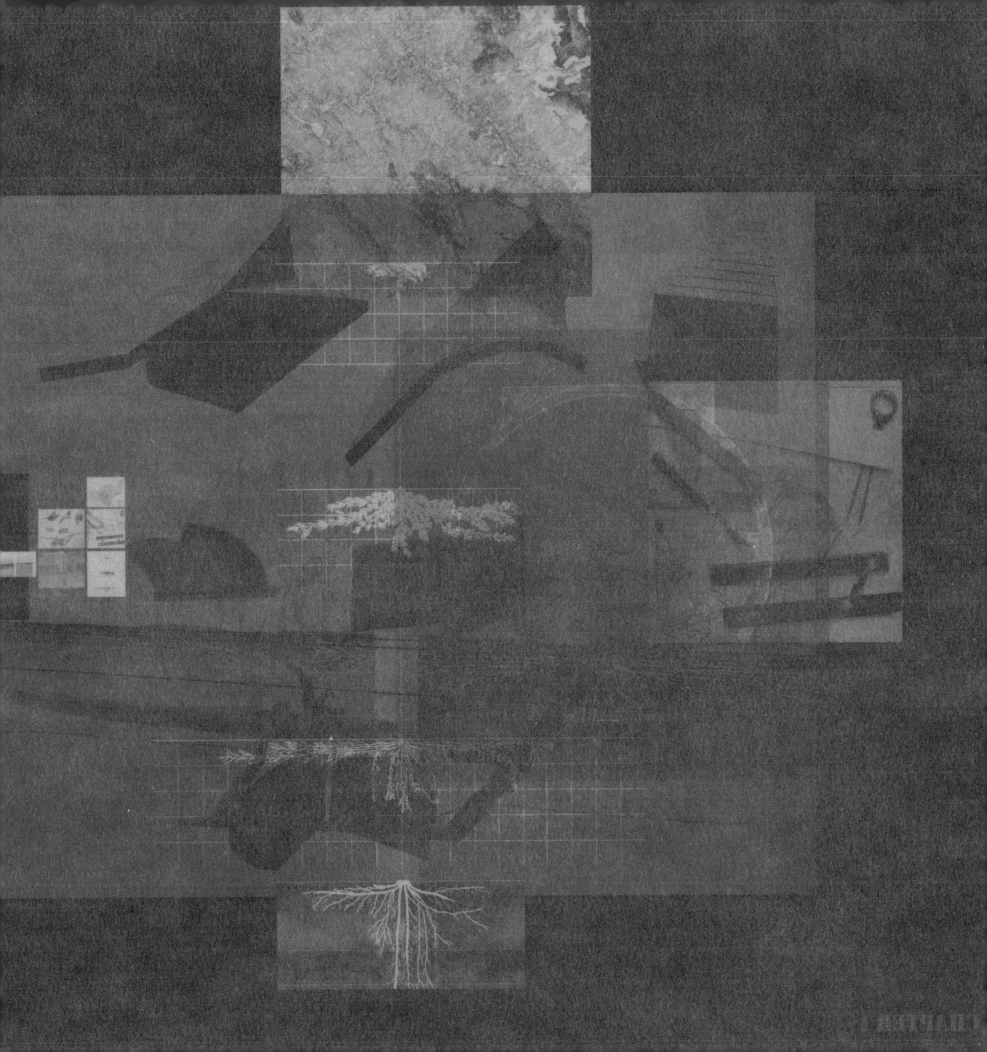

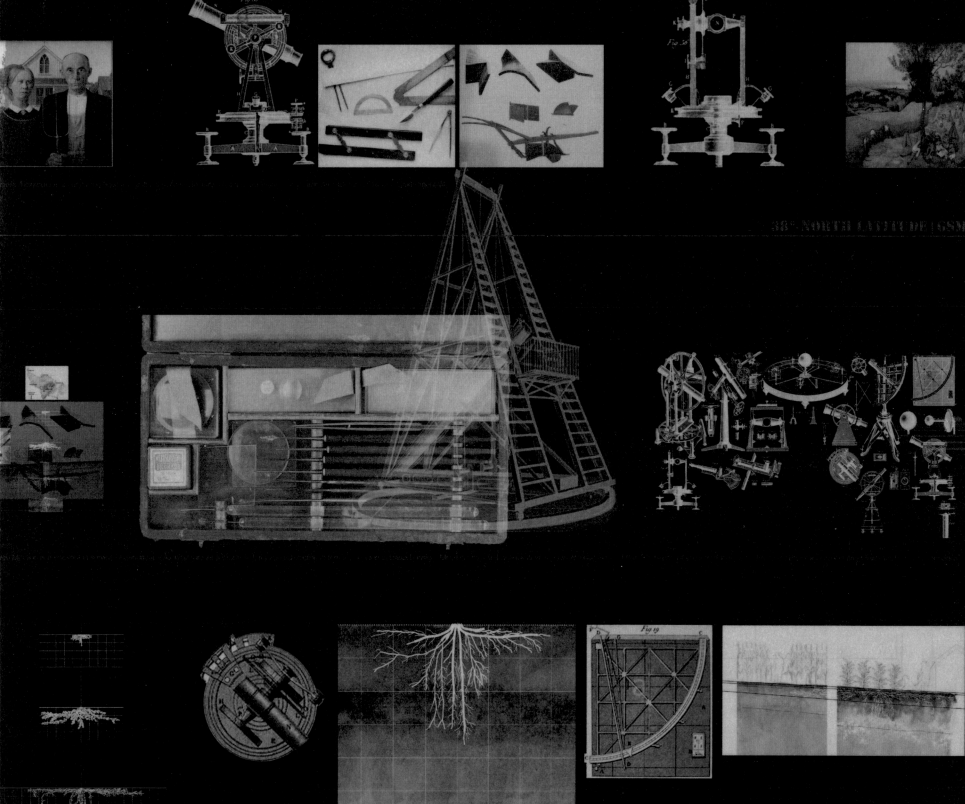

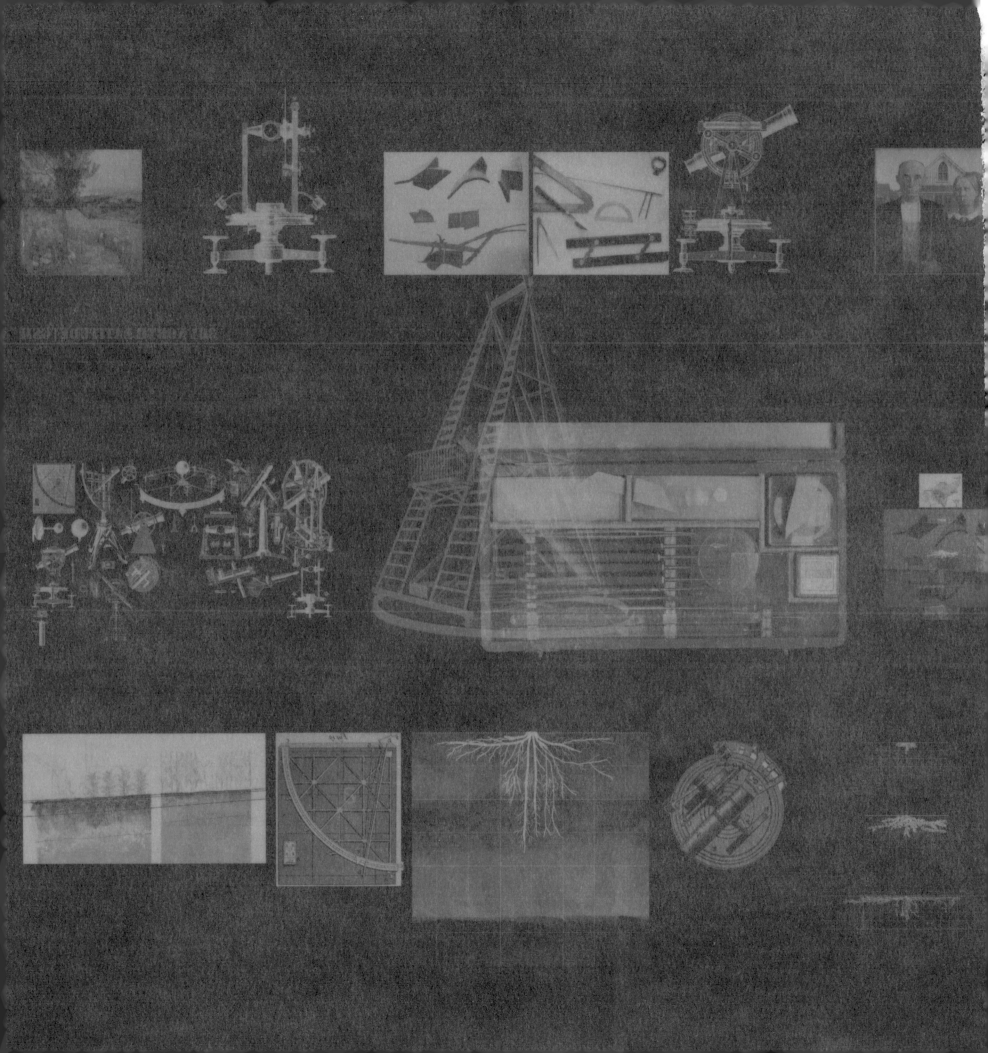

CHAPTER ONE: PRECONDITIONS

Earth as a Tool for Revealing, by Danielle Alexander

Roots and Routes, by Gwen McGinn

Connective Tissue #1 Preconditions: On Scientists First and then Magicians Last, by Peter Waldman

Danielle Alexander is an anthropologist and cultural historian in service of re-envisioning Landscape Architecture in terms of instrumentality.

Gwen McGinn is a scientist in service of Landscape Architecture as a grounded, rigorous discipline in terms of evidence-based design.

McGinn offers first an inventory and typological matrix of tree Roots before she introduces us to the possibility of an Urban Forest reiterated

in the Colonnades.

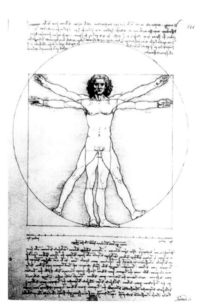

Earth as a Tool for Revealing
Danielle Alexander

The plough is to the farmer what the wand is to the sorcerer. Its effect is really like sorcery.
Thomas Jefferson to Charles Wilson Peale, Monticello, April 17, 1813.

Technology is a way of revealing. If we give heed to this, then another whole realm for the essence of technology will open itself up to us. It is the realm of revealing, i.e., of truth.
Martin Heidegger, The Question Concerning Technology, 1954.

Earth is many things: a material, a planet, a substrate, a home.

A house on a hill, a university on a ridge, a retreat in a forest: these are a few of the architectural works Jefferson carved a space for in the ground and set into the world. These actions were experiments with the ground, which enchanted him. The site revealed to him its architectural potential, and it is through tools he allowed his imagination to work into the ground and the ground worked back through him. It was a character Jefferson held discourse with, as well as the preconditions by which he molded his vision, and in turn, his vision was molded.

In order to commune with the earth, Jefferson was dependent upon tools. Jefferson made assiduous notes about his tools. He calculated all they could assist him in accomplishing. He measured their inputs and outputs. A lover of investigation and experimentation, he envisioned greater potentials for them and conjured up improvements.

Our human relationship with tools has been investigated over time: we are fascinated with it. Why do we use tools? What does it say about us? What are they made of? What do we do with them? What do they do to us?

FROM THE BEGINNING

One of the very first images we saw in this course is Corbusier's sketch of the night view from the Rio de la Plata. In the dark of the universe, we are not only oriented to our world through the horizon, but also our own insertions into this space. It is through tools that we can create these forms. To begin this exploration of our relationship to tools, I will first recall some other images that you have seen through the course and provide an alternative reading through their depiction of tools.

In the very first week, regarding spatial tales of origin, we encountered many characters that demonstrated the origins of our views of the accountability of architecture, the construction of our histories, and relationship to the unknown. Each of these depictions of characters is laden with messages about tools as well. The sphinx and pyramid demonstrate tools crafting the same material into different forms. The solid material of earth and stone, dug and carried from a distance, has been crafted by tools and human hands to form the rational pyramid as well as the expressive sphinx. George Washington, in this painting by Grant Wood, is depicted with his axe, an instrument that gives way to a story of shaping one's environment and character. Parson Weems the author of the fable, writes:

When George was about six years old, he was made the wealthy master of a hatchet! Of which, like most little boys, he was immoderately fond, and was constantly going about chopping everything that came in his way. One day, he unluckily tried the edge of his hatchet on the body of a beautiful young English cherry tree, which he barked so terribly, that I don't believe the tree ever got the better of it. The next morning the old gentleman, finding out what had befallen his tree, came into the house. With much warmth asked for the mischievous author. Presently George and his hatchet made their appearance. His father said, George, do you know who killed that beautiful little cherry tree yonder in the garden? This was a tough question; and George staggered under it for a moment; but quickly recovered himself. Looking at his father, with the sweet face of youth brightened with the inexpressible charm of all-conquering truth, he bravely cried out, I can't tell a lie, Pa; you know I can't tell a lie. I did cut it with my hatchet.

Grant Wood depicted Washington as an adult and master of a tool. Another North American hero, Sassacus, Chief of the Pequots, led his tribe in the Pequot War in 1637 against the settlers of the Pilgrim Colony and Massachusetts Bay Colony. He was captured in battle and executed by a rival tribe that fought on the side of the English. Here he is shown with his staff and ornaments, depicting his relationship with the beasts and tools that crafted his legacy before he was executed. The Vitruvian man, Leonardo da Vinci's drawing inscribing the body simultaneously in both a circle and a square, illustrates geometries and proportions and shows the body itself as tool of measurement.

The boy scout, in Norman Rockwell's painting, demonstrates two individuals, with their walking sticks for the journey into the unknown, but also the pack containing the tools needed to complete it. And Robinson Crusoe, also a character in the unknown, having been washed ashore by shipwreck only to encounter cannibals, captives, and pirates. He holds an umbrella, a mechanical tool protecting him from the elements; a tent. He also holds a gun, a hybrid of the chemical and mechanical, metal and wood, which requires a mechanical pull of the trigger and chemical reaction of gunpowder. Like Washington has a hatchet.

Peter also showed the Limbourg Brothers illustrated manuscript. Not only do we see scenes depicting peasants and tools, but the scenes operating within systems of technology and measurement. Peter then explored built works such as the Eric Goodwin Memorial Passage. It taught us lessons of giving and grace, as well as ways of orienting ourselves in the world. It also displayed sensitivity to tools and tectonics, as well as methods of making.

Most recently, in Catharine's essay, we jumped scales and were offered 10 lessons that can just as easily be interpreted in tools as through the human experience. Tectonics, the inner logic of construction, demonstrates the effectiveness of tools and identifies their applications. Weathering, through the lessons of subtraction and addition outlined by Catharine, provides a revealing of the marks of the tools as well as what is not immediately shown, such as embedded materials. All the exemplary walls referred to by Killien in her essay on Two Hands and Ten Digits, are an immediate response and display of the tool upon the surface of the material.

Now here these illustrations of tools of evolving layers illustrate the archaeological imagination of tools used in construction. The aggregation of materials, the addition of steel to wood and brick, allows us to look back in order to move forward. Choreography performs in two ways: in relating scales through a spatial sequence as well as performance of a space in time. Each of these also engages different kinds of tools in their production. The first shows not only the scales of space, but also that different scales of construction would require the same tools, as with the shaping of stone in its bench and slab for seating. The second, through the many performances of clipping flowers, the execution of Caesar, and the slicing of pizza throughout time conjures the tools required for these actions: this plaza is one of many blades.

Materiality, like tectonics, identifies the applications and potential for tools to reveal the textures, weights, temperatures, scales, and sensations made possible by tools. The action of the tools deepens the meaning of the material. The scale and pace of the human reveals the alteration by tools along a path. Early in the journey, handmade bricks line the runnel, where later they are replaced with materials manipulated by finer tools.

Maintenance implies the use of specific tools in order to prevent the deterioration of the work of the original tools and craftspeople. Here we see the wood, which required tools unique to that of the stone louvers to construct, and will require equally unique tools to maintain.

Monumentality in experience presences us to the manipulations of tools. The formwork in contrast to the stonework strikes us with astounding clarity and the tools used to shape this experience are evident in the markings they leave behind.

Lastly, some tools are not as apparent upon first notice. Here, the tools are not just the steps, but the water itself, providing a way of registering the climate events of the season. Also, the rich patina reveals the embossing by instruments and fingernails. These lessons remind us to be awake and present when experiencing architecture. We must read our world and reorganize our views in many ways to see what lessons there are to learn.

TOOLS AND TIME

Moving on, let us look now to how we use tools in the naming of our histories. Tools mark important developments for humans over time. In archaeology, three ages define the development of humans through the tools they used and the materials they worked with, the Stone Age, the Bronze Age, and the Iron Age. The dates that I have shown are rough, just intended to give you a general sense of their span, though each of these ages does not necessarily have a specific beginning or end and certainly overlap, differing with location.

The Stone Age is loosely defined by several eras of human history. Its name refers to humans working with stone to craft tools or as material. Here are two images of Stone Age tools, showing marks where they were shaped to be sharper for stabbing, scooping, grinding, and cutting. These tools were mechanically shaped. Some would have had wooden handles, while others would be held directly in the hand. The Bronze Age is the first age defined by a material chemically shaped by humans. Tin would be mined, then smelted, then added to molten copper to make bronze. This process produced more refined tools and works of art. Here the presence of the handle is more obvious due to the void where the wood became dislodged and deteriorated. The Iron Age continues our human development into the realm of chemical processes to shape our tools. Here we see knives and blades made of iron form this period.

Each of these ages did not have to be so named. The Stone Age could have easily been defined as The Age of the Genus Homo. The Bronze Age could have been named The Age of the Development of Trade. The Iron Age could have been named The Age of Writing, due to the introduction of written characters and the development of literature in many cultures in this period. Yet, we name them for tools and materials which we developed.

Throughout the ages we have continued to document tools, how they are used, and what we can accomplish with them. Our fascination with tools has worked its way into our art forms, which substantially document our evolving relationships.

Jumping forward a few eras, let us look to a few drawings created during the Age of the Enlightenment. This age, a cultural movement in the seventeenth and eighteenth centuries, sought to define human history and reform society using reason and knowledge. All that was known was catalogued. Denis Diderot, a French philosopher, writer, and art critic wrote and drew extensively on tools and the development of technology and science. Here in these two images, he demonstrates building techniques, but also people working with tools to accomplish them. He draws the construction images and documents the tools and processes. There is no building without the tools required.

In the very same catalogue, he demonstrates the processes of agriculture, natural history, and geology. In the first slide, we see an understanding of a person's relationship with the deep section of the ground as they perform their work. The miner is in search of these crossing and intersecting mineral seams. Also, the surveying of the surface is demonstrated as can be seen by the crisscrossing guidelines. Lastly, we see an illustration of agriculture. Iterations of a plow are drawn, and above, people are drawn using the plow to work the land.

Now we still see an interest in documenting and cataloguing tools. Clemens Wimmer is a German art critic who documented the history of garden tools. Not only does he show images that were created to demonstrate the variety of tools needed for gardening activities, but he also shows that these tools were valued to demonstrate one's status, a relationship going beyond the instrumentality of the tool. He also shows many catalogues of tools and how they have been iterated over time. Many of the tools he documents would have been similar to those used by Jefferson's laborers on Monticello.

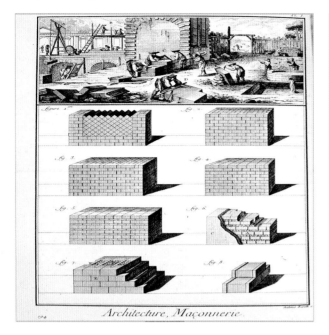

Architecture, Maçonnerie.

Tuilerie.

Histoire Naturelle, Fig. 1 Maniere de tracer les Concessions des Mines.

Minéralogie, 7.me Collection Filons et travaux des Mines. Pl. III.

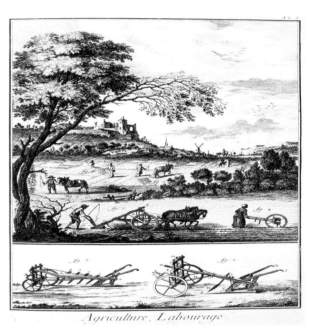

Agriculture, Labourage.

TOOLS IN ART

I'd like to now show some artworks I find particularly inspiring in their depiction of tools and their relationships to us. Earlier we saw a painting by Grant Wood depicting George Washington with his axe. This painting, American Gothic, is one of the most famous of his paintings. Here we see a man and his daughter, the man holding a tool. The tines of the pitchfork are metal, the handle, wood. His hand molds to the wood, which is split or capped by the iron of the tines, which then cut into the earth to turn, aerate, and shape it. The forms of his tool are reflected elsewhere in the work, as seen in the folds and seams of his overalls as well as inverted in the structure of the mullions. The materials too are reflected in his glasses as well as the wood of the building.

Pieter Bruegel the Elder, a Flemish Renaissance painter, created many works in the mid-1500s of peasants in their landscape. In each of them, the peasants work with tools to shape the land, harvest crops, or build. The Tower of Babel narrates peasants at work in the construction of the tower described in Genesis. It is written, "Then they said, Come, let us build ourselves a city, and a tower with its top in the heavens, and let us make a name for ourselves, otherwise we shall be scattered abroad upon the face of the whole earth." We see in the painting that this was not to be, that there are pieces crumbling as the peasants attempt this Sisyphean task. Tools here are at work shaping our construction sites at the scale of the city and humans relationship to nature. It is also demonstrating the ephemerality of their affects as the works fall into decline.

In Haymaking, each of the characters is shown with a tool—and again—a beast facilitates some of the action. The tools are worked into the land and bring about bounty. This painting is one of six in a series, demonstrating the use of tools throughout the year. The characters stay the same, but they depend upon different tools to work the land. In The Harvesters, we see peasants at work and at rest. Both the work and the rest are narratives made possible by the tools. Their tools in the form of a plow have initially shaped the land. In the foreground, we see the removal of the wheat at harvest time, in the middle ground is situated the prerequisites of a watering hole, and in the background, this same story is extrapolated.

This one is my favorite of them all. This painting, made circa 1555, displays the fall of Icarus. The fall of Icarus is a Greek myth. It is told that Icarus's father, Daedalus, made him wings of wax so he could fly. Icarus chose to ignore his father's warnings about the material of the wings and flew too near the sun, which caused the wings to melt, and as you can see from the painting, Icarus fell to the earth and drowned in the sea.

What interests me is the placement of the peasant in the foreground and his activities. He pushes a plow, and we see a rough cliff face be made smooth and terraced by the actions of the plow, man and beast. The man holds the wooden handle, which connects to the metal blade, which connects to his beast. The whole is a working technological system. The blue of distance here is twofold, the sky and ocean meeting. The sun, setting where the two met, may have betrayed Icarus but it is the peasant's ally in working the land and cultivating crops. I hope you all have noticed that there is a statue of Icarus right here on campus, and if not, you should go find it – it is not very far from here.

JEFFERSON AND HEIDEGGER, OR TOOLS AND THE EARTH

Now we move to Jefferson. A house on a leveled hill, a university on a ridge, a retreat in a forest between two mounds: these are a few of the architectural works for which Jefferson carved a space in the ground and set into the world. These actions were experiments with the ground, which enchanted him. The site revealed to him its architectural potential, and it is through tools he allowed his imagination to work into the ground and the ground worked back through him. It was a character Jefferson held discourse with, as well as the preconditions by which he molded his vision, and in turn, his vision was molded.

In order to commune with the earth, Jefferson was dependent upon tools. Jefferson made assiduous notes about his tools. He calculated all they could assist him in accomplishing. He measured their inputs and outputs. A lover of investigation at Monticello, the Lawn, Academical Village, and Poplar Forest.

In order to have a better grasp on Jefferson's interactions with technology and how it creates a dialogue between him and the land, let's take a deeper look into the philosophy of our human relationship with technology. We tend to think of technology as a means to an end, such as in the manufacturing of an object. If we seek a definition beyond this, we might be able to further unpack how Jefferson interacted with technology to shape his sites and the agency the tools he used had.

For Heidegger, our relationship to technology is an essential way of interacting with the world, and a way of understanding the agency of objects. He claims that all objects have an "essence." "When we are seeking the essence of 'tree', we have to become aware that what pervades every tree, as tree, is not a tree that can be encountered among all other trees." What he means here is that essence does not necessarily define an object, but it is its quality of operating in the world. This demonstrates philosophy here.

It isn't about technology being about the technological, it is about how we interact with technology and what it means. However, because we interact with it every day, our understanding of it is compromised. This also grows more complicated by our desire to get in control of technology. We are continually struggling to use it to solve problems and solve the problems it creates. He observes, "The will to mastery becomes all the more urgent the more technology threatens to slip from human control."

For a moment, I would like to return to a set of images we saw earlier in the semester. Here are Serlio's Comic, Tragic, and Satyric theatre sets. Our desire for control through our tools and the construction of our city set the stage for the drama of life to play out before us.

Notice how the city constructed in the most orderly fashion, with the heightened sense of perfect perspective, is the set used for the tragic.

Earlier I demonstrated examining the elements of the tools as wood and metal, mechanical and chemical. Heidegger also breaks down an element into examinable parts. He calls these elements "causes", drawing upon earlier philosophers. He writes, using a chalice as an example of an instrument.

Monticello

The Lawn and Academical Village

Poplar Forest

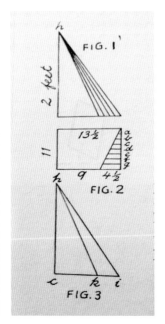

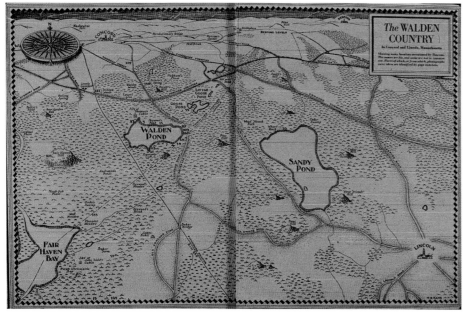

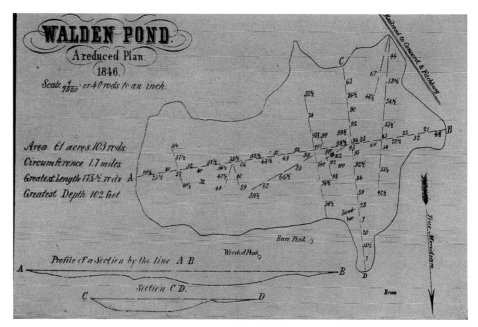

For centuries philosophy has taught that there are four causes:
1. The *causa materialis*, the material, the matter out of which, for example, a silver chalice is made;
2. The *causa formalis*, the form, the shape into which the material enters;
3. The *causa finalis*, the end, for example, the sacrificial rite in relation to which the chalice required is determined as to its form and matter;
4. The *causa efficiens*, which brings about the effect that is the finished, actual chalice, in this instance, the silversmith. What technology is, when represented as a means, discloses itself when we trace instrumentality back to fourfold causality.

So again, to reiterate, we will look at a model of Jefferson's plow at Monticello. Its *causa materialis*, the actual material out of which an element is made, are iron, wood, and the rope that connects it to the ox or horse. Its *causa formalis*, the form the material is made into, are how those tectonically come together in the shape of a plow at the angles and joints he designed. Its *causa finalis*, the system in which it operates, determining its form and material, is the system of shaping the earth which entails movement and force. Its *causa efficiens*, that which enacts the operation of the element, are the actors that bring it into operation.

These *causa* set up relationships between the tool and its user. To examine this, Heidegger analyzes how a tool is indebted to its user and the user responsible to the tool. A tool is only really a tool when it is being enacted. If it is just present at hand, it demonstrates the *causa materialis* and *causa formalis*, but not the *causa finalis* or *causa efficiens*. So right now, this plow is but a sculpture. It is the idea of a plow, but it lacks the true essence of a plow.

Bringing forth brings out of concealment into concealment. Heidegger says, "Technology is no mere means. Technology is way of revealing. It reveals whatever does not bring itself forth and does not yet lie here before us, whatever can look and turn out now one way or another." Heidegger has come to somewhat of a conclusion. I show the Maverick plan of the university here as a reminder that this was not originally designed to be this size. It was designed to be much larger, with a square lawn. However, through the shaping of the earth through various technologies, the form of the lawn was revealed as it is now.

So, this all seems simple enough by this point. Technology allows us to reveal the potential forms of things. Jefferson used technology and tools to reveal things here that otherwise could have been one way or another, a university opening its arms out to the world, a house on a hill with rows of gardens. It almost seems too easy to understand. Which is why as soon as you have a grasp on what Heidegger's talking about, the ideas wax in complexity through the introduction of opposition to these ideas of technology. They most readily apply themselves to a craftsman's technologies and potentially not modern machine-powered technology.

This sets up the essence and definition of technology anthropologically, which Heidegger also acknowledges. He calls this enframing.

That which is primally early shows itself only ultimately to men. Therefore, in the realm of thinking, a painstaking effort to think through still more primally what was primally thought is not the absurd wish to revive what is past, but rather the sober readiness to be astounded before the coming of the dawn.

Our orientation to tools is essential to our orientation to the world, and vice versa. In excavating this knowledge, we are not delving into nostalgia, but preparing ourselves for an awakening of our senses about what is to come. Thus, Heidegger jumps into an understanding of our orientation to the world. Our experience of the world is mediated through our relationship to technology. Technology allows for us to enact our intentions.

However, the enframing created, especially through modern technologies, has the potential to impede the more "primal truth." Technology and what it makes possible or impossible, as we struggle for mastery over it, defines then how we shape the world, due to what is known and how it enframes our relationship to the world. Heidegger therefore posits that perhaps it is this, therefore, that makes possible the revealing, which is the essence of technology.

Many of these conclusions put forth by Heidegger are reflected in a work many of you may have read in high school or otherwise. Walden; or, Life in the Woods details the daily experiences of Henry David Thoreau as he lived simply and self-sufficiently two miles outside of Concord, Massachusetts. Like Jefferson, he plotted out and examined his land as a surveyor, seeking to use it optimally.

Here are his simple living quarters, where he dwelled for two years while writing and farming his land.

Just as Jefferson deeply connected with the plow, Thoreau also had a tool he wrote extensively about: the hoe. He spent much of his time cultivating a bean field and writing about it. He writes,

> It was a singular experience that long acquaintance which I cultivated with beans, what with planting, and hoeing, and harvesting, and threshing, and picking over and selling them -- the last was the hardest of all -- I might add eating, for I did taste. I was determined to know beans. When they were growing, I used to hoe from five o'clock in the morning till noon, and commonly spent the rest of the day about other affairs.

His pursuit of farming was a pursuit of knowledge facilitated by tools. He calls the experience an acquaintance, indicating he is only scratching the surface of understanding, though he would spend seven hours a day each day working into the earth to cultivate them.

Thoreau's way of knowing is a thing he questions throughout. He writes,

> The intellect is a cleaver; it discerns and rifts its way into the secret of things. I do not wish to be any busier with my hands than is necessary. My head is hands and feet. I feel all my best faculties concentrated in it. My instinct tells me that my head is an organ for burrowing, as some creatures use their snout and fore paws, and with it I would mine and burrow my way through these hills. I think that the richest vein is somewhere here- about; so, by the divining-rod and thin rising vapors I judge; and here I will begin to mine."

He compares intellect to a tool, a cleaver. His description is very much alike to Heidegger's expression about truth, in that questioning and understanding uncover the concealed essence of things. A deep understanding of the earth is what motivates him, and he uses the metaphor of the divining rod in seeking truth.

Lastly, he makes a direct statement about how tools define us:

> But lo! men have become the tools of their tools. The man who independently plucked the fruits when he was hungry is become a farmer.

Through our engagement of tools, our societal roles are defined. Also, this returns to Heidegger's concept of enframing, in that once we have built our relationship to technology, it defines our way of acting in the world. If technology is so dependent on our enactment of it, then where do we draw the line between our tool and ourselves? We envision the ends of the technological cycle, in which we have hammered a nail into a board or pushed a plow through a field. Tools thus become the conduit for our intentions and imagination.

Now I will reiterate some of these lessons in the evidences of tools and their marks left on Jefferson's projects. Jefferson's imagination ran wild on the lawn, at Monticello, and at Poplar Forest.

If technology is affected by enframing, these sites have their own methods of enframing due to the technologies applied to them. The lawn here is somewhat abstracted from the surrounding landscape, but displayed within the bounds of the pavilions are the terraces cutting across the lawn. These cuts serve to produce a stepping down from all that is known in the world to all that is unknown. Through tools a ridge has been turned into a series of flat surfaces. This method was applied throughout the piedmont of Virginia, as it was the prime technology for sculpting the land into inhabitable space. Here we see this action in the earth from the side. The stepping down of the ground is reflected in the stepping down of the brick, and the angled connections of the woodworking lattice of the porch railings. We see this again at the backside of the eastern pavilion gardens.

In a letter to James Madison, Jefferson wrote: "I set out on this ground, which I suppose to be self-evident, 'that the earth belongs in usufruct to the living'". In his shaping of the earth with tools, he enables it to be a tool for the living to inhabit it and perform within. These spaces then recycle themselves over time. Here the anatomical theatre deconstruction provides bricks that were used for the reconstruction of serpentine walls and other academic buildings at the university. Here we see the process of construction of the walls using recycled bricks

By now you all have been to Monticello as well. We see in this topographical drawing that not only did he use tools to level the hill, but to sculpt the ways to access the site. Monticello demonstrates the many ways in which Jefferson played with tools on the land. Using the same earth-moving techniques, he terraces, and sets walls to retain his terraces.

Some methods required more discrete and calculated tool usage, such as in the construction of a French drain here. His garden, a place of botanical experimentation, also served as a site of tool experimentation yet again. While at times tools yield just another flat terrace, at other times they reshape the earth into

different surfaces. Monticello is full of experiments with the earth, and a building full of tools, reminding us that Jefferson's visions were crafted through his obsessions with tools. Tools made of metal and wood, and have cases and moveable parts.

Lastly, I will return to a few images that Paul Golisz showed of Poplar Forest. This first image shows the house between the two mounds of earth. Paul noted that a shovelful of earth would become brick, but we also see that a shovelful of earth becomes constructed earth, earthen mounds flanking and orienting his retreat. A sunken lawn in the center, created through the same terracing techniques as at Monticello.

In these images, we see tools at work in the construction of the structure itself. Different masonry methods are revealed on the inside than on the outside. The joining of materials is apparent in the exposed ceilings during renovations. Lastly, the property pays homage to construction and tools through maintaining the formworks and models for the gutters that line the offices.

The more we enter this field, the more digital technologies become our tools for creation and enframe our ways of designing. Malcolm McCollough discusses the relationship of our hands to tools to our digital practices as architects in Abstracting Craft. He writes, "Hands are underrated. Eyes are in charge, minds get all the study, and heads do all the talking. Hands type letters, push mice around, and grip steering wheels, so they are not idle, just underemployed. This is a sorry state of affairs, for hands can contribute much to working and knowing."

By pointing, by pushing and pulling, by picking up tools, hands act as conduits through which we extend our will to the world. They serve also as conduits in the other direction: hands bring us knowledge of the world. Hands feel. They probe. They practice. They give us sense, as in good common sense, which otherwise seems to be missing lately. McCollough accuses industry of being "a beast without hands, whose dull and monotonous products remain only at the threshold of art." But he usually praises hands without any explicit critique of industrialization, and celebrates tools as a way of probing the world. "I do not know if there is a break between the I and the mechanical orders—I am not very sure of it—but the implement at the end of his arm does not refute man's existence." This is to say that tool usage, even when machine-powered, can remain very much humane.

As you move through your careers as designers, many of you will go on to produce beautiful drawings that then are handed off to contractors instructing how and what to build, which are then inhabited by people who will care (or not care) for them. You may never know what it is like to physically construct the bracings and frameworks, or craft the details of a handrail once you leave this building of investigation and iteration. You will use your mouse, produce an image, laser cut it, 3d print it, route it. I encourage you to deeply engage with the tools not only of construction of building and earth, but of your concepts as well. Make use of your pencils and woodshop, and keep in touch with your humanity through the tool you hold in your hands. Be a surveyor, with your compass and rod. Be a nomad, with your walking staff and flint. Be a lunatic, with your astral instruments and magic wands. Be inspired by tools.

Roots and Routes
Gwen McGinn

There is an entire living landscape below ground that we can't see. Seeds germinate, and roots grow. These roots are thought to grow in every direction to find a balance of available air, water, and nutrients. Roots often extend laterally more than twice the height of a tree. The thickest of the roots support the tree, but much of the root system is composed of finer roots. Many grow upward from the lateral support roots towards the surface of the soil, where air and nutrients are most abundant. Roots exude chemicals that alter their surroundings. These chemicals can inhibit the growth of other plants, or even support other plants by transferring carbon to them. Below ground, roots may communicate with each other in ways that we are only beginning to understand. The ground is thick. The ground is alive.

The ground has been built by the plants that were there once before. Each plant alters, consumes, and creates the ground that it grows within. Each plant absorbs minerals and releases others through its roots. When the plant dies, it decomposes, and becomes part of the soil. On both geologic and human time scales, different communities of plants have altered the existence of the Academical Village. The hardwood forests that once grew on the Lawn would have been dense with roots. Once the forests were cleared to create fields for agriculture, the decomposing roots would fertilize the fields of tobacco and corn. These crops would have been planted annually—a constant quick cycle of nutrient absorption and depletion. Today, the trees and the turf of the Lawn each seem stately and permanent. In reality, they will continue to evolve and be replaced as trees age, climates change, and pests and diseases move through our forests.

The different plant communities that have lived on the Lawn will each have altered and manipulated the ground in different ways. The ways in which each plant and their respective communities have formed the ground will be cataloged in this essay to create a composite of what has shaped the ground of the Academical Village.

1. Route to The Lawn

In 1734, Peter Jefferson was appointed Surveyor of the Road from the Mountains to Licking Hole Creek. This colonial road travelled mostly along ridgelines from Richmond to the Shenandoah Valley, as most colonial roads often followed ridgelines or rivers, seeking the most efficient form of travel. The erosional processes of weathering wears ridgelines into well drained routes. Surveys of colonial roads speak toward the topography of the lands that they traverse.

At the time of purchase from John Perry in 1817, the Lawn was "an impoverished, disused corn field, rising high and dry by itself and without any obstructions in the way of trees and bushes." It also happened to be located beside the road that Peter Jefferson had surveyed.

2. The Ground

The Lawn is located at the western edge of the central Piedmont; a geographic region that lies between the coastal plain and the Blue Ridge Mountains. Geologically, the Piedmont is a peneplain; a plain formed through fluvial erosion during a time of relative tectonic stability. The rocks beneath the peneplain have been folded and tilted; striations facing toward the Blue Ridge Mountains and pointing downward in the direction of the Atlantic Ocean. These geologic formations are generally comprised of weathered and eroded crystalline rock. Creeks and streams meander through the peneplain, slowly carving and reforming the ground. As described in the 2001 Charlottesville Comprehensive Plan:

The Charlottesville formation, which makes up over a third of the bedrock found beneath the city, contains fine-grained metamorphic rocks that were created during the Precambrian Age. The formation contains large amounts of quartz-biotite gneiss and a few beds of sericitic and graphitic gneiss. The Charlottesville formation is about one mile wide and runs through the center of the city in a southwest to northeast direction.

As the formations of rock shift along faults, cracks form. A dyke is the seam of rock that forms within the crack of a pre-existing rock. The Lawn is underlain by an 830-foot wide amphibolite dyke. This vertical seam of rock was created when igneous rock from below pushed upward through an existing fracture in the surrounding rock of the Charlottesville formation. Close to the surface, this dyke is visible as a seam of quartz that can be traced from nearly the center of the Rotunda to Clark Hall, it has been aptly named the University Amphibolite Dyke. The University amphibolite dyke was formed during the Precambrian Era and faults are located on both sides. According to the 1998 University of Virginia Landscape Master Plan:

The soils of the Piedmont are primarily residual soils, formed in place, through the process of the underlying decomposed and weathered rock (saprolites) mixing with the decaying organic, surficial matter. As a result, the soils of the Piedmont are generally clay with significant range of depths. Most of the campus is comprised of the Hayesville-Ashe-Chester Group, a deep and moderately deep well-drained soil with a clayey or loamy sub-soil, formed from material weathered from granite and gneiss.

3. The Lawn as Forest

As noted in the 2013 University of Virginia Academical Village Cultural Landscape Report, the climatic changes that concluded the Pleistocene Epoch (around 12,000 BCE) and began the Holocene Epoch resulted a shift of forest species in Virginia. As the climate became warmer and drier, boreal woodlands dominated by native spruce (Picea) and pine (Pinus), transitioned to mixed deciduous and coniferous forests that resembled closely the forests of Virginia that exist today.

Assumptions can be made about the condition of the Lawn before it became a field for farming by observing the conditions of surrounding forest. By looking to Observatory Hill, we can begin to imagine the character of forest that would likely have been a pre-condition of the Lawn. The 1998 University of Virginia Landscape Master Plan describes this condition:

Two mature forest types comprise the woodlands of Observatory Hill. The predominately mature oak and chestnut-oak groups are found on the upper and south facing slopes, the poplar-oak and poplar groups generally follow the middle and lower slopes along the streams or where damp hydric soils are present . . . The understory is comprised of red maple, black gum, holly, and dogwood with bands of mountain laurel.

The Lawn is sited on a south facing slope, a ground that would have once supported populations of either an oak dominated forest or of a poplar-oak forest. The understory might have contained red maple, black gum, holly, and dogwood; a similar condition to the slopes of Observatory Hill. The United States Department of Agriculture Forest Service's Agriculture Handbook 654, titled Silvics of North America, offers descriptions of the root systems of American forest trees that enable us to begin to imagine the life of the roots below ground:

Chestnut oak (Quercus prinus) seedlings initially develop a deep tap root but as the trees establish, the root system architecture changes. Saplings and larger trees have a root system consisting of six to ten main lateral roots extending 10 to 33 feet from the root crown at depths from near the soil surface to 36 inches. Numerous secondary roots branch off these main laterals, and a dense mat of fine roots develops near the soil surface. The root system extends over an area approximately five times that of the crown area. The roots of chestnut oak are slightly deeper than those of northern red oak but not as deep as the white oak.

White oak (Quercus alba) is deep rooted, a trait that persists from youth to maturity. White oak seedlings produce a conspicuous, well-developed taproot but this gradually disappears with age and is replaced by a fibrous root system with well-developed, tapered laterals. Most of the main branches away from the central stem were within 2 feet of the ground surface. Fine roots are typically concentrated in dense mats in the upper soil horizons usually close to trunks but occasionally lying beneath the base of neighboring trees. Root grafts between neighboring trees are common, especially under crowded conditions. Yellow poplar (Liriodendron tulipifera), also known as tulip tree, has a rapidly growing and deeply penetrating juvenile taproot, as well as many strongly developed and wide-spreading lateral roots. It is considered to have a "flexible" rooting habit, even in the juvenile stage. The Woodland period is a label used by archaeologists to designate pre-Columbian Native American occupations dating between roughly 1,200 BCE and 1,600 CE in eastern North America. The 2013 University of Virginia Academical Village Cultural Landscape Report, provides a history of the region prior to European colonization:

Location of Woodland period sites in the central Virginia Piedmont document a continued preference for floodplain and riverine setting, on higher and lower order streams in the region including along the Rivanna River near the site of the future Academical Village. Holland's study of Albemarle County sites suggests that settlement within the Rivanna River floodplain may have begun or, at least, intensified during the Middle Woodland period. By the end of the Late Woodland period, Siouan speaking peoples lived in autonomous villages . . . throughout the Piedmont of Virginia. Within the central Piedmont of Virginia, the Monacans were the predominant cultural group. Archaeology of Late Woodland sites in the central Virginia Piedmont has documented the presence of domesticated corn and squash. Likewise, studies have also revealed a strong reliance on a corn based diet, suggesting a stable agricultural economy within Monacan society.

Although Virginia's first English colonists had been told about the dominance of the Monacans and the location of their villages in the beginning of the seventeenth century, by the 1720s when European and African American settlements began to permanently penetrate the region that was to become Albemarle County, the Monacans appeared to have largely disappeared from the landscape.

4. The Lawn as Field

The economy of Colonial Virginia was defined by tobacco (Nicotiana tabacum). The high profitability of tobacco offered little incentive for Virginians to plant a variety of crops or carefully tend to the health their soils. By the middle of the eighteen century, the production of tobacco in the Virginia Piedmont was the result of the labor of enslaved people. David R. Montgomery's Dirt: The Erosion of Civilizations provides a detailed narrative of the conditions of the ground and the treatment of soil in Colonial Virginia:

New land was constantly being cleared and old land abandoned because a farmer could count on only three or four highly profitable tobacco crops from the newly cleared land. Tobacco strips more than ten times the nitrogen and more than thirty times the phosphorous from the soil than do typical food crops. After five years of tobacco cultivation the ground was too depleted in nutrients to grow much of anything. With plenty of fresh land to the west, tobacco farmers just kept on clearing new fields. Stripped bare of vegetation, what soil remained on the abandoned fields was washed into gullies during intense summer rains. Virginia became a factory of turning topsoil into tobacco.

A pre-condition of the Lawn would have likely been a tobacco field. The chestnut-oak forest would have been cleared, the soil would have been tilled, and tobacco would have been planted. Five years later, the soil would have been depleted as productive yields fell, and the fields would no longer able to support the growth of tobacco. Once tobacco production was impossible on the field, corn (Zea mays) would be planted until the soil was completely exhausted. Following years of tobacco and corn cultivation, the soil would have been acidic. Once abandoned, acid-tolerant species such as pine, sedge, and sorrel would have taken over the fields. After years of cultivation, any remaining soil would have been left to fully erode. In Dirt: The Erosion of Civilizations, Montgomery continues:

About the time of the American Revolution, some of the founding fathers began to worry about the impact of mining the soil on the country's future. George Washington and Thomas Jefferson were among the first to warn of the destructive nature of colonial agriculture. Ideological rivals, these prosperous Virginia plantation owners shared concern over the long-term effects of American farming practices.

Native Americans of the Woodland period would have cleared forests near the Rivanna River for agricultural fields of diverse crops including corn and squash. The nutrients in these soils would have been replenished during flooding events. But Colonial Americans continually cleared forests, exhausted their fields of nitrogen, and left the soil exposed to erosion by wind and rain. Instead of tending fields with manure and rotating crops, the profitability of tobacco production lead to deforestation and soil depletion that is still visible today.

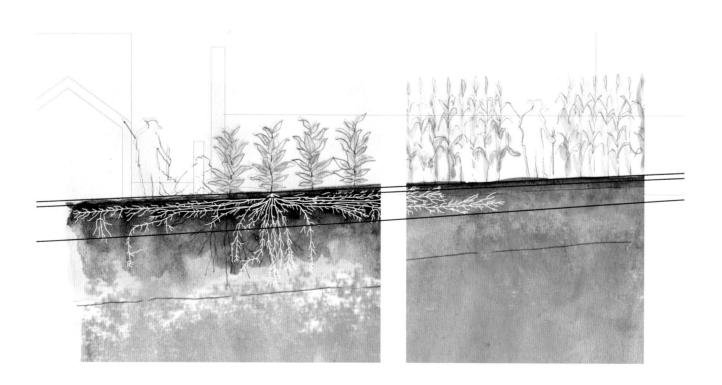

5. The Lawn of Grass and Trees

The initial construction of the Academical Village was under the direct guidance of Thomas Jefferson. In Jefferson's 1810 letter to the Trustees of East Tennessee College, he describes his early vision for the architecture and landscape architecture of the University of Virginia: "a small and separate lodge for each professorship, with only a half below for his class, and two chambers above for himself; these lodges to be joined by barracks for a certain portion of the students, opening into a covered way to give dry communication between all parts, the whole of these arranged around an open square of grass and trees."

In his History of the University of Virginia, Philip Alexander Bruce describes the condition of the property when land was first purchased for the University of Virginia:

The first parcel of land, which covered an area of 47 acres, was, at the time of purchase, an impoverished, disused field. The second parcel, amounting to one hundred and fifty acres, and situated about five-eighths of a mile from the first, contained a large quantity of valuable timber and stone for building—the reason in part for its acquisition, since it was not needed as the site of any of the projected structures. It was also expected to form the watershed for the reservoir which was to supply the cisterns within the precincts.

Black Locust

The "Historical Sketch of the Trees and Grounds of the University of Virginia," an unpublished 1961 manuscript by Edwin M. Betts and Sylvester H. O'Grince, pieces together the landscape history of the university. From this manuscript, the history of the ground of the Lawn can be told. In 1823, Jefferson purchased 100 black locust (Robinia pseudoacacia) trees for the university. For this study, we will assume that by 1831 there were double rows of young locust trees, planted on each side of the lawn.

Black locust usually produces a shallow and wide-spreading root system. Nitrogen-fixing bacteria are associated with nodules on the roots of black locust; these bacteria increase nitrogen content of the soil in which the tree grows. For this reason, it can grow on poor soils and is an early colonizer of disturbed areas. As is true of all tree roots, the process of initiating and aborting root growth adds organic matter to the soil. Eventually the roots build the soil and attract additional beneficial micro-organisms. The presence of the black locusts on degraded soil will have improved the condition of the soil and aided in the subsequent establishment of hardwood trees.

It is unclear whether the positive effect of black locust on the soil was a reason for choosing the tree. In 1823, black locusts were a common ornamental tree. They would have been readily available from nursery production, and relatively inexpensive. The trees were also useful for their quick growth. They were often used for wood for fence posts.

Cows and Pigs

According to Betts and O'Grince, during the time between Jefferson's death in 1826 and 1856, the planting of trees and maintenance of the Grounds was under the supervision of the proctor. "The proctors had no particular training for this task, and the condition of the landscape often went through periods of neglect and moments of attempted restoration . . . In 1858, the Board of Visitors created a position separate from the position of proctor to establish and maintain the grounds. William Abbott Pratt was elected to be the first Superintendent of Buildings and Grounds; he was trained as an architect and civil engineer."

By 1859, Jefferson's "open square of grass and trees" also included Charlottesville's wandering cows and pigs who grazed and compacted the Lawn. The southern end of the lawn was gated to keep the animals out, but as a prank, students would remove and carry off any gate that was installed on the fence.

Virginia University Magazine, Editor's Table, January 1859:

> We have an occasional dingy lamp-post, a sickly locust, a good sized common for the Charlottesville cows, while the members of the Medical and Law classes are compelled to snuff a breeze redolent with the perfume of decaying tomato vines, cabbage stalks, etc. Mr. Pratt will correct most of these abuses, if the students will lend him their hearty co-operation, desist from taking off the gates, and other mischievous acts; if not, his labours must be futile.

Virginia University Magazine, Editor's Table, February 1859: The much-abused Pratt, our Superintendent of Public Grounds, is certainly hard at work doing something. He has been accused of not knowing what he is about. He tells us that he knows exactly what he is about, and that he will soon make such an improvement in the general appearance of the University, that its old friends will hardly know it again . . . There is plenty of room for improvement, and we wish every success to Pratt and his plans. We will assist him so far as to make known his earnest request that the gates be carried off no more. He has asked us to say that he considers it useless to begin his plantings, as long as the habit of carrying off the gates is persisted in; because everything that he plants will be destroyed by the Vagrant Stock that will find its way into the enclosure.

Colonel John E. Johnson was appointed the position of Proctor on August 10, 1866; the positions of Superintendent of Grounds and Proctor had been combined once again. He decided to plant lines of spruce trees on each side of East and West Lawn. This caught the attention of students, who under the cover of darkness, pulled up all the young trees, and piled them against the door to Johnson's home on the East Range. After this incident with the spruce trees, there is no record of Johnson attempting to plant anything else. Instead, he continued to attempt to enforce an enactment that prohibiting the keeping of cattle, horses, or hogs within the walls of the University.

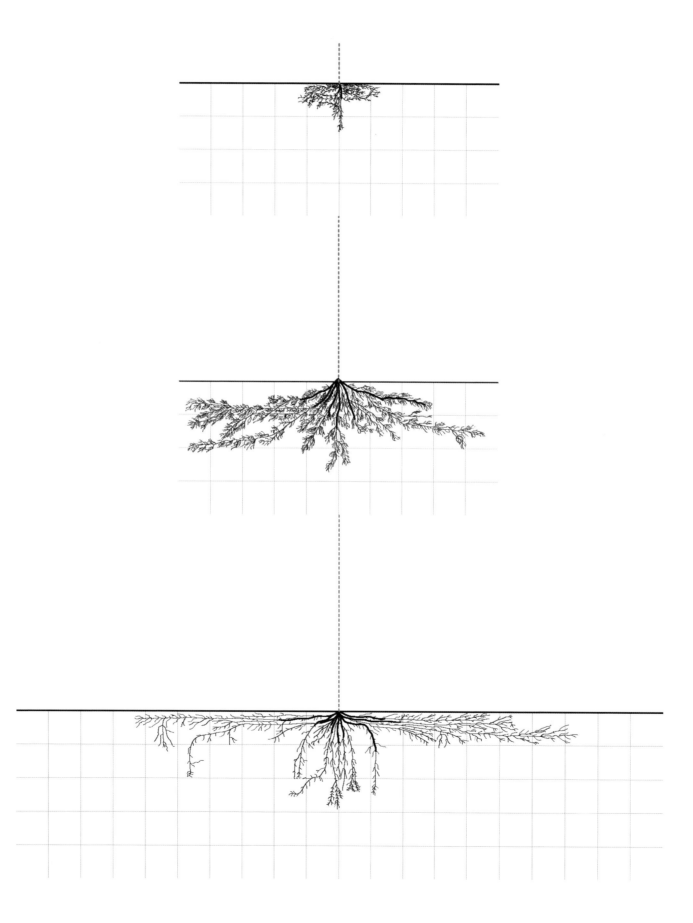

Ash and Maple

On December 4, 1867, Major Green Peyton, an engineer and financier replaced Johnson as Proctor and Superintendent of Buildings and Grounds. Betts and O'Grince speculate that in early 1868, the gaps between the trees on the Lawn were replaced; again, in December of 1869, some of the remaining damaged and old trees were removed and replaced. By May of 1871, the editor of the University of Virginia Magazine wrote in praise of "the young trees planted on the Lawn and in other parts of the college during the fall and winter." It was noted that in a few years they would provide a desired shade. "They should have been planted twenty years ago instead of the locusts that now disfigure the Lawn; but better late than never."

Two genera of trees were planted on the Lawn by Peyton: ash and maple. In 2014, at the time of writing, these are still the only genera of tree present. There are three species of ash planted on the Lawn: white ash (Fraxinus americana), green ash (Fraxinus pennsylvanica), and blue ash (Fraxinus quadrangulata). Of maple, there are two species planted on the Lawn: red maple (Acer rubrum) and sugar maple (Acer saccharum). A third genus, dogwood, is planted south of Pavillion IX, it marks a transition from the enclosed Lawn to a space of other. There is only one species of dogwood planted on the Lawn: the flowering dogwood (Cornus florida). All three species of tree demonstrate an opposite branching pattern (the only other tree to branch this way is the Horsechestnut), but their root systems are distinctly different.

Green ash is often a floodplain species in Virginia. It is adapted to survived saturated soils for extended amounts of time, often supported by a shallow root system. White ash is typically an upland tree, with a deep root system that allows it to access water between rocks below the drier soils of the forest floor. While both species of ash tree are adapted to different forest conditions, they can both tolerate the soil conditions of the Lawn when planted there. Referring again to "The United States Department of Agriculture Forest Service's Agriculture Handbook 654":

Green ash (Fraxinus pennsylvanica) roots to penetrate about 3 feet deep in sandy and clay soils. In the southern part of its range, green ash has a root system that is typically saucer-shaped with no distinct taproot; roots penetrate to depths of 3 to 4 feet. The extensive root system of this species makes it relatively windfirm. Green ash seedlings, and probably older trees, have certain rooting habits or adaptations that enable them to withstand flooding. Young green ash has been shown to have the ability under flooded conditions to regenerate new secondary roots from the primary root, develop adventitious water roots on the submerged stem, accelerate anaerobic respiration rate in the absence of oxygen, and oxidize its rhizospheres. These root adaptations enable it to withstand flooding regimes of several months during the dormant and early growing season that would kill other species.

White ash (Fraxinus americana) generally forms a taproot that in turn branches into a few large roots that grow downward. From these vertical roots, single lateral branches develop at intervals. Intraspecific grafting is common. The distribution of roots is strongly influenced by soil type. On a loamy sand, most of the roots, both large and small, were in the A horizon. On a fine sandy loam, the majority of the fine roots were in the B, horizon, and the large roots equally in the A and B1.

Similar to the ash trees, there are differences in the environments that red maple and sugar maple are adapted to. Sugar maple is an upland tree that cannot tolerate flooding. While, red maple is an extremely adaptable tree that can thrive in upland conditions but can also adapt to floodplains or even swamps. More specifically, from The United States Department of Agriculture Forest Service's Agriculture Handbook 654:

Red maple (Acer rubrum) trees grow well and are generally capable of growing as well as or better than their associates on sites with less than optimum moisture conditions, either too wet or too dry. Roots of maple seedlings are capable of developing differently in response to various environments, so that the seedlings can survive in situations ranging from swamp to dry upland. This characteristic root system adaptability is maintained as the trees grow older. Under flood conditions, many adventitious roots develop, but the root systems recover quickly upon drainage. Red maples seem to tolerate drought through their readiness to stop growing under dry conditions and by producing a second growth flush when conditions improve again, even after growth has stopped. Red maple roots are primarily horizontal and form in the upper 10 inches of soil. After germination, a taproot develops until it is about 1 to 2 inches long, then it turns and grows horizontally. As the woody roots extend sideways, nonwoody fans of feeder roots extend upward, mostly within the upper 3 inches of mineral soil.

Sugar maple's (Acer saccharum) root system has strong, oblique laterals with extensive branching. Roots on the upper side of the laterals grow upward into the humus layers and those on the lower side grow downward. Most of the fine feeder roots remain within the general area of origin. Intraspecific root grafting is common. Sugar maple roots are extremely sensitive to flooding during the growing season. The roots of maple form both endotrophic and ectotrophic mycorrhizae.

Flowering dogwood's (Cornus florida) extensive root system is extremely shallow. This fact undoubtedly accounts for the susceptibility of this species to periods of drought.

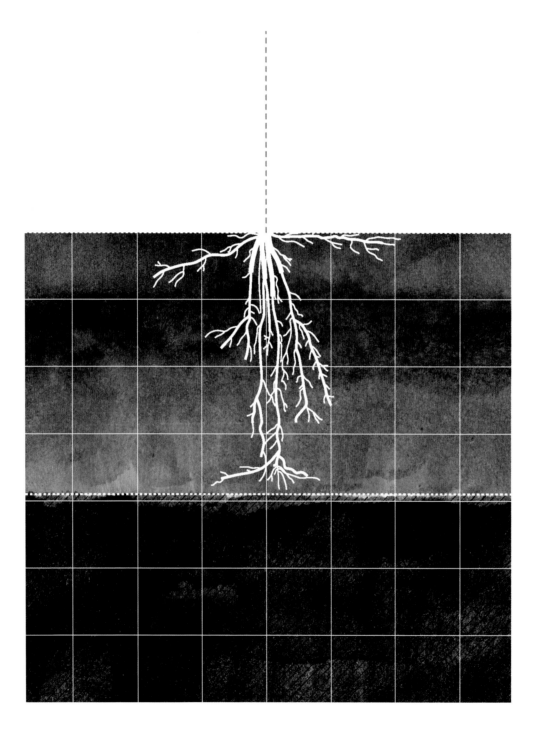

6. The Lawn of the Lawn

Betts and O'Grince mention an attempt to maintain the grasses on the Lawn for the first time in 1872 as "every effort was made to stop the students from making paths across the Lawn. In order to curtail this practice, wire fences and barricades of different sorts were placed across the paths to protect the grass." J. K. Campbell served temporarily as proctor from June 28, 1882 to 1886. In October of 1884, Virginia University Magazine reported that "the maples on the Lawn are reddening" and in 1885 "the trees are trimmed and much in the line done recently." It seems that Campbell maintained the Lawn without altering it. Once political control shifted in the state, Major Green Peyton was re-elected Proctor in 1886, and the Lawn seems to have been neglected by 1888.

Virginia University Magazine, October 1888: It is a fact well-known to the students generally that to traverse the Lawn at any time is a hazardous under-taking. The long-matted grass entangles the feet and seriously incommodes one's progress in the day-time, but when night has settled down over this wilderness, the Lawn possesses all the intricacies and difficulties of an Indian Jungle[.]

Perhaps these complaints of neglect were beneficial, in the spring of 1890, the Lawn had been partially re-sodded. The Lawn became a popular place to "spend an idle hour" as it is still today

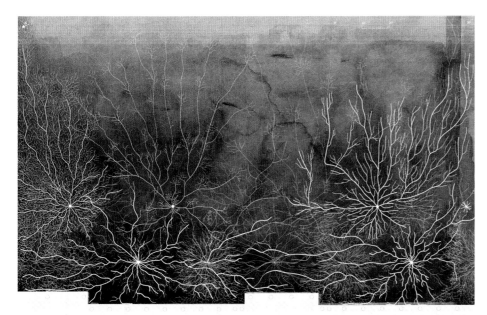

7. Lessons from the Lawn

In 2014 I had the opportunity to lecture about the ground of the Lawn in Peter Waldman's Lessons of the Lawn. Following my lecture, the students were assigned the following:

As a lunatic, delve a hole into the darkness of the earth. With what tools did you do this? What do you find? How many things do you find? What are the layers? If you dig with a pencil, how many grains of soil, layers of earth, or dwellings of insects do you find? If you dig with a spoon, how many grass roots connect to each other? Are the blades of grass separate plants or all one? If you dig with a trowel, what is the total length of tree roots that you find and at what depths? What does the soil feel like and smell like? What lives there that you cannot see? Diagram the contents and structure of the hole. Survey it's reality and imagine what might exist in the depths below the reach of your chosen tool. Diagram the relationship between the hole and its context. Is it a wide but shallow hole in a large flat plane, or a narrow but deep hole beside the foundation of a building? What did you dig it for? Did you leave anything behind? Is the dirt returned to the hole or left beside it? If you leave a mound, is it larger than the hole? What marks were left? Think Pistachios and Chili Peppers. How must one implant the notion that Architecture is a Covenant with the World, Again? For at least one day, and for the time it takes to write one essay, the ground was deeply considered.

As students fill the Lawn on graduation day, year after year, below their feet are layers of stories. Drainage pipes and irrigation systems are hidden below the lawn to support our current interpretation of Jefferson's "grass and trees." The roots of white ash are reaching deep into any fissures in the igneous rock of the Amphibolite Dyke, the layer of rock below the Lawn that happens to be different from the geologic formations to the east and west of the Academical Village. Roots of the green ash trees are just below the surface of the soil competing with the grasses for moisture and nitrogen. Roots of the black locust trees purchased by Jefferson in 1823 might still be below ground slowly adding organic matter back to the soil that had been completely exhausted. In the ground are stories of the enslaved people forced to work the tobacco fields, harvesting the crop, and sending with the dried leaves a part of Virginia's earth to Europe in the form of nicotine. There had been centuries of forest decomposition that formed the rich soil that once blanketed the landscape but have been lost from erosion. Deep in the ground there are always stories, it's just a matter of digging and taking a look.

Connective Tissue #1 Preconditions: On Scientists First and then Magicians Last
Peter Waldman

The First Architectural act is to break the Ground, by Gottfried Semper

Today, in North America, in politically correct elementary school texts, to describe the available site of the Academical Village as barren ground. The selected site offered by the Commonwealth was an example of Colonial America's widespread, unwise and shortsighted agricultural practices resulting in brownfield degradation. Rarely, does prefacing research reveal that the indigenous, yet nomadic peoples and their Wilderness were simultaneously clear-cut by early settlers to yield arable fields for the shortsighted planting practice of single species crops made possible by the institution of the European slave trade. This succession of crops, greedily ignored the wise medieval practice of leaving land fallow, and soon depleted the viable capacities of the soil evidencing an unsustainable cultural practice of short-term greed which foreshadows still today Jefferson's new republic.

Long before the Lawn, and that short-lived Brownfield Condition, the Pre-Condition of the site of The Academical Village was a vast North American hardwood forest in which the first people carved out small clearings to cultivate simultaneously corn, squash and beans. And long before those People and that Forest, there were the geological transformations of Glacial frictions of the last Ice-Age which repeatedly negotiated its southern boundary through Gneiss formations of Virginia's Piedmont, eroding the ancient Appalachian Mountain Range and splintering off the Blue Ridge and the so-called South West mountains which were to frame Jefferson's future project. The structure of the Ground, some call Soil, if not Dirt, and the hydrological processes therein have been scientifically interrogated by Gwen McGinn in "Roots and Routes". In this investigation we attempt to understand the multiple scales of the collective Colonnades as a reconstruction of that once and future Forest for a Spatial Tale of Origin for the newly minted American Republic. The locally resourced specifications for the foundation of the buildings are considered in parallel with the scientific components of root structures and evolving temporal processes of soil evolution.

Coincidental with construction, while Observatory Hill served as the source of Lumber, and Madison Bowl resultantly served as quarry for clay and then foundation stones, the same Hill also served as arboretum for the fast-growing Black Locust and later the deeply rooted Ash and Maple specimens which have endured on the Lawn for centuries. In Serlio's stage sets of 1654 for Tragedy and Comedy, there is also the Satiric setting, of forests to be lumbered and mountains to be quarried. The Satiric setting is the Pre-condition to the City and was referenced in Jefferson's time by Hudson Valley School painter (1836) Thomas Cole series on "The Course of the Empire". The Enlightenment's fascination with the temporal, if not progressive promise of Arcadia is the intellectual context why Jefferson made first a clearing in the Wilderness, then juxtaposed two distinct landscapes: one native species again on the resultant Lawn with exotic fruit bearing species in Gardens framed by Serpentine if not Edenic walls between the Pavilions and the Range Hotels. We conceive this Jefferson project of curiosity to be an enlightenment covenant with the world, again—conceived by Scientists to appear as the work of Magicians. Jefferson's project is significant in the idea of variant multiplicities, there is no typological consistency, rather signifying multiple scenographic components, and serves also as an essay on the source of materials, close at hand and the methods of assembly of a society of both freemasons, journey men and the enslaved.

The Lewis and Clark expedition (1803) initiated by Jefferson, as our third President, initially mapped the continental vision of Arcadia for a coastal nation of former Atlantic colonies. This expedition used thc Tools of Rod and Compass, Sextants to triangulate the stars and to mark twain along hydraulic courses to confirm Gravity and Orientation.

Science was the instrument of spatial discovery from which the Tools of Plow and Hearth established the fictions of claiming this nation as resource full from sea to shining sea.

This first Connective Tissue intends to make a case for the useful collaboration of earth scientists and agents of change by the tools they employ. It is speculated for this exercise in recurrent dualities that magicians are the most knowledgeable and pragmatic of all as they employ fast science. The first tool was the finger, some call digit now, the second was the hand, proceeding onto the scales of the Ice-Age and correspondent hearth, residing in the Age of Enlightenment in the investigative instruments of the telescope and the microscope. Jefferson's Rotunda is the mythic universe where both latter instruments were lodged distinctly in the Attic and the Basement.

Our digits and then our hands might have been the first instruments of engagement, if not fabrication. On our way down from the forest canopy, we would grasp at branches, swing from limbs, steal eggs from nests and eventually dig deeply into trunks and roots for grubs to sustain us. By a stream our ancestors would cup their hands to quench thirst and then learned to grasp at fish. Nimble fingers learned to pick berries and gather fruit. At some point an inquisitive hunter-gatherer pushed an indexical finger into the rich dark soil and dropped a seed or a pit bearing witness to agriculture. It is rumored that the corn kernel was accompanied by a fish head by the first people of the Americas and then covered over with the thanksgiving blessings of one's hands.

Danielle Alexander's essay on "Earth as a Tool for Revealing" traces civilization's advancement from the material succession first from Stone and Wood to Bronze and then Iron, and eventually composite assemblies to arrive in Jefferson's Age of Enlightenment with the Sextant and the Plow. Surveyors, Nomads and Lunatics have used these tools for ages to trace from where we have come and where we now find ourselves. By these tools we evolved from Nomads to Settlers who then built massive hearths and dug deep wells. Thomas Jefferson's father, Peter, was a surveyor of Colonial Virginia's mountain ranges and watercourses and was awarded thousands of acres of Arcadian forest in return from King George II. A generation later, Thomas Jefferson, who was to author the Declaration of Independence specifically addressed to King George III, later encouraged the newly–minted Commonwealth of Virginia to acquire a worthless brownfield site for the construction of the Academical Village, now known as the University of Virginia.

Danielle Alexander is an anthropologist and cultural historian in service of re-envisioning Landscape Architecture in terms of instrumentality. In my teaching of Lessons of the Lawn, the Pre-Conditions of Site must be first exhaustively researched as scientific and cultural landscapes with the ethical premise that it is our task to reveal the site not as empty, but full, consequently, architecture must frame that, which is already there.

We come to a site to explore a New World each time as we are reminded that Architecture is a Covenant with the World Again. We frame this pedagogic methodology early on with Rebecca Solnit's *A Field Guide to Getting Lost*.

Danielle Alexander's first image is set in darkness, as is Genesis, where the depiction of five digital towers articulates for Le Corbusier the precise space between the night sky and the reflective surface of the Rio de la Plata. Corbusier's first vision of the New World City of Buenos Aires was grounded in Terra incognita, in the Southern Hemisphere, in darkness read against the space of human-made prisms of silvery reflection. The earth we know as either generative ground, or simply dirt, is not rendered in this vision. Here scale-less prismatic towers are offered as visions of the work place of a New World Citizens now estranged from the toil of the soil. Soon thereafter, Le Corbusier would travel to the Northern Hemisphere and write on that counterpart vision. In "When the Cathedrals were White," he noted Chicago's skyscrapers, Silos and Grain Elevators and the vast dimensions of America's emerging manufacturing facilities, as reflective landmarks, and sextants framing the vast monumental landscapes of the emerging economy of North America. At the same time Charles Scheeler recorded the same monumental visions of "The Classic American Landscape" (1930) juxtaposed coincidentally by Grant Wood's pre-occupation with the tools of human-scape in *Arbor Day*. Walter Lippmann in *A Preface to Morals* calls America in 1927 "Barren Ground", because we have separated ourselves from our ancestral agricultural roots, the endurant processes of nature and time on our way out of our culture and out of our class enroute to become simultaneously cosmopolitan citizens in the world of estrangement we call the Modern City. In a primal sense, tools are inseparable from earth from which they were fabricated, and from generative processes of soil formation nurturing roots. There is an essential temporal imperative in both Alexander's anthropological tracing and McGinn's interrogation of soil enroute to understand roots as a once hidden, or overlooked determinant of planted form.

Gwen McGinn is a scientist in service of Landscape Architecture as a grounded, rigorous discipline in terms of evidence-based design. McGinn offers first an inventory and typological matrix of tree Roots before she introduces us to the possibility of an Urban Forest reiterated in the Colonnades. This inventory soon necessitates a reconsideration of the earth as generative ground clarifying the processes of making soil from geological frames of reference to the immediate implications of the currency of acid rain and climate change. Finally, the term Routes traces an essential pre-occupation of Jefferson as a pragmatic farmer, as well as a world traveler in fact and in his imagination. On the micro- scale, Jefferson was pragmatically resourceful by acquiring Observatory Hill as a second-thought after the brownfield site of little resourceful value. Observatory Hill offered a reliable source of water, timber and the adjacent Madison colluvial tract yielded rich red clay deposits for brick. But the route is extended on the telescopic or macro-scale beyond resources at hand to Lewis and Clark's Osage Orange trees from Missouri, as well as Magnolias from China and design guidelines, paradigms and models from Ancient Rome, onto Palladio's Four Books of Architecture, and contemporary French Connections of Labrouste, L'Enfant, and Ledoux. One of Jefferson's treasured tales was Cervantes' *Don Quixote* where the elegant Don and earth-bound Sancho Panza encountered and engaged both Machines and Myths through Landscapes of Aggression re-echoed in both the Colonnade and juxtaposed Range arch passages framing meandering pathways along serpentine walls. The Routes manifested in Enlightenment Literature, William McClung reminds us in *Western Literature from Eden to Jerusalem, Paradise Lost and the Promise of the Enduring City*, might be read in the Academical Village as construction site envisioned by an ancient farmer on his Hill still equipped with both telescope and microscope held optimistically high by red clay stained digits. McGinn and Alexander provide connective tissues for subsequent essays of rigorous inventories inspiring the instrumentality of action played out by and for generations of citizens and strangers in dialogue.

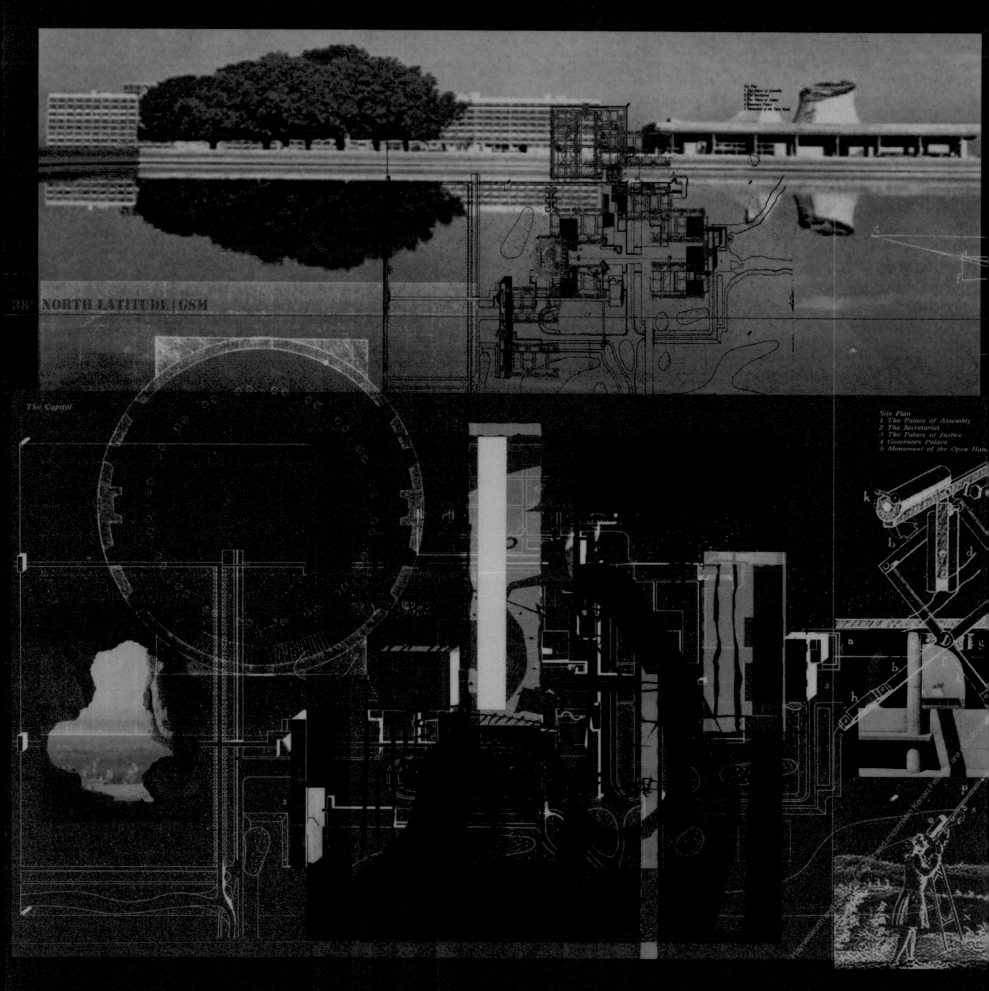

The Capitol

Site Plan
1 The Palace of Assembly
2 The Secretariat
3 The Palace of Justice
4 Governors Palace
5 Monument of the Open Hand

CHAPTER 2

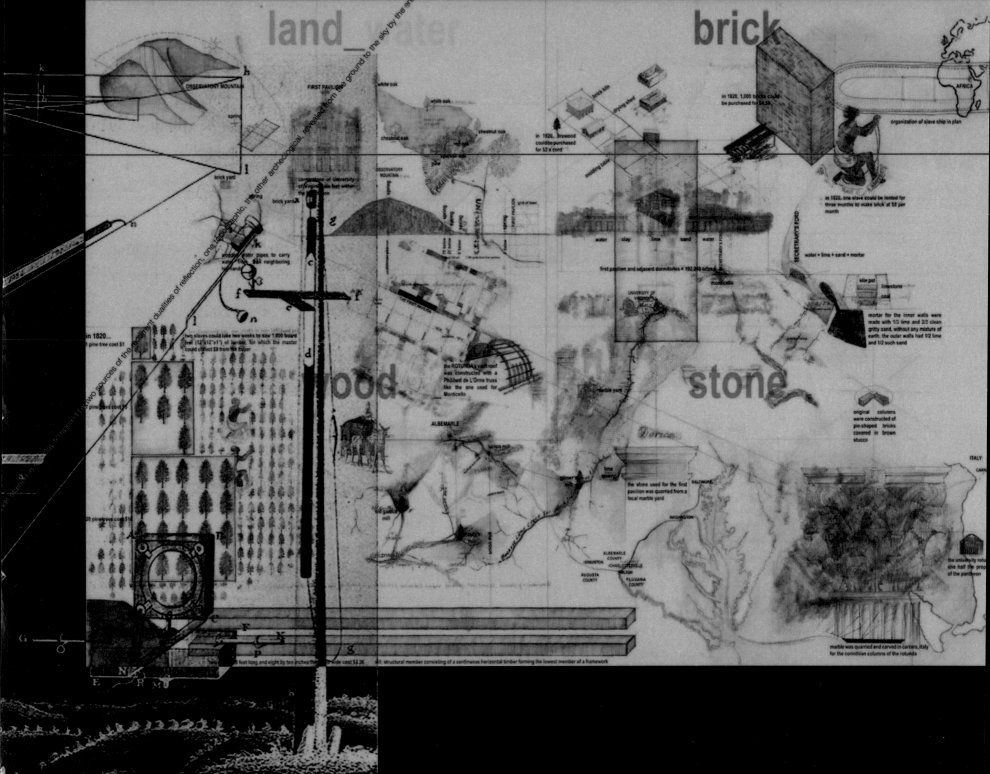

land_water

brick

wood

stone

AFRICA

ITALY

organization of slave ship in plan

in 1820, 1,000 bricks could
be purchased for $4.50

in 1820, one slave could be rented for
three months to make brick at $8 per
month

brick kiln

drying shed

molding table

in 1820, firewood
could be purchased
for $2 a cord

water   clay   lime   sand   water

water + lime + sand = mortar

first pavilion and adjacent dormitories = 192,230 bricks

mortar for the inner walls were
made with 1/3 lime and 2/3 clean
gritty sand, without any mixture of
earth, the outer walls had 1/2 lime
and 1/2 such sand

kiln pot   limestone
            coal

OBSERVATORY MOUNTAIN

spring

FIRST PAVILION

white oak

white oak

chestnut oak

red oak

chestnut oak

spanish oak

OBSERVATORY
MOUNTAIN

cornerstone of University
of Virginia, 600 feet within
the corporation

SECRETARY'S FORD

monticello

UNIVERSITY
VIRGINIA

THE FIRST PAVILION

brick yard

brick yard

wooden water pipes to carry
water from a neighboring
headland

two slaves could take two weeks to saw 1,000 board
feet (12"x12"x1') of timber, for which the master
could collect $9 from the buyer

the ROTUNDA's vault roof
was constructed with a
Philibert de L'Orme truss
like the one used for
Monticello

marble yard

the stone used for the first
pavilion was quarried from a
local marble yard

original columns
were constructed of
pie-shaped bricks
covered in brown
stucco

Dorica

in 1820...
1 pine tree cost $1

17 pine trees cost $1

ALBEMARLE

lime
quarry

BALTIMORE

20 pine trees cost $10

old grist
mill

WASHINGTON

ALBEMARLE
COUNTY

STAUNTON

CHARLOTTESVILLE

AUGUSTA
COUNTY

FLUVANA
COUNTY

the university rotunda
one half the propor
of the pantheon

feet long and eight by ten inches thick and wide cost $3.36

sill: structural member consisting of a continuous horizontal timber forming the lowest member of a framework

marble was quarried and carved in carrara, italy
for the corinthian columns of the rotunda

N

E   R   U

CHAPTER TWO: INVENTORIES

Haynsworth Woodcock and Hackney the first and midstream Kenan Fellows, are in dialogue with, hands stained in red clay tempered by

two sources of the recurrent dualities of reflection, one topographic, the other archeological, revealed from the ground to the sky by the

enduring scaler utility of the telescope and microscope.

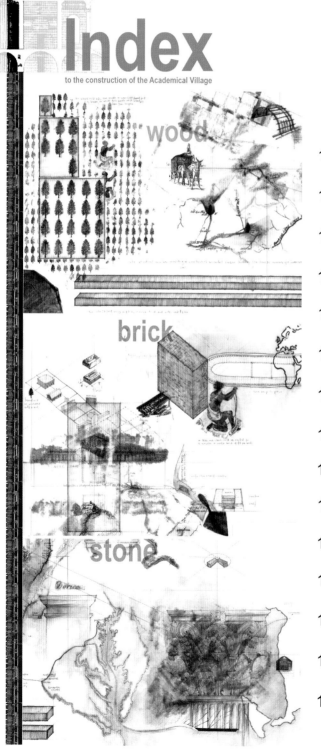

Index
to the construction of the Academical Village

wood

brick

stone

construction timeline *

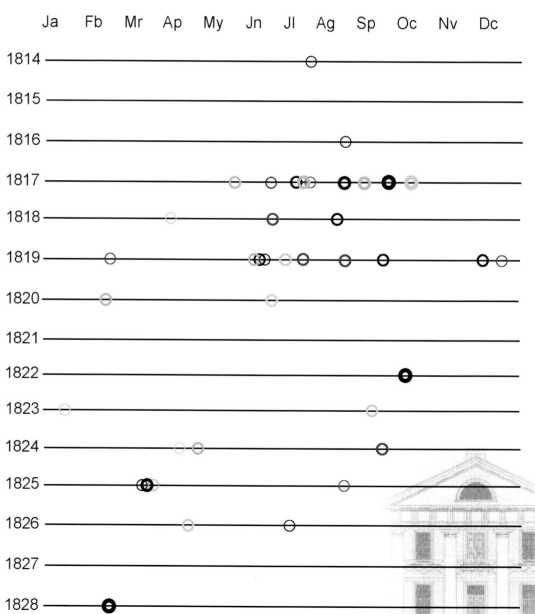

	Ja	Fb	Mr	Ap	My	Jn	Jl	Ag	Sp	Oc	Nv	Dc

*A key to this construction timeline can be found at the end of this inventory.

Index to the Construction of the Academical Village 1817-1828
Spencer Haynsworth Woodcock

For much of Thomas Jefferson's adult life in politics, he promoted the idea of creating a three-tiered public education system in the newly formed country, which included primary, secondary, and university levels. Jefferson succeeded in the formation of a state-chartered university. The University of Virginia in Charlottesville, VA, called the Academical Village, was designed by and constructed under the supervision of Jefferson, and its construction was an occupation that consumed much of his time after his presidency and until his death in 1826.

A formal examination of the Academical Village reveals a very rational neoclassical plan. A hierarchical, U-shaped space is capped by a prominent domed Rotunda, connected by pavilions and smaller rooms, opening out to a long, narrow green square. Pavilion VII, the first building designed and constructed at the university, stands out as the smallest and least impressive of all the buildings in the complex. But this first pavilion in fact is revelatory in terms of understanding the history of the Academical Village. Pavilion VII was an experiment in construction for Jefferson, a means for testing and learning from the mistakes of its production, which informed the improvements, subsequent iterations, and the landscape and structures that are celebrated today as a highlight of American architecture.

Drawing from the formal and documentary histories of Frank Edgar Grizzard and Richard Guy Wilson, this text looks beyond the formal plan of the Academical Village to examine the discrete building materials of the site, namely land, water, brick, stone, and wood, to tell a history of the university's origin that is both exploratory and experimental. The material processes of burning and laying bricks; felling timber and sawing it into plank; quarrying and hauling rock; measuring and clearing land; piping and creating reserves of water; and the workers engaged in its construction connect to the immediate site, country (the newly formed Colonies), and world (Africa, Italy, and Europe), revealing a history of interactions that extend far beyond Jefferson's original plan as well as what first appears to the visitor today.

Measurement

For Jefferson, architecture was an experimental and iterative process. He was a self-taught architect, who learned from his vast collection of books, travel within the country and abroad, and self-funded design and construction projects. Jefferson once said that architecture was his delight and that putting up and pulling down one of his favorite amusements.[1] By the time he began work on the Academical Village, he was very knowledgeable about laying out buildings, making bricks, woodcutting, and stone carving.

Jefferson envisioned the model of the Academical Village as a repeated module consisting of a single pavilion and dormitories. He spoke of this module as a "germ from which a great tree may spread itself."[2] The first pavilion, commonly referred to as Pavilion VII because of its position among the ten pavilions in the Academical Village, along with its twenty adjacent dormitories, were the seed from which the entire university sprung. The first pavilion was an experiment in construction, in which Jefferson's conceptual plan was tested against the realities of the construction site and served as a datum for the surveying of springs, topography, as well as the construction materials of the local site and beyond.

Jefferson drew a first ground plan of the Academical Village in the summer of 1814 for the Albemarle Academy, of which Jefferson was a trustee.[3] The plan existed conceptually on paper for three years until it served as the precursor to the Academical Village. Jefferson's concept of a large open square containing a series of individual pavilions connected by student dormitories on three of the square's four sides is illustrated there. The open square was noted at 257 yards.

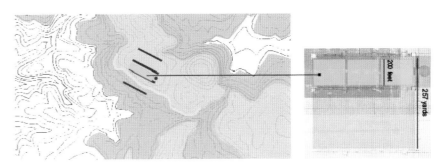

Jefferson's early study of a "typical" pavilion was realized in a drawing of Pavilion VII showing the elevation and floor plans for a two-story pavilion measuring 26 feet by 34 feet on the exterior and connected by dormitories measuring 10 by 14 feet. These drawings, the earliest of his college- or university-related drawings, were most likely the plans that Jefferson presented to the Board of Visitors of the Central College for its consideration in May 1817. After receiving advice that the size of the pavilions was too small—especially if the professors were married and would want more than two rooms—Jefferson decided to leave the back side of the pavilions without windows so that two or three rooms could be added when needed.

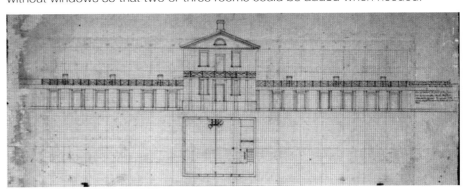

The initial prototype transformed when Jefferson received the drawings from his architect friend, Benjamin Latrobe, a Philadelphia based architect, and additional space was provided in all the pavilions that followed. The size of the first pavilion in relation to the others can be seen in the Maverick Plan engraving ca. 1821, the first formal plan of Jefferson's Academical Village.

Latrobe's elevations showed large order porticos, where the columns extended the full two-story height of the pavilions, and in designing the preceding pavilions, Jefferson would use Latrobe's porticos. Through these alterations, Jefferson maintained his vision of the ten pavilions referencing the cannon of ancient roman architecture and serving as a learning tool for the students: "Now what we wish is that these pavilions as they will shew themselves above the dormitories, shall be models of taste and good architecture, and of a variety of appearance, no two alike, so as to serve as specimens for the Architectural Lectures."[4]

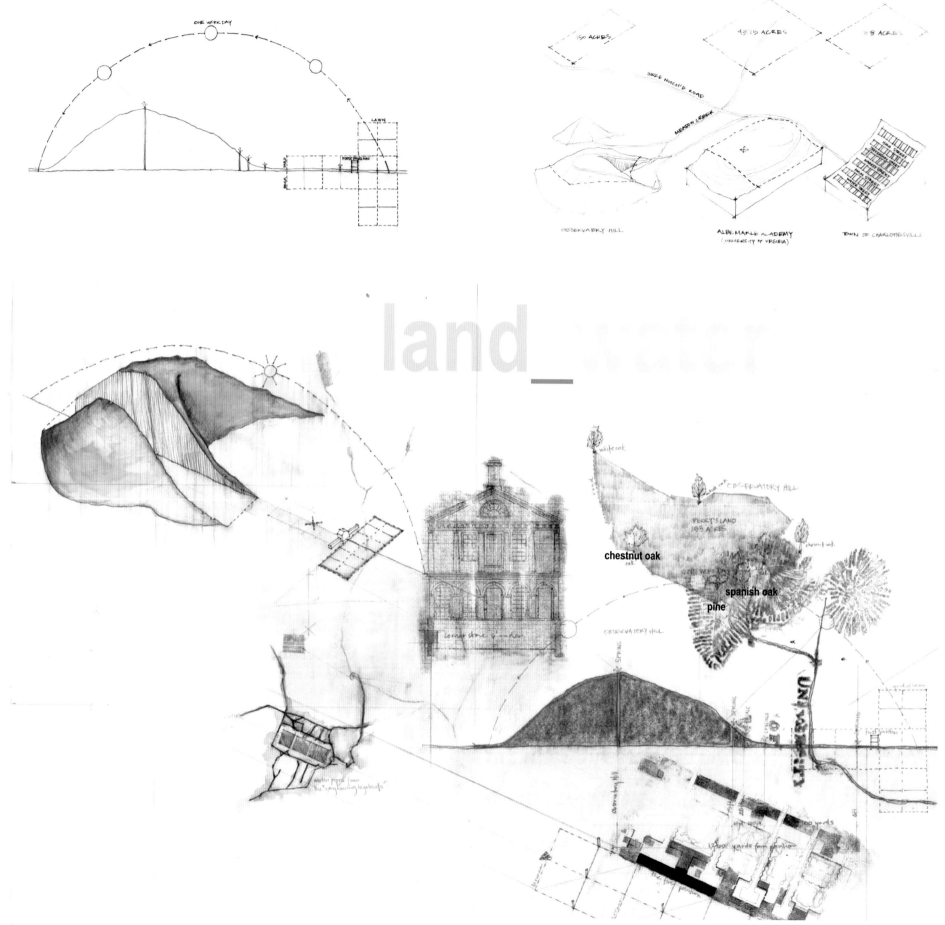

Land

The Academical Village was located on a 43 acre tract of Albemarle County land about a mile above Charlottesville. Jefferson bought the land from John M. Perry, a carpenter that worked on the university construction site as a stipulation in the purchase agreement, for $12 per acre or $525 for the parcel. It was a fallow agricultural field in an ideal location. Perry sold the college another tract for $1,421.25.[5] This other tract was 153 acres located about 5/8 mile from the first site, encompassing the top and part of a mountain, now known as Observatory Hill. As a point of reference, the nearby town of Charlottesville was only 38 acres at the time.

A third tract of land was bought in 1820 that bordered the Three Notch'd road and the 43-acre parcel that the Perry's had sold to the Central College.[6] This second tract increased the assets of the university, but was $50 an acre totaling $6,600, much more than the original land purchase. The 1825 land agreement allowed Jefferson to move Three Notch'd Road, the public road to Staunton, Virginia, along to the new boundary so that it passed parallel to the northern side of the university, making room for an entrance to the Rotunda and the central lawn.[7]

In 1817, Jefferson requested permission from the Board of Trustees of the Central College to begin construction of the original plan of the Academical Village with a plan and elevation of a typical pavilion, which later became Pavilion VII. The board approved the construction of a single pavilion on Jefferson's plan with stipulations that "the lots of the said pavilions be determined on the ground [with] the breadth of [an undetermined number of] feet with two parallel sides of indefinite length. That the pavilion first to be erected be placed on one of the lines so delineated."[8]

Jefferson had not yet surveyed the site to determine the exact width of the lawn, so it was necessary to have the flexibility in the dimensions of the building layout. On July 18, 1817, when Jefferson measured the site, he was surprised to discover that the central lawn would need to be considerably narrower than he had previously designed for in his original concept. In reality, the open "square" measured only 200 feet and needed to be reduced to a rectangular swath. At that point, he indicated on his sketch that the center of the north side, which he had initially intended for three small, uniform pavilions, would now become the focal point for a grand pavilion.[9]

Benjamin Latrobe had previously suggested a variation from Jefferson's original plan, which would require closing off the north end of the square with "some principal building." Latrobe sent Jefferson a sketch of a cubical "center building" fashioned after Andrea Palladio's Villa Rotunda. In the sketch, Latrobe placed two pavilions on each side of the Rotunda and one in each corner of the square's northern end. Jefferson later told Latrobe that the addition of a principal building to his original concept was necessary because of the "law of the ground", but one can assume that Latrobe's suggestion contributed significantly to Jefferson's architectural response to site conditions.[10]

According to his specifications book, "Operations at & for the College", Jefferson divided the 43-acre site into 12 smaller rectangles that measured 100 by 127-1/2 feet where each square was a leveled terrace with a pavilion at each end. By referring to Jefferson's original survey one can follow his written specifications, A locust stake was located at the center of the middle square where additional stakes where driven at the corners of the first pavilion. A pile of stones was placed around each of theses stakes. The place where the theodolite was fixed being the center of the Northern Square and the point destined for some principal building in the level of the square."[11]

Edmund Bacon, overseer at Monticello from 1806 to 1822, described the scene when Jefferson laid the foundation for the first pavilion: "As we passed through Charlottesville, I went to old Davy Issacs' store and got a ball of twine, Dinsmore found some shingles and made some pegs, and we all went on to the old field

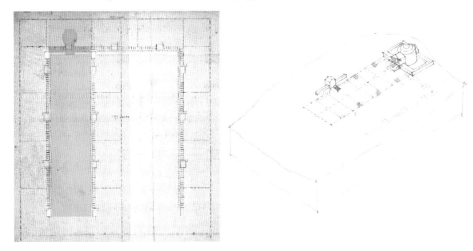

together. Mr. Jefferson looked over the ground for some time and then struck down a peg in [the location of the first pavilion], and then directed me where to carry the line, and I stuck the second. He carried one end of the line, and I the other, in laying off the foundation of the university. He had a little rule in his pocket that he always carried with him, and with this, he measured off the ground and laid the entire foundation, and then set the men at work." Architectural historian Frank Grizzard considers it highly doubtful that Jefferson laid out the foundation for Pavilion VII with a pocket ruler, though it does make for a fascinating story.

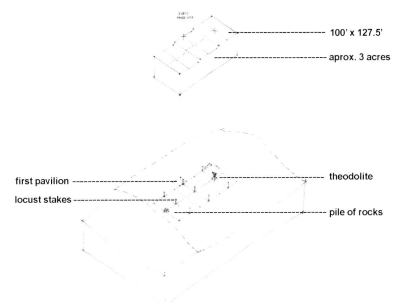

100' x 127.5'

aprox. 3 acres

first pavilion — theodolite

locust stakes

pile of rocks

The resulting lawn is a "gently terraced square" made so by the "law of the ground" with an increasing number of dormitories between each pavilion moving south, which creates a forced perspective view looking north towards the Rotunda. "From the closed north end, the pavilions appear to be spaced evenly apart and from the south end looking northward one's attention is forced toward the grand central building."[12] Architectural historian, Richard Guy Wilson, asserts that the optical illusion was not planned but a fortunate outcome resulting from the "constraints of the site and the need to provide more pavilions for the professors."[13]

Water

The first pavilion served as a datum from which five springs were measured to Observatory Mountain. James Dinsmore and John Perry, the leading two contractors at the university construction site, submitted a report informing the Board of Visitors that after they leveled the ground from Pavilion VII, the first two springs were about 1,100 yards from the pavilion and 6 feet above the water table. One hundred yards further was another spring that was 26 feet deep, about 60 more yards was a spring that was 75 feet, and the deepest spring on Observatory Hill was 1,260 yards from the pavilion.

Water was needed not only for the construction operation but also for the infrastructure to service the Academical Village. Wooden pipes to transport water from the "neighboring highlands" were constructed in the late fall of 1819. By mid-June 1820, the proctor reported that "the pipe borers were laying down the logs … in a covered ditch at the end of which is a reservoir where the water is taken."[14]

The construction manager suggested in the spring of 1824 that reservoirs "nearly the depth of the Attic and as large in diameter as the space will admit of be placed in the two north corners of the attic" so that in case of fire, water could be thrown by pipes or hose to any part of the building beneath the dome of the Rotunda. These reservoirs were never built.[15]

Brick

Jefferson described where the materials were located in order to make and lay bricks, "The lime kilns are about 9 miles distant along the public road, and the price of lime has been generally about 16 cents the bushel at the kilns; but it is believed that better lime, and on better terms, may be had from more distant quarries. Good sand is two miles distant. The wood lands commence at about half a mile, and the brick yard with water is about 30 to 40 rods distant: space for the yard, earth for the bricks, sand for mortar, and water for both will be given."[16]

In mid-July 1817, in a small brick kiln near a large spring on the west side of the

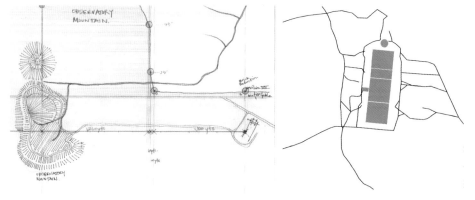

central lawn, bricks were being made in preparation for construction of the first pavilion of Jefferson's Academical Village. The spring closest to the first pavilion was also the location where the first brickyard was laid out. A young student described the brickyard in a detailed letter to his father,

> The yard is laid off in a more regular manner than I ever saw one, and everything seem to go on with perfect order. They do not make up their mortar as we do with Oxen but with a spade and make it in large piles and cover it with planks a day before they use it, the hole is near a branch, and they always have a good deal of water in it. They have the

table near the place that they lay down the bricks and move it as they lay them down, and the mud is rolled to it. I have not yet seen them molding brick as I went there just as they began to kiln; they hack all the bricks in single hacks and under a large shelter which is erected for the purpose, which effectually keeps off the sun and rain. The kiln which I saw, was lined with a stone wall about a foot thick, about half way and the other part with brick.[17]

The process of brickmaking was in full force by early summer in 1818, and bricks were being laid for the first pavilion. The first pavilion and its adjacent dormitories required 192,248 bricks to build, which cost approximately $892 given that at the time 1,000 bricks could be purchased for $4.50. It is probable that Jefferson used slaves to manufacture the bricks for the Academical Village, given the fact that one slave could be rented for as little as $8 per month to make brick.[18]

Wood

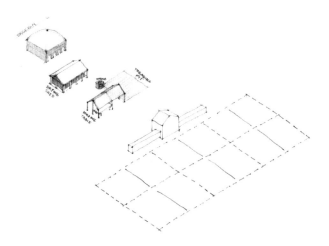

Wood was used for house carpentry and joinery as well as for the roofs of all the buildings including the Rotunda. The Rotunda's wood roof was constructed with a Philibert de L'Orme truss like the one used at Jefferson's Monticello home.[19]

The carpenters' work was at pace with the amount of lumber that could be delivered to the site. Wagon loads of plank from Gilmore's, Garth's, and Maury's sawmills located in Albemarle County were hauled to the construction site regularly. The boards were delivered unseasoned and had to be sufficiently kiln dried by the carpenters.[20]

In 1818, a pine tree could be bought for $1, seven for $5, and twenty trees for $10, and a thousand feet of sawing cost from $7.50 to $9. It should be noted that two slaves could take two weeks to saw 1,000 board feet of lumber, for which a master could collect $9 from the buyer.[21]

On June 20, 1819, one of the carpenters at the site, purchased standing timber located about four to five and a half miles from the first pavilion. James Oldham, a master carpenter and joiner, wrote: "I expect to have all my large timber hewn this [week], the logs are [ready], but the water is too low to [work the] mill . . . On Monday last I made a [purchase] of seven or eight thousand feet of lumber, the quality I have no doubt you will be [satisfied] with.[22]

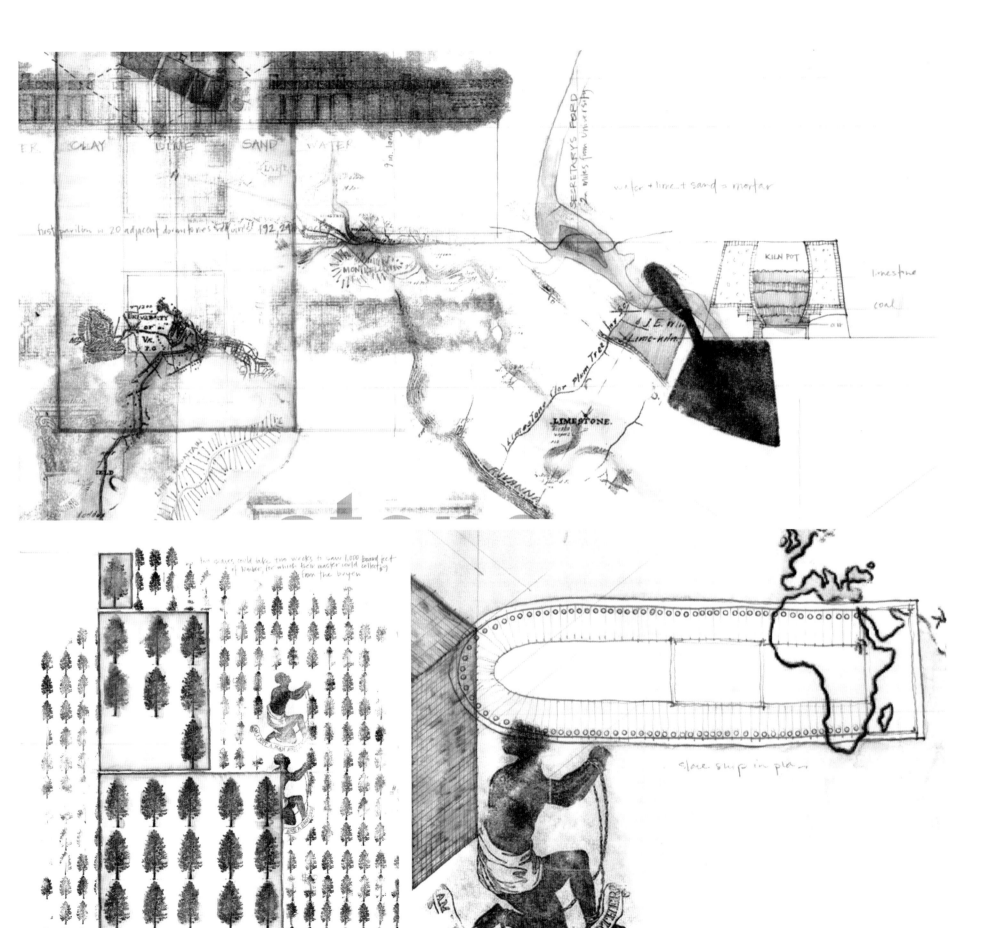

CLAY   LIME   SAND   WATER

SECRETARY'S FORD
(2 miles from University)

water + lime + sand = mortar

KILN POT

limestone

coal

first pavilion w 20 adjacent dormitories required 192,29...

MONT...

UNIVERSITY OF VA.

J.E. Wm
Lime-kiln

Limestone (or Plum Tree)

LIMESTONE.

Two slaves could take two weeks to saw 1,000 board feet of timber, for which their master could collect $9 from the buyer

slave ship in plan

AM NOT A
MAN AT A BROTHER

In 1820, one slave could be rented for 3 months to make brick at $8 per month.

Stone

On October 6, 1817, the cornerstone of the Thomas Jefferson's Academical Village was ceremoniously placed six feet within the foundation of the first pavilion commencing the entire construction operation. The Widow's Son Masonic Lodge No. 60 and Charlottesville Lodge No. 90 conducted the ceremony. For the cornerstone laying ceremony, the grand master applied [the square, the plumb, and the level] to the stone, struck the stone three times with a mallet while saying, "this stone [is] well-formed and trusty," and then a band played Hail Columbia, one of the unofficial national anthems of the United States until 1931. The grand master scattered corn, wine, and oil over the throne and offered another prayer, "Assist in the erection and completion of this building. Protect the workmen against every accident, and long preserve this structure from decay, and give to us all in needed supply, the corn of nourishment, the wine of refreshment and the oil of joy. Amen."[23]

Early on in the process, the [Board of Visitors] agreed "that it be expedient to import Stone Cutter[s] from Italy" because they had the first degree of skill but went for one-third of what local/regional stonecutters asked.[24]

It was imperative to Jefferson that the stonecutters arrived in Baltimore and were transported quickly to Charlottesville because he feared that if they were "permitted to stay in Baltimore a single day as they will learn there the wages of that place, and would not come on, or stay when come."[25]

The sculptors finally arrived at the university on the last day of June 1819, and Jefferson wrote, "this requires the Quarriers to get to work raising the stone, common stonecutters to prepare the blocks and other arrangements to get them underway."[26] The Italian stone sculptors had been at the university only a few days when they examined the local quarry and, in Jefferson's words to the Board of Visitors, "pronounce it impossible to make of it an Ionic or Corinthian capital."[27]

It should be noted that the same commission for the six Doric bases and capitals for the first pavilion were given to both the Raggi brothers from Italy and a local stone carver. Though it is unclear what happened, it can be inferred from the surmising of other historians and the record that the Giacomo and Michele Raggis were paid for the same task that was most likely carried out by a local Lynchburg-area artisan at a later date. Jefferson stated in a letter that every dollar paid to the Raggis was sunk cost at that time.[28]

The stonecutters were shipped back after a disappointing year and were instead commissioned to carve the Ionic and Corinthian capitals from Carrara marble in Italy with the intention that they ship the Carrara marble capitals to the construction site in Charlottesville, VA as they were finished.

In the end, the Doric columns for the first pavilion were carved locally with marble from a local marble yard. The specific Doric Order Jefferson used for the portico of the first pavilion is the Palladian Doric shown in Freart's and Errand's Parallel de l'architecture Antique avec la Moderne (1766).

In July 1823, Jefferson learned that the marble capitals from Italy were being shipped to Richmond from New York aboard the Draco. Upon arrival in Richmond, several of the capitals were so enormous and heavy that the university's commission agent did not know what to do with them. "They are too heavy to be [towed]," he informed the proctor, "and the locks are not in order to admit the passage of boats from the basin to Tidewater, and again, I fear they are too heavy for boats, particularly those of the north river, and when the water is low."[29]

A Richmond merchant managed the difficult and dangerous job of loading the massive marble capitals onboard the small vessels that would carry them by water from Rockett's Landing, a significant wharf on the James River in Richmond, to Milton, the busy village on the Rivanna River just east of Charlottesville near Monticello.[30]

The last shipment of marble, which had been ordered in October 1823, arrived at Boston from Leghorn, Italy in August 1825, 31 bases and 37 cases of paving squares on board one ship, and 24 capitals on board another ship. It was then transported from Boston to New York City, where the bases were placed on board a sloop and the capitals on a schooner, for their voyage south.[31]

John Gorman set the last capitals in place nearly three years later only a few weeks before Jefferson's death on July 4, 1826.[32]

Cornerstone and Capstone

On March 7, 1825, the day of its official opening 30 or 40 students had arrived at the university, and by April 12, 1825, Jefferson boasted to his future grandson-in-law that the number had risen to 65.[33] All the pavilions were occupied except Pavilion VII because it was the smallest and inadequate to suit even a single professor. Despite its shortcomings, Pavilion VII, held a prominent position on the lawn for a short time. The cornerstone served as the capstone of the Academical Village and was a temporary substitute for the principal building being constructed on the far north end of the lawn.

Pavilion VII was designated the "book room" while the Rotunda was being built

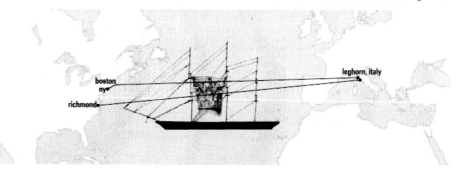

and stored all the books that would ultimately sit on the shelves of the Rotunda's great library room. The pavilion also housed the great bell and clock to be installed in the Rotunda upon its completion. Jefferson instructed how these two ornaments should be located temporarily in his letter to a trustee,

The bell should be placed on the ridge of the roof of the pavilion in which the books now are, on a small gallows exactly as the tavern bells are. You will contrive how the cord may be protected from the trickish rings of the students. When the clock comes from Richmond it should be placed before a window of the book room of the same house, the face so near the window as that it is time may be read through the window from the outside.[34]

This inadequate solution underscores the necessity for some principal building to complete Jefferson's vision, an element which was transformative to his original plan for the Academical Village. Jefferson described the architectural and spatial significance of the Rotunda to a friend, "the [Rotunda], not yet begun, is essentially wanting to give [the university] unity and consolidation as a single object. The

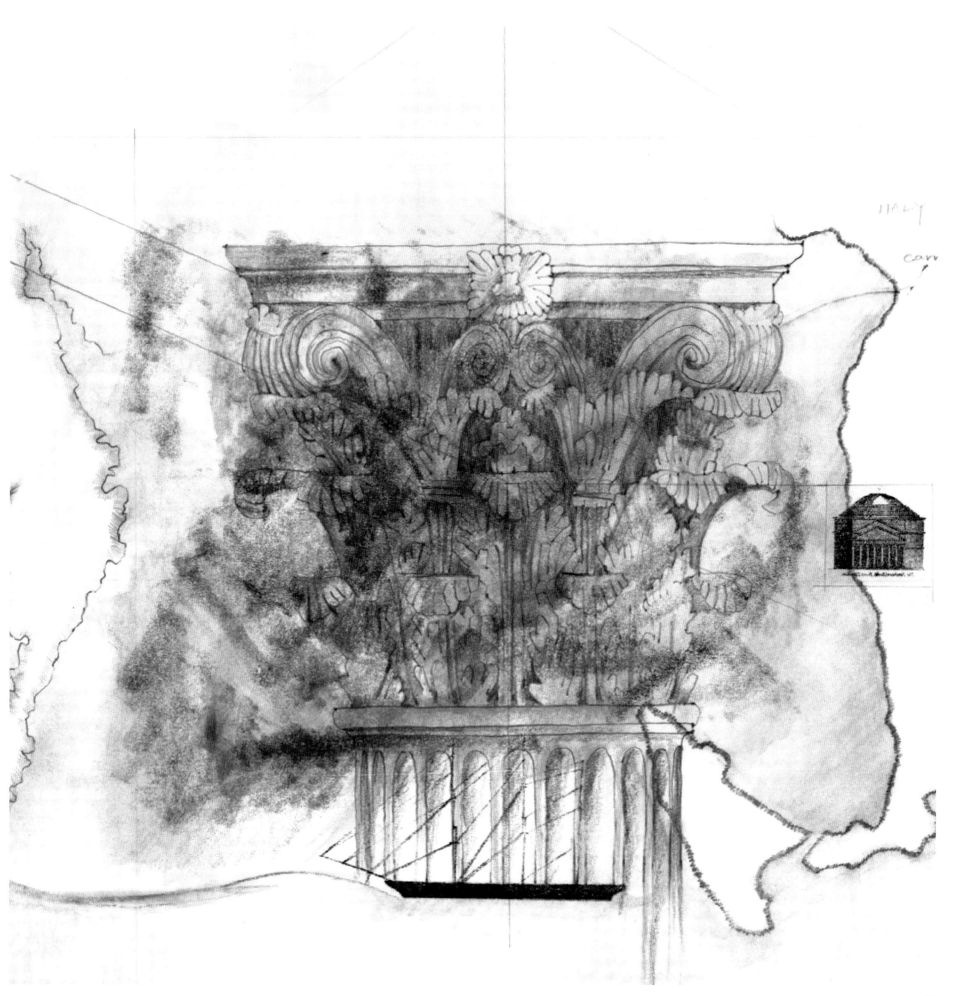

ITALY

corr

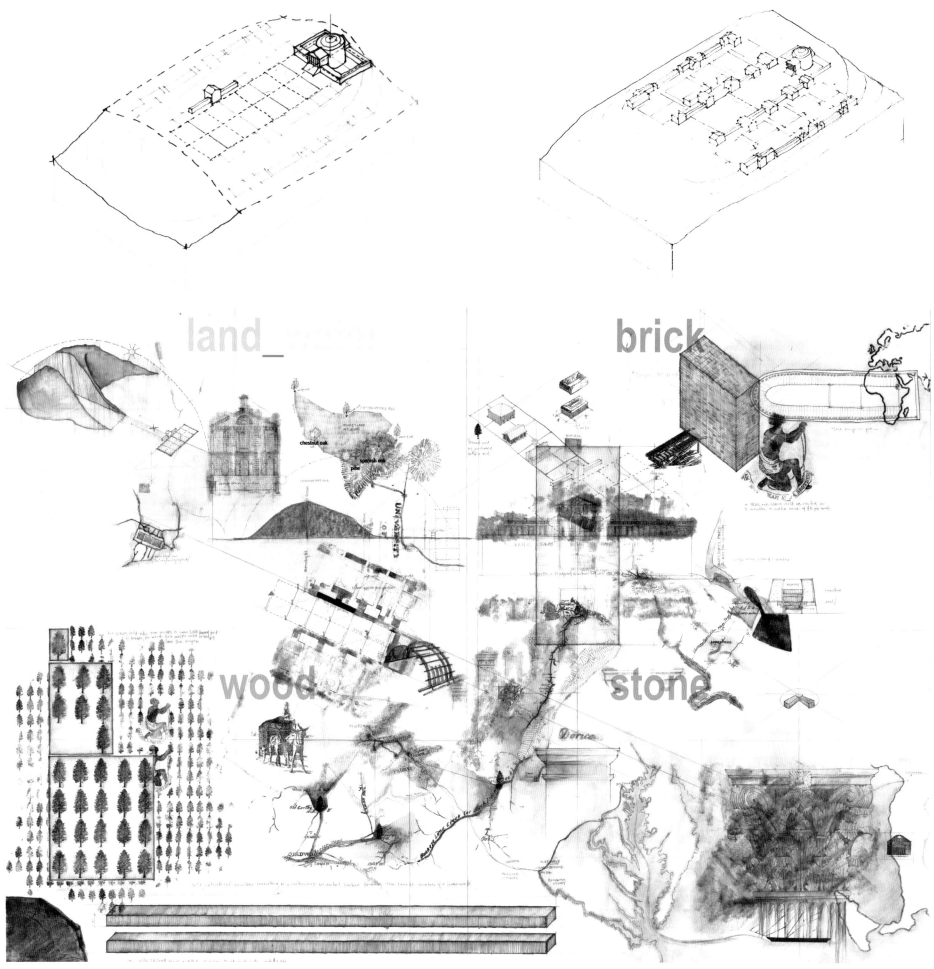

land_

brick

wood

stone

[Rotunda] is to be on the principle of the Pantheon, a sphere within a cylinder of 70 feet diameter—to wit, one-half only of the dimensions of the Pantheon, and of a single order only. When this is done you must come and see it.[35]

On October 7, 1826, after Jefferson's death, the Board of Visitors prepared its annual report of the recent progress of the work and what remained to be done on the Rotunda. The portico of the Rotunda was complete, and the library was nearly finished with books on the shelves. Various rooms and the entrance hall were still unfinished. In 1828, the capstone of the Academical Village was complete and set at the northernmost point of the lawn, concluding eleven years of construction at the site.

Jefferson's Academical Village provides a dual reading. The first pavilion and the principal building, the cornerstone and the capstone, provide two distinct foci. Most obviously, the village is a hierarchical space where a central figurehead, the Rotunda, encloses a swath of open space, in which smaller pavilions and single-room dormitories proceed down a lawn flanked by a secondary series of hotels and rooms. A more layered interpretation surfaces when one excavates the material index of the site, which points to the building campaign from 1817 to 1828 and pivots around the conception and construction of the first pavilion.

Pavilion VII was the "germ" that gave birth to the "great tree." Some might assume that this culmination is the completed Academical Village, the exemplary model of American architecture that stands today, in which the magnificence of the creation overtakes the significance of the seed. Instead, imagine another interpretation, a different species of tree–the first pavilion originating a vast network of material flows, workers engaged in construction, and processes of production connected to Albemarle County land, the newly formed thirteen states, Europe and Africa.

Note to the Reader

When this research was completed in 2006, I had not fully explored the troubling subject of the African slaves and their essential involvement in the construction of the Academical Village. I encourage any future Kenan fellows to begin piecing together a real and complete history of the Academical Village, which might serve as a form of reparations for the brutalities of the system of slavery and help to break down the current systemic racism that still exists today.

This essay stems from the body of research developed through the Kenan Fellowship, that took the form of an illustrated guidebook and material construction map of the Academical Village from 1817-1828. The majority of research so integral to this project is credited to architectural historians Richard Guy Wilson and Frank Edgar Grizzard, Jr. for his effort in compiling the Documentary History of the Construction of the Buildings at the University of Virginia, 1817–1828.

Endnotes

1 Malone, Jefferson 3:222.
2 Thomas Jefferson to Col. Yancey, 6 Jan. 1816.
3 The Albemarle Academy was an institution chartered by the Commonwealth of Virginia in 1803 and never was an operational institution but served to develop the design of Pavilion VII and the subsequent pavilions.
4 Thomas Jefferson to William Thornton, May 9, 1817.
5 Pierson, Rev. Hamilton Wilcox, Jefferson at Monticello: The Private Life of Thomas Jefferson, from Entirely New Materials, 1862, 19-22.
6 See Thomas Jefferson to the Board of Visitors, 15 April 1825, in ViU:JHC
7 Brockenbrough's agreement with Daniel A. and Mary A. Frances Piper, 22 September.
8 May 5, 1817 – Meeting of Board of Visitor of Central College. Vol. 1, p. 2
9 http://www.iath.virginia.edu/wilson/uva/pavilionVII/History.pdf, p 29
10 Operations at and for the College, 18 July 1817, ViU:TJ, and Thomas Jefferson to Latrobe, 3 August 1817, DLC:TJ
11 Operations at and for the College, 18 July 1817, ViU:TJ, and Thomas Jefferson to Latrobe, 3 August 1817, DLC:TJ.
12 See Patton, Jefferson, Cabell and the University of Virginia, 187.
13 See Patton, Jefferson, Cabell and the University of Virginia, 187. The west, VII, is 104 feet, then IX is 122 feet, and for the east, numbers VIII and X, nearly the same dimensions hold. The small differences result from the different widths of the pavilions" ("Jefferson's Lawn: Perceptions, Interpretations, Meanings," in Wilson, Thomas Jefferson's Academical Village, 90).
14 Minutes of the Board of Visitors of the Central College, 26 February 1819, in ViU:TJ.
15 Brockenbrough to Jefferson, 4 June 1824, ViU:PP
16 http://www.iath.virginia.edu/wilson/uva/pavilionI/hsrpav1.body3.html
17 John Hartwell Cocke, Jr. to John Hartwell Cocke, 27 August 1819, ViU:JHC
18 The Reshaping of Everyday Life, 107.
19 See http://www.iath.virginia.edu/wilson/uva/pavilionVII/History.pdf, Apendix A
20 http://www.iath.virginia.edu/wilson/uva/pavilionI/hsrpav1.body3.html
21 Documentary History of the Construction of the Buildings at the University of Virginia, 1817–1828, Frank Edgar Grizzard, Jr., Appendix B: A Note on Prices.
22 Oldham to Brockenbrough, 20 June 1819, ViU:PP.
23 The description of the cornerstone ceremony on October 6, 1817 is taken from Alexander Garrett's undated Outline of Cornerstone Ceremonies, in ViU.
24 Minutes of the Board of Visitors of the Central College, 28 July 1817, PPAmP: UVA Minutes.
25 Appleton to Thomas Jefferson, 20 December 1817, DLC:TJ.
26 Thomas Jefferson to Brockenbrough, 2 July 1819, ViU:PP; see also James Dinsmore to Brockenbrough 2 July 1819, in ViU:PP.
27 Thomas Jefferson to James Breckenridge, Robert B. Taylor, James Madison, and Chapman Johnson, 8-26 July 1819, ViU:TJ
28 Thomas Jefferson to Appleton, April 16, 1821. DLC.
29 Peyton to Brockenbrough, 7 July 1823, ViU:PP.
30 See Thomas Jefferson to E. S. Davis, 27 August, in ViU:TJ, and Peyton to Brockenbrough, 8 September 1823, ViU:PP.
31 See Henry A. S. Dearborn to Thomas Jefferson, 6 September, in ViU:TJ, and 20 September, in DLC:TJ, and Jonathan Thompson to Thomas Jefferson, 9 September, and 3 October 1825, in ViU:PP.
32 See Thomas Jefferson to Brockenbrough, 5 May 1826, in ViU:PP
33 Thomas Jefferson to Coolidge, 12 April 1825, ViU:TJ. Joseph Coolidge, Jr. (d. 1879), married Jefferson's favorite granddaughter, Eleanora Wayles Randolph (Ellen; d. 1876), in the drawing room of Monticello on 27 May 1825.
34 Thomas Jefferson to A. S. Brockenbrough, Jan 3, 1826. ViU:PP.
35 Thomas Jefferson to Short, 24 November 1821, printed in Whitman, Jefferson's Letters, 362-63. "[The university] will have cost on the whole but 250,000 dollars"

Source: Le Corbusier. *Global Architecture 30: Le Corbusier - Chandigarh*. Yoshizaka, Takamasa., Futagawa, Yukio., ed.
GA A.D.A. Edita Tokyo, 1974

Source: UVA Library Kore Collection, Slide Number: In-20-Je-3-9. Digital Image Number: AS071103_0034. Artist Authority ID: 15899. IRIS Work No: 197097
Slide Repository: FAIC-UVA, 115188. Data from: University of Virginia

Chandigarh Capitol Complex + City Plan
Lauren Hackney

FIGURE : GROUND

figure | *percept, maneuver, play, perception, perceptual experience, design, pattern, flesh, frame, human body, soma [Hindu deity], physical body, terra fluxus.*

ground | *antonym of figure* | *terra firma, establish, anchor, found, land, earth, solid ground, perceptual experience, perception, percept, surface, soil, primer coat, place, position, background, connect, instruct, set, footing, basis.*

figured ground | *dynamic inhabitation of layered physical, political, cultural ground.*

Chandigarh manifests an idea of figured : ground as the structuring theme for inhabitation of the earth and sky. By interweaving temporal and enduring cycles of human, civic, monumental, and site operations, Le Corbusier establishes a complex relationship between the individual and the collective through Modulor, a proportional ordering system based on human proportions.

Four interrelated themes illustrate this relationship of individual to collective. The first theme is the relationship of figure to ground: where humans structure an ordering system of center and edge. This permits the strata of constructed ground by articulated layered foundations some call basements or grottoes. Upon this constructed field the figures of iconography and identity provide relationships to cultural and collective memory. This crucial connection of semantic content connects the modern to enduring cultural traditions. Precedent is the spatial manifestation of these connections through Le Corbusier's synthesis of intrinsic and extrinsic modern, ancient, classical, and vernacular influences.

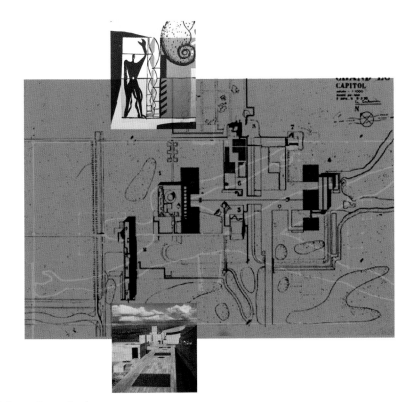

capitol complex + city plan
chandigarh, india | le corbusier
city plan, 1950-57; capitol complex 1950-1965

CONTEXT

Chandigarh responds to political and cultural turmoil of Indian independence and, more broadly, to the post-war condition of the world through its reaction to modernity. Drawing of boundaries between Pakistan and India generated an extremely volatile political situation in the region, with the worst violence in Bengal (where Ghandi staged his protest fast) and in Punjab, where there were millions of refugees. Lahore, the ancient capital of Punjab, was annexed to Pakistan, leaving the region of Punjab without a capital and administrative center. In 1948, the government decided to build a new capital city that P.L. Verma, the chief engineer of Punjab, described as "possessing sufficient magnificence and glamour to make up for the psychological loss of Lahore."[1] Chandigarh, named for the ancient temple *Chandi Mandir* in the territory's vicinity, was to have an important and far-reaching symbolic purpose in building national identity. Nehru, the first prime minister of independent India, issued a "call to modernization" and what he termed an "aggressive effort to catch up with the west" – and, specifically regarding Chandigarh, he called for a "new city, unfettered by the traditions of the past, a symbol of the nation's faith in the future."[2]

Le Corbusier was commissioned in 1950 for the city Master Plan and Capitol Complex, and he worked on the project until his death in 1965. Chandigarh represents many recurrent themes in his later work, especially his disenchantment with modernism's detachment from social, human agency.[3] Le Corbusier's post-war work draws from vernacular, cosmological influences and traditions, an interest in the connection between Man and Nature, and an interest in the mathematical abstraction and regularity of organic forms and enigmatic figures, particularly that of the human figure. Spatially, the recurrent theme of these figures registered against precise geometries, meters, and datums, particularly the horizon, characterizes his later work: the subversive new landscape in the sky at the Unite d'Habitation— the mythical and spiritual geometries and forms of the chapel at Ronchamp— and the enigmatic figures in the courtyard that register against the building and the sky at La Tourette.[4]

The political condition of Punjab profoundly shaped Le Corbusier's vision for Chandigarh as the dialectic of meter (the push toward Modern) and figure (ancient cultural traditions caught by this effort).   Noted architectural historian + theorist Kenneth Frampton described Le Corbusier's reaction to the place and of the people as a "synthesis of modern technology with a timeless ... culture, the insertion of the one with the maintenance of the other, to the benefit of both."[5] The Capitol Complex addresses this duality between the transitory state of India, exemplified by Nehru's catalytic ideas about a "transformative modernism to counter stasis" through progress, and what Frampton terms an "antique civilization with its rhythmic, cyclical notion of time and place."[6] This cultural and political duality weaves through the project's conception and making.

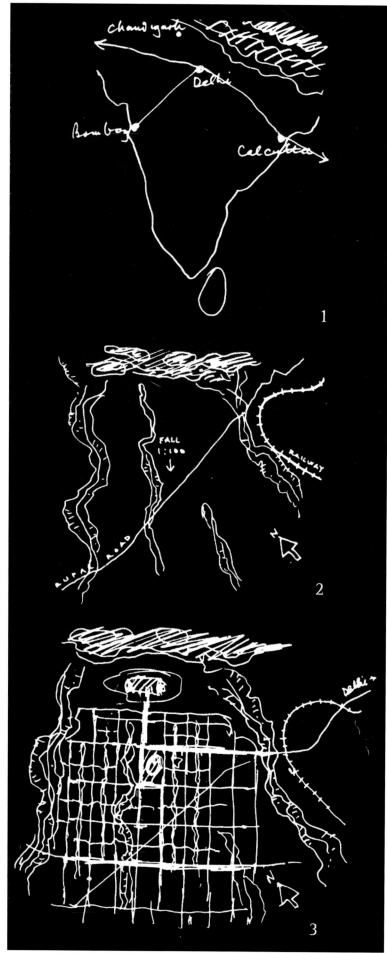

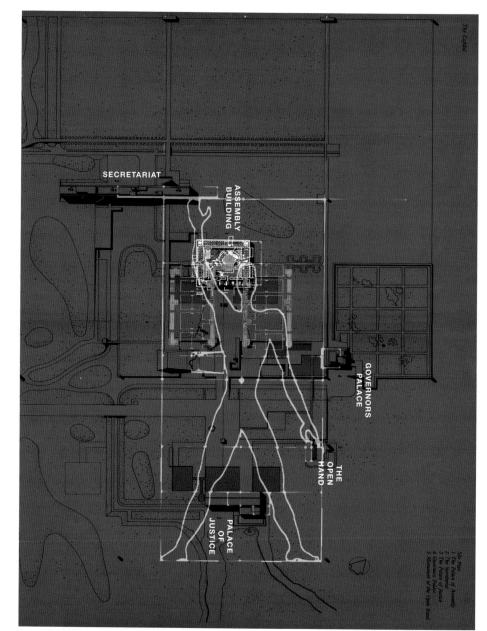

Source: Original site plan: Le Corbusier. Global Architecture 30: Le Corbusier - Chandigarh. Yoshizaka, Takamasa., Futagawa, Yukio., ed. GA A.D.A. Edita Tokyo, 1974
Modulor overlay adapted from Gast, Klaus-Peter, "Chandigarh General Plan," in Le Corbusier, Paris—Chandigarh Gast, Klaus-Peter, "Chandigarh General Plan," in Le Corbusier, Paris—Chandigarh, 98-113.

Ordering of the Capitol Complex: The overlay of the Modulor Man on the site plan registers the proportional system of the composition and also the relationship of pieces to parts of the body – the Assembly Building, where Parliament meets, is at the head. An overlay of the Academical Village illustrates the monumental scale of the Complex's buildings and public spaces.

Structure of the City: The grid juxtaposed with the alluvial landscape registers the sinuous form of existing streams, and recalls the agricultural precondition of the site. Layered systems of circulation connect the infill of independent urban sectors.

Modulor proportions (right) show the figure in an architectural space, metered with a dynamic/fluid condition. Humanscapes provide the frictional dynamics framed by static public institutions.

MODULOR: PROPORTIONAL SYSTEMS OF ORDERING

Modulor was a proportional system devised by Le Corbusier that is based on the module of a 6' man, as well as the principles of Golden Section/Spiral and the Fibonacci series. Modulor references two historical proportional/geometrical representations of the human figure as a system for ordering: the classical Vitruvian man and the Renaissance re-drawing of the Vitruvian Man by Leonardo daVinci. The human figure is first inscribed in a square + circle as a static object demonstrating ideal geometries; the daVinci figure becomes more dynamic with the grounding square breaking the circle and the arms and legs of the Vitruvian man in motion.

The Modulor Man is drawn relative to a double square and a double rectangle derived from Golden Section. The figure is dynamic and asymmetrical in its geometries, engaging its context and reaching.[7] The explicit relationship between this representation of Man and Vitruvius's drawing is manifest in the single square vs. double square relationship, in the diagonals that frame rather than cross the figure's center of gravity. Here and at Chandigarh, Le Corbusier reframes classical ideas of proportion and of the figure in space: the city plan juxtaposes figural and geometric systems, such as the overlay of the grid of transport over stream corridors.

Le Corbusier's deployment of Modulor as a structuring, ordering system at Chandigarh reflects his concern for what he calls "the fundamental base which unites man with the cosmos."[8]

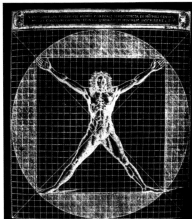

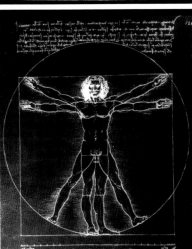

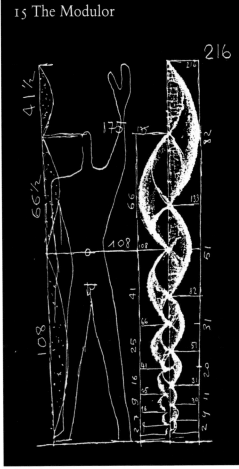

SITE AND CITY / HUMAN ESTABLISHMENTS

Sited in an alluvial floodplain at the foothills of the Himalayas, streams etch Chandigarh's territory, making legible the relationship between source (the Himalayas) and resource (the streams that feed this agricultural plain). The Capitol Complex is sited at the city's northernmost point and the land slopes away from the complex to the southwest. The Chandigarh city plan is a grid of 400x800m sectors of varying densities, bounded by two rivers to the East and West and the Capitol Complex to the North. Farmland and smaller villages surround the city.

In *Three Human Establishments*, written in 1942 and applied at Chandigarh, Le Corbusier identified the radiant village, or the unit of agricultural production as the first human establishment, in service of the peasant and the cooperative; the linear industrial city, or the place where habitation, work, and self-cultivation occurs as the second; and the radio-concentric city of exchange, the most urban unit, founded upon what Le Corbusier terms man's relationship to nature.[9] One might think of the three human establishments as the utopian urban manifestation of First, Second, and Third Nature in landscape, the gradation from wild to civilized landscape.[10]

The plan of Chandigarh was an opportunity for Le Corbusier to test principles of modern urban design, codified in his writings in *Three Human Establishments*. Each 400x800m sector -- a double square -- was designed as an autonomous community within the city, with its own economic, dwelling, and recreation zones, described anthropomorphically as "organs and functions" in a new "biology of building", connected by layers of vehicular and pedestrian circulation that Le Corbusier described as "irrigation of territory by transport."[11] This references the precondition of the site: the network of etched streams irrigates as an agricultural resource; the overlay of systems of movement irrigates the city. The urban form is a network of autonomous sectors, interwoven by strata of transit/transport connections.

Le Corbusier saw the pedestrian as the most important mode of circulation in the city. As the human body is the fundamental unit of measure in Le Corbusier's Modulor system, so does the pedestrian become the fundamental unit of measure of movement in the city. Le Corbusier described the primacy of the pedestrian in his vision as such:

> Things which we believe Utopian, are now present: the royalty of the pedestrian. This silence of the street, this serenity of the walker, this possibility of looking, of raising the eyes towards upper stories endowed with fine proportions. This unity of stones, and this unity of windows, the scale of which is the result of a tournament between human needs and the techniques of building.[12]

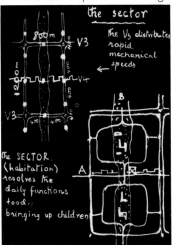

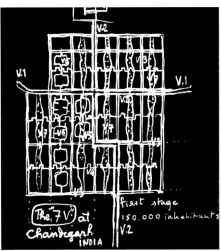

Source: Collectif. Chandigarh, la ville indienne de Le Corbusier. Le Capitole, une oeuvre inachevée... (Coédition Musée). Somogy éditions d'art, 2002.

Le palais des Ministères (en gratte-ciel)   L'Assemblée   Le palais du Gouverneur   La Main ouverte

The Parthenon, "a sovereign cube facing the sea" (courtesy FLC)

"Nothing existed but the temple, the sky, and the surface of paving stones damaged by centuries of plundering. And no other external sign of life was evident here, except, far off in the distance, Pentelicus, creditor of these stones, bearing in its side a marble wound, and Hymettus, colored the most opulent purple."

"I think the flatness of the horizon, particularly at noon when it imposes its uniformity on everything about it, provides for each one of us a measure of the most humanly possible perception of the absolute."

Source: Le Corbusier. The Parthenon. Journey to the East. See Endnotes.

Source: View of the University of Virginia from Lewis Mountain by E Sache, 1856

ENCOUNTERING THE CAPITOL COMPLEX: SURVEYOR, NOMAD, LUNATIC

In the scope and form of his post-war work, Le Corbusier searched for permanence in the face of upheaval. He looked to cultural traditions to foreground his intentions. On Le Corbusier's first trip to Punjab, he met villagers and observed vernacular and cultural traditions of the region; these observations are manifest throughout the Capitol Complex in its proportions, materials, siting, construction, and occupation.

Le Corbusier also referenced the physical geography that shaped these cultural operations through the juxtaposition of artifice and nature embedded in the ordering of the land. The rational Surveyor observes this juxtaposition, datum registered against figural, as dialogue rather than imposition: the grid juxtaposed with stream corridors registers their sinuous form and recalls the agricultural precondition of the site; layered systems of circulation connect the infill of independent urban sectors.

The Capitol Complex is located at the terminus of a main street, Jan Marg, above the city. Mounded landforms obscure the view from the city into the complex; the processional axis terminates off-center, in a composition of slipping axes and shifting centers, where edges are at once immediate and distant, defined by layered horizons of structures and mounds, and the Shivalik range of the Himalayas and its foothills. The peripatetic Nomad encounters borrowed scenery, or *shakkei* - a landscape painting technique - that encompasses the Himalayas as an orienting device and as a bounding horizon, creating tensions and ambiguities between immediate and distant elements and situating the Complex in its precondition.

In composition, the Capitol Complex references Jantar Mantar, an astronomical observatory built in 18th century that consists of collection of elements placed within composition to measure time, track orbits, and measure celestial altitudes.[13] The landscape of Chandigarh is a collection of elements that cut and mound the earth. These Mounds and Valleys obscure and reveal views and axes, reflecting pools mirror the sky and reference traditional cycles of rebirth and emergence, while attics and basements enclose spaces. The dialectical Lunatic understands the themes of ground, water, sky, and horizon as not only cosmic but cosmological, referencing Hindu and Christian philosophy.

Le Corbusier recorded his formative travel experiences in *Journey to the East*, his travel journal and first publication. As we look pedagogically to the Academical Village and to the characters who inhabit and narrate it – Surveyor, Nomad, and Lunatic – Le Corbusier drew lessons from the Acropolis. Looking to this ancient precedent situates Chandigarh and its promise of Indian democracy in the same temporal continuum.

In 1911 at the Parthenon, he observed:

> Having climbed steps that were too high, not cut to human scale, I entered the temple on the axis...turning back all at once from this spot once reserved for the gods and the priest, I took in at a glance the entire blazing sea and the already obscure mountains of the Peloponnesus...The steep slope of the hill and the higher elevation of the temple above the stone slabs of the Propylaea conceal from view all traces of modern life, and all of a sudden, two thousand years are obliterated, a harsh poetry seizes you...sparkling and elusive above the sea, a spectral past, an ineluctable presence.[14]

This description of his first encounter with the Acropolis suggests a more profound understanding of 'ground', one that Robin Dripps describes in 'Groundwork' 50 years later:

> Metaphorically, ground refers to the various patterns of physical, intellectual, poetic, and political structure that intersect, overlap, and weave together to become the context for human thought and action.[15]

The thread of shaping and constructing the ground weaves through Le Corbusier's conceptions of both the city through the three-dimensional grid of transit and plan of sectors, and the Capitol Complex, where the ground obscures, structures, and scales the buildings of the complex. On approach, the mounding of the earth sets apart the Capitol Complex as another autonomous sector with its own systems and shifting axes, and landform obscures the Secretariat and the Assembly Building. Consider this arrival sequence in dialogue with the Lawn or the Acropolis – the processional axis terminates not in a singular capitol, but toward the east and the horizon. Rather than giving hierarchy to a single building or civic function, the buildings are perceived on the oblique, indicating their relationship within the monumental composition and to the larger whole. Le Corbusier framed this relationship at the Acropolis: "I think the flatness of the horizon, particularly at noon when it imposes its uniformity on everything about it, provides for each one of us a measure of the most humanly possible perception of the absolute."

There is a relationship among the Capitol Complex's porous edges, the shifting axes of the Lawn, and the layered views of the Acropolis. In one of Le Corbusier's earliest sketches of the Capitol Complex, the horizon is referenced and broken at various points in the composition, alternately overtaking and receding. To draw in the horizon, Le Corbusier utilizes shifting axes and centers. These shifting axes and centers can be examined both in plan and in precedent. At the Lawn, the north-south axis is intended to be continuous, opening to the mountains beyond

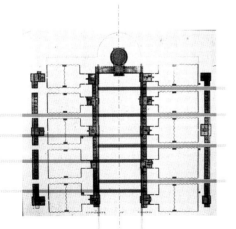 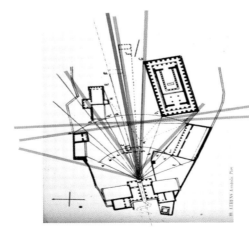 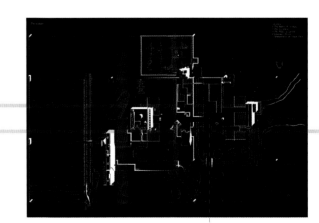

Axial relationsihips compared across precedents, from left-right: The Lawn, the Acropolis, the Capitol Complex.

Le Corbusier intended that a single ray of light hit a column of Ashoka, the first emperor, on the speaker's rostrum on the opening day of Parliament. Through this vertical axis mundi, the sky begins to penetrate the constructed ground of the building through a mythical ray of light.

Iconography explores the connection of sky, horizon, ground, figure, and water connected by the axis mundi. The Enamel Door, the ceremonial entrance to the Assembly Building, symbolizes the transition from dark to light in its rotation and pivots about an abstraction of the tree of knowledge.

to enclose the site; columns and by walls truncate east-west axes, except for one on the first terrace that runs all the way through; at the Acropolis, all elements are brought into the composition, and the composition related to the landscape, by shifting axes and layered views.

CENTER, EDGE, AND STRATA: ELEMENTS CONSTRUCTING DEMOCRACY

According to the Indian constitution, the fundamental elements of democracy are the Assembly, the Secretariat, the High Court, the Governor's Palace, the Tower of the Shadows, the Monument for the Victims of the Partition of the State, and the Open Hand. These elements of democracy, evolved from ideas of democratic engagement from both Nehru and Le Corbusier, construct identity in their forms, relationships, and references.[16] Reflecting pools connect particular elements – the Assembly Building, the High Court, the Open Hand – to the sky. Operating at a spectrum of scales, from engulfing space to body-scaled *brise-soleil*, the spaces of the Capitol Complex are all scripted by Modulor and manifest representational strategies -- proportional systems, *chiaroscuro*, figure-ground -- deployed in the negotiation among figure, ground, and sky, measured against the horizon. The Assembly Building, the main meeting hall of Parliament, exemplifies broad themes of center, edge, and strata that explain the overall site strategy of the Capitol Complex. In plan, Le Corbusier organized the Assembly Building as a gridded system and a forest of columns, read against the floating, subtracted volume of the Forum (the main meeting room of Parliament). Re-oriented to the cardinal points from the NE/SW orientation of the rest of the building, the Forum is celebrated as the symbolic gathering place that is at once poetic and rational. Sections of the Assembly Building reveal the depth of its constructed ground and the stratification of the horizon.

Entering the Assembly, there is a duality between inhabiting the ground and denying the ground. Buildings are of the earth, permanent, constructed in concrete; vertically stratified circulation engages the depth of the ground, recalling the Chandigarh city plan and its 7V circulation system. The reflection of forms by the reflecting pool denies the ground, instead drawing the sky to the earth. Again, Dripps's "Groundwork" provides a reading for this strata:

[Providing] protection and a sense of permanence...the wall is part of the ground. It grows from the making of terraces and thus reveals the underlying topographical structure of its earthen context and grounds local place in a larger world. [The ground] forms one pole in a spatial construct linking earth to sky that he considers one of the fundamental relationships guiding human thought and action. The attic, with its clearly articulated structure exposed to view, its removal from the particularity of the ground, which gives it its greater sense of perspective on things, and its mnemonic capacity coming from the contents typically stored within, is considered the rational part of the house.[17]

At the Assembly, Modulor weaves together several operations: the constant registering of monumental versus human scale; the juxtaposition of static ordering and dynamic sculptural elements; the geometrical abstraction of figures; *chiaroscuro*, the poetic carving of volumes of light from a space of shadow, and painting as a method of study; and iconography. Le Corbusier studied the spatial operations of the Capitol Complex through daily painting to investigate space and qualities such as movement and perception; he devoted afternoons to architecture. In his method, you can see a continuum from the hand wielding a paintbrush to the way space is delineated and stratified at the scale of the city by Modulor's multi-scalar application. Paintings of the Modulor man situated at the threshold between earth and water, mythical scale versus distant horizon, establish him as belonging to both realms.[18] This duality persists in reading the Assembly Hall and the Complex more broadly.

The painting technique of *chiaroscuro*, where light is created by carving white/light from a dark canvas is a connective thread between Le Corbusier's paintings and his attention to the sacred and monumental qualities of space at the Capitol Complex. This is manifest at the Assembly in the subtractive quality of volumes of light carved from the building – scholars have noted the symbolism of the oculus as related to the Pantheon, and also to Hindu temples and the idea of the regenerative power of light that punctures the darkness of a masonry-walled space. Le Corbusier intended that a single ray of light hit a column of Ashoka, the first emperor, on the speaker's rostrum on the opening day of Parliament. Through this *axis mundi,* vertical connection from sky to ground, the sky begins to penetrate the constructed ground of the building through a mythical ray of light. This connection draws several precedents of study in the class – the Pantheon, the Rotunda, and now this democratic sacred space.

Source: Le Corbusier. Global Architecture 30: Le Corbusier - Chandigarh. Yoshizaka, Takamasa., Futagawa, Yukio., ed.
GA A.D.A. Edita Tokyo, 1974

Source: Le Corbusier. Global Architecture 30: Le Corbusier - Chandigarh. Yoshizaka, Takamasa., Futagawa, Yukio., ed.GA A.D.A. Edita Tokyo, 1974

The reflection of forms by the reflecting pool denies the ground, instead drawing the sky to the earth. Vertically stratified circulation engages the depth of the ground, recalling the Chandigarh city plan and its 7V circulation system that separates and prioritizes pedestrian movements.

Source: Le Corbusier. *La poeme du l'angle droit.* Tériade Publishing, Paris, 1955.

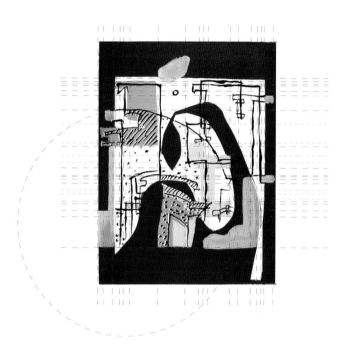

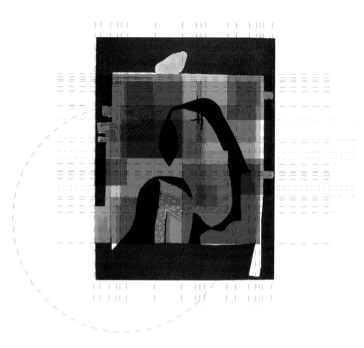

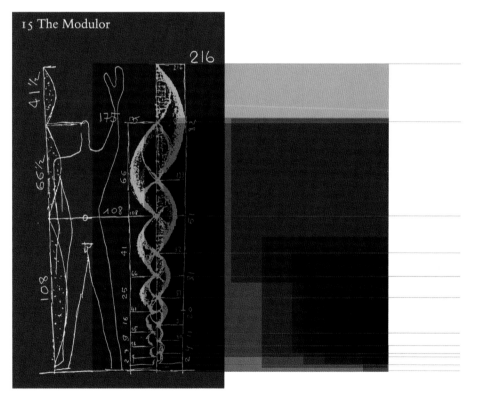

Source: Le Corbusier. "The Modulor." *Three Human Establishments.* See Endnotes.

This analysis connects Le Corbusier's method for study, daily paintings, to strategies at the scale of building and site. First, the analysis discerns the painting's ordering strategy and identfies scales of proportional relationship and references that are manifest. Next, proportions guiding Modulor - the golden section - further derive geometries. Finally, the analysis is applied at site scale.

This painting, as with many of Le Corbusier's paintings, applies to plan and sectional relationships and directionalities and expresses the dialogue between the figural and datum.

METHODOLOGICAL ANALYSIS: TRANSLATING METHOD AND INTENTION

This analysis superimposes the Assembly Building and a key painting to analyze the deployment of Modulor and Golden Section in terms of this superimposition of scales. This painting, from *Le poeme de l'angle droit*—a composition of verses, paintings, musings published by Le Corbusier in 1955—expresses many of Le Corbusier's interests at the Capitol Complex. The volume of white is carved from the heavy, dark ground of a figural element; an orthogonal grid pulls the ground into the carved volume of white as a structuring grid; fragments break through frames and weave in and out of the structuring grid. The dominant figure morphs from the ground to shape both interior and exterior space in the painting.

Applying the Modulor ordering system to the site reveals proportions of the composition that deal with how one moves through and perceives space. The layering of methods and scales manifest in the painting are also manifest in the buildings of the Capitol Complex as scalar densities facilitate the registration of human scale against monumental/infinite scale through the layering of bench, balcony, window; water and horizon. The individual is read within and against the monumental at the site scale. At the building scale the metering of the facade is read against a forest of columns in the hypostyle hall. At the scale of the room individual microphones and seats are registered against the tapestries. In the Forum of the Assembly there is a constant overlay of systems of inhabitation and civic purpose.

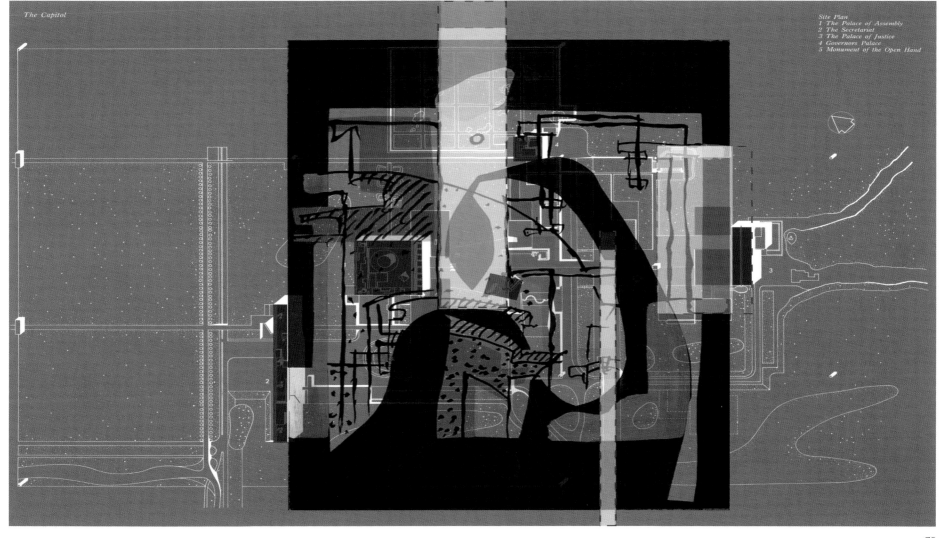

The Capitol

Site Plan
1 The Palace of Assembly
2 The Secretariat
3 The Palace of Justice
4 Governors Palace
5 Monument of the Open Hand

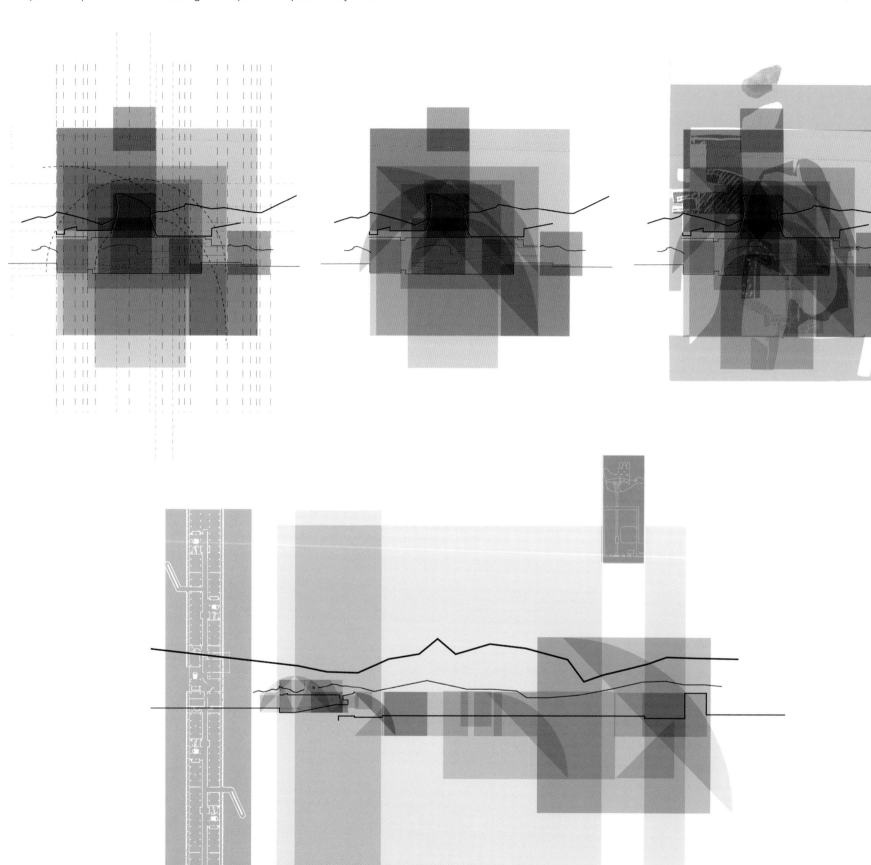

The peripatetic Nomad encounters borrowed scenery that encompasses the Himalayas as an orienting device and as a bounding horizon, creating tensions and ambiguities between immediate and distant elements and situating the Complex in its precondition.

ICONOGRAPHY, IDENTITY, + PERMANENCE

Le Corbusier grounds the Capitol Complex in iconography and human scale, referencing not only the cultural traditions of the region, but also his painting methodology and translation. The Enamel Door is the ceremonial entrance to the Assembly Building, symbolizing the transition from dark to light in its rotation. There is transference and echoing of forms between the approach to the Assembly and the ceremonial door: the abstraction of the sun in the Forum and in the sun on the door, the geometrical abstraction of the pyramid and the abstracted geometries of the tree of knowledge; the vertical columns that meter and define the entry, reaching to the ground, and the pivot that connects floor and ceiling on which the door rotates.[19] In a dialogue between modern and ancient civilization, cosmic cycles and geologic time, iconography connects ancient ritual with democratic progress.

Vernacular influences manifest through materials, typologies, and climate further this dialogue, registering human agency against monumental scale. At Chandigarh, the roughness and imprecision of materials – concrete packed between rough planks, highly labor-intensive construction – leaves space for the tactility of the hand, for weathering and patina that are an expression of permanence. The appreciation of vernacular tradition and material craft can also be seen at the Lawn, in the formation and use of brick, incorporating local practices and reinforcing the Lawn as of the earth. The *brise-soleil* of the Complex's Secretariat, a thickened zone that mediates between fluctuating shadow and light, is a threshold inhabitable by one person that breaks down the façade's monumental scale through its meter, and moderates Chandigarh's hot climate over the course of the day and seasons. The colonnades of the Lawn create a similar threshold between inside and outside, shadow and light, individual and collective. The combination of modern and ancient references seeks permanence in the face of political turmoil.

FIGURED GROUND, AGAIN

Sited in its social and political context, Chandigarh is a subversive landscape that places the condition of Man before the trajectory of politics, defying the directive for the Modern to erase the ancient and refuting the separation of modernization and tradition by grounding the Capitol Complex, and the city of Chandigarh, physically, materially, and culturally. The constructed, figured ground of Chandigarh is suggestive of ruins and timelessness.[20] Through this conception of figure : ground, Le Corbusier situates the Capitol Complex within a continuum of time, place, ritual, and complex horizons.

POSTSCRIPT: THE OPEN HAND

"It was not a political emblem, a politician's creation, but an architect's creation, a symbol of peace and reconciliation, open to receive the wealth that the world has created, to distribute to the peoples of the world. It ought to be the symbol of our age. The Open Hand will affirm that the second era of machinist civilization has begun; the era of harmony."[21]

Source: Collectif. Chandigarh, la ville indienne de Le Corbusier. Le Capitole, une oeuvre inachevée... (Coédition Musée). Somogy éditions d'art, 2002.

Source: Le Corbusier. La poeme du l'angle droit. Tériade Publishing, Paris, 1955.

Endnotes

1   Prakash, Vikramaditya, "Introduction: The 'East-West' Opposition in Chandigarh's Le Corbusier," in *Chandigarh's Le Corbusier: the Struggle for Modernity in Postcolonial India*. Mapin Publishing Pvt. Limited, 2002. pp 7.

2   Prakash, pp 9.

3   Curtis, William J R. *Modern Architecture Since 1900*. 3rd Ed. Phaidon Press, 1996. pp 377.

4   Curtis, pp 424.

5   Frampton, Kenneth. *Celebrating Chandigarh*. Ed. Jaspreet Takhar. Illustrated edition. Chandigarh Perspectives in association with Mapin Publishing. 2007. pp. 37.

6   Frampton, pp. 36.

7   Cresti, Carlo. "Le Corbusier." *Twentieth-Century Masters*. Hamlyn: 1970. pp 34.

8   Le Corbusier. *Les Trois etablissements humains*. Éditions Denoël, Collection ASCORAL, Paris, 1945. pp 167.

9   Le Corbusier. *Les Trois etablissements humains*. pp 98-165.

10 For further discussion, see Hunt, John Dixon. *Gardens and the Picturesque.* Cambridge: MIT Press, 1992. pp. 3-16.

11 Le Corbusier. *Les Trois etablissements humains*. pp 51.

12 Le Corbusier. *Les Trois etablissements humains*. pp 165.

13 The Jantar Mantar at Jaipur, India. *Portal to the Heritage of Astronomy, in partnership with UNESCO World Heritage Site*. <https://www3.astronomicalheritage.net/index.php/show-entity?idunescowhc=1338>

14 Le Corbusier. *Journey to the East*. Ed. Ivan Zaknic. Cambridge: MIT Press, 2007. Originally published by Forces Vives (Paris) in 1966 under the title *Le Voyage d'Orient*. pp 210-239.

15 Dripps, Robin. "Groundwork." Site Matters, ed. Burns, Carol, and Andrea Kahn. pp. 59.

16 Prakash, pp. 19.

17 Dripps, pp. 66-67.

18 Zimmer, Heinrich. *Myths and Symbols in Indian Art + Civilization*. Princeton: Princeton University Press, 1974.

19 Prakash, pp. 94.

20 Frampton, pp. 36.

21 Curtis, pp 429.

Further Reading:

   Gast, Klaus-Peter, "Chandigarh General Plan," in *Le Corbusier, Paris—Chandigarh*, 98-113.

   Venturi, Robert, "Contradiction Juxtaposed," in *Complexity and Contradiction*, 56-70.

   Blee, Michael, "Criticism: Chandigarh and the Sense of Place," in *Architectural Review* (March 1958), 201-203.

   Rowe, Peter G. *Civic Realism*, 46-58.

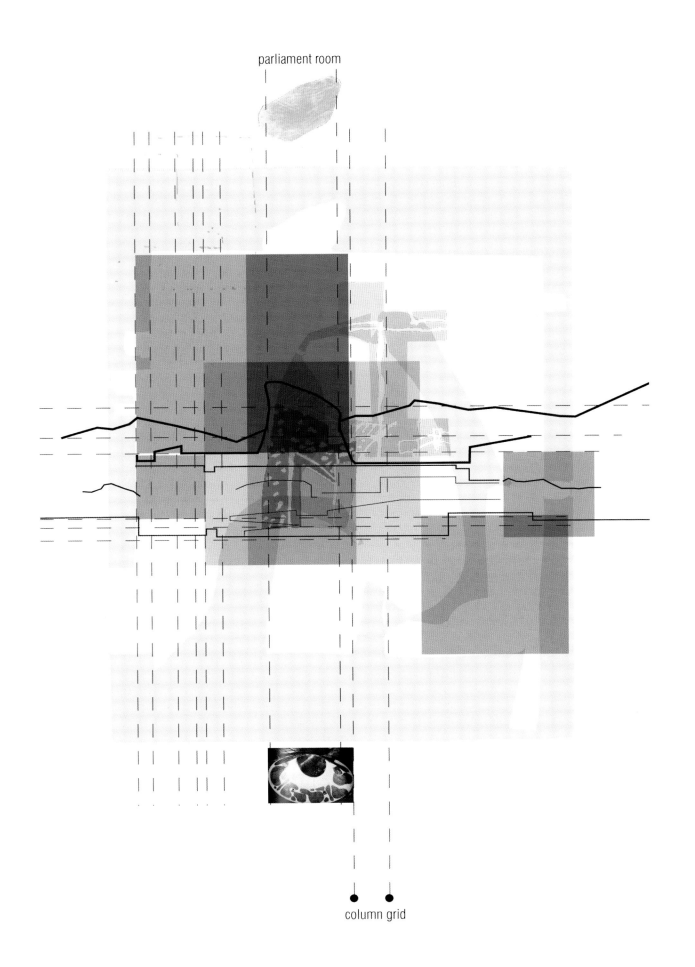

parliament room

column grid

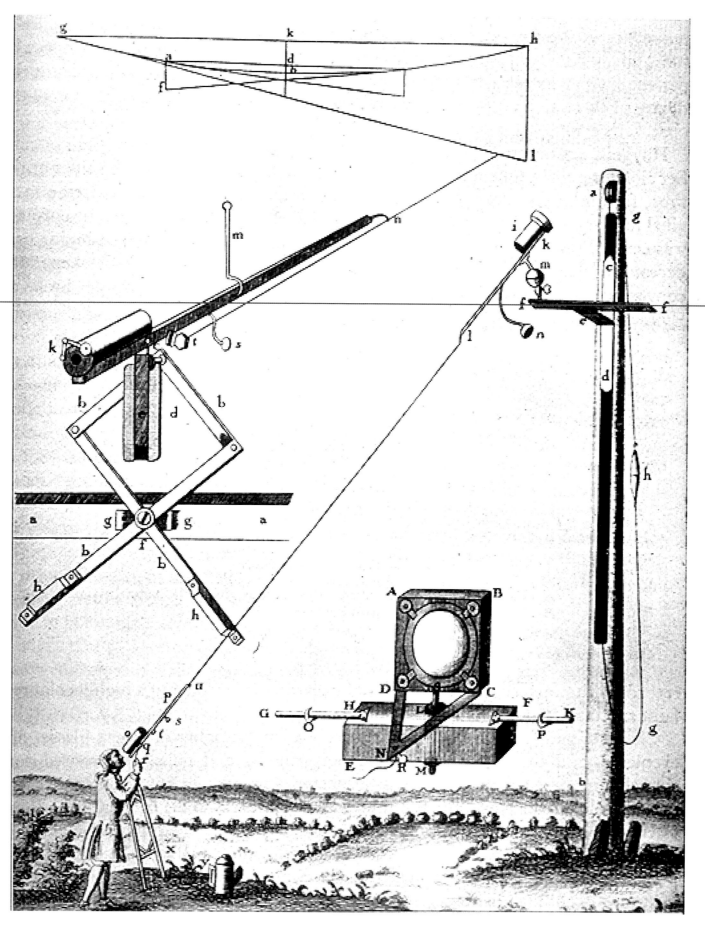

Connective Tissue #2 Specifications for Construction

Peter Waldman

I once sought to radicalize our curriculum in this School of Architecture by emphasizing the dual requirements of the construction site: material inventories and performance sequences. I imagined that the banal structure of Specifications for Construction could set up a useful dialogue of Land as Resource and Building as a Verb. My colleague, Elizabeth Meyer from Landscape Architecture confronted my assumption early on as I appeared to project the Nature of Site as a passive resource rather than a primal source of embedded cultural histories. Rather, through dialogue, Meyer and I realized that the flows of sites and systems should be revealed through the frames of architecture. Challenged to take on a deeper understanding of site, I sought refuge in the knowledge base of my first students here in 1992, all descendants it seemed of the First Families of Virginia. Surely, they could inform me where the bricks were made and lumber milled. One hundred feet East from Campbell Hall was a great excavated swale, quarried for red clay, topographically transformed through brick kilns with an enslaved labor force supplied by the local plantation system. To the South was Jefferson's pedestal base at the Rotunda's North Front overlooking Madison Bowl.

The Pre-Condition of the Lawn's construction was not focused initially onto the continental view shed, but pragmatically on resources to be claimed close at hand. Jefferson must have had eyes on both sides of his head then as Janus, double-facing if not crossing the dual site conditions of source and resource toward the intended construction of the national frame of Manifest Destiny.

A dialogue between two familiar citizens Lewis & Clark and a pivotal stranger along the way, Sacajawea, provided appetites and maps to new sources and resources for a continental national imagination. Close at hand, in parallel memory, this immediately enslaved as well as highly skilled labor force was renowned for the finest masonry work in the South under the apprenticeship of the First Families of Virginia, no doubt Free-Masons all. This site, now known as Madison Bowl, was previously a level field renowned for the famed peach orchard and subsequent preserves of the Widow Carr who cultivated Carr's Hill prior to its Brownfield demise. From a once lovingly cultivated Cartesian Field to excavated Bowl, from sweet preserves to the salty sweat of brick production, this site was to be subtracted, blistered and scarred. In 1895 when it became the brick yard once again for post-fire reconstruction yielding this time quarried gneiss stone for the huge foundations of Cabell Hall after the local clay ran out, an architecture was driven by both retained image and opportunistic evidence of circumstantial new resources which helped to sustain a deeper understanding of the Grounds.

Haynsworth Woodcock and Hackney, seven years apart as Kenan Fellows, are surrogates for the Widow Carr and the Wise Sacajawea in dialogue with Lewis & Clark. The former always close at hand cultivates and curates the construction site of the Academical Village as a sustainable garden with microscopic attention. The latter has an appetite to tell haunted stories of new lands beyond our colonnades and ranges, and opens an oculus to the sky some call a telescopic imagination.

Spencer Haynsworth Woodcock, acquired both a Masters of Architecture and Landscape Architecture as a dual degree candidate, and was one of the original Kenan Fellows. She began logically with building an inventory of facts while attempting heuristic narratives to be read in her fleshed out story boards. Acquisition of site which yielded the beginning inventory, stresses that most of the materials were derived from materials at hand, that the red brick columns were never white, but routinely masked and maintained by stucco with river run sand from the Rivanna, that roofs were shingled first in tin and then in local Buckingham County Slate, while Observatory Hill was purchased as an after-thought to provide timber and a reliable water supply.

Lauren Hackney arrived from West Virginia seven years later in a fallow year and generated explorations far afield from Jefferson's brownfield site through 20th century urban speculations from the heretofore intense interrogations of the Academical Village through her speculations far away and into the late 20th Century project of Lo Corbusier's Chandigarh Capital Complex + City Plan. As both a University of Virginia architecture undergraduate and later with the longest tenure as Kenan Fellow for four years in her graduate years, she intensely extended her research as a dual degree candidate of both Architecture and Landscape Architecture by this analysis of an urban if not regional scale. She helps us to extrapolate for the first time beyond previous focused analyses of the Lawn a new understanding of the relevance of topographic and archeological imaginations onto a 20th century case study projects such as Le Corbusier's Capitol Complex at Chandigarh, India, Gehry's Guggenheim, Bilbao, Spain, and Tschumi's Parc de La Villette, Paris, France.

Haynsworth Woodcock focuses on the Brick in Hand, the powerful art of measurement, from deep in the Earth as hidden foundational figures, and now in dialogue metering the sky in multiple syncopated hearths aligned with the ethereal void of the Rotunda oculus. Haynsworth Woodcock is a meticulous accountant. Hackney takes the position of an archeologist tracing with overlays the lessons from a handful of pivotal catalysts: from Athenian Acropolis to urbane Academical Village, onto the footprint of the Rotunda superimposed onto the great Assembly Hall, all contained in the superimposed collage of le Corbusier's Poem to a Right Angle where the timeline has become a Full Circle. Haynsworth Woodcock and Hackney, the first and midstream Kenan Fellows, are in dialogue with, hands stained in red clay tempered by two sources of the recurrent dualities of reflection: topographical and archeological imaginations revealed from the ground to the sky by the enduring scaler utility of the telescope and microscope. Haney and Symborska would smile on their engagement.

This connective tissue collage is distinct from others in that they are primarily a diptych of the two juxtaposed authors. Hackney's image elements on the left anchors her own overlays of the Lawn onto the Capital master plan absorbed by Le Corbusier's painting of The Poem to the Right Angle. On the right facing page, Haynsworth Woodcock's pictogram of the source materials for inventories is episodic enough to hold its own as an archaic message in contrast to Le Corbusier's stream of consciousness set of cubist hallucinations Hackney assembles for us. Finally, the telescope is inserted as a foil to these landscapes to set them in dialogue with the sky which is the intention of Jefferson's oculus.

Hackney engages Meyer in dialogue on reading the ground as full, echoing Carol Burns' in prioritizing Construction of Site as the first set of Specifications for Construction, and critically Dripps in Trouble in Paradise joins in, no demands in the light of failure of the Age of Enlightenment, now at the brink of the consequences of the Anthropocene, that we give free range to the flora and fauna some call wildlife who arrived in Eden long before Adam and Eve took up a short-term encampment. Haynsworth Woodcock has the last word in this dialogue and reminds us that Jefferson's first acts were to break the ground and to timber Observatory Hill permitting a new assemblage of distinct coastal states to imagine The Blue of Distance through the Lens of this new Arcadian nation replete with Ranges and a Lawn and approximations of gardens as permutations in-between the precision stage sets of Serlio and West Coast musings of Solnit in A Field Guide to Getting Lost.

38° NORTH LATITUDE | GSM

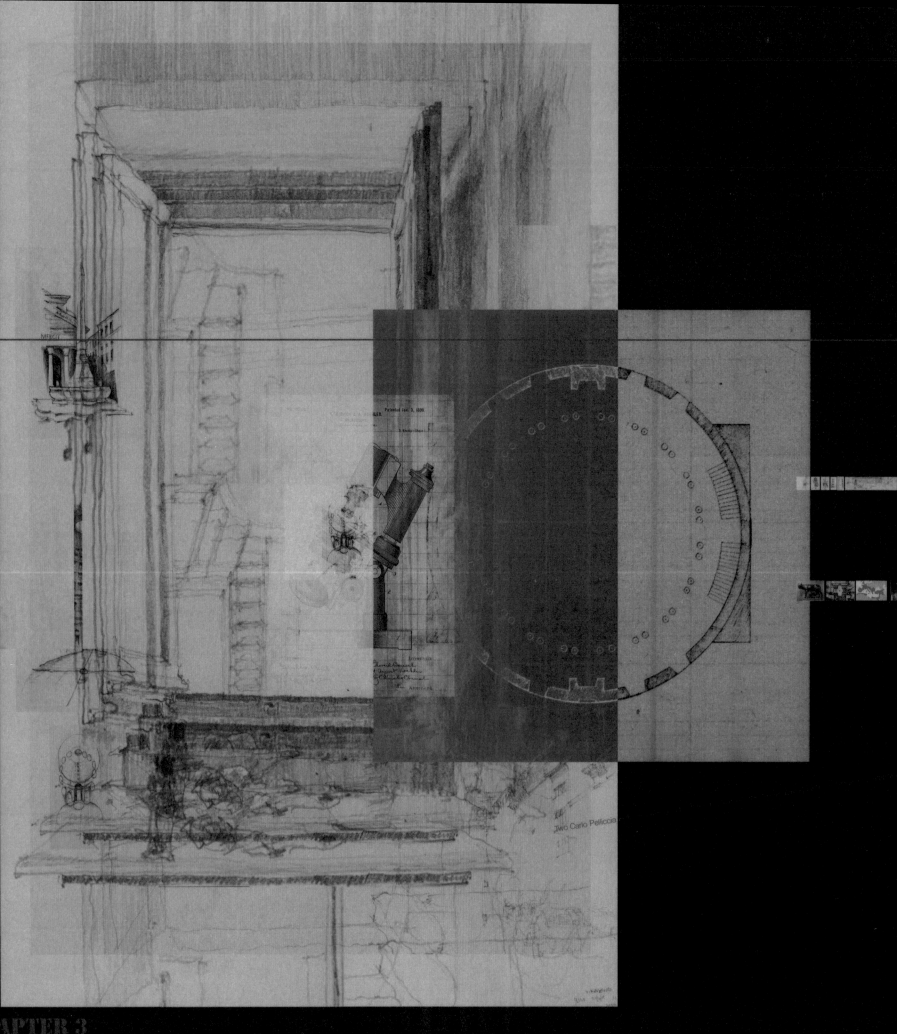

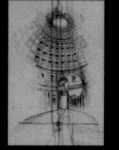

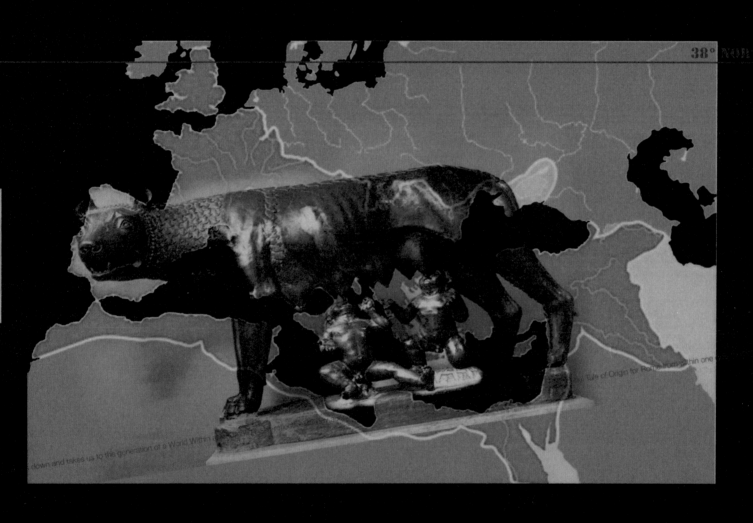

...down and takes us to the generation of a World Within ... Rule of Origin for Rome from within one ...

CHAPTER THREE: COMPOSITION

Two Carlo Pelliccia Fellows journeyed to Rome to measure the external world from within as contemporary pilgrims.

Jim Richardson's essay slows us down and takes us to the generation of a World Within as a Lunatic's self-reflective 28-day account centered on the June Solstice.

Maria Bninski rendered an alternative Spatial Tale of Origin for Rome from within one Good Window frame and Substantial Sill.

The Lens of the Pantheon
Jim Richardson, AIA, LEED AP BD+C

INSPIRATION | THE INTERIOR SPACE OF THE PANTHEON

The Pantheon, the best-preserved monument from Roman antiquity, eludes historical certainties. Surrounded by mysteries such as which emperor to credit for its design, or how the largest unreinforced concrete dome on earth was constructed, the Pantheon is open every day except Christmas to citizens and strangers alike. Inspired by the space of the Pantheon, and thanks to a Carlo Pelliccia Fellowship from the University of Virginia, I set out to spend the summer in Rome, to experience first-hand the magical space of the Pantheon, to investigate the Pantheon's deeper connections to place and culture, and ultimately as a practicing architect, to make better architecture. I embrace the dialogue between Rome and the Pantheon, of history and legend, of the archeology of ruins and the temporal landscape of the city. This anthology of investigations and shared experiences delights in the Pantheon.

LESSONS OF THE LAWN AS METHOD
We all experience architecture everyday. Lessons of the Lawn is both an introduction to architecture itself, and a method of understanding the world through architecture. Using both narrative and graphic explorations, we are taught to use Jefferson's Academical Village as a tool with which to appreciate architectural relationships with creativity, enthusiasm, and insight. My proposal for study in Rome suggests the Pantheon as a similar template. As a lens through which to experience and interpret the city of Rome, the Pantheon is a center of the rituals and routines of daily life.

The best works of architecture, including both the Pantheon and the Academical Village, can be immediately enjoyed at a glance, yet invite deeper investigations and reward continued attention with moments of fresh understanding. As a Spatial Theater, visitors to the Pantheon are entranced by its form, proportion, and sense of coherence. As an Urban Portico, the Pantheon and its porch are places of passage, thresholds of experience that can transport us. The Pantheon is the reconciliation of individual and collective expressions coming together into a community. As a Civic Ruin, the Pantheon has endured over time and embodies a rich history. Its meaning and circumstances continue to change over time, just as it continues to last and be loved.

Jefferson never visited the Pantheon in person, and yet, the Pantheon and its lessons are a model for the Rotunda and the University of Virginia's Academical Village. As Spatial Theaters, both the Pantheon and the Academical Village strive for an elusive beauty of form, space, and experience. As Urban Porticoes, the Pantheon and the Academical Village are places for people that invite belonging. As Civic Ruins, the Pantheon and the Academical Village create for students and citizens a home.

THE ORIGINS OF THE PANTHEON (AND ROME)
Rome was founded as a series of camps atop seven hills adjacent to the Tiber River. The hills of *tufa*, the thick crust of volcanic lava and ash, provided both protection and formal structure for the early settlements. As the camps got bigger, the swampy terrain between the hills was drained to create the forum, Rome's meeting ground and market place. The dual spatial structure of Rome, created by the vernacular settlements clustered to the topography, merged against the ritual and legendary crossing of the Cardo and the Decumanus, became Rome's symbol of civilization, and likewise the diagram of the Pantheon. More than just political or business centers, cities are cultural places that live in the minds and stories of their citizens.

Conceived on the site where Romulus ascended to heaven, the Pantheon reinforces Rome's foundation. The Pantheon was built in the lowest spot in Rome, specifically with the intention to let its dome rise above the other seven natural hills of Rome. However, they permitted the floor of the Pantheon to flood regularly by the water pressure of the Tiber rising through perforations in the center of the floor. The Cardo of the Pantheon is in line with the axis on which the heavens turn, and its Decumanus, the oculus, is oriented toward the passage of the sun. As a new ideal center, the Pantheon expresses in concrete form the common ideals of harmony, majesty, and equality. Within the Pantheon, individual and collective expressions alike reconcile into a form, and a place, where wonder is infused into everyday life, given more meaning by its setting.

The Roman Empire extended through a series of military campaigns, and concurrently made civic improvements within its city walls to benefit everyday people. As the world's first roadway system begged for new destinations, upgrades such as sewage systems, aqueducts bringing fresh water to public drinking fountains, and public baths revolutionized the daily life of Roman citizens. Just as the Lawn ends in two solitary student rooms as an ethical symbol of the individual's responsible identity, the city of Rome highlights the role of the individual speculative imagination.

The Pantheon | Shared Imaginings With Jefferson's Academical Village

Inspiration | The Interior Space of the Pantheon

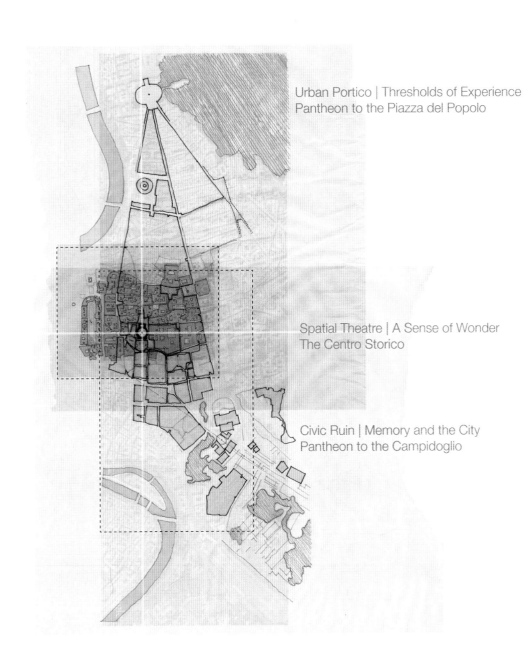

Urban Portico | Thresholds of Experience
Pantheon to the Piazza del Popolo

Spatial Theatre | A Sense of Wonder
The Centro Storico

Civic Ruin | Memory and the City
Pantheon to the Campidoglio

SPATIAL THEATER | A SENSE OF WONDER

The most distinctive and striking feature of the Pantheon is the perfect geometry of its massive, spherical interior space. Inside of its domed drum fits a 150-foot diameter perfect sphere, which is the size of a 10-story building. No other space like this exists today, or has ever existed in the 2,000 years since the Pantheon was built. This incredible atmosphere inspires a unique sense of wonder that, everyday, makes visitors feel alive. At the top of the dome is a 30' diameter oculus, a circular hole and the Pantheon's only opening to the outside, through which sunlight enters the space. As the earth moves around the sun each day, the sunbeam travels across the Pantheon's interior, and people are invited to watch. Morning and evening, rain or shine, cloudy or clear sky, the atmosphere is constantly changing. Your attention is awakened to your surrounding, grounds you in the moment, and you can feel a profound connection to the world.

ATMOSPHERE AND PHENOMENA

Hadrian, the first bearded emperor, used the Pantheon as the seat of his empire. Hadrian proclaimed himself as a sun king, associating himself with the sun's most compelling power entering through the Pantheon's oculus. The circular interior stood for the energy of the sun, and the collage of lavish materials represented the many lands of the world that were Roman. From the shadowy southern side of the Piazza Della Rotunda, the Pantheon showcases the phenomenon of atmosphere and time. Sunlight becomes a playful, kinetic element to stimulate our creative faculties. It's not just the form of the Pantheon that matters, but the cinematic motion of the sunbeam and its effect on our immediate awareness of knowing that we are intensely alive right here, right now. Watching the sunlight moving is intensely enchanting and promising, and also mysterious.

FORM AND COHERENCE

Hadrian spent much of his 21-year reign traveling around the empire on a series of journeys, gaining a level of first hand experience of the Roman empire. He reconstructed Rome's center and assimilated all his knowledge into the universal space of the Pantheon. While Hadrian's Villa, sited outside of Rome, is a loose conglomeration of collected travels, the Pantheon is a unification of ideas into one great space.

Every day the experience of the Pantheon is different, based on the weather, the time of day, and the group of people inside. While the space is huge, a 150-foot inscribed sphere, somehow it doesn't make you feel small. The space inspires a moment of clarity for me unlike anything else I have experienced. It is a space of centering oneself within the fabric of Rome, between the ground and sky, where we can actively crave wonder and beauty.

Architecture is the setting of our daily lives, and our everyday experiences are made up of various influences. Personal accounts, research, exaggerations, and tall tales can all be valid contributions.

A LEGEND OF ORIGIN

Hadrian was a particularly benevolent emperor, adored by the citizens of Rome. To build the dome, the interior of the Pantheon's circular brick and concrete drum was filled with a mound of earth. A fortune of golden coins was mixed into the earthen tumulus. After the dome was poured atop this earthen formwork, and had cured, the doors of the Pantheon opened for the first time, and citizens of Rome were invited to carry the earth away and keep the coins that they found.

EMAIL DISPATCH | FIRST RAIN

It's raining this morning in Rome. Not a downpour, rather just a steady sprinkle. Intrigued by this first rain, I threw on my rain jacket and strolled over to the Pantheon to see the rain come into the space through the oculus. Rain entered the space in a cylinder of droplets, gently slapping the floor. Inside, it rained for a while, then the clouds would part to allow the sun's disc to illuminate the interior. Then clouds and rain again. This cycle created for me a kind of inverted lighthouse, monitoring the sky with a curious Morse code. The polychrome floor, coated with a sheet of water, became a mirror that completed the spherical interior. A little lady with a squeegee chased misbehaved puddles into one of 22 tiny drains in the floor. Also fascinated by this magic were Kirk Douglas and Goldie Hawn. Both were wearing jeans and sneakers, Kirk with a blue blazer and Goldie with big sunglasses and a brown checked Pashmina. Kirk pointed around the dome with his umbrella. Speculating on the positioning of the sun throughout the course of the day and year, he performed little dance, using his umbrella as a prop. Embarrassed, Goldie pulled her collar more closely around her head and face.

Hope you are well,
- Jim

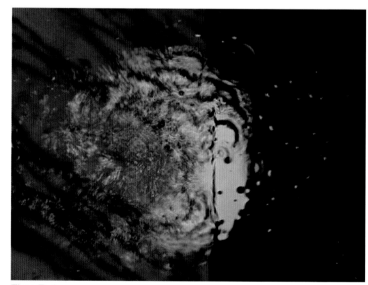

First Rain

  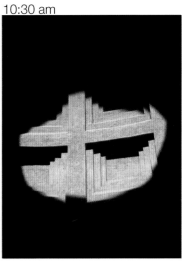 

Templum Morning   Mundus Afternoon   Pomoerium Evening

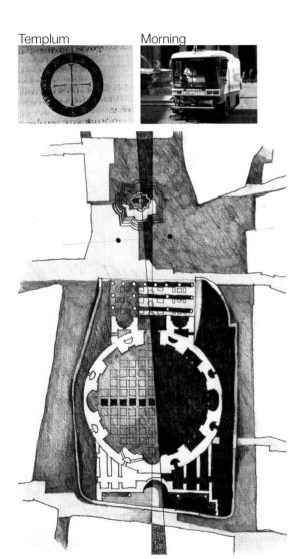 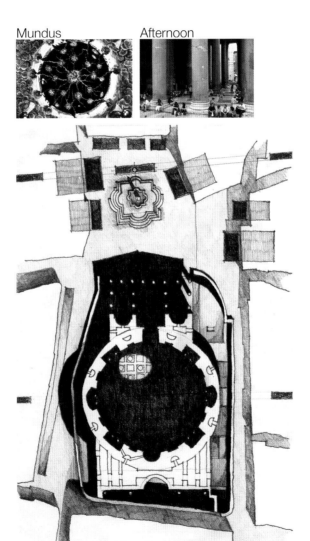   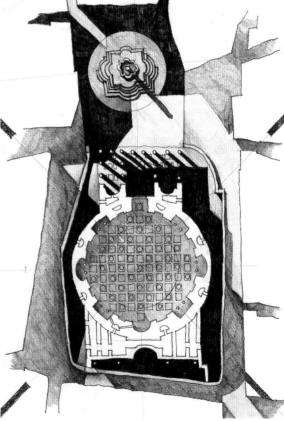

First, in the morning, to establish the center of Rome and the Pantheon, a mystical surveyor used a tall bronze rod to draw on the ground a diagrammatic crossing of two lines. Shadows cast by the rod onto this "templum" became the origin of the new structure: the Cardo, in line with the axis of the sky, and the Decumanus, in line with the course of the sun.

Next, in the afternoon, a circular and shallow ditch called a "mundus" was dug and filled with the fruits of habitation. The first architectural act of Rome and the Pantheon was to mark and break ground as an offering to the underworld. The formation of cities and buildings is not only physical, commercial, and political, but also ritual.

In the third act of inauguration, by the evening, the Surveyor used a bronze plow to establish the city boundaries. This "pomoerium" is the first furrow of threshold of inside vs. outside city limits. The ritual, legendary formation of Rome is echoed each day by the path of sun and shadow across the Piazza Della Rotunda and the Pantheon's interior, and by everyday use.

10:00 am

10:30 am

11:00 am

11:30 am

12:00 pm

In the afternoon, as the sun shining through the oculus makes a space on the floor, the temple is crowded with groups of tourists. It is an active space of congregation in the heat of the Roman sun. Other than a solitary line at the Piazza's fountain to refill a water bottle or two, people avoid the direct sun of the Piazza Della Rotunda. Groups of schoolchildren, identifiable with matching neon hats, carry value meals from McDonald's across the Piazza to picnic within the forest of columns that support the Pantheon's shaded porch. Behind the Pantheon, I sit on a wall and eat a slice of Pizza Margherita, served as a sandwich folded carefully in a wax paper envelope. I seek the city's shadows and frequent an air-conditioned bookstore.

01:00 pm

01:30 pm

In the evening, tourists sit in the amphitheater created by the steps of the fountain. In the orange light of dusk, people enjoy dinner along edges of the Piazza Della Rotunda. The Piazza is alive with conversations over wine and a secondi. Street vendors draw attention to their knocked-off designer watches and purses, carefully arranged on cardboard boxes that easily fold up in case the Caribinieri come around. I walk to Geolitti for a two scoops of melon gelato.

12:30 pm

THE MAGIC OF EVERY DAY EXPERIENCE

In the morning, the Pantheon's bronze doors, still on their original hinges, open to allow the first visitors to enter this temple of light and shadow. Between cigarettes, a round man wearing green overalls buffs the granites, porphyries, and marbles on the floor. A street-sweeper circulates around the base of the fountain, leaving a trail of soapy water behind. Delivery trucks unload the day's supplies to the adjacent cafes and trattorias that unlock their doors for the days. As a waiter unfolds a white tablecloth, I order a cappuccino and sit to sketch in the welcoming sunlight.

02:00 pm

02:30 pm

03:00 pm

30 pm

04:00 pm

04:30 pm

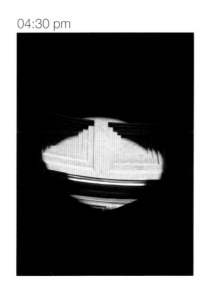

05:00 pm

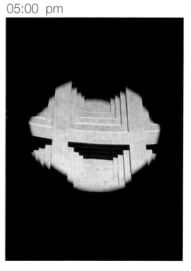

05:30 pm

CIVIC RUIN | MEMORY AND THE CITY

Buildings and cities are made of materials. To be meaningful and memorable, architecture must make an emotional connection, not just an aesthetic one. Materials and the details of their assembly deliver the message of architecture. The materials are what people make contact with, and the materials register architecture's use over time. The Pantheon is a marvel of structural innovation and material composition that has magically endured in a changing world.

CONSTRUCTION & INGENUITY

The unity of the Pantheon derives from the skill with which a variety of parts have been assembled. The great task of construction was accomplished by a series of smaller acts, and we can get a lot from small details if we're willing to look. We delight in the complexity to which genius has lent an appearance of simplicity. Materials are densely packed with significance.

Since previous structures were burned in the great fire of 80 AD and then again by lightning in 110 AD, the Romans invented a fireproof building material called concrete to construct the Pantheon. By adding *pozzolano*, a granular volcanic stone, to their mix, concrete could be molded into virtually any shape and stand alone as a building material. Monolithic granite columns too were fireproof, and bronze cladding covered the wooden porch structure.

The structural walls of the Pantheon were built by pouring concrete into trenches formed by inner and outer brick walls. These walls are not solid, but rather composed of systematic networks of cavities and relieving arches that transfer the loads of the structure to eight massive piers. Amazingly, the concrete contains no steel reinforcing, as would be required today for strength and tensile forces.

The Pantheon is a marvel of Roman construction sequence and logic. The dome was poured on a complex wooden formwork. Twenty-eight rows of five coffers each, like the five planets known to the Romans and the twenty-eight lunar days in the Roman month, substantially decrease the weight of the dome and guide the loads to the ground. As the thickness of the rotunda walls diminishes from 20' at the base to 4'-11" thick around the oculus, the specific weight of the aggregate in the concrete likewise decreases in clear zones. Brick and stone aggregate within the foundation transitions to porous volcanic pumice at the dome.

A TREASURY OF MATERIALS

The volcanic eruptions that put the ground under Rome's feet made the Roman countryside a supply yard of wonderful building materials. Likewise, materials from afar were brought to the Pantheon for citizens to enjoy. Materials have a role to play in making buildings just as architects do.

While the brick and concrete of the Pantheon are distinctively Roman, the building's other materials represent the many lands of the Roman empire: granites and porphyries of Egypt, colored marbles of Africa, white marbles of the Aegean, and stone from Asia Minor. Every material has a story to tell, and every detail is in itself a world of bewildering activity and infinity.

The materials of ancient Roman buildings, including materials that clad the Pantheon, were used to build Renaissance Rome. Many Renaissance buildings in the Campus Martius were destroyed by barbarian sacks of the fifth century, a devastating earthquake in the sixth century, and recurrent floods. While sparcely populated in the Roman perod, the Campus Martius became the population center of Medieval and Renaissance Rome. During the pontificate of Pope Boniface IV, the Pantheon was transformed from a temple for all the gods to to a Christian Church, Santa Maria Rotunda, and it was protected from further plundering. The broad appeal and wonder of the Pantheon has lived on.

WEATHERING AND THE PATINA OF AGE

Rome is a city of cavities, a compressed city where slices between walls and the narrow vertical spaces between buildings are utilized daily. As the current horizon of the ground peels back to uncover the foundations of the Pantheon, a liminal trench connects the city to its layered history. Citizens and tourists alike line the moat created between the city and the Pantheon to eat lunch or hail a taxi. As in most protected ruins in Rome, a parallel city of cats dwells in this in-between realm. These spaces are museums of the imagination. The city's history of flood, rubble and reconstruction is chronicled as this depth of surface. Within this occupiable horizon of time, fallen building elements and exposed ruins delineate paths, become benches and shape garden walls.

Mysteries and incompleteness fascinate us. By inducing fascination, the Pantheon's ruinous form encourages interpretation without beginning or end. The chronicles of life accumulate in materials. A weathered wall might allow us to peer into its history, turning a surface into a site for probing the mysteries before us. Weathering and use over time magnify these depths with patina. The Pantheon is not a fixed state but remains a work in progress. It is a place of possibilities. The Pantheon exceeds any single moment in time, and embodies the motion of life as a process.

A LEGEND OF RUIN

A priest named Barackas met the Devil outside the Pantheon. The Devil offered a deal to the priest: his soul for a book of spells that would offer to the Priest many desires. Before the deal was final, Barackas used the spell book to fly to Jerusalem and back in one night. Upon his return, Barackas had second thoughts about finalizing the deal, and again met the Devil outside the Pantheon. In an attempt to renege, Barackas distracted the Devil by sprinkling walnuts along the ground around the Pantheon's drum. He then sneaked inside, fell to his knees, and begged for forgiveness inside the domed space. The Devil was so angry at being thwarted that he flew in circles around the Pantheon like a cyclone, digging the gap between the building and the city that still exists there today.

06:00 pm   06:30 pm

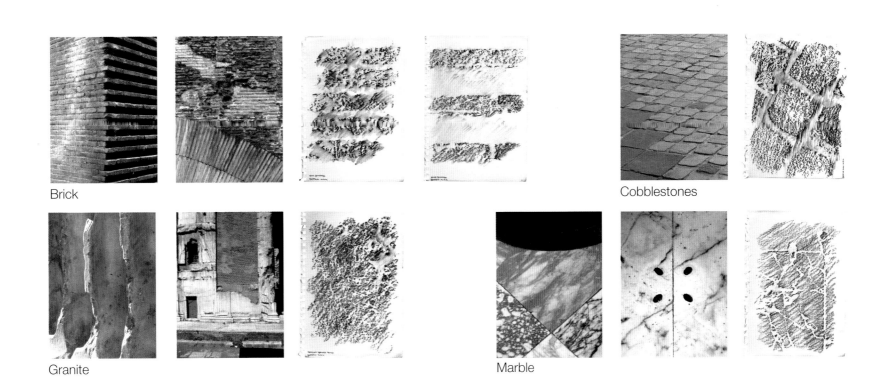

Brick

Cobblestones

Granite

Marble

The Excavation Between the Pantheon and the City

Active Archeology at the Back of the Pantheon

URBAN PORTICO | THRESHOLDS OF EXPERIENCE

We all experience architecture every day. Architecture is the making of places for people, providing a physical common ground for meaningful exchange in an increasingly divided and digital world. The Pantheon is an open and inviting place that strives for universal cultural ideals, and a place for shared experiences. The Pantheon's thresholds choreograph and dramatize the Pantheon's public presence.

A PLACE OF PASSAGE
The five-inch gap between the Pantheon's circular drum and the Pronaos is a result of the formal and structural innovation of this new building type. While circular buildings, like the tholos and the tumulus, were fairly common in antiquity, they were forms without entrance. The Pantheon is the first circular building that invites the public inside, and the porch is the threshold of entrance.

The Pantheon operates between the streets of Rome and the otherworldly. The porch is both the transition from the city to the Pantheon's spherical interior, and itself a complete environment. When you move through the Portico, pausing so that your eyes can adjust, and pass through the massive bronze doors, suddenly your gaze is invited upward and an entirely new space, like a new world, unfolds magically. To enter is not only to gain passage, but also to bring an unforgettable event into being. The porch transitions from public to private, from light to dark, from enclosed to open, from busy to still.

THRESHOLDS AND EXCHANGE
Architecture can move people from different backgrounds and views, and search for something universal in an increasingly divided world. The Pantheon's focus, through architecture, is on what unites rather that what divides us. Thresholds in architecture are not sharp dividing lines, but interchanges in which each side and its properties mingle, helping people to find their place in the world both physically and spiritually. The Pantheon is a social place, a new urban and architectural space where people come to meet.

At the Pantheon, I find myself surrounded by people of all faiths, colors, languages and cultures, everyone attentive with a shared sense of wonder, all admiring the simplest of miracles - sunlight and shadow. Throughout the ages, people have always gathered to watch the very same spectacle. The Pantheon is alive, and lives on through its relationships with people.

THE DRAMA OF ARRIVAL
The Pantheon originally stood at the end of a rectangular forecourt, paved with travertine slabs. The forecourt's purpose, in addition to a public plaza, was to increase the dramatic sense of arrival to the Pantheon. The forecourt's size, proportion, and colonnades were carefully designed to conceal from view any part of the Pantheon's drum and dome. Once inside the forecourt, only the Pantheon's facade would have been visible from the ground, heightening the surprise of the spherical space within. The effect is not to aestheticize but to empower the threshold.

The level of the Piazza Della Rotunda has risen considerably over time, burying the seven steps of the porch with Tiber mud and Medieval refuse. The added elevation of the Piazza reveals the dome to the city. Now access to the Pantheon is via steps leading downward from the city to the porch.

TWO LEGENDS OF THE PORCH
The front facade of the Pantheon consists of two separate triangular pediments, one above the other, that to many appear as a mistake. The mystery of the double-pediment is the source of speculations about its intentional or accidental origins, which suggest how the porch ended up shorter than originally desired.

1. When the giant granite monolithic columns arrived at the Pantheon, it was realized that there wasn't enough lay-down space for the tall shafts to be tipped into position. Regardless of sequence, the columns were too long to be positioned on the ground in a workable configuration, including the necessary clearances required on the sides for pulling and pushing, without interfering with each other. They could not fit diagonally, nor could they be raised into position upright. Engineers determined that by cutting off roughly ten feet, the columns could be sufficiently sequenced and tipped into place. The double pediment that you see today illustrates the difference between the planned height and the actual height of the columns. The extra cut drums articulate the Pantheon's floor surfaces.

2. The giant granite monolithic columns of the Pantheon's porch were quarried in the hills of Egypt and transported systematically on rollers and carts to the port of Alexandria, where ships were waiting to sail them to Rome. When the rough-cut granite drums arrived in the port of Alexandria for shipping, the first two columns were too heavy for the boats, which sunk to the bottom. Port engineers determined that by cutting off roughly ten feet, the remaining columns and boats could be safely loaded and sailed to Rome.

Approaching the Pantheon

Plastico di Roma Imperiale, Italo Gismondi, 1969
Depicts Rome in the 4th Century AD including the Pantheon's Forecourt, and the curious double-
triangular pediment that has led to several stories of its intentional or accidental origins

Drum | Intermediate | Porch | Plazza | Block

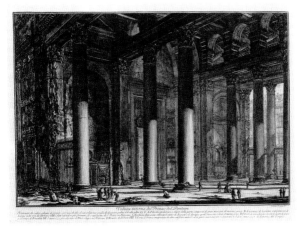

Interior of the Pronaos of the Pantheon,
Piranesi ,1769
The Complete Environment of the Porch

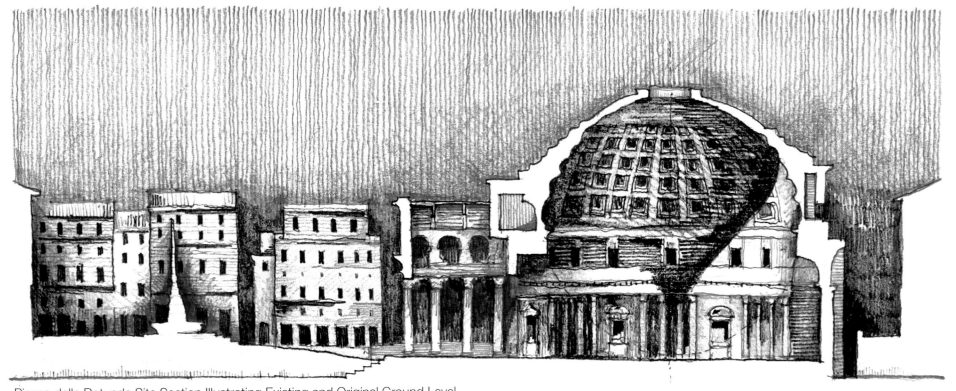

Piazza della Rotunda Site Section Illustrating Existing and Original Ground Level

THE PANTHEON | SHARED IMAGININGS
WITH JEFFERSON'S ACADEMICAL VILLAGE

At a glance it's easy to appreciate that the Rotunda at the University of Virginia is based on the form of the Pantheon as a model. The brilliance of the Lawn is that the Pantheon's most meaningful themes are appropriated not just into the Rotunda's domed form, but throughout the Lawn's many component parts as a wholc.

In the Virginia Piedmont, rather than an urban center like Rome, the Academical Village at the University of Virginia is a center for a collegiate ideal of students and teachers living and studying together.

Jefferson believed that an educated citizenry, and thereby public education, was the key to the survival of his new Republic. He appropriated the form of the Pantheon, and its authority of time and knowledge, for the purposes of a university library in a domed Rotunda, where the universals of education expressed and supported democracy. With a diameter of 77', Jefferson's Rotunda is h alf the diameter and height of the Pantheon.

Through the design and construction of the Lawn, Jefferson wanted to reform both Virginia's education and its architecture. Like Hadrian, Jefferson was influenced by all that he saw. His architecture was eclectic, while also remaining highly creative. With the Rotunda at its center, he made a village that emulates the idea of community. As a village, buildings and landscape are given equal attention. The Lawn draws us in, inspires learning, and opens to nature and the world beyond.

The architecture of the Lawn expresses in concrete form a community of scholars coming together, with an orderly systems of parts, into a coherent form where learning is integral to life. Still in regular use, like the Pantheon, the Lawn is constantly changing and evolving. Citizenship is not a fixed state, but an ongoing work in progress.

As Spatial Theaters, the Pantheon and the Lawn are places that can take your breath away, places that can inspire, places that can calm. By striving for beauty, architecture can encourage our better selves.

As Civic Ruins, the Pantheon and the Lawn foreground materials, showcase design innovation, and honor craftsmanship. By providing a home that adapts over time, architecture can link place and memory.

As Urban Porticoes, the Pantheon and the Lawn forge open and inviting common ground for the exchange if ideas from different points of view. Belonging through architecture allows people to make connections.

Both the Pantheon and the Academical Village are vital symbols, while remaining actively in use every day to citizens, students, strangers and tourists alike. When architecture provides a memorable home, strives for beauty, and encourages belonging, it can invite belief. Belief allows architecture to be effective, lasting, and loved.

Opposite, Upper Left
Aerial Imagery of the Campus Martius
From above, the aerial illustrates the Pantheon's scale and materiality in relation to the urban logic of the Centro Storico. The dome and oculus are unique forms that distinguish the Pantheon within the surrounding city fabric. Buildings and city blocks within Rome's monumental core are connected by a friction of spaces and streets.

Opposite, Upper Right
Pianta Grande of Rome, Giambatista Nolli, 1748
The Nolli plan renders all public spaces of the city, both interior and exterior, as white. The Pantheon, public and open, is one of many such amenities in the city. At street level, the Pantheon's shape and interior space are hidden, latent, and surprising upon entrance.

Opposite, Lower Left
Imaginary Plan of the Campus Maritius, Giovanni Bautista Piranesi, 1762
Piranesi's fanciful reconstruction of the Pantheon's urban precinct creatively mixes together history and imaginative urban speculations. The Pantheon's spatial magic is given a creative urban prominence. Self-contained, individually harmonious building complexes are simply accumulated together about interlocking urban spaces.

Opposite, Lower Right
Forma Urbis Romae, Rodolfo Lanciani, 1901
Lanciani's plan chronicles with accuracy the city from antiquity through the 19th century. The Campus Martius is rendered as an excavation, rich with layered histories. Alongside Baths, Libraries, and Markets, the Pantheon has been a regular part of the daily life of citizens for many years. Between and underneath the the Centro Storico's infill developments are massive buildings of formal geometry, laid against one another and related to each other by sheer inertia and their mass.

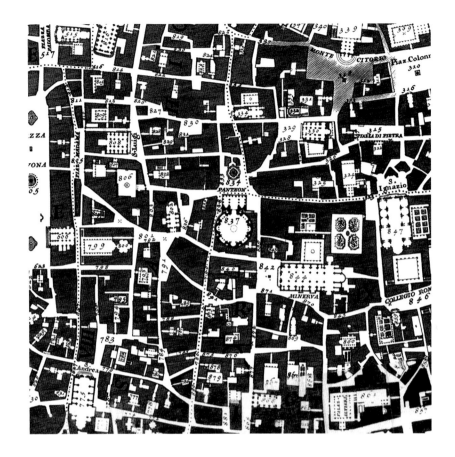

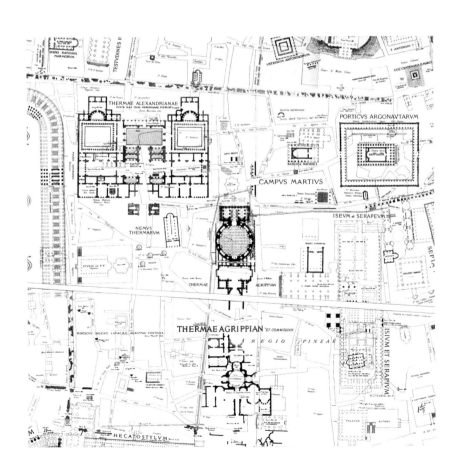

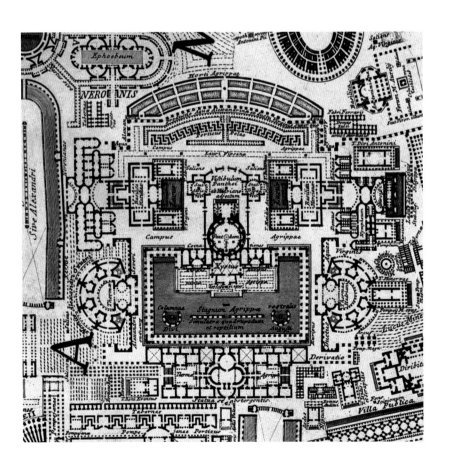

Bibliography
Based on the nature of this essay, and the nature of the Pantheon itself, this bibliography is inclusive rather than specifically noted. All sources listed below have made a modest and real contribution.

Arnheim, Rudolph. *The Symbolism of Centric and Linear Composition.* Perspecta: The Yale Architectural Journal. Volume 20, 1983.

Brown, Dan. *Angels & Demons.* Pocket Books. 2000.

Bacon, Edmund. *Design of Cities.* Penguin Books. 1976.

Burns and Kahn, ed. *Site Matters: Design Concepts, Histories, and Strategies.* Taylor and Francis Books, Inc. 2005

Calvino, Italo. *Invisible Cities.* Harcourt, Inc. 1974.

Calvino, Italo. *Marcovaldo, or the Seasons in the City.* Harcourt Brace & Company. 1983.

Campbell, Malcolm. *Piranesi, Rome Recorded.* Malcolm Campbell and the Arthur Ross Foundation. 1989

Dewey, John. *Art as Experience.* The Penguin Group. 1934.

Eisenman, Peter. *Feints.* Skira Editore S.p.A. 2006.

Heene, Gerd. *Baustelle Pantheon.* Verlag Bau + Technik GmbH. 2004.

Holl, Steven. *Questions of Perception.* a+u Publishing Co., ltd. 1994.

Kostof, Spiro. *Roman Concurrences. A History of Architecture.* Oxford University Press. 1995

Kultermann, Udo. *The Oculus of the Pantheon in Rome.* A+U. Nov 1979.

La Regina, ed. *Archaeological Guide to Rome.* Electa. 2005.

Licht, Kjeld Do Fine. *The Rotunda in Rome.* Jutland Archeological Society Publications VIII. 1966.

Lombardo, Alberto. *Views of the Pantheon Across the Centuries.* Palombi Editori. 2003

Lombardo, Alberto. *Views of Piazze de Roma Across the Centruries.* Palombi Editori. 2005.

Lugli, Giuseppe. *The Pantheon and Adjacent Monuments.* Bardi Editore Roma. 1963.

Macdonald, William. *The Pantheon: Design, Meaning, and Progeny.* Harvard University Press. 1976

McGregor, James H.S. *Rome from the Ground Up.* Harvard University Press. 2005.

Morrish, William. *Civilizing Terrains: Mountains Mounds and Mesas.* William Stout publishers. 2005

Mostafavi and Leatherbarrow. *On Weathering, The Life of Buildings in Time.* Massachusetts Institute of Technology. 1993.

Norberg-Schulz, Christian. *Genius Loci, Towards a Phenomenology of Architecture.* Rizzoli. 1984.

Rowe and Koetter. *Collage City.* The MIT Press. 1968.

Rossi, Aldo. *The Architecture of the City.* The MIT Press. 1991.

Rykwert, Joseph. *The Idea of a Town: The Anthropology of Urban Form in Rome, Italy and the Ancient World.* The MIT Press. 1998.

Sennet, Richard. *Building and Dwelling, Ethics for the City.* Farrar, Straus and Giroux. 2018.

Tanizaki, Junichiro. *In Praise of Shadows.* Vintage, 2001.

Taylor, Rabun M. *Roman Builders: A Study in Architectural Process.* Cambridge University Press. 2003.

Vighi, Roberto. *The Pantheon.* Tipografia Artistica. 1962.

Wilson, Richard Guy. *Thomas Jefferson's Academical Village: The Creation of an Architectural Masterpiece.* University Press of Virginia. 1993.

Image Credits
Images not credited by image caption within the body of this essay, or by below, are by the author.

Page 4: "Templum," from Rykwert, the Idea of a Town, page 48. The Tempum of the Sky. Miniature illustrating Hyginus Gromatcus's "Constitutio Limitum" in the most ancient surviving manuscript of the Corpus Agrimensorum, the "Codex Arcerianus," a sixth century collection of writings on surveying Corpus Agrimensorum Veterum, Wolfenbuttel, Herzog-August Bil., Guelferb 2403, Aug.f.36, 23, p41 recto.

Page 4: "Pomoerium," from Rykwert, the Idea of a Town, page 64. A Ritual Poughing Scene, with ithyphallic figures and ornaments. Objects made up of Villanovan or primitive Etruscan fragments by an eighteenth century Italin antiquarian or forger. British Museum, London.

Mike, Jonathan, and Clinton at the Piazza Della Rotunda

Laura at the Piazza Della Rotunda

Mom at the Pantheon's Porch

On One Good Window
Maria Bninski

Prologue/Precondition.

Some would locate the definition of Rome in the growth Roman Empire. Others would reference a mythical founding by a fratricidal twin, born at the crater lake Albano to the daughter of King Numitor, ruler of Alba Longa, and sent down the river in a basket when the king was overthrown and the twins' lives threatened. In either case, one must approach the city in terms of its larger territory. A city does not make sense on its own, but only in terms of what surrounds it. A recent thread of urban analysis has posited "city" as a concentration of flows and materials; by this definition, the city is identifiable only in relationship to the normative condition of its context – that which is not concentrated or intensified.

The name Rome is used to refer to both the city as it exists today, and the larger territory of the Roman Empire, a linguistic overlap which emphasizes the difficulty of discussing the node without referring to the network. Rome helps us understand the meaning of a city. The unique experience of a particular city is formed by phenomena from the geologic scale to the scale of the fingertip, or even smaller. Rome is also defined by phenomena of wildly disparate time scales – from forms, structures and stories that have endured from the beginnings of recorded human history, to constructions, gatherings, and forms that are ever-changing, enduring only weeks, hours, or minutes. Let us take a journey through these scales, a tour that will use microscopes alongside telescopes to find ideas that illuminate the nature of the city. We will begin with the smallest scale beside the largest, and progress from both ends toward the middle-scale of the building in the city.

top: Political Map of the Roman Empire at its greatest extent, 100s CE;
below: Lake Albano, birthplace of Romulus and Remus.

1. A City's Spatial Tales of Origin, From Mother Wolf to Shifting Tectonic Plates

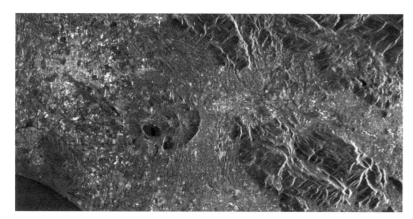

left: Aerial with Rome, Lake Albano, and the Apennine Range
right: She-Wolf, bronze, early 5th century BCE; figures of Romulus and Remus added c. 1472

Mountain Ranges and Volcanic Crater Lakes

> Rome's landscape is best understood as a plateau of soft rock (primarily tufa, a sedimentary rock of volcanic origins) that has been worn down by the Tiber River about 30 km. from its mouth. This erosion created, in the case of the Palatine, Aventine, and Capitoline, free-standing hills along the riverbank almost detached from the plateau. The other hills traditionally included in Rome's seven ... are rather finger-like extensions of the plateau.
>
> - Rome Alive: A Source-Guide to the Ancient City, vol. 1, by Peter J. Aicher

The region which Rome inhabits has its origins in two kinds of geologic movement: first, a Cretaceous Era collision of the African plate with the Eastern European plate, which pushed up limestone and other sedimentary strata, forming the Apennine Range which runs the length of the Italian peninsula; second, the explosion of lava through fissures, creating volcanic mountains like the one whose crater today holds Lake Albano, the site of the Pope's summer retreat from Rome.

This kind of dramatic movement of molten stone and earth structured the spatial precondition for all future development of biological, cultural, and political life in Rome. The land is not just a physical resource, but a source of myth and identity.

Bodies

A succinct account of Rome's origin at the scale of the body, this statue of Romulus and Remus with their surrogate mother she-wolf edits out all but the most minimal context. However, the relationship of the babies' bodies to the land is still essential. In the act of nursing portrayed here, the wolf is the salvific link between the hungry infants and the flows of material and energy in the surrounding environment.

Before Rome had an architectural form of any kind, it had a relationship with the the ridges of the Apennines and the water they shed to the river basin; with the fertility of the soft volcanic plateau worn down by the Tiber to make its seven hills; with the protecting and nourishing body of a wolf mother. Rome's architecture can seem so ancient and inevitable that we accept it as almost geologic; but we must remember that it too interpreted and modulated this supportive precondition of mountains, forests, rivers, plains, plants, and animals. Even in this statue, the mother wolf is the precondition to the arrival of Romulus and Remus; the form of the wolf is an Etruscan sculpture from the early 5th century BCE, joined by the twins almost two millennia later, during the Renaissance.

2. Supportive Land

below left: The hills of Rome. (After Enea nel Lazio, from R. Ross Holloway, The Archaeology of Early Rome and Latium, Routledge 1994)
below center: Seven hills of Rome with ancient monuments: schematic representation in the form of an oval, woodblock, Rome, print from 1538, 21.7 x 12.8 cm;
right: Romulus and Remus, Peter Paul Rubens, 1615-16, 213 x 212 cm.

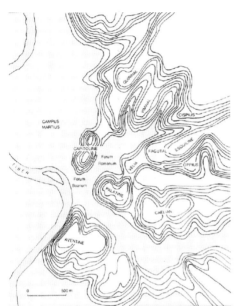

Gathering Boundary: Finding Hills, and Building Walls

Rome was founded upon and within the protective embrace and formal structure of seven hills. The various landforms played different roles in the urban terrain. The Capitoline had been the seat of the Republic. The Palatine, the seat of Imperial power, and the valley floor contained the various public forums. The Roman urban terrain extends from its early land-forms to include the plain.
- W. Morrish, Civilizing Terrains, "Capu Mundi," drawing 15.

"The town within its walls, the densely built-up urban area girdled by this circumvallation . . . During the Middle Ages painters represented the town as a single, uniformly shaped building . . . The walls were the most expressive symbol of the town."
-E.A. Gutkind, "The Town was a work of Art in the Middle Ages," Urban Development in Southern Europe: Italy and Greece.

Rome's local topography was created by the preconditions set up by the tectonic and volcanic events mentioned before. These maps show two ways that we can think of the local topography making the city of Rome. One emphasizes the landforms as a boundary gathered around the lowlands, the other emphasizes the constructed boundary of the city – the wall – and treats landforms as objects of interest contained within it, associated with particular cultural and political uses.

Gathering People: Nestling within Topography

In a mythic and prearchitectural moment, Rome instructs us about a relationship between human persons and the land that architects must interpret and develop. Cheerily collapsing time and space, Rubens' painting of Romulus and Remus shows us at once two joyous fat babies attended by an adoptive wolf mother, kindly birds, a thoughtful shepherd, and the babies' biological parents. The group sits comfortably nestled into the elements of ground and vegetation by the edge of a gentle river. In a less idyllic version of this story, which admits danger and contingency, Romulus and Remus are abandoned on the flooded Tiber and deposited on the foot of the Palatine Hill by its receding waters. There they are adopted by a she-wolf who takes them to her cave; outside the social and architectural structures of family life, they are sheltered by the wild wolf and the complexities of a topography shaped by the erosive forces of the river which deposited them there.

Romulus and Remus act out a tale of origin for Rome's engagement with its topography over time, saved from the flooding waters of the Tiber by the structure of the ground, and dwelling against a hill's mass as a sheltering boundary.

3. Connecting from Within and from Without – Origin and Interface ------------------------------------

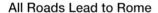
above: Map of the Roman Countryside, Eufrosino della Volpaia, engraving, 1547, 1.1 x 1.2 m

All Roads Lead to Rome

This map by della Volpaia gives another account of the landscape which supports the city, emphasizing the way it contains a field of connections and resources in which the city is embedded: roads, waterways, fertile soils, crops – the multiple conditions which must converge to support the concentration of people in an urban condition. The hills are evident as both an embracing boundary and something to dwell upon.

One Good Window

While Rome, ancient and contemporary, has its own spatial tales of origin, those who dwell in it have their own. The dwelling is the space from which we originate each day. It orients us to the condition of the city as we direct our first blinking gaze out of one good window into the gathering daylight. This simple moment is supported by the kind of intense connection between the city and its territory that we see in Volpaia's Map of the Roman Countryside; the fruit bowl on the table is filled by the fertility of unseen fields, the breeze floating by the window was cooled or heated and tinted with particles and scents from the land it passed over on its way.

Sometime we consider the connection with the outside in all its intensity and complexity; flows of resources, nutrients, energy. Sometimes we must consider it in terms of one good window for one room, and then realize that it is the same thing.

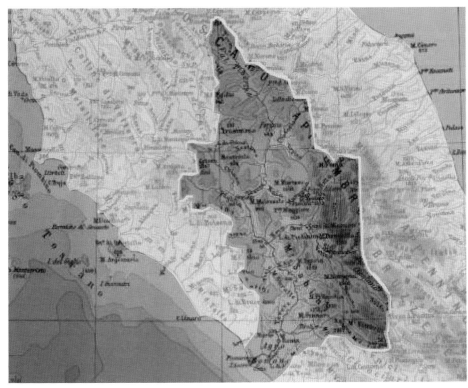

above: Watershed of the Tiber River

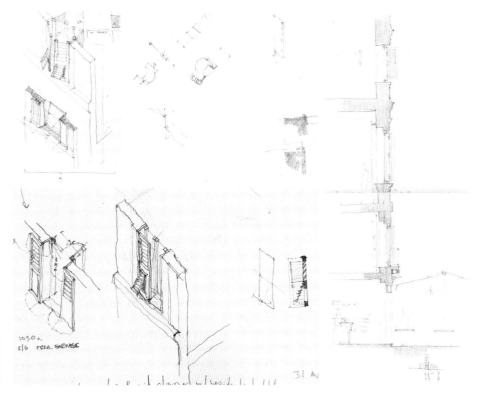

River path, between Mountains and City

In mythology under each mountain on the end of the axis mundi lie the waters of life. Water and Mountain are balanced opposites. The mountain's role is to collect, store, and distribute the water from the sky to the field, houses, and cities which it protects. The mountain is the urban reservoir. The mountain through its power and function to capture the water from the sky is the guardian of civilized life as it monitors and replenishes our urban water resources. (W. Morrish)

On the regional scale, topography acts as interface between the city and the sky; the form of the distant mountains determines what is inside and outside the reservoir for the city. The moment of geologic origin, the shifting of tectonic plates, created a form which today determines that one drop of rain in the mountains will eventually join others in the Tiber, passing under the bridges of Rome, past the Castel Sant' Angelo, and finally out to the Tyrrhenian Sea - while another drop ten feet away will never see Rome, taking a much shorter trip east to the Adriatic Sea.

The simple pieces: Shutters, Latches, Curtains, Panes of Glass

A window may seem like a simple idea, but to design it is to design an interface between here and there, inside and outside, mine and not mine. The tightness and intensity of inhabitation of both inside and outside in Rome means that the task of the window there is particularly important and complex. Even Rome's modest windows are hardly simple; they are multilayered and employ wood, glass, heavy and light fabrics, and an endless variety of metal hardware to create the potential for many different configurations that admit or exclude light, sound, views, breezes, scents.

There is nothing inevitable about the way the boundary between inside and outside is made. The method varies according to time, climate, and culture. Compare the configuration of the Roman window to an aboriginal Australian walless domestic structure, where the boundary of the private domain is indicated by a change in the ground's surface texture, effected by sweeping around the shelter two or three times a day.

What is in? What is out? What forms the interface between the two? Depending on the scale under consideration, the answer may be determined by tectonics, by massive infrastructural efforts like earthworks and canals, or by the daily work of hands and fingertips: the drawing of a lace curtain, the rhythmic movement of a broom.

5. Finding the "Beyond" Right Here

below left: Plan of Rome with Figures of Jupiter, Mars, Apollo, and Minerva, Taddeo di Bartolo, fresco in Palazzo Pubblico (Siena, Italy).
below right: Map of Rome, Piero del Massaio, c. 1453-56.

Only later did I come to think that the street of that afternoon was not mine, that every house is a branching candlestick where the lives of men burn like single candles. Borges, "Calle Desconocida"

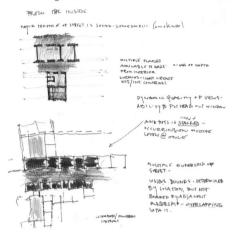

City + River

The city is never isolated. The river is the undeniable connection between the city and the beyond, whether one imagines the city wall as the end of terra cognita, or at least terra interesante - such as in Taddeo di Bartolo's 15th century map of Rome - or understands the city wall as merging and interlocking with a significant preexisting landscape of form, place, and flow. Under the name of the Tiber River, topography, water, and gravity coincide to introduce the flux of exterior conditions into the constructed space of the city, at times for trade and profit, at others flood and devastation.

Amidst Branching Candlesticks

We have seen that at the scale of the city, we are never isolated. There is always something that reveals an interface between what is here and there, our place, and the beyond: the Tiber flowing through the city, or the topographic context which shapes patterns of construction and inhabitation. At the scales of the building and the street, this is also clear. Rome teaches us that boundaries are not simple, and we can seem to be in two places at once. The space of the street, or an apartment, is not only itself but is also partially composed of the many adjacent domestic and public territories where the lives of citizens and strangers unfold.

6. Finding the "Here" Beyond

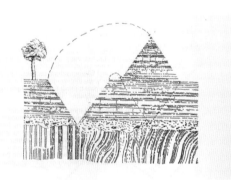
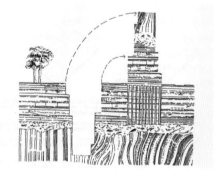

left: "Geologic Agents," W. Morrish, Civilizing Terrains, drawing 5.
right: Waste was Frequently Emptied Into Street-Side Openings to the Roman Sewers. The sewers carried off sewage, urban runoff, and drainage water together (based on Macaulay).

Consuming and Disposing

At the scale of the building and the individual, we see that life in the city has almost always involved the generation of materials considered to be "waste" – no longer useful, and to be thrown "away." This section of an Imperial Roman street shows the integration of sewers into the composition of public and private space. These are a public infrastructure and represent an urban ethic of sending "used" materials out of the city, into the same flowing river which brought "new" materials in, fresh and full of promise.

Excavating and Constructing

Just as the river brings the conditions and news of the beyond to the interior of the city, so the interior of the city leaves its mark on the territory beyond; see W. Morrish's powerful diagrams above. Rivers have often been used as conduits to move elements of the larger landscape into a concentration in the space of the city. The channels of communication between the city and its resources mark the extents of the corollary landscape that is created as the city constructs itself from its context, near and far. The urban topography of Rome's walls, streets, and buildings has a geomorphic impact on its context.

This ethic is not without consequences. Today, as our use of our territories' resources becomes ever more intense, our planet's ecological health emerges as a true "common good": a good achievable only via collective human cooperation. We can no longer design the city to manage material flows as if there is a neutral "away" place for our waste. The waste we send downstream is always upstream of someone else. The Tiber, once a source of clean water and fish to eat, became polluted by waste. Even in the way we design our streets, we must engage the material flows of daily life that connect us to local and distant terrain, which in turn sustain our existence.

7. Being Inside and Outside

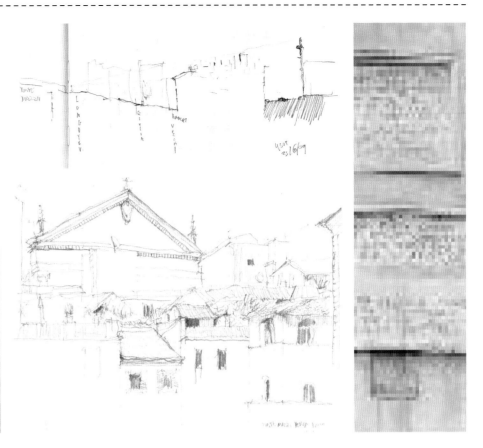

A river in the city points to the distance

The intense interiority of central Rome is broken by a giant canyon of space. In the midst of Rome's density, two steep masonry embankment walls miles long channel the Tiber River through the city. These walls were built in the 1870s after Italy's unification and the choice of Rome as the new country's capitol in the early 1860s. The political function of the capitol city demanded a guarantee of environmental stability, safety from the violent fluctuations of the Tiber River as it carried the rains and spring waters of the region to the Tyrrhenian Sea. As a result, the space of the Tiber River in the city is something quite other. Its scale is in tune with the scale of the whole watershed, yet it intersects with the tight urban fabric of Rome's center, some of whose streets transform from narrow channels of movement through the packed city to solid stone fingers reaching across the broad expanse of river.

The quantity of evidence that this great volume belongs to territories beyond fluctuates with events and seasons. Sometimes the city seems to own the river; during the summer small festival stands encamp on the riverside walkways and even the surface of the water becomes a place for the life of the city to play out. But at other times the Tiber's connection to the outside and the unseen is made clear by distant heavy rains that transform the Tiber into a dangerous space, swollen and muddy with the region's runoff, carrying broken fragments of the beyond swiftly under Rome's bridges.

The Apennines and the view from Ponte Mazzini

Despite the undeniable power of planimetric geometries and the focus on them in the historiography of urban planning, the ground has another equally important type of geometry, one indisputably significant to the visitor with tired calves making her way up 124 relentlessly steep steps to the Basilica di Santa Maria in Ara Coeli. The sectional geometries of the ground, its topography and microtopography, are a defining element in the experience of urban space.

Tuned to flows at the scale of the regional landscape, the high embankment walls of the Tiber form a defining topographic feature at an urban scale. Moments of crossing this canyon reveal the separateness of its logic from those that govern the rest of the city. Here, the distant topography of the Apennines creates a corollary urban topography outside of Rome's norm.

Crossing the Tiber on foot over Ponte Mazzini toward via Giulia, one is in the stone-embanked canyon of the river, outside the city's fabric. But suddenly, at the end of the bridge, also up- inside the world of roof terraces. The height of the river embankment creates a vantage point from which the upper stories of two parallel streets ahead– via del Pellegrino and Corso Vittorio Emmanuele - are collapsed against each other. These buildings were designed to be seen from the ground plane, facades addressing the lowly pedestrian approaching on the street; but from the height of Ponte Mazzini suddenly the pediment at Chiesa Nuova mingles with potted plants and satellite dishes on the roof terraces of small apartments. Ninety seconds later, descending from the height of the bridge into the city, order is restored and buildings can only be seen from their proper streets.

Into the city and out of sight of the Tiber, there are still traces of the river's presence. Some walls bear marks of the river's highest floods.

8. Making the City between Historied and Pure Geometries

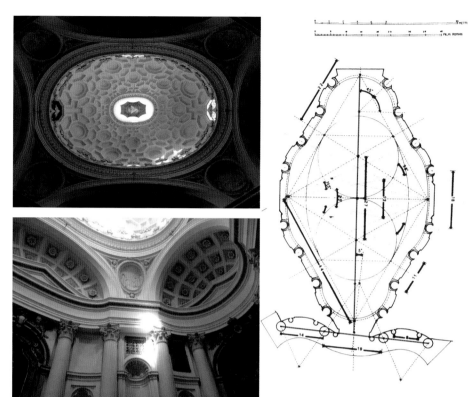

left: Marble map of Rome at time of Septimius Severus, fragment: area of Via Portuense, 203-211 CE.
right: Map of Sixtus V's Urban Plan for Rome, Bacon

above: plan & photographs of San Carlo alle Quattro Fontane

City streets

> The Baroque planner transformed the utopian ideal plan into a concept of set-pieces or ideal fragments inserted into existing city fabric as nodal points along, or terminating, lines of movement . . . The large scale network derived from ideal-city polemics and the set-pieces provided for an organizational framework for the arbitrarily-placed, separately conceived, dissonant forms of the existing medieval city of Rome. (J.M. Schwarting)

We have looked at two defining constructed elements of Rome: its city walls and its river walls; now on to the network of channels of human movement within the confines of those walls: the streets. An examination of Rome's streets reveals the coexistence of two very different types of plan geometry: one which refers to non-local rules, invoking the authority and recognition of a timeless, portable, self-supporting logic of pure geometries to govern space; and one in which the negotiation of multiple parameters and demands has led to a particular geometry that makes sense in local conditions and histories, but not necessarily anywhere else.

This second type of fragmented geometry is typically associated with the medieval city. In the stone map fragment above, we see an example from the third century where the negotiations between private, shared, and public space is the juxtaposition of recognizable geometries with a regular and thus unrecognizable composite forms. In Rome these two conditions (those referring to self-defined geometrical forms like the circle and square and those referring to unique, local geometrical conditions) overlap, cross, transform, and interpret each other.

City buildings

Intensely enveloping, highly controlled in its connections to the exterior, and close to obsessive in the self-referential geometries of its interior, Francesco Borromini's exquisite Baroque masterpiece San Carlo alle Quattro Fontane would seem to utterly refute the condition of connection and embeddedness just discussed. Upon first examination, it has completely avoided the kind of negotiation with or concession to context that we noted in the urban condition recorded in the 3rd century map of Rome, choosing instead a non-local context of abstract or "pure" geometries to reference. However, Borromini has made one geometrical concession to the urban form around him; in order for the church's facade to align with the street, it is canted a few degrees from perpendicular to the main axis of the church. At the building scale, control of a particular lot of land allowed the development of a complex, interrelated geometric architectural composition; at a single, selective point this composition is adjusted to interface with the geometrical context of the street.

The street that San Carlino's facade addresses is actually one of the axial routes defined by Sixtus V's urban plan for Rome in the late 1500s. It is instructive to note the proportional differences in geometric complexity and scale between Borromini's building-scale effort here and the Sixtus' urban plan. Both schemes invoke the power of abstract geometry to communicate significance and an idea about the relationship of the parts and the whole. However, the simplicity of the Sixtus plan, relying on the power of the point and the line, allows it to operate on an urban scale in a context of inherited forms and limited resources, while Borromini's strategy of geometrical intricacy, so convincing at the scale of a building, would demand total formal control over the city to achieve legibility at an urban scale.

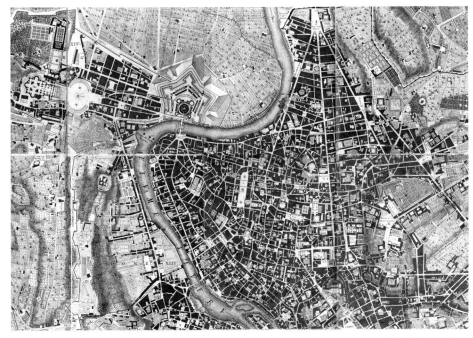

above: Giambattisa Nolli's 1748 map of Rome

The public ground

The urban forms resulting from the negotiations between symbolic geometries, utilitarian geometries, inherited geometries, and accidental geometries collectively define the shared realm of Rome's streets and piazzas. Giambattisa Nolli's 1748 map of Rome introduces us to the idea to both the complexity and the moments of clarity available on the ground plane. Nolli helps us see how the private interiors withheld from the public realm contribute to the shape of that realm. The boundaries of interior domestic spaces do not merely enclose the life within, they define much of the perimeter of the life without. In Nolli's map, this relationship is clearly seen, as the solidly held volumes of the interior carve out figures of white space. Nolli's famous map is a drawing that defines shared urban space as corollary, in the strictest sense, to the private space of the interior. Through the discipline of two tones, the dense blackness of interior space and the whiteness of the exterior are direct, unavoidable corollaries of each other. This drawing of the relationship of private and public space is a tantalizing beginning to an investigation of the space of urban dwelling. The enclosure of the public realm here is only represented in solids and voids in plan - we understand the shape of the public ground, but not the full four-dimensional volume of these public spaces.

Urban space as deep space

The space of the street, its volume and the nature of its boundary, is created by the facades which address it. But the tale does not end here. Punctures, transparency, domestic infrastructure, decoration, and the half-open door connect the shared realm of the street to the private volumes of space beyond the facade. Moving across the shared exterior ground plane results in a realization of the city's spatial depth and one's position inside of it. In Complexity and Contradiction in Architecture, Venturi discusses the baldachino (the covering for an altar inside the volume of a church) to illustrate the idea of intense interiority. This example—which emphasizes vertical enclosure, or canopy, as the defining enclosing element— could be counter-balanced by a reading of the street as interior. While open to the sky, the street and piazza are wrapped laterally in the layered solids and spatial volumes of the adjacent buildings, offering a sense of embeddedness in deep space, and in the activities, materials, and territories of others.

Nolli's map reveals the embeddedness of much of Rome's public space, but once again, the variation in section, elevation, light, temperature, sound, and smell which define these spaces cannot be explained by the map. Repeated embodied experience of these spaces is necessary to apprehend their multiple thresholds, their shifting and sometimes contradictory sensory cues of interiority or exteriority.

10. The Enclosure of the Public Realm ---

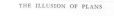

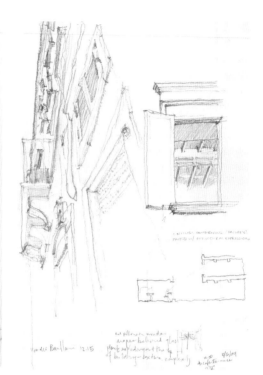

The Exterior is Always an Interior

The walls of private buildings are answerable to the exterior as well as the interior. The multiple facades along a street or on a piazza unite with the shared ground plane to contain a volume of space which has often been interpreted as an urban "room." In the center of Rome, the density of built form outweighs the uncoordinated character of the facades to result in a strong unity of the street wall, "And like the sculpture which consists of compressed automobiles by John Chamberlain and the photographs through telescopic lens in Blake's God's Own Junkyard, they achieve an ironically compelling kind of unity" (Venturi, "The Inside and the Outside").

Giambattista Nolli's map offers us great clarity in its explanation of the composition of the city's public realm. However, it must do so at the expense of description of the totality of surfaces which complete the three-dimensional enclosure of Rome's urban rooms. This enclosure can be interpreted purely in terms of mass, of solid and void, in a way that unites the horizontal and vertical as a containing volume for activity. Or distinctions of material composition can enter in to help us interpret the ground, the wall, and the ceiling. The ground is designed for and formed by very different types of pressure and abrasion than the "vertical patience of a massive wall . . . interrupted by a solitary and miniature cage of clarity" (Holl, "Anchoring"). In Rome, surfaces on the horizontal ground and on the vertical building walls set up a dialogue between materials of Baroque stone and planar stucco. These surfaces call and answer each other in many ways between dawn and dusk, winter and summer, congestion and emptiness. They conspire to create luminous and acoustic environments in which the impulses of light, movement, and sound of the city are played out.

The eye and the beholder are on the move

It is becoming clear that the urban exterior and urban domestic interior must always be considered in terms of one another. Their adjacency means more than a shared territorial line - their nearness instead implies an ongoing exchange of bodies, views, screens, breezes, scents, produce and refuse that modulates according to time of day, season, and occasion. It is in this dynamic exchange that both the dwelling spaces of all scales which float above the street and their corollary spaces of dwelling tied to the ground plane can be interpreted in terms of the corolla, or garland - pieces and twining flows which emerge not as rigid, mutually exclusive counterparts, but as complementary interpenetrating realms, layered, mutable, seasonal, multi-determinate, and processive.

In Towards a New Architecture, Le Corbusier notes that

> The human eye, in its investigations, is always on the move and the beholder himself is always turning to the right and left, shifting about ... at once the problem spreads to the surroundings. The houses near by, the distant or neighboring mountains, the horizon low or high make formidable masses which exercise the force of their cubic volume.

In addition to the patterns and events of life within buildings which transform their appearance, the movement of the individual through exterior urban space, the variety of angles from which he or she will view the elements of the built environment makes the nature of urban enclosure dynamic. The undersides of things become significant, much-viewed surfaces. From below, even modest relief on a facade stacks into an enveloping sea of protrusions. A glimpse up through a window on via dei Baullari reveals the thickness of the building's wall, the direction and dimension of its primary and secondary floor structure, a design painted into the metered spaces between structural elements on the ceiling.

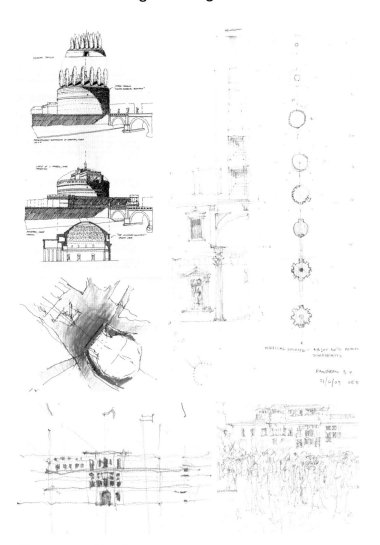

From ground to sky

We can study how Rome's building facades mediate not only the adjacent conditions of inside and outside, but also the dynamic conditions of sky and ground. Rome's buildings, which seem self-referential in their bilateral symmetry are in fact asymmetrical about a horizontal axis, in response to the asymmetry of the conditions associated with ground and sky – like the activity and movement on the ground plane and the availability of sunlight, views, and satellite signals above. From the public ground plane, these different vertical zones fade in and out of our consciousness at different times of day and year. For example, in the moment depicted above, the thick summer crowd blocks the view of the busy stores and cafes on the ground floor of Piazza Navona, and one is enclosed in a space of jostling bodies with apartments quietly floating above.

Vertically-organized logics are significant for singular as well as collective forms, as they are integral to tectonics, to issues of solar access, and to the preconditioning human experience of ground and sky. This is illustrated in William Morrish's depiction of the architectural "sacred mountain" form, and in the distinct vertical zones of the Pantheon's interior. A series of plan cuts from the floor to the top of the Pantheon's dome reveal the varying of geometry and the hierarchy of governing lines at each level. The Pantheon's interior, a composite of ancient Roman and Renaissance architecture, calls out across time to teach us the difference between down and up; it tells us that a preoccupation with ground and sky, basement and attic, is at once elemental, human, architectural, and urban.

From public to private

The difference between down and up, expressed monumentally at the Pantheon, is important in organizing the spaces and activities of everyday buildings as well as exceptional ones. In Rome and many other cities, the ground floor, with its connection to the street and piazza, is different in form and in use from the floors above; a building's most public functions are accommodated on the ground floor, with spaces becoming gradually more private the higher one goes in the building. However, at the very top of the building, even a small roof terrace creates an opportunity to emerge from the confines of the building and reconnect with the surroundings – often a view to a whole second ground of the city composed of rooftops and terraces.

The facade of the convent and church of Santa Brigida at Piazza Farnese reveals the combination of a larger, more public volume of space (the church) with the repetitive, cellular, and more private rooms of the Sisters. However, there is some complexity here in the negotiation between interior space and exterior facade form. The portion of the facade associated with the church extends the full four stories of the building, from ground to sky, expressing its importance in relation to the activities of the convent. But a glimpse through the small ironwork lunette in the church's pediment reveals that the actual interior volume of the church is only two and a half or three stories tall, and sitting on top of the church, behind its pediment, is a small roof terrace for the Sisters.

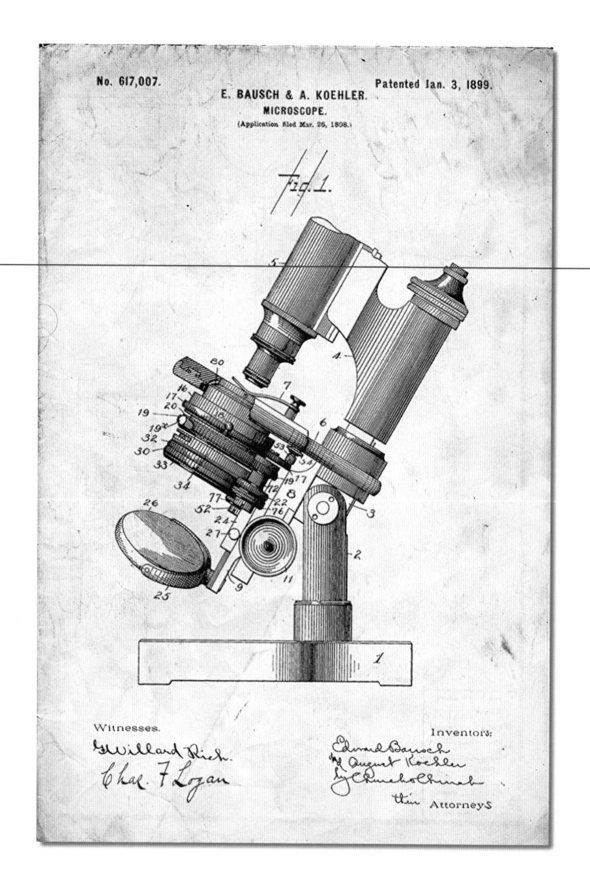

Connective Tissue #3 Center and Edge
Peter Waldman

We pause now to pivot the huge hinges of the monumental portals of Rome to appreciate the intimate residual voids within labyrinths. Daedalus taught us to delight in being lost in the cacophony of shadows, only to be cast down by the clear light of Apollo's chariot. Both these authors from the middle years of the Kenan Fellowships (2005-2010) come to Rome from afar. Richardson from Pittsburgh and Bninski from Poland. They found themselves at the University of Virginia as Master of Architecture graduate students and were awarded Carlo Pelliccia Traveling Fellowships in consecutive years to sojourn to Rome to read the city by drawing with both 6H and 2B sensibilities.

We encounter Richardson first, genuinely posturing as a life guard now turned wise young archeologist/architect as he observes at sunrise a street cleaner scrubbing the fountain out in the Piazza. Richardson then pauses within to note an elderly custodian shepherding rain drops from the oculus down into 22 drainage holes. This young architect succumbs to a gravitational attraction, some call star struck moment, to Kirk Douglas and Goldie Horn. He now volunteers as Huckleberry Finn, or is it Aeneas, as a self-appointed guide. Only then, he takes a break outside for a cappuccino and a cornetto early in the day. Once again he returns to trace the path of the sun, now read as light-tower in reverse. Then he is driven out by the heat, to a mid-day melon gelato down the street. Then back again he renders precise contours and deepening shadows on coffers. Only now he seeks out a final retirement leading to a late afternoon Spritz out by the multi-tiered fountain in the Piazza Della Rotonda. Water haunts this landlocked oasis in the accounts of one accustomed to measure the tides. There are frequent precise coordinates with the everyday present, with a proper respect and/or humorous delight for rumors from the past, and hallucinations of the future. Richardson documents the Pantheon as construction site over millennia and simultaneously in the light of a one-day solstice cycle. His essay of gait and pause, self-reflection and encyclopedic provocations is a masterful story told of intimacy and a respect for Solnit's provision of The Blue of Distance.

Bninski reads the city of Rome first from afar and then intimately strategically from within, from the Cardo to the Decumanus. This is expected in plan, but then surprisingly extrapolated in section, in the contained city of both archeological and topographic imaginations. Classified early on within coherent walls, and then as if in response, Bninski takes notice of the containment of excavated voids within monumental blocks. Bninski's essay, as was her well-framed lecture, consistently offered the origins of Rome as an idea in the juxtaposed mythic narrative of a she-wolf In service of Romulus and Remus and the vast coordinates of the Roman Empire under Hadrian. Our collage superimposes the bronze statue over the map of the empire and found Romulus could suckle Italy while Remus suckled Greece. We dwell on "One Good Window" as Bninski's Observatory counterpart to Richardson's Oculus, as she notes the bowl of fruit that reimagines distant landscapes of fecundity, of linen curtains which dance in celebration of sea-scented breezes, of the labyrinthine fecundity of hardware, material inventories, and spatial choreographies of closing in and opening out to the city. Bninski promises to take us through Rome from its enormity down to the intimacy of this window, only to arrive in this syncopation to the ambiguity of "building" itself, both verb and subject. We end up with not only in the reconstruction and re-inhabitation of Rome as the verb Roam, a journey through evolving place at the modest chiesa of Brigida where the Blue of Distance is revealed at the scale of our digits. Is this not the story our own Daedalus, Jefferson who is trying to offer in the ideogram of the Academical Village? Bninski offers her essay on Rome as a device to read the Jefferson project as a good window and an open gate to a continental nation, from our own juxtaposed Appalachians and Rockies standing for the Apennines, from sea to shining sea with serpentine walls recalling the twisting Tiber. Her essay confirms that Architecture is a Covenant with the World, again and again.

These two juxtaposed essays are a study in the power of recurrent dualities as facts and fictions, of monumentality and intimacy. Composition implies the arrangement of parts in balance, often equilibrium. For Jim Richardson and Maria Bninski, their appreciation of Rome is through the frictional intentions of recurrent dualities. Richardson dwells within the Pantheon and reveals the world as far as destinations of the Piazza del Popolo and the Roman forum. He takes us within the cavities of innovative Roman Construction and reveals that the Pantheon was built in the lowest spot of Rome, where an eighth hill of Rome was raised to construct the dome without reinforcing. Bninski powerfully allows the interrogation of one good window of many coordinates and coordinated parts and operations to reveal the world through Rome.

This juxtaposed connective tissue occupies a pivotal position as Chapter Three, which is located in the middle or fulcrum between Chapter One and Chapter Five. A microscope is juxtaposed to a telescope here as it is superimposed Bninski's open window to foretell in Hildner's Epilogue Jefferson's multi-scaled capacities for continental as well as adolescent imaginations.

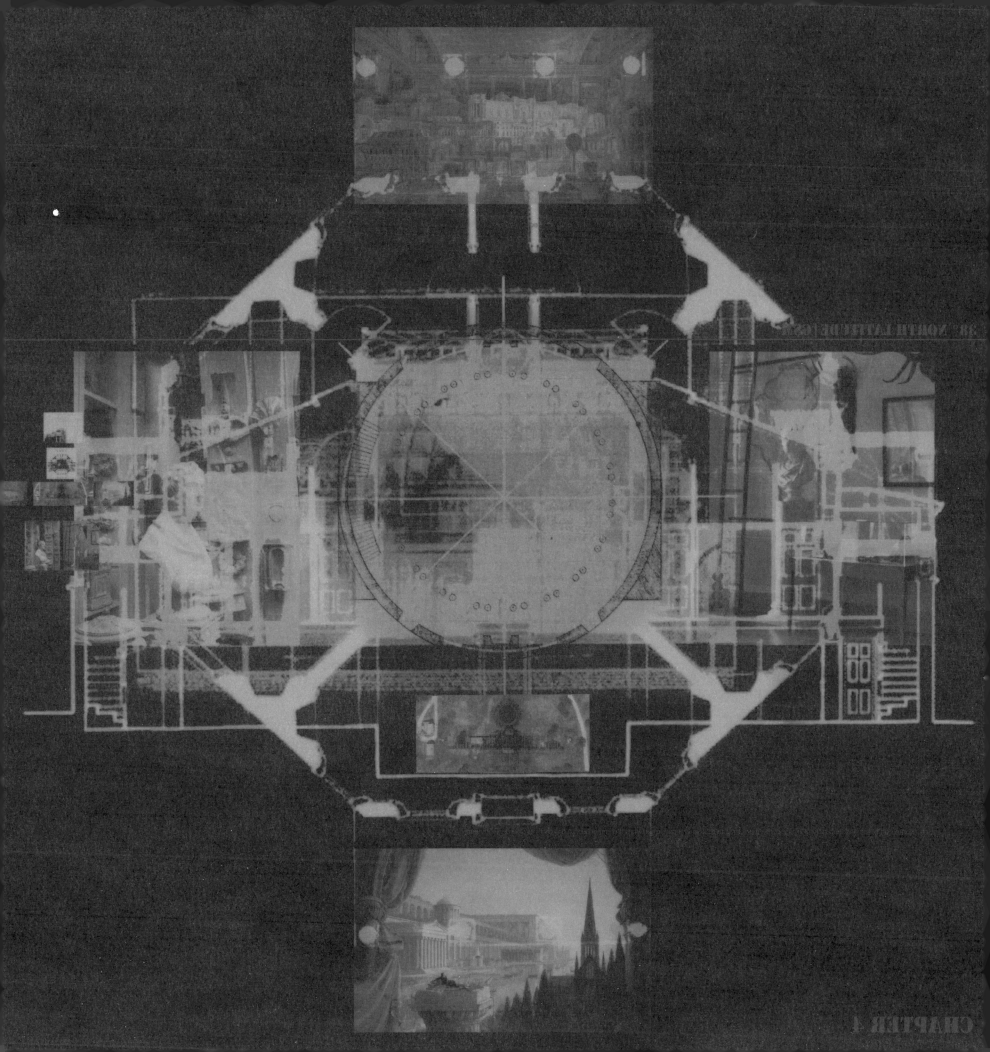

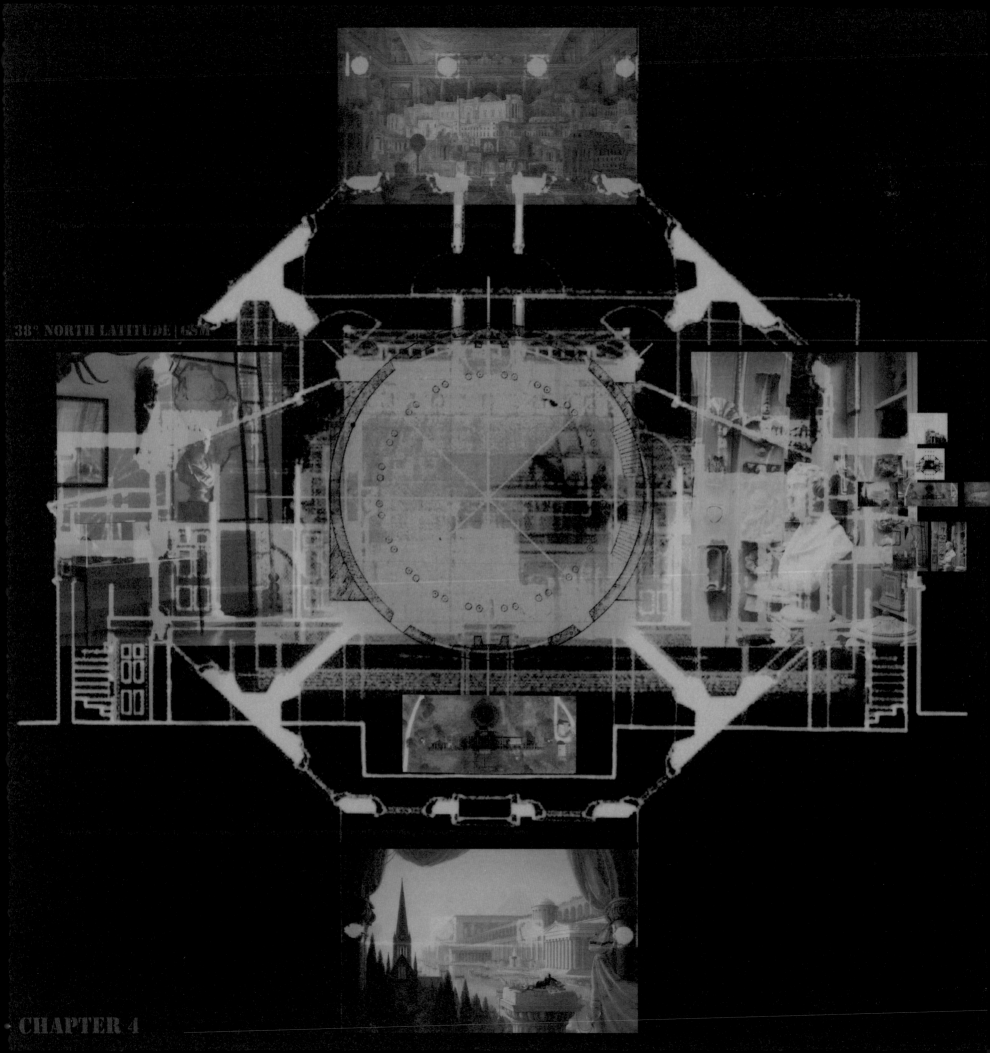

...nal artifacts and second hand representations of archeological fieldwork

CHAPTER FOUR: TRANSFORMATON

These are self-reflective spatial essays with a great sense of the Intimate Interior,

Cabinets of Curiosities, while both architects were also preparing their most public of civic theaters.

Soane's father was a master bricklayer, Jefferson's father was a surveyor.

Both worked off of the accountability of digits, of the modular with materials transformed from the immediacy of the earth as source.

But both were in the world trade of unearthing the past in both the original artifacts and second hand representations of archeological finds.

The Curious Homes and Collections of Jefferson and Soane
Danielle Willkens

Preface

Originally developed for the Lessons on the Lawn, this essay was composed in the fall of 2007, following travels sponsored by the American Architectural Foundation and the Soane Foundation Traveling Fellowship. After more than a decade of research, this project developed into a PhD dissertation at the Bartlett School of Architecture, under the supervision of Dr Barbara Penner, and is now a manuscript in preparation with the University of Virginia Press. Although recent research and analysis yielded a more developed, nuanced thesis about the parallels in the formative years, architecture, and legacies of Jefferson and Soane, this essay has not been heavily edited. Instead, it retains the voice of a young and eager transatlantic researcher who was in the process of discovery through design and the initial explorations of rich archives. Just like preliminary sketches for a project, the essay presents emergent ideas and questions. The essay is flawed and raw, but still serves as a treasured starting point for a project that has captivated so much of my time and attention.

2007

Initially, my interest in the parallels between these two multi-faceted designers was sparked by key similarities: they were both architects influenced by the Enlightenment, their birth and death dates were separated by a mere ten years, and both gentlemen took more than forty years to complete their own home. Throughout my investigative, architectural journey to discover the motivations, anomalies and connections between Monticello and Sir John Soane's Museum I have discovered so much more than design parallels. The journey, for me, became an opportunity to explore my own theory of architectural drawing and caused me to question exactly what makes architectural pilgrimages sites like Monticello and the Sir John Soane Museum so captivating to designers and the general public. The journey has left me grasping for more ways to understand Jefferson and Soane, searching with a critical eye for revealing details in their homes, books and collections.

My work is greatly indebted to the Sir John Soane Museum and Thomas Jefferson Foundation. I thank all of the staff at the Soane Museum for so warmly welcoming me into their family over the summer of 2007. In particular, thanks to Stephen Astley and Stephie Coane for answering my endless questions and allowing me to access the library and drawing collections; and to Sue Palmer for her guidance through the archive. At Monticello, I thank Gary Sandling for his support and enthusiasm as well as the security staff and curators for being so accommodating to my odd drawing schedule. Thanks to all the warders of the Soane Museum and interpreters of Monticello who are an inspiring community with priceless information on not only the architects of their respective places of employment but on the operations and eccentricities of a house museum. At the University of Virginia, I owe a great deal to Professor Peter Waldman for his unwavering encouragement and counsel. Above all else, I thank the Soane Foundation for giving me the opportunity to meet two seminal architects through an intimate study of their homes.

Introduction

The edifice has a thousand stories. Here and there one beholds on its staircases the gloomy caverns of science which pierce its interior. Everywhere upon its surface, art causes its arabesques, rosettes, and laces to thrive luxuriantly before the eyes. There, every individual work, however capricious and isolated it may seem, has its place and its projection. Harmony results from the whole. (Victor Hugo)

Within the grand history of architecture, Thomas Jefferson's Monticello and Sir John Soane's Museum are infantile. The two edifices were the result of decades of design and labor, not centuries, yet both house museums represent a lifetime of study and contemplation from their respective designers. Monticello and Sir John Soane's Museum each took more than forty years to construct; arguably, construction was truncated only by the death of the respective architect. Like cathedrals constructed over the centuries, both Monticello and Soane's Museum are building with rich narratives. They are organic edifices that seem to have a life of their own beyond the assembly of brick and plaster. These buildings continue to inspire others, welcoming thousands of visitors each year.

Thomas Jefferson and John Soane spent the majority of their adult lives editing and evolving their homes. Both gentlemen lost their wives and never remarried, they instead became wedded to their intricate house museums. The homes and eclectic, personal collections held within have been preserved, to varying degrees of cohesion, at both Jefferson's Virginia home Monticello and Sir John Soane's Museum in London. Although both gentlemen left behind a copious paper trail, most of Jefferson's in written form and Soane's through drawings, the homes and contained collections of these two men illuminate their personalities, insecurities, ambitions and legacies better than any singular record of pen on paper. These two homes give an intimate glimpse into the design theories, daily operations and sometimes contradictory actions of two of the most notable architects, especially in their respective countries of residence, inspired by Enlightenment thought.

According to the Oxford English Dictionary, Enlightenment is defined as, "the action of enlightening or the state of being enlightened or a European intellectual movement of the late 17th and 18th centuries emphasizing reason and individualism rather than tradition." The act of becoming enlightened was derived from reading, writing, corresponding, conversing, listening to music and looking at pictures. Therefore, the endeavor was partially an act of individual study and partially a sociable art. This Janus-faced theory of learning is acutely critical to understanding the program and arrangement of Jefferson's Monticello and Sir John Soane's Museum. At both Monticello and the Soane's Museum there is a strong public program in the form of a museum: Jefferson's was one of the first private museums in America and Soane's was the first architectural museum in England. Both gentlemen made their homes a place of investigation and discourse. Conversely, each home had a distinct spatial arrangement that provided for quiet, individual study. According to John Locke's theory of introspection, enlightenment was a product of a talk with oneself, not the outside. Therefore, the act of introspection was imperative. For an architect, designing one's own home may be the most introspective act of all: both Jefferson and Soane could isolate themselves within the studious cocoons they created. Additionally, the designed privacy found at Monticello and Sir John Soane's Museum was a rare convenience of eighteenth-century domestic architecture.

The house museums of Jefferson and Soane are now, somewhat, frozen: walls are not continually "put up and pulled down" and the collections do not move within the home unless under the watchful eye of curators clad in protective gloves. The vibrant design process at Monticello and Sir John Soane's Museum was a never-ending exercise for Jefferson and Soane. Unfortunately, the best record of this multi-decade design process is the current state of each house museum. Since each house museum had architects that lived on-site, many decisions were made without record, whether written or drawn. The paper trail for both Monticello and Sir John Soane's Museum is sparse given the more than forty-year long design and construction process for each home. Therefore, to understand how Jefferson and Soane designed their own homes as illustrative examples of Enlightenment thought it is important to outline the education and evolution of the each architects, the paper trail of each home as recorded through drawings and written accounts from both architects and visitors, and finally examine the homes with a modern eye, tracing the scars of past changes and the wear of time.

The Formulation of an Architect: Education and Exploration

Thomas Jefferson was born at Shadwell, a farm located at the base of the mountain now known as Monticello, on April 13, 1743. John Soane was born across the Atlantic Ocean a little over ten years later in Reading, England on September 10, 1753. Both young men lost their fathers at the age of fourteen but went on to have transformative educational experiences as young men. They evolved into bookish, introspective students, and eventually pursued successful careers in the public realm: Jefferson as statesmen and Soane as architect.

Both Jefferson and Soane had fathers that were accomplished in professions tangentially related to architecture: surveyor and bricklayer, respectively. Therefore, both Jefferson and Soane grew up in an atmosphere where drawings were present in map, diagram, or plan form. Additionally, both gentlemen grew up in an atmosphere where the measured detail was critical. Their eyes were trained to perceive space in a quantitative manner; their qualitative skills would be developed through reading and observation. Jefferson never abandoned the legacy of his father's occupation, surveying pieces of his property throughout his life and applying a surveyor's mathematical precision to his building book by calculating measurements to the sixth decimal place in some instances. Soane's bricklayer-heritage informed his construction knowledge and arguably led to his characteristic manipulation of brick surfaces in unconventional manners. He learned the rules of brick construction at a young age and was therefore comfortable with breaking them as an emerging architect.

In their teenage years, both Jefferson and Soane ventured away from their country homes for educational purposes. As a law student at the College of William & Mary in Williamsburg, Jefferson had the opportunity to interact with the colonial elite, and he acquired his first architectural book. Although the colonial capital was home to such buildings as the Governor's Mansion and the Wren Building, Jefferson's architectural palette was not satisfied with Williamsburg, noting that "the genius of architecture seems to have shed its maledictions over this land." While in Williamsburg, Jefferson was also exposed to the political life of the city. In particular, a friendship with Governor Fauquier inspired Jefferson's entrance into governmental service. Jefferson rose from land lawyer to Governor of Virginia in only twelve years. During that twelve-year period Jefferson was also working on what he called his "essay in architecture," his mountaintop home Monticello. The

name for the home reflected Jefferson's early love of neoclassical design: the term monticello was used in Palladio's Quattro libri as a description for the site of Villa Rotunda in Vicenza. At Monticello, the process of designing and building was slow: for one year, the only edifice that stood on the mountaintop was the South Pavilion. In a 1771 letter Jefferson wrote:

I have here but one room, which, serves me for parlour for kitchen and hall. I may add, for bed chamber and study too. My friends sometimes take a temperate dinner with me and then retire to look for beds elsewhere. I have hopes however of getting more elbow room this summer.

Construction continued on Jefferson's first iteration of Monticello through the 1770s; however, the two-story, eight-room, restrained neoclassical home was a derivative model of designs Jefferson studied in architectural books like James Gibbs or Robert Morris. In 18th century Virginia, there were four ways of understanding architecture: pattern books, self-initiated travel, apprenticeship, and previous experience from abroad. Jefferson only knew the architecture of books and poor models constructed in colonial and Georgian America. However, in 1784 this would all change: Jefferson experienced the world of European architecture. His architectural style would never be the same and the concept of Monticello as we know it today was born.

Jefferson's only experience aboard was granted by his appointment of Minister to France from 1784-1789. He took the position to escape the melancholy he found at Monticello due to the recent passing of his wife after only ten years of marriage; however, Jefferson's excursions abroad proved to be more than emotional respite. While in Europe, Jefferson met key figures of the Enlightenment, saw the architecture of the ancients, watched the construction of new architectural innovations and met contemporary designers. France was enlivened with the architectural explorations of Boulleé and Ledoux, two key figures that Jefferson most likely met while at the French court.

During Jefferson's diplomatic tenure in France, he traveled to various sites in Europe. He made an extended visit to England, partially to visit John Adams who was serving ambassador and partially as a design-driven trip to explore estates and gardens. Additionally, Jefferson spent fifteen weeks visiting various towns and sites in France and northern Italy; his journeys were extended a year later to encompass Amsterdam, parts of Germany, and the Netherlands. Despite Jefferson's fevered travels throughout Europe, he never traveled to the Veneto to see the works of Palladio in person, nor made it to Rome to see the work of the ancients. Nonetheless, Jefferson was able to see classical design in France, "here I am gazing whole hours at the Maison quarrée [sic], like a lover at his mistress." The pseudoperipteral hexastyle temple, then-turned church, was constructed by Marcus Vipsanius Agrippa from 19-16 BC.

While Jefferson was in France, he was approached to design the Virginia State Capitol and quickly took the opportunity to introduce his fellow Americans to the classical designs that had attracted his architectural attention at the Maison Carrée, "a specimen of taste in our infancy, promising much for our maturer age." The idea that architecture could elevate the culture and international reputation of a nation was one shared by Jefferson and Soane; this topic will be addressed later with particular reference to the collections that furnished the respective house museums of Jefferson and Soane.

Jefferson did not think that his sole experience in Europe would be during the years of 1784-1789. When he returned to America, he was immediately asked to take the position of Secretary of State under Washington. Jefferson continued to serve the nation, eventually as Vice President and then President, until 1809 and finally took permanent retirement from political life at the age of sixty-six. Despite Jefferson's demanding national posts he never abandoned work at Monticello. In fact, when he returned from France, he approached the project with renewed enthusiasm. After experiencing the invigorating architecture of Europe, both ancient and contemporary, it was also no coincidence that Jefferson's initial version of Monticello was almost completely demolished. He came home with new ideas and ambitions that could not be contained within the polite architectural frame of his initial home that adhered to a strict Palladian ideal. Armed with the experience of visiting both ancient and contemporary buildings, Jefferson came to better understand the rules of classicism, and more importantly, he began to break those rules. Nonetheless, it is important to note that Jefferson did not bring his mountaintop to a tabula rasa. Jefferson demolished, altered, and expanded upon the conception of his original Monticello. Design and construction at Monticello melded into a sine curve of peaks and valleys. One could infer that such an erratic process meant that Jefferson was indecisive or never had a holistic conception of his mountaintop home. On the contrary, I assert that Jefferson's ability to continually revisit his design displayed the flexibility of a mature architect, secure in his craft. Jefferson was able to edit, add, and manipulate his home without the impulse to literally go back to the drawing board every time an idea or dilemma presented itself. Additionally, the fact that Jefferson retained portions of Monticello I's plan illustrates that his initial design parti was not completely abandoned due to his educational experiences abroad.

John Soane had similar series of early, transformative events to those of Jefferson: urban exposure, higher education, and foreign travel. Soane deliberately obscured his early life and education since he thought his humble beginnings would be detrimental to his career as a notable, professional architect. Therefore, the knowledge of Soane's early life is relegated to the vague statement in his autobiographical Memoirs on the Professional Life of and Architect, privately printed in 1835, that he was, "led by natural inclination to study architecture at age fifteen." As a fifteen year-old, Soane entered the office of surveyor James Peacock through the association of a 'near relative.' Eventually he found a job in bustling London as a messenger boy at the office of George Dance the Younger and eventually moved in with the family on Chiswell Street in London. Under the apprenticeship of Dance, who inherited the position of Clerk of City Works in London from his father, Soane was exposed to a vast architectural library, prominent contemporary architects, met future clients and made connections to eventually enroll as a professional student. While at Dance's office Soane saw the groundbreaking work at Newgate Prison, a project that Jefferson wrote about in letters to friends and possibly saw while visiting England.

Six weeks after his eighteenth birthday, Soane became a student of architecture at the newly formed Royal Academy. Although the Academy had been open for three years, Soane was only the twelfth student to enroll in the architectural program. According to his professors he was not a natural draftsman, "at no period was Soane distinguished for mastery of his pencil and his reputation has rested on the design, not on the drawings, of his conceptions." The lack of technical facility with

architectural drafting was something Soane shared with Jefferson. When Jefferson returned from his duties as Minister to France he brought back with him what he considered one of the most brilliant innovations of the modern age: graph paper. Despite Soane's lack of natural draftsmanship, his tireless efforts over the drafting board would eventually win him the opportunity to develop his architectural education abroad.

Unlike Jefferson who inherited thousands of acres of land from his father, Soane's fortunes as a young man were extremely limited. Therefore, it was a critical turning point in Soane's career that he won the Gold Medal from the Royal Academy: under this honor Soane was afforded a trip to Italy by King George III. Soane embarked on the trip at the age of twenty-four and spent 18 months traveling, studying, and drawing. When Soane visited Pompeii it was deemed illegal to draw so he supposedly climbed the walls at night to sketch the ruins in the moonlight; lessons learned from Pompeii would later appear in the design for his home. While in Italy he also had the fortune of meeting Piranesi. While visiting with the ailing artist and antiquarian, Soane was presented with four engraved plates of Paestum. These engravings were instrumental additions to the humble beginnings of Soane's pictures gallery that would later become a critical element of his home at Lincoln's Inn Fields.

Soane returned from Italy in 1780 and set up his own architectural practice the following year. Twelve years of flurried activity passed between Soane's return from Italy and his first designs for Lincoln's Inn Fields: Soane took on his first architectural student, he married, saw the birth of four sons (two would live into adulthood), had several architectural commissions and was appointed architect to the Bank of England. Soane was well practiced as a designer before he dove into the task of designing Lincoln's Inn Fields, unlike Jefferson who tackled Monticello as his first endeavor. This chronological difference highlights a key distinction between Jefferson and Soane as architects of their own homes: Jefferson was a gentleman architect whereas Soane was a professional architect. Jefferson's fortunes, or lack thereof given the exorbitant debt that would accumulate towards the ends of his life, were not dependent on his designs. Therefore, as a self-trained, gentleman architect—Jefferson was his own first client. Monticello was not designed to impress investors in order to procure future architectural commissions. The home was designed by a trained surveyor and practicing farmer as a working plantation, self-catered to the needs of an eclectic bibliophile, politician and family man. As a professional architect, Soane had the ability to completely devote himself to the study and practice of architecture; however, he had to earn a living from the profession. Soane had to establish a career, client base and income before he could be self-indulgent and tackle the design of his own residence. Although Soane was successful as a professional architect, it was the death of Eliza's uncle George Wyatt in February 1790 that finally afforded Soane the financial flexibility to design his own home. In 1792, Soane purchased no. 12 Lincoln's Inn Fields and immediately began demolition and design. Site Selection: Place as a Personification

At first glance, Jefferson's plantation home in the Blue Ridge Mountains and Soane's townhouse in the bustling metropolis of London have little in common: one man sought solitude while the other chose to surround himself with the chaos of urban living. Jefferson began with a picturesque mountaintop; although not without constraining factors. Jefferson selected the site for his residence as a young boy when he told friend Dabny Carr that he would one day build his home on the little mountain west of the Jefferson family homestead, Shadwell. As a fourteen year-old, it is doubtful that Jefferson thought about the problems such a site would pose: water was constantly low on the mountaintop, skilled craftsmen had to be solicited for the rather remote location and many building materials had to be transported up the treacherous mountainside since the existing natural resources were not sufficient. Furthermore, for a designer, a blank slate can prove the most problematic and difficult of tasks although seemingly ideal. The issues of too many options can drive the designer to functional and aesthetic disarray. Soane's site selection, however, resulted in the exact opposite of problems. His site was already stamped with a townhouse with a meandering parti wall and the building codes that governed Lincoln's Inn Fields were strict and numerous. Although seemingly desperate, the site selections of Jefferson and Soane share crucial ideals. Both gentlemen chose sites that were most conducive to their personalities: Jefferson, the ever-introspective naturalist, sought a place for solitude, study and expansive connections with nature while Soane, the ambitious self-promoter, chose to be in the center of professional, social and bureaucratic circles. For both men, the site was a personification.

Monticello

In many of his own writings, Jefferson asserts himself as a reluctant statesman; however, the fact that his career spanned more than forty years adds doubt to this claim. Jefferson often writes of his current position or appointment as his last only to find himself again in the throes of governmental service,

> I had retired after five and twenty years of constant occupation in public affairs, and total abandonment of my own. I retired much poorer than when I entered the public service, and desired nothing but rest and oblivion. My name, however, was again brought forward [for the Presidency], without concert or expectation on my part.

Although Jefferson's actions seem to prove contradictory to that of an adverse representative, the site selection for his home resonates the ambitions of solitary man that wanted nothing more than to escape the public eye and enjoy the quiet pursuits of a farmer and family man. Jefferson was an ingrained Virginian by the time he broke ground at the mountaintop and familiar with the plantation lifestyle after a childhood spent at residences like Shadwell and Tuckahoe. Throughout Jefferson's career he was constantly pulled away from his home to fulfill the duties of his appointed post: Williamsburg, Richmond, France, Philadelphia, and Washington. It is irrelevant to speculate whether Jefferson predicted that much of his life would be spent away from his chosen place of residence; however, it is important to note that he never abandoned Monticello as his permanent residence and dwelling of choice in favor of the convenience of city life. The mountaintop was a retreat for Jefferson, a landscape reminiscent of his childhood that looked upon the nation's urban growth rather than existed within it. Jefferson's hermetic site selection illustrated his search for Pliny's concept of *otium*, a villa for retreat. Conversely, Soane extricated himself from the quietude country living and inserted himself in the matrix of the urban milieu.
Sir John Soane Museum

Soane's selection of a townhouse on the north side of Lincoln's Inn Fields was the result of careful site study. By selecting the townhouse at no. 12 Lincoln's Inn Fields, Soane put himself in proximity to many of the larger building initiatives in London as well as the social circles where patrons operated. Additionally, he secured a site with generous southern light and a pristine view of the largest garden in central London. While in London Jefferson presumably walked by the urban garden and his passing presence was at a crucial juncture for Lincoln's Inn Fields. The program of the fields was changing from a simple, green garden to that of an organized and designed landscape of paths and a central basin. Although Jefferson would have passed Lincoln Inn's Fields six years before Soane purchased his first townhouse, it is easy to imagine that Jefferson the naturalist recognized the spatial benefits that homes adjacent to the fields reaped in contrast to the congestion of London's typical urban fabric.

Soane's move to central London displayed his architecturally driven initiative to insert himself into the culture of a growing, vibrant city:

> London is the place where an impression as to the state of art is first made, from whence the art itself is expected to emanate. It is the place wherein the wealthy and enlightened of every class are congregated. It must therefore be considered as the great theatre best suited for displaying the abilities and calling into action the talents of the learned of every description.

For Soane and his evolving architectural career, his residential location was crucial in establishing his presence as a legitimate architect. Nonetheless, it must be noted that although seemingly an ideal location, Soane's selection of Lincoln's Inn Fields posed many problems. The townhouse at number 12 Lincoln's Inn Fields was constructed in 1657 and the parti wall followed the medieval farming plots. Therefore, the east parti wall was angled to the northwest, creating a plan that narrowed drastically on the northern end of the residence. Unlike Jefferson who leveled a mountaintop, excavated and then freely built upon Virginia clay, Soane was forced to design his residence within a strict set of parameters. Lincoln's Inn Fields was run by a Board of Trustees established by an Act of Parliament. The homes surrounding the fields were governed by stringent design parameters and eventually Soane went to court over alleged infractions. Although Soane tested the limits of the architectural review board, the majority of his creative impetus spent was away from the leering public eyes focused on the facade of his townhome. His design was internalized, and he spent more than forty years shaping and reshaping the interior of his home and its connections to the ground and sky.

Distinctive Elements: reading the design of Monticello and Sir John Soane's Museum in parallel

Axes

As noted earlier, both Jefferson and Soane created realms within their homes for quiet study and contemplation. These realms are composed of a series of rooms with views to the public areas of the house. Although the realms are situated away from the main entry axis of the home both afford the designer a visual command of the activities of the home, both inside and outside.

At Monticello, nearly one-third of the ground floor plan is designated for Jefferson's private use. The series of rooms that compose Jefferson's private realm are the Library, Cabinet or study, Bedchamber, Greenhouse, and the interstitial spaces known as the Venetian Porches. Jefferson's quadrant of private space completely occupies the southern side of Monticello, providing him with optimal light year-round. In many ways, Jefferson's design for his private rooms in the home labels him a selfish architect. At times there were more than twenty-three family members living in Monticello; their cramped conditions were in stark contrast to the spacious accommodations Jefferson resided in behind closed doors. Additionally, one of the most used public spaces in the house was relegated to the worst solar orientation: the Dining Room faces north and was subject to both harsh prevailing winds and little solar gain in the winter. Arguably, this rash design decision was primarily based upon the fact that Jefferson wanted his personal spaces to be the most occupiable in the home since the bulk of his day was spent in his Library, experimenting in the Greenhouse and pouring over the writing desk.

From Jefferson's personal quadrant in Monticello, he formed a command center for monitoring the outside activities of the mountaintop. From windows in the four rooms Jefferson could observe the east carriage path, south terrace, portions of Mulberry Row (the light industrial area of Monticello where many slaves lived and worked) and the West Lawn. Additionally, from his studious cocoon, Jefferson had access by two doorways into the Entrance Hall. These two doorways, however, were not simple thresholds. Each door leading from Jefferson's private realm was attached to a liminal space. The south hallway from the Library to the Entrance Hall was seemingly redundant. However, this second door is another assertion of Jefferson's control of lines of vision within the home. If the door between the Entrance and south hallway was left open, Jefferson had a clear view into the museum area of the home through the Library's glazed door. Thus visitors, both friends and uninvited guests, had a vista into Jefferson's cosseted spaces. The Entrance Hall doorway provided for privacy between the public and private areas. With this opaque door closed, Jefferson was shielded from the prying eyes of visitors; yet, he could still monitor the private activities of the south hallway, particularly the stairs, from behind his glazed Library door. The second door leading from Jefferson's private realm is in the Bedroom. However, there is not just a singular door separating this bedchamber from the Entrance Hall but rather a second one assuring a spatial pocket. This spatial sequence is repeated at the entrances to the Octagonal Room and North Square Room, the only two guest bedrooms in the home on the ground floor. The sequence of two doors may have simply been a result of Jefferson's constant design changes to Monticello. However, I would argue for the purposeful placement of these sequences: they provide a thermal buffer within a home notoriously difficult to heat and the redundant doors act as spatial signifiers that space one is about to enter is private.

The architectural composition of Jefferson's private realm in Monticello is the most complex in the home. The linear connections, constructed vistas, geometries and sectional relationships between the four enclosed rooms of Jefferson's introspective realms are also the most intriguing in the home. The energy Jefferson spent creating his ideal working and resting environments were manifest in the details. The undulating character of the polygonal rooms defines individual zones but also creates fluidity and a sense of unencumbered, open space. Typically, one would expect a bedchamber to be the most sheltered, womb-like space within the sequence. However, Jefferson's bedchamber is the most luminous and elevated. The bedroom is, nonetheless, the "relaxed" space of Jefferson's realm in comparison to the contained, focused room of the Cabinet.

A similar condition of designed isolation with the benefit of prime views exists at Sir John Soane's Museum. Soane's private realm was located on the ground floor, like Jefferson's residence. Also, like Jefferson, the sequence of rooms was located directly adjacent to one of the most public rooms in the house: the Dining Room. Soane's realm for privacy was a linear series of spaces containing an office, dressing room and privy. This linear progression, rather than the massing approach at Monticello, causes an experiential blur in the zone as to whether it is a corridor, or a series of spaces intended as pauses within the flow of the home.

The north-south axis of Soane's realm bridges the area between the arranged formality of the Dining Room and Library with the chaotic condition of the museum area. Soane had the ability to monitor visitors to the home from the south-facing door. To the north, Soane had a prime view of the juncture between the museum and the Picture Gallery as well as the stairway to the Student's Room. Any unadvised activities on the part of his young pupils could be detected immediately. On the east-west axis Soane's spaces for reflection and study separated the two courtyards of the home. To the west Soane had a prime vantage point into the Monument Court and its unique *pasticcio*. The planar character of the windows facing this courtyard as well as the composed architectural cacophony of the *pasticcio* created a modernist composition of exterior spaces. Directly across the small court Soane could peer into the Breakfast Room of no. 13. The Breakfast Room was the domestic heart and arguably the most architecturally influential space in the home. To the east, Soane's Dressing Room looked upon a contrasting condition to the modern Monument Court: the contrived ruins of Monk's court. Through arrangement of the two courtyards Soane literally surrounded himself with architectural inspiration from the past and present.

Stairs

The staircases at both Monticello and Sir John Soane's Museum are design curiosities. The stairs are not on the central entry axis of the home; therefore, their presence is secondary to the linear circulation of the ground floor plan. Nonetheless, the constrained, elegant staircases create powerful vertical extrusions within the homes. The stairs are not grandiose or processional, yet they are captivating through their irregular rise and run rhythms, curvilinear character and unexpected illumination from skylights. Finally, in homes with distinct hierarchies ranging from owner/architect to family to acquaintance, student, servant, and even slave, it is important to note that there is not a distinction between the servant's vertical movement and that of the rest of the household. There is only shared vertical circulation with implied boundaries.

Jefferson's initial designs for the stairs of Monticello were awkward and uninspired. Early study plans that date 1768-1770 show a simple rectilinear ground plan with a matching, prescriptive stair arrangement. If the plans are read in a similar manner, taking note of the first study plans annotation that the "front [is] to the south if convenient", the drawings are oriented with the top of the page signifying north. The stairway on both study plans is in the northeast corner of the home, illuminated by one window on the east. A door to the north is also within the stairway corridor. Between the two study plans it is evident that Jefferson was debating the axial alignment of the stair corridor within the composition of the ground floor plan since one plan has a southern, interior doorway on axis with the exterior stairway corridor door and one plan slightly shifts the southern door off this axis. The study plans show a stairway arrangement that is banal and almost labyrinthine in comparison to fluid circulation between rooms on the ground floor. The subsequent surviving study plan for Monticello from 1770 shows a drastically different, more dynamic ground floor arrangement lacking stairs. This possibly infers that Jefferson was considering designing only a one story home or could signify an unfinished plan. The drawing is devoid of the poché that Jefferson typically used in his architectural drawings. Therefore, the plan may illuminate the problem Jefferson was grappling with in terms of designing an interesting, efficient stair arrangement. The next set of study plans, from 1771-72, display Jefferson's introduction of the semi-octangular rooms and dual porticos. These plans represent what most historians refer to as Monticello I. A small annotation on the right of the page labels the "North Bow-room". This signifies a change in the orientation of the drawings: the previous study plans were oriented true north; however, now the top of the page is west. This possibly explains why contemporary orthogonal drawings of Monticello are not cardinally oriented. Nonetheless, more critical than the altered orientation of the plan is the new configuration of the stairs. Instead of the standard, single-run rectangular stairs of the earlier study plans, the 1771 plan shows a smaller, dog-leg stair adjacent to the primary north-south circulation axis. The stair is still illuminated by a single window. The subsequent plan of the ground floor and dependencies, c.1772, shows that the east-facing cubical protrusions now each contain a wrapping switchback square stair. Although the stairs turning the corners have been replaced with square landings, the turning detail later returned in the final design of the home. Jefferson's insertion of a set of symmetrical stairs within a defined geometric solid, a square, show the influence of Palladio's' designs. The design evolution of stairs at Monticello show that Jefferson moved away from the linear, colonial arrangement of stairways connected to an entry corridor in favor of a more refined, neoclassical configuration of stairs tucked away from the central, axial circulation of the house.

Between the evolution of Monticello, I to the current configuration of the home, the stairs were moved from protruding square bays of the east facade to be tucked along north-south axis that bisects the home. The quarter turn stairs are economical in size at only twenty-two inches wide. The nine-inch risers emphasize the vertical extrusion of the stairs and the treads that irregularly turn the corners make the stairs somewhat difficult to navigate and accentuate the sense of spiraling in the narrow procession between floors. The steep stairs were designed

to Jefferson's specifications as noted: "The risers are to the treads 3 to 4, to wit 7 ½ & 10. This is the ancient proportion, and preferable to the modern of 2 to 1, which is so tedious that every person prefers going 2 steps at a time, tho' that be rather laborious."

Throughout the study plans Jefferson drew windows adjacent to the stairway; in the final design the windows were manifested vertically in the form of skylights. Through the use of skylights Jefferson was able to internalize the stairs without comprising his desire to naturally illuminate the vertical circulation of the house. Although small in scale, no detail of the staircases was left unfinished by Jefferson: a rare, surviving interior elevation shows the constrained stair as well as a detail for the balusters.

The two identical stairways of Monticello were used by all members of the household. Instead of a grand central stair to occupy the Entrance Hall paired with hidden service stairs, Jefferson's stairs were a democratic design compromise. Within Monticello the act of ascending or descending was not a spectacle, but rather one of necessity within a busy household. Just as Jefferson's site selection was a personification, the stairs also expressed his personal convictions. Numerous quotes from Jefferson illuminate his stance against all forms of wastefulness. The stairs of Monticello were a supreme exercise in efficiency in terms of space, heat, and light.

The same themes of utility, compression and illumination are present within the configuration of stairs at Sir John Soane's Museum, albeit in a more expressive, dynamic manner. As stated earlier, Soane's first townhouse at no.12 Lincoln's Inn Fields proved to be a challenging design exercise. The drastically narrowing plan made light precious and circulation difficult. The townhouse's plan was further encumbered by a large stairway. Soane spent a little over a month drawing options to reconfigure the ground plan for a more efficient use of space, diffusion of southern light into the deep site, and cohesive circulation system in place of the existing weighty stairway. Soane's masterful reorientation and geometrical manipulation of the stairway in no. 12 Lincoln's Inn's Fields asserted his ability as an architect to sequence spaces and control light. As illustrated in the 1796 plan, the oval stairway followed the angle of the medieval parti wall, proving both an entry sequence and a break in massing between the public and private portions of the small townhouse. Like Jefferson's stair, the no. 12 oval well staircase turns the corners fluidly to emphasize the spiraling character of the space and the stairway itself is illuminated by a generous skylight.

With the acquisition of no. 13, Soane was able to expand both the house and museum as well as design another unique stair. The stairway of no. 13 was designed as a manipulation of Soane's asymmetrical oval stairway of no.12. Unlike no.12, the stairway was located off the entry axis of the home and obscured by two small thresholds. Study plans from the summer of 1812 show that Soane experimented with an axial service stair, small and tucked within a rectangular recess adjacent to the northwest corner of the courtyard. These study plans show Soane's design struggle regarding the vertical circulation with the home verses that of the museum area. Various stairways would be added and destroyed within the museum area as Soane grappled with the two distinct programs of house and museum competing for circulation space. The final design of the home as it stands today is composed of four stairways: the unique asymmetrical oval stairs of no.12, no.13, and no.14 (detached from the program of the house museum and used for the rented residence) and the constrained switchback stair used for the

Museum and Student Room. The asymmetrical oval stairs of each townhouse give a greater sense of space to the fairly small square footage. The switchback stair on north wall of the museum is jarringly similar to the tight spiral of Monticello's stairways. The risers are steep but illuminated from a skylight above. Much like Monticello, the character of the stair changes drastically from the stone-clad bowels of the home to the light, plastered attic space of the upper stories.

For both Jefferson and Soane, the staircases at their respective homes were not simply means to get from floor to floor but also expressions of each man's social theories. Jefferson's stairs were democratic and utilitarian; Soane's were an expression of aesthetic hierarchy. Soane's eighth lecture as a Royal Academy professor detailed his theories on vertical circulation. He stated that the six things to attend to in regards to the design of staircases were situation, magnitude, form, lighting, decoration and construction. Soane also stated that, "stairs in country homes are secondary in consideration since they lead to inferior apartments but more important in homes in towns because the best rooms are usually on the first floor." The staircases of Soane's house museum illustrated the aforementioned statement. The staircases of no. 12 and especially that of no. 13 were intended to be architectural objects, vertical extrusions lit by distinctive skylights. However, these architectural objects are not on the entry axis or were obscured by walls thereby making the full revelation of the staircase's unusual forms a process of discovery within the progression of the home. The staircase along the north wall of the Museum is diminutive in size, materiality, and placement to the stairs of no. 12 and no. 13 but I argue that this is not because the museum stair is a service stair but rather is aesthetically diminutive to the collections of the museum space. Soane did not place an 'object' stair in his museum as to not distract from the architectural fragments and sculptures: the simplicity of the stair compliments the chaos of the collections.

Today the stairs of Monticello and the Sir John Soane Museum still retain a certain hierarchy between the "servant and served". Both house museums are instruments for the education and exploration of the public; the curators and staff within serve this program. At both house museums, curators and staff occupy the upper floors of the homes as offices, workrooms and spaces for additional collection storage. The bowels of each home still serve utilitarian, domestic functions as kitchens, break rooms, and storage areas. Instead of doors or thresholds that signify "employee only" areas, the stairs serve as the privileged boundary between the activities of the general public visiting the house museums and the employees. These boundaries, however, are not implied as they were in the times of Jefferson's or Soane's residence, but rather chains and alarms now mark the line between the servants of the public programs and the served.

Light

Natural light enlivens both Monticello and Sir John Soane's museum causing dramatic chiaroscuro. Light is an active participant in the character of each home and much of the natural light is brought into the home through the unexpected incorporation of skylights. Jefferson and Soane were known connoisseurs of the quality of natural light within their homes: Jefferson's daily routines were sculpted around the seasonal changes in light and Soane was known to dismiss visitors to his home on a dark and dreary day in favor of their return on a day with optimal natural lighting conditions. Both architects wanted to capture as much natural light as possible for their residences to enliven the architectural spaces and showcase the contained collections. Light is harvested, filtered and manipulated at both Monticello and Soane's home through a variety of methods. Jefferson's triple sash windows provided grand views into the landscape, natural ventilation through their operability, and could be encased by exterior shutters or interior wainscot shutters that could be pulled from the thickness of the wall. Soane used a similar shutter system for the southern facing windows of his town home.

Soane's use of windows seems to be ruled by convenience and composition; however, the meticulous mathematician Jefferson derived a "Light Rule" that was recorded in his building notebook. Although both architects incorporated skylights into the design of their homes, certainly an unconventional aperture for the time, both used these light sources in distinctly different ways. Jefferson's skylights are utilitarian, lighting spaces that would otherwise be devoid of glazing such as the staircases, attic hallway, bedrooms on the third story. Of the three most intriguing skylights in Jefferson's design: his bedroom, the Dining Room, and oculus of the Dome Room, only one is located in a room designated for public use. Soane's skylights were utilitarian, illuminating interior spaces without access to natural light given the narrow townhouse site. However, Soane's skylights, with the exception of those in his Dressing Room and Breakfast Room, were located in portions of the house museum intended for public and student use. For Soane, each skylight was an opportunity to highlight his experimentations with form and color.

Jefferson's initial encounter with the use of skylights was in France at his rented home in the Hôtel de Langeac. Jefferson's final iteration of Monticello contained thirteen skylights, including the Dome Room's oculus that measures fifty-four inches in diameter. With the exception of the oculus, the skylights are composed of clear rectangular panels of glass, layered much like a shingle. The layered composition of the skylights was possibly utilized for ease of construction or due to Jefferson's hesitation to use a solitary, fragile piece of glass over such a large expanse. The odd shape of the skylights that taper in three dimensions towards the sky in Jefferson's Bedroom and the Dining Room were supposedly designed so that a person standing six feet tall could see the glass of the opening from any point in the room. Although the tilt of the skylights in Jefferson's bedroom and the Dining Room correspond to the slope of the roof, from the interior of the each room the angle is perceived as a gestural slant within the space.

Just as Jefferson's neatly composed, strictly balanced facades conceal the irregular sectional character of the house, the rigidly symmetrical roof plan masks the asymmetrical placement of some of the skylights within the interior composition of the home. The large skylight in Jefferson's Bedroom is not in the center of the ceiling, like that of the Dining Room, even though the bedroom forms the symmetrical counterpart in plan. The reason for the discrepancy is that Jefferson's alcove bed, with a storage closet framed above, separates the bedroom from the semi-octagonal Cabinet room. This additional form breaks the massing of the larger square composition of the room in plan. The third floor is lit only by the presence of skylights; however, two of the three bedrooms located on this floor do not have their sole lighting source placed symmetrically within the space. The central bedroom and south bedroom of the third floor both have skylights place in the southeast corner of the room. The skylights are not visible from the exterior on the ground; however, Jefferson's desire for a balanced roof plan determined the placement of the apertures within the interior spaces of the home. It is as if Jefferson anticipated the aerial photographs that capture the pure symmetry and order of the roof within the irregular natural landscape.

While studying and drawing in Rome and its environs Soane undoubtedly saw the skylights and oculus forms that were incorporated in ancient architecture. Buildings such as the Pantheon, illuminated only by the twenty-seven-foot diameter oculus, must have inspired young Soane in his future architectural projects that were so consumed with natural light and chiaroscuro. For Soane's home at Lincoln's Inn Fields, the incorporation of skylights was an act of necessity. Natural lighting was constrained by the townhouse's arrangement: there were parti walls to the east and west and the north facade faced the undesirable alley conditions of a carriage drive. The only facade Soane could puncture with windows was the south. Although Soane would eventually create two small courtyards within the plan of the three, combined townhomes, the primary method for bringing light into the house museum was the insertion of skylights. Unlike the symmetrically arranged skylights of Monticello, the skylights of Soane's home are all varied and placed sporadically along the roofline. Looking upon the roof of the museum area from the Drawing Room or upper floors of the private residence, the skylights and transparent domes occupying Soane's roof form the skyline of a futuristic city of glass.

Many of the earliest design sketches and perspectives for the house museum, composed mainly by Soane's students, incorporate skylights. The spaces, vividly illustrated with pen washes to denote light and shadow, are illuminated only by an overhead source. Many sketches do not include an image of the skylight itself thereby rendering spaces with mystical light qualities. The use of mysterious light would also appear in Joseph Gandy's iconic and alluring watercolors of the house museum. Through the use of diffused light, the collections and architectural spaces of the museum meld into a cohesive whole. Today, visitors can see more than thirty different skylights and domes in the house museum. Additionally, the skylights of Soane's home reflect his interest in manufactured objects. Unlike the simple panes of glass placed within counterweighted wooden frames at Monticello, the skylights of Soane's home are all uniquely molded with lead sealants and iron details.

Skylights were not the only unconventional apertures utilized at Monticello or Soane's Museum. Jefferson placed small, square windows in three of the metopes of the frieze on the southern façade, directly above the Greenhouse. These small windows correspond to the nursery on the second floor. The windows are carefully placed within the design constraints of the classically-modeled Doric frieze; however, they add a modernist detail to the home. An additional design anomaly of Monticello incorporating glass is the double-glazed transom separating the Dining Room and Tea Room. At Soane's home there are several metal grates in the dome-museum area. These grates, varying in size, puncture the floor and allow light from the top-lit Museum to penetrate into the crypt level. The use of grates allowed Soane to retain circulation within the tight confines of the ground floor of museum and created a relationship between the cavernous spaces of the crypt and light-filled dome-museum area. The rough, tunnel-like spaces of the Crypt at Soane's home are mirrored in the all-weather passageway of Monticello. This linear service corridor recalls a similar, excavated character. The passageway is a cryptoporticus lit by half-moon windows that connects the domestic operations of the home. The subterranean spaces of the all-weather passageway at Monticello and crypt of Soane's Museum illustrate that each architect wanted to create spaces in their homes that seemed out of place and time, illuminated only by small punctures.

Mirrors

At Monticello and Sir John Soane's Museum mirrors are used to extend spaces and sometimes disorient the viewer. It must be noted prior to discussing the use of mirrors at Monticello that the interior furnishings and arrangements of the house have been altered since Jefferson's lifetime. Due to Soane's wonderful forethought through the Act of Parliament to preserve the house museum, one can walk through the home today with the eerie feeling that Soane has just stepped out for the moment. Unfortunately, the preserved placement of objects does not exist at Monticello. Following Jefferson's death, his possessions were liquidated at a dispersal sale in order to settle for the massive debt he had acquired during the course of his lifetime. Therefore, the placement of many objects in Monticello is based upon an inventory by his daughter Martha, a sketched plan by his granddaughter Cordelia, visitor accounts and Jefferson's own written records.

Jefferson's Monticello does not match the disorienting number of mirrors at Soane's home, but at both homes the viewer encounters concave and convex mirrors, large looking glass sections and has a distinct impression that mirrors are not objects utilized for grooming but rather spatial manipulation. Jefferson's Cabinet has a large concentration of mirrors that accentuate the angles of this semi-octagonal space and making it appear larger. A lunette mirror in Jefferson's Bedroom is adorned with candles to reflect light at night and is affixed to the wall at a height too elevated for even the tall Jefferson to use the piece as a shaving mirror. In both his bedroom and the Parlor there are large, multi-paneled mirrors placed directly across from triple sash windows. This arrangement continually pulls the viewer's gaze towards the landscape. The room with the most complex use of mirrors in the home is the Dome Room of the third floor. This octagonal room has large bull's eye windows on six walls; two of these windows have mirrors on the bottom halves in order to conceal the fact that the Dome Room intersects with the roof line of the home. The placement of mirrors creates an illusion that the room is an isolated construction.

The small space of Soane's Breakfast Room in no. 13 Lincoln's Inn Fields contains more mirrors than all of Monticello. Soane used small convex mirrors along the ribs of the canopy dome and tall, thin looking glass panels adjacent to the piers and window jambs to create an illusion of space in an otherwise small room. Two small "windows" separate the Breakfast Room from the Museum Dome; both of these panels are covered with mirrors that create a dynamic illusion between the Breakfast Room and Museum Dome. The rooms can appear in isolation when the windows are closed, and the mirrors reflect the room's architecture. When these windows are open, there is an opposing balance between the Breakfast Room and Museum Dome. The warm tones of paint, carpet, colored glass, and wood in the Breakfast Room contrast with the cool atmosphere of stone, plaster, lead and clear glass in the Museum Dome.

Additional retreats

Although Jefferson and Soane invested more than forty years into the design and alteration of their house museums each gentleman also owned a retreat property. In the early 1800s Jefferson began designing Poplar Forest, a 5,000-acre plantation home located approximately ninety miles south of Monticello. Jefferson designed an octagonal home raised on a piano forte and flanked by earthwork, dependencies and freestanding octagonal privies. Jefferson left a small amount of documentary evidence about the design and evolution of Monticello; unfortunately, he left an even smaller amount of drawings and writings about Poplar Forest. The design process at Poplar Forest was fast-paced compared to that of Monticello. Jefferson's political career kept him away from Monticello for years on end, yet he took a two month break from residency at the President's house in Washington to oversee the laying of the foundations at Poplar Forest. Unlike Monticello, Poplar Forest actually functioned as a profitable plantation and the residence truly served as a retreat for the retired statesman. Through his retirement, Jefferson annually would spend a few months at Poplar Forest, but Monticello always remained the center of his architectural focus. At the same time Jefferson was designing Poplar Forest, Soane was engaged in the design of Pitzhanger Manor. He purchased the 'country' house in 1800. The property consisted of twenty-eight acres and the existing home had a wing designed by George Dance the Younger, Soane's mentor for a period of time. Envisioning the property as a prime location to receive clients and participate in the rich artistic culture of London Soane rapidly made adaptations to the home and even commissioned Joseph Gandy to create a series of watercolor images depicting the sublime residence. Soane finished his alterations to the existing home around April 1804 and even constructed Roman ruins on the grounds. He viewed the property as an ideal location to cultivate his own architectural dynasty and hoped that his young sons would be captivated by their surroundings. Regrettably, his sons were not enamored with Pitzhanger; he sold residence in 1810 and turned his personal architectural attentions to the alteration of no. 13 Lincoln's Inn Fields.

Creating Curiosity: Museum Collections and Libraries

The Age of the Enlightenment was a philosophical movement that questioned conventions, morals and religion. Largely centered in France, England and Germany the movement later spread through Europe and eventually crossed the Atlantic. The pedagogy of enlightenment, derived through public discourse and private study, directly related to shifts in built space. Under the patronage of the Enlightenment the museum and library became prevalent architectural programs. Until the Enlightenment, most structurally innovative, ornate and spatially awe-inspiring works of architecture were either sacred spaces or projects sponsored by empires. Architects of the Enlightenment challenged the precedent of architectural hierarchies and introduced inspirational spaces intended for non-secular, public use. For example, the British Museum, opened in 1759, was the first purpose-built national museum opened to the public. Architecture in the private realm also evolved during the Enlightenment: French architects of the mid-eighteenth century like Étienne-Louis Boullée and Nicolas-Claude Ledoux penned innovative designs for the cooper, surveyor and industrial worker. Suddenly, spaces designed by trained architects were not solely reserved for wealthy aristocrats. As for the architecture of introspection, libraries became more common outside of the secular world. Quiet study was no longer reserved for the cloistered as it was in the Age of Humanism and for the first time silent reading, as opposed to reading aloud among a group, was prevalent. Public structures like the British Museum opened magnificent reading rooms and libraries became part of the programmatic language of private residences.

Jefferson and Soane shared a lifelong passion for education as evidenced by their varied collections, extensive personal libraries, and dedication to the edification of their respective countrymen. Jefferson and Soane were both dedicated nationalists that hoped to improve their contemporaries by providing worthy architectural models. For example, while Jefferson was in France he was consulted on the design of the new Virginia State Capitol. Adamantly against the traditions of American colonial architecture he was familiar with from the once-capitol of Virginia, Williamsburg, Jefferson called for a new approach to the architecture of the emerging nation, "how is a taste in this beautiful art to be formed in our countrymen unless we avail ourselves of every occasion when public buildings are to be erected, of presenting to them models for their study and imitation?" Jefferson even saw his own residence as an architectural model: when he was in the process of building his second plantation residence of Poplar Forest, Jefferson said that new plantation would be the best home in the state with the exception of Monticello. Budding American architects like Robert Mills made journeys to Monticello to draw the home and study the wealth of Jefferson's architectural library, the best in the nation at the time. Soane had a similar, nationalistic approach to his architectural work,

The time, not distant far, shall come
When England's tasteful youth no more
Shall wander to Italia's classic shore,
No more to foreign climates shall roam
In search of models better found at home

By surrounding his students with models, casts and recreations Soane created a rich working environment for the young architectural interns. Additionally, Soane's own architectural work in London broke down the conventions of English neoclassicism and paved the way for new, modern architecture in England. For Jefferson and Soane, edifices were not just important for their beauty and programmatic functions; buildings were the keys to unlocking the potential of a country and building an empire of citizens that valued not only aesthetics but also knowledge and nationalism.

Jefferson and Soane both opened their collections of their museums to the public. Jefferson's Entrance Hall at Monticello was filled with maps, Native American "tokens of friendship", fossils and other natural specimens. Although Jefferson had architectural instruments as well as a select number of prints and models, the architectural imagery of the house was largely contained within the neat framework of the entablatures. Jefferson used different architectural orders in different rooms as examples just as Soane placed architectural fragments on the walls of his Museum. As a professional architect, Soane's collections largely related to the built environment: he had casts of details and friezes from ancient buildings, models, drawings and architectural instruments. Soane diversified the collections with items such as sculptures, paintings, gadgetry and natural history samples. Both gentlemen took a varied approach to the arrangement of objects within their private museums. For the most part, items were not arranged thematically or according to size or chronology. The pairing of disparate items next to each other spurred unusual conversations and parallels. Unlike the arrangement of many modern museums where a viewer steps into a room with tight interpretive constraints clearly labeled on the walls (e.g. Impressionist paintings or Assyrian culture), the museums of Jefferson and Soane presented viewers with natural and man-made objects ranging from ancient to modern times all within a single vantage point. They created collages for intellectual exploration.

It is impossible to discuss the collections at Monticello or the Sir John Soane Museum without mentioning books. It is not surprising that two architects of the Enlightenment had similar books in their personal libraries. Although Jefferson had the largest architectural library in America, his titles paled in comparison to Soane's collections. Jefferson library was more varied; the extent of his political and historical texts spoke to his profession as statesman rather than the theoretical and visual resources essential to the library of a professional architect. Although Jefferson had multiple copies and editions of certain architectural texts, such as Palladio and Vitruvius, Soane's repetitive collections were necessary for granting his students access to the most seminal texts. Among architectural authors and theorists shared in the libraries of Jefferson and Soane were Inigo Jones, J. Gibbs, Robert Morris, Edmund Burke, Claude Perrault, A. Desgodets, M.A. Laugier, Alberti, Vignola, and Serlio. Both gentlemen held a large collection of books related to antiquity as well as landscape architecture and gardening. For example, Soane acquired Thomas Whateley's 1770 Observations on modern gardening in 1784; Jefferson used the text as a guidebook while traveling through the English countryside in 1786 and made notes in the margins.

Jefferson knew of a portion of Soane's architectural work through books. Conversely, it is impossible that Soane knew of Jefferson's architecture through books since the statesman was not truly credited as an architect in published, scholarly works until the early twentieth century. However, it was well known in England that Jefferson was the primary author of the Declaration of Independence and a politician. Soane even owned a copy of Cyrus R. Edmond's The life and times of General Washington that contained a facsimile of a draft of the Declaration of Independence. Soane's library contained books published by the American Philosophical Society, an intellectual organization founded by Benjamin Franklin and based in Philadelphia but also largely affiliated with Jefferson. He was elected to the prestigious organization in January 1780 and held the position of President within the organization from March 3, 1797- January 20, 1815. Soane owned the works of Francis Bacon, Sir Isaac Newton and John Locke, the three men represented in Jefferson's "trinity" of paintings in Monticello's Parlor featuring the men Jefferson considered the greatest the world ever produced. Soane also owned a text by a gentleman Jefferson did not hold in such esteem: natural historian George Louis Leclerc, comte de Buffon. The French naturalist argued in his 1785 publication that the humidity of the New World would foster weaker and inferior plants, animals and even people. This concept infuriated the scientific and nationalistic sensibilities in Jefferson to the point that the avid patriot sent Buffon the entire skeleton of an American moose to prove the vast diversity, and sometimes superiority, of American species in relation to those of Europe. It is clear, from even a small sampling of books at both sites that Jefferson and Soane operated in the same intellectual circles and were consulting some of the same texts.

Jefferson and Soane shared a few practices related to the acquisition of books: both gentlemen were attracted to texts with prominent previous owners and went through certain periods of avaricious book collecting. The fortune of inheritance in 1788 gave Soane a flexible income to begin seriously building his library. During the same time period, Jefferson was avidly buying books in France and England. Jefferson was enthralled with the selection of European bookstores during his time as Minister to France, 1784-1789. In those five years abroad, he purchased more than 2,000 volumes. By the early 1800s both gentlemen were receiving books from friends and catalogues from booksellers; their status of collectors was well established.

At both Monticello and Sir John Soane's Museum books were more than static collections on droll shelves. Books represented the variety of interests held by Jefferson and Soane, their lifelong dedication to self-education and their desire to eventually create reference libraries for their fellow countrymen. The libraries at Monticello and Soane's home were open to students and they continue to operate as research libraries for contemporary scholars. Although both Jefferson and Soane had dedicated library spaces, books occupied shelves, mantles and spare places on the floor throughout the home. The varied placement of books throughout rooms of each home displays that the libraries were not exhibits, merely showcasing an investment, but were active collections. At Monticello, Jefferson's fascination with gadgetry even pervaded his library: a custom-designed revolving book stand allowed Jefferson to view five books open at once, "I make it a rule never to read translations when I can read the original."

In both homes, book shelves were integral to the architecture. Monticello's custom-fabricated bookshelves were actually book boxes, individually stacked for easy removal. With the attachment of a piece of wood each book box became a traveling case allowing the peripatetic Jefferson to take a portion of his collections with him. These book boxes differ in height to accommodate volumes from pocket to folio size; stacked one upon another the units fit perfectly within the architecture of the undulating walls in Jefferson's library. Soane's bookshelves contained a similar dynamism through the use of mirrors that multiplied the effect of the ever-growing collections. Additionally, the book cases in the yellow Upper Drawing Room form piers within the hippodrome shape of the room; knowledge literally fortifies the architecture.

There was some semblance of order with the chaos of library collections at Soane's home; however, Jefferson's obsessive personality led to a strict system at Monticello. Jefferson's compulsion for cataloguing fueled his three-prong system of classification for the library: reason, memory and imagination. These classifications can be applied to the subjects of history, philosophy, and the fine arts, respectively. Within these categories Jefferson further specified the division of topics. Jefferson displayed a librarian's consistency towards the arrangement of his collections: he granted certain people access to his collections but was very specific his preferred library etiquette. For example, in a letter to Mr. Ogilvie Jefferson stated that any texts pulled from shelves should be placed on the Cabinet's desk rather than re-shelved improperly.

Although Jefferson spent nearly a lifetime collecting his ideal library, he parted with the majority of the collection in 1815 when he sold 6,487 volumes to the Congress of the United States for $23,950. Soane's library totaled 6,857, only a few hundred books more than the shipment Jefferson sent to Washington. Jefferson's books became the core of the Library Congress, an institution that is currently the world's largest library, acts as a copyright depository for the United States and contains texts in more than 450 languages. The scope and diversity of the contemporary holdings at the Library of Congress were largely influenced by Jefferson's bibliomania, "you know my collection, its condition and extent. I have been fifty years making it, and have spared no pains, opportunity or expense, to make it what it is."

One curiosity of the Library of Congress sale is that Jefferson included his most precious books in the shipment. As a young man he spoke of the difficulty of obtaining certain architectural books and praised the wealth, and bargain, of bookstores in Europe. However, he parted with his carefully acquired texts in order to broaden the collections of the nation. Nonetheless, the sparse shelves of his library must have been distressing to the bibliophile. After sending a letter to friend and fellow statesman John Adams in 1815 stating that he, "cannot live without books," Jefferson began amassing his retirement library. His shelves received collections once again but only with a fraction of the titles he once possessed. Arguably his collection of books on the fine arts was most impacted by the sale. For example, when Jefferson was designing the University of Virginia, he was forced to look outside of his own library for even the most essential architectural references. In 1817 Jefferson wrote to hobbyist architect and former President James Madison, we are sadly at a loss here for a Palladio. I had three different editions, but they are at Washington, and nobody in this part of the country has one unless you have. If you have you will greatly aid us by letting us have the use of it for a year to come." Jefferson at one point called Palladio's books on architecture 'the bible'; yet he parted with the volumes in his 1815 sale to the Congressional Library.

Common Threads: Interpersonal Connections

Throughout my research I pursued the question of whether Thomas Jefferson and John Soane ever met. The only window of opportunity for their acquaintance would be Jefferson's brief visits to England while serving as Minister to France during the years 1784-1789 since Soane was not in France during Jefferson's tenure nor did Soane ever make the journey across the Atlantic. My interest in whether Jefferson and Soane ever met was not the primary focus of my research but rather a question that needed to be addressed: did the two men ever know that they both made such personal architectural laboratories and foundries of knowledge? Although construction at Jefferson's "Essay in Architecture" began twenty-three years before Soane's initial alterations to his first townhouse at Lincoln's Inn Fields, it is an interesting exercise to imagine a conversation on methods, theories and lessons learned that Jefferson could offer Soane over tea in a London coffee house in 1786. Would Jefferson have been confident enough to share his ideas with a professional architect? Would Soane have taken the advice? If the conversation ever meandered outside of the arts, the two gentlemen would have found themselves at a crossroads in terms of their personal lives: Jefferson had taken a post overseas to escape tragedy of his wife's recent death while Soane was just beginning his family.

My research thus far has proved that the two never stood and shook hands, nor exchanged private correspondence. Soane was just beginning to make a name for himself as an architect while Jefferson was in Europe, and their social circles did not overlap or coincide. It was disappointing to confirm with substantial certainty that the two never met; however, the goal of my research was not to investigate their personal relationship but rather to explore the architectural similarities and contrasts of their homes. Nonetheless, after examining the respective social circles of Jefferson and Soane outside of the five short years Jefferson was in Europe, I have discovered interesting interpersonal threads between the two. It is not surprising that two men of the Enlightenment, well-known in their respective countries, would share friends and acquaintances; what is extraordinary about these common threads are some of the particular personalities both gentlemen knew. This section gives a brief synopsis of the person and their connection to Jefferson and Soane. The names are alphabetical, not in order of importance or chronology, but represent the most intriguing connections during my research.

Marquis de Chastellux (1734-1788)

Francois-Jean de Beauvoir, Marquis de Chastellux, came to the United States in 1780 to serve as Major-General with the French troops under the command of the Comte de Rochambeau. During his three-year tenure he traveled and wrote a narrative on life in the newly formed nation that was originally published anonymously in 1781 under the title Voyage de Newport à Philadelphie [sic], Albany. The first enlarged and authorized version of the text was printed in 1786. Soane purchased a copy of the 1786 edition, from John Cumming in Paris. The possession of the book in Soane's library does not ensure he ever read the text, especially considering Soane kept nearly every book, pamphlet and piece of paper he encountered. Nonetheless, a pencil inscription on the front free-endpaper denotes that Soane at least opened the book. Had Soane read Chastellux, he would have discovered a description of Jefferson's Monticello. After spending seven days at Monticello and discussing Jefferson's future plans for the home, Chastellux concluded that the planned revisions would give Monticello ranking among, "the most pleasant mansions of France and England." Monticello, at its present state during Chastellux's visit, was less than appealing:

> [Monticello] of which Mr. Jefferson was the architect, and often the builder, is constructed in an Italian style, and is quite tasteful, although not however without some faults; it consists of a large square pavilion, into which one enters through two porticoes ornamented with columns. The ground floor consists chiefly of a large and lofty salon, or drawing room, decorated entirely in the antique style; above is a library. It resembles none of the others seen in this country; so that it may be said that Mr. Jefferson is the first American who has consulted the Fine Arts to know how he should shelter himself from the weather. [Jefferson] an American, who, without ever having quitted his own country, is Musician, Draftsman, Surveyor, Astronomer, Natural Philosopher, Jurist, and Statesman.

Chastellux did not attribute the poor condition of the home on the tastes of his host but rather commented that the destitute state of affairs at Monticello was due to Jefferson's public service. He complimented Jefferson's design as superior to all other houses in America. If Soane read the commentary on Jefferson and his Monticello it is hard not to imagine Soane's interest in a self-trained architect across the Atlantic that was constructing a house worthy of Chastellux's attention.

Charles-Louis Clérisseau (1721-1820)

Clérisseau was an artist, architect, and expert on the ruins of Rome. Jefferson owned Clérisseau's 1778 publication Antiquités de la France, Prèmiere partie: Monumens de Nismes. The ownership of this book that contained Clérisseau's engravings, nine of which illustrated the Maison Carrée, may have been the reason Jefferson sought out Clérisseau while in France. When Jefferson selected the Maison Carrée as his model for the Virginia State Capitol he enlisted Clérisseau to prepare the finished drawings that would eventually be sent across the Atlantic to be used as construction drawings for the project. Soane's connection to Clérisseau was two-fold. The inside right plane of the north side of Soane's Picture Room contains scenes by Clérisseau of classical ruins. Additionally, Clérisseau instructed one of the most prominent architects of Soane's lifetime: Robert Adam (1728-1792). Clérisseau toured Adam in Rome in 1754, enriching Adam's training as a legitimate architect. In return, Adam was Clérisseau's patron for more than twelve years. Adam went on to become a supremely successful architect in Scotland during the later eighteenth century and in 1833 Soane purchased an archive of more than 9,000 of Adam's drawings. The drawings are still retained by the Soane Museum and will find a new home in Education Centre in no. 14 Lincoln's Inn Fields that will be opened in the near future.

Maria Cosway (1760-1838)

Maria Cosway was an Anglo-Italian musician, artist and wife of a popular and notoriously flamboyant painter. She captured the romantic attention of Jefferson while he was in France. John Trumbull, artist of the life-sized Declaration of Independence painting in the United States Capitol, introduced the two in Paris. Trumbull, later painted for Cosway a miniature of Jefferson in 1788. The miniature was left by Cosway to the Collegio delle Grazie di Maria SS. Bambina in Lodi, Italy, the convent where she spent the remaining years. This miniature portrait displays a well-groomed diplomat serving as a memento of the fleeting Parisian encounter between them. Jefferson and Cosway corresponded, with varying frequency and "affection", from 1786 to 1824, even though the last meeting between the pair was on December 7, 1787. Through their prolonged correspondence, Cosway knew of Jefferson's mountaintop architectural experiment, Monticello; however, she never crossed the Atlantic to see the home in person.

Soane met Cosway, then known by her maiden name Hadfield, at the age of eighteen when he was in Rome studying under the Royal Academy's Gold Medal. The two retained a lifelong friendship as both were involved in London's vibrant arts society. When Cosway eventually moved back to Italy to oversee her convent school she continued communication with her friend. The private correspondence of Soane, held at the Soane Museum, consists of forty-five letters from Maria Cosway, dated from 1806-1834. The majority of the correspondence occurred after 1830 and were typically addressed, "My dear Sir". Many of the letters are written in Italian and include discussion of drawings, paintings, and young architects. Although the letters reveal that the two discussed personal matters, such as friendships and Soane's loss of sight, there was never a mention of Jefferson. Cosway never prompted a discussion of the eclectic American architect nor the redheaded diplomat that may have once captivated her interests, if not her heart.

King George III (1738-1820)

George William Frederick, King George III, formally initiated Soane's career as a professional architect by granting him the funds to travel to Italy, a fundamental excursion for any architect hoping to truly make a name for himself among the elite. Later in life Soane claimed that he showed plans for his designs for the new House of Lords to the King in person. Following disappointments and the difficulties of politics in the later 1790s, Soane seemed to realize that the early promise of George III's architectural patronage was a misapprehension. Jefferson earned an ill reputation with the monarch in 1776 as the primary author of the Declaration of Independence. The document criticized the monarch, even though the prose in Jefferson's original draft softened following edits from the Continental Congress' Committee of Five.

Jefferson's ill perception of the king did not fade with the end of the American Revolution, "our friend George is rather remarkable for doing exactly what he ought not to do." Nonetheless, when Jefferson was visiting his colleague John Adams in London in 1786, he made a diplomatic visit to the English court; here, the patriot was snubbed when presented to the king.

Continuing Connections

I had the fortune of studying at Soane's home during a particularly interesting period due to the museum's impending occupation of no. 14 as a new Education Centre. The fact that a construction dumpster was parked on the street outside of Soane's cluster of Lincoln's Inn Fields townhouses and numerous workers were going in and out of the home during the day was a contemporary reminder of what Soane's neighbors experienced for nearly forty years while he was altering and enlarging the form of his home. The finish work in no. 14 was being concluded; the all-important processes of testing alarms and logistical planning for moving offices were beginning. The new Robert Adam Study Centre required the fabrication of cabinets and furniture; interestingly, the American Black Walnut harvested for the fabrication of the new pieces comes from a piece of land that was once part of Thomas Jefferson's farms.

Lasting Legacy Without Their Home?

After spending countless hours at Thomas Jefferson's Monticello and a sizable amount of time in the home of Sir John Soane, I have been internally debating the following question: would these two men exist in our memory without their respective homes and contained collections? According to the book "The Destruction of Memory", architecture is the primary legacy of culture; when destroyed our understanding and a significant part of that culture's place in history is erased. This premise struck me as particularly pertinent when referring to the homes of Jefferson and Soane.

Without Monticello Jefferson, without a doubt, would still hold a significant place in history because of his writings and political career. I also believe we would still know Jefferson as an architect; however, his body of work would be limited to the somewhat derivative but nonetheless influential Virginia State Capitol building and the obscurity of smaller projects like Farmington and Barboursville. Poplar Forest would possibly attract more attention due to its unique intimacy and distinctive design in his small oeuvre of built work. Would the University of Virginia still receive significant attention if not related to Jefferson's Monticello? The University would be known to architects for its innovative programmatic planning and translation of an ancient Roman temple, the Pantheon, into a temple of knowledge called the Rotunda that once housed the University's library. As a resident of Charlottesville for nearly six years I can certainly say that I cannot imagine the University without Monticello looming above the valley. Much of the University's architectural presence and intrinsic sense of place is derived from the fact that the author of the Declaration of Independence and third President established one of the nation's first public universities in his own backyard. In the winter months, when the trees are bare, you can still envision Jefferson using a telescope on the North Terrace of Monticello to watch construction of the Rotunda, a process he unfortunately did not live to see completed. The legacy of Jefferson is an ever-present one at the University and consequently the University owes much of its architectural importance to the survival of Jefferson's home.

If Soane had not taken steps towards the preservation of his house, his legacy, and his place in history as an architect and collector, would we know him today? The canopy structures and natural lighting principles of many of his buildings, especially the Dulwich Picture Gallery, would probably still receive attention in architectural history courses. It is a fruitless exercise to ponder what would have happened to Lincoln's Inn Fields and his collections, particularly the drawings, without the Act of Parliament. However, I am sure many would shudder at the thought, suspecting with certainty, that the home would not resemble anything that we know today. Even with Soane's conscientious preservation of his place in history through the maintenance of his residence at Lincoln's Inn Fields, the world has witnessed the loss of many of his architectural projects due to wartime destruction, careless alterations and even purposeful dismantlement.

Speaking as architect-in-training, architectural historian, and student of Mr. Jefferson's University I have come to discover that the legacies of Jefferson and Soane are closely tied to their homes. Monticello illuminates the character of Jefferson: without the innovations, contents and unique character of his 'essay in architecture' we may only know Jefferson as a gifted man, especially with the written word, a tentative public speaker, a reluctant politician and an otherwise lackluster introvert. For Soane, his home and museum give the public a glimpse into the world of a professional architect, collector and peculiar curiosity of a man. Clearly, the preserved house museums of Jefferson and Soane are the anchors of their architectural legacies.

Decay and rebirth

Jefferson made no major attempt to preserve his home or its contained collections; conversely Soane took specific actions during the later years of his life to ensure his life's work would endure his own mortality. Regardless of these disparate approaches to preservation, both Jefferson's Monticello and Sir John Soane's Museum went through periods of disrepair. The once vibrant air of Monticello and its chaotic household changed dramatically after the Jefferson family was forced to leave the property and part with the collections of their patriarch. The majority of Monticello's collections were auctioned in the large dispersal sale of January 1827 where slaves were sold alongside furniture. The art collection was sent to Boston in hopes that the elevated character of aesthetics in New England would bring higher revenues; Jefferson's retirement library was sent to a bookseller in Washington, D.C. Jefferson's 'essay in architecture' and its adjoining property was sold in 1831 in order to pay off a portion of the extraordinary debt. Washington socialite Margaret Bayard Smith visited Monticello during Jefferson's lifetime and criticized the former President for his odd tastes and experimental architecture. However, her letter to Anna Bayard Boyd and Jane Bayard Kirkpatrick from August 12, 1828 illustrated a different tone and lamented the loss of Monticello's splendor: "We entered the Hall once filled with busts & statues & natural curiosities—filled to crowding—now empty!—bare walls & defaced floor—from thence into the drawing-room—once so gay & splendid—whose walls were literally covered with pictures—like the Hall—bare & comfortless."

James Barclay, the new owner, made an unsuccessful attempt at a silkworm farm. Consequently, Monticello changed hands once again in 1834. Uriah Phillips Levy, a United States Naval officer, took on the charge of restoring and preserving both Jefferson's home and its surrounding property. Unfortunately, by the time of Levy's occupation the rich collections of the interior of the home had already been lost.

Jefferson's Monticello was starting to decay just as Soane's life was coming to a close. Unlike the haphazard sale of Monticello, Soane's residence was carefully placed in the hands of a curator and Inspectress after the architect's death. Across the Atlantic, Monticello continued its decline and experienced the ravages of the American Civil War. Although no major battles occurred in Charlottesville, Monticello faced the traffic of Confederate soldiers curious about the home of one of the Founding Fathers; they left their marks in the etchings of tin shingles on the roof and graphite notes on the walls. During this time, the Levy family was in a heated battle for the ownership of the house and years of neglect did nothing to improve the weathered condition of railings, crumbling bricks, decaying plaster, or shattered glass. The first known photographs of Monticello from the 1870s capture more of a ruin than a home. Towards the turn of the century Monticello was revived by Levy's nephew, aptly named Jefferson Monroe Levy. In 1923 he sold the home to the current owners: a non-profit called the "Thomas Jefferson Foundation". Through many years and careful investigations, the Foundation discovered the majority of Jefferson's possessions that once adorned the walls and shelves of Monticello; about one-quarter of the collection can be found in the home today. The architectural structure of the home continues to undergo careful restoration. Due to the tattered history of Monticello's ownership and maintenance the home required significant attention in order to open the property to public visitation. However, the contemporary visitor to Monticello must view the house museum with a cautious eye in order to understand the line between restoration and recreation. There is almost a too-pristine nature to the home; today's Monticello is better manicured than it ever was during Jefferson's lifetime. Through its labyrinthine character as well as ongoing exhibitions, Soane's house museum does not seem to possess this sterile element of curation. As mentioned earlier, the home feels as though Soane just left the property.

Although Soane ensured the survival of his museum through the Act of Parliament in 1833, his home was subject to unfortunate events and litigation. Some of the home's furnishings were sold and the property of no.14 Lincoln's Inn Fields was lost in 1784. Thankfully numerous addition and renovation proposals in and around the museum were prevented, such as a railway line underneath the home and the addition of a fourth story to no. 13. Modern interventions still crept into the home, such as the restroom in the Tivoli Recess. A portion of the collections was moved during the air raids of World War I; however, heavy bombings and proximity of the museum to major railway targets forced the evacuation of the majority of the museum's collections during World War II. A bomb that landed in the corner of Lincoln's Inns Fields in 1940 damaged the home and destroyed much of the original glass on the north facade. War damages were eventually repaired and grants during the latter half of the twentieth century allowed the museum to restore elements such as crumbling portions of the Monk's Court and purchase the property at no.14. One particular element of Soane's house museum that remains unchanged is the educational program: the library still accommodates scholars, the collections are still drawn by students of art and architecture during class trips and continuing education seminars, and the Model Room is active as a space of creation and restoration for items in the home. Scholars do not work in the same way at Monticello: the interior of the home is only accessible with an interpretive chaperone and access to Jefferson's library and papers are available, but down the winding road from Monticello.

Conclusions

Although the design of one's own homes is an intimate act, Jefferson and Soane tackled an additional design challenge that questioned their aesthetics, priorities and insecurities: a funeral monument. Buried close to their respective residences, each man designed his own tombstone and wrote his own epitaph. Jefferson was buried on the property of Monticello in a cemetery that was established after his childhood friend, Dabny Carr, was laid to rest in 1773. Jefferson's gravestone will as simple obelisk of rough stone elevated on a square plinth and adorned with a single phrase:

Here was buried
Thomas Jefferson
Author
of the Declaration of American Independence,
of the Statute of Virginia for Religious Freedom, and
Father
of the University of Virginia

Ironically, the owner of over 600 slaves chose to highlight three life accomplishments that emphasized different elements of freedom; political, religious and educational. It was also no linguistic error that Jefferson used the term 'father' rather than 'founder' in reference to his University of Virginia; Jefferson had no surviving sons with his wife Martha therefore he aspired to be an educational patriarch within the Commonwealth. Soane's tombstone in the churchyard of St. Pancras Old Church was much more elaborate in design than Jefferson's, reflective of a literal final charrette for a professional architect. Soane's monument was a nested design of rectilinear elements capped by his signature canopy dome. The monument shares inscriptions to Soane's wife and his eldest son, yet his own epitaph adorns the 'front' of the monument. Despite his profuse body of architectural work, he named only one commission on his epitaph: architect of the Bank of England. Unfortunately, the inscription on Soane's tomb lasted longer than his crowning achievement. Soane's designs for the Bank of England were largely demolished by 1933.

As architects Jefferson and Soane designed their homes as perfect illustrations of Enlightenment principles: designated museum spaces contributed to the diffusion of knowledge through a public program and private zones with premium views, light and enclosure encouraged introspection and self-initiated study. Although Jefferson and Soane appear serious and even somber in many of their writings, both must have possessed a sense of humor considering they each placed portrait busts of themselves in their homes in comical locations. Jefferson's larger than life Roman-style bust is situated was in the Entrance Hall across from his political nemesis Alexander Hamilton; he told his grandson the two politicians would be opposed in death as they were in life. Soane superciliously placed his own bust above small sculptures of the Renaissance masters Raphael and Michelangelo in his Museum's domed atrium space.

Modern visitors cannot escape the frozen gazes of the multifaceted creators of Monticello and Sir John Soane's Museum and it seems wonderfully appropriate that Jefferson and Soane placed themselves among the curious artifacts of their unique house museums.

1. Throughout this text Monticello will always be before the Soane Museum in comparative listings simply for chronological reasons; Monticello was begun in 1769 and the first townhouse that would later compose the Soane Museum was purchased in 1792. This document is composed in the Chicago Manual Style of citation with American spelling.

2. Dorinda Outram, Panorama of the Enlightenment (London: Thames & Hudson, 2006), 56.

3. Outram, 184.

4. Jack McLaughlin, Jefferson and Monticello: The Biography of a Builder (New York: Henry Holt and Company, 1988), 255.

5. "Architecture is my delight, and putting up and pulling down, one of my favorite amusements." Jefferson as quoted in Rayner's Life of Jefferson, 524.

6. A profuse amount of students' drawings of Soane's house museum are preserved. These drawings, however, mostly showcase the collections and their alternating locations rather than major spatial changes or design diagrams.

7. McLaughlin, 58.

8. Anne M. Lucas, "Ordering His Environment: Thomas Jefferson's Architecture from Monticello to the University of Virginia" (M.A. Thesis, University of Virginia, 1989), Appendix 1, 47. In 1768 Jefferson acquired a 1742 edition of Palladio's Four Books of Architecture with notes by Inigo Jones. The book was later part of the 49 architectural books Jefferson sold in 1815 as part of the Congressional Library sale.

9. Notes on the State of Virginia from John P. Foley, ed, A Comprehensive Collection of the Views of Thomas Jefferson (New York: Funk & Wagnells, 1900), transcribed by the University of Virginia Library Thomas Jefferson Digital Archive of the Electronic Text Center, Viii,394. E-text 436. Hereafter referred to as E-text.

10. The use of Palladio's terminology is notable considering Jefferson referred to Palladio as 'the bible' in a letter to General John Cocke from February 23, 1816. Lucas, 1989.

11. The first known written reference to the 'south pavilion' is in a letter dated January 1798 from Jefferson to his daughter Martha. Jefferson references the building as the 'outchamber' in subsequent letters until 1806; after this date he always refers to the building as the 'pavilion' or 'south pavilion'. See Koester, viii.

12. Letter to James Ogilvie, 1771, as quoted in William Howard Adams, Jefferson's Monticello (New York: Abbeville Press, 1983), 60-63.

13. Lucas, 7.

14. "I had folded myself in the arms of retirement, and rested all prospects of future happiness on domestic and literary objects. A single event [Mrs. Jefferson's death] wiped away all my plans, and left me a blank which I had not the spirits to fill up. In this state of mind an appointment [Minister to France] from Congress found me, requiring me to cross the Atlantic." Jefferson to M. de Chastellux 1782, E-text 7441.

15. Buford Pickens, "Mr. Jefferson as Revolutionary Architect," The Journal of the Society of Architectural Historians 34, no. 4 (1975):, 259.

16. Hugh Howard, Thomas Jefferson Architect: The Built Legacy of Our Third President (New York: Rizzoli, 2003), 42.

17. Pickens, 277, argues that Jefferson did not visit Vicenza or Rome because he was more concerned with visiting contemporary developments in architecture. I would argue that Jefferson's explorations were a reflection of both time constraints and priorities: Jefferson was visually familiar with the architecture of the Veneto and Rome through engravings in architectural books. Although not equivalent to firsthand experience, Jefferson possibly viewed a broad agenda for his architectural travels that included the lesser known and/or undocumented edifices of the Netherlands, Germany, and England. This theory asserts the claim by Wilson, 671, which states Jefferson tended to take his knowledge of the world from books rather than direct experience.

18. Jefferson letter to Madame La Comtesse de Tesse. Nîmes,1787. E-text 442.

19. Jefferson letter to James Madison. Paris, 1785. E-text 450.

20. Robert F. Dalzell, Jr., "Constructing Independence: Monticello, Mount Vernon, and the Men Who Built Them," Eighteenth-Century Studies 26, no. 4 (1993): 548, argues that Monticello II was not a pure reflection of Jefferson's lessons learned abroad because the home was not a blank slate for the designer.

21. The wife of architect William Thornton wrote in 1802 of the home, "he [Jefferson] has altered his plan so frequently, pulled down and rebuilt that in many parts it looks like a house going into decay from the length of time it has been erected." Descriptions of Monticello vol.2, 34.

22. Soane added the 'e' to his name in 1784. See Gillian Darley, John Soane: An Accidental Romantic (New Haven: Yale University Press, 1999), 74; Kristyna G. Olsen "Giovanni Battista Piranesi: Eighteenth-Century British Architects and the Roman Ideal" (MA Thesis, University of Virginia, 1997), 55.

23. John Soane, Memoirs on the Professional Life of an Architect Between the Years 1768 and 1835. (London: James Moyes Castle Street Leicester Square, 1835), 11.

24. Margaret Richardson and Mary Anne Stevens, eds, John Soane, Architect: Master of Space and Light. exh.cat. (London: Royal Academy of Arts, London, 1999), 78.

25. Richardson and Stevens, 78.

26. A letter from 1821 recounts Jefferson's thoughts on a prison in England from 1785 and potentially refers to George Dance the Younger's remodeling of Newgate Prison following the Gordon riots of 1780. For the letter see E-text 446.

27. Richardson and Stevens, 86. The architectural program was a compliment, not an intended substitution, for apprenticeship in an architectural firm.

28. Darley, 17, see note 72.

29. Jefferson's lack of drafting abilities is noted in Pickens, 279; McLaughlin, 57-64.

30. See Nichols catalogue of Jefferson's drawings; most dating after 1789 were completed on graph paper (labeled in the catalogue as CX).

31. Soane was in Pompeii in 1779 and supposedly made sketches and measured drawings, 'by the stealth of moonlight'. Watkin 1996, 525.

32. Olsen, 60. Soane didn't immediately seek out Piranesi because he wanted to improve his Italian before meeting the famous engraver.

33. Olsen, 60. Soane met Piranesi at Palazzo Tomati. The letter of introduction was produced by Williams Chambers; see Hurwitz, 9.

34. For a comprehensive chronology of Soane's life, by Susan Palmer, and architecture projects, by Stephen Astley, see Richardson and Stevens, 282- 288.

35. John Wilton-Ely, "The Rise of the Professional Architect in England," In The Architect: Chapters in the History of the Profession, ed. Spiro Kostof (Oxford: Oxford University Press, 1977), 194, calls Soane the father of the modern profession of architecture.

36. Alice Gray Read, "Monticello's Dumbwaiters," Journal of Architectural Education 48, no. 3. (1995): 174, argues that, "Monticello as an intended model of agrarian self-sufficiency within a pastoral landscape and a model of healthy living."

37. Soane had 'practiced' certain elements of the design for his own home on preceding architectural commissions. Praed's Bank on Fleet Street from 1801 was a trail run for the linear façade arrangement of Lincoln's Inn Fields. I thank Steven Astley for this discussion and his insight.

38. See Darley 95-96.

39. During Jefferson's tenure as Secretary of State he wrote to a friend that he wanted, "to be liberated from the hated occupation of politics, and to remain in the bosom of my family, my farm and my books…I have my house to build". Howard, 46; "However ardently my retirement to my own home and my own affairs, may be wished for by others, there is no one of them who feels the wish once where I do a thousand times." Jefferson to Francis Eppes, April 1792, E-text 7743.

40. Jefferson to Edward Rutledge, December 1796, E-text 7442.

41. Dalzell, 559, explores this idea through the lens of Palladio's Book II.XII, that states the country villa is where, "one whose spirit is tired by the aggravations of the city will be revitalized, soothed, and will be able to attend in tranquility to the study of literature and quiet contemplation; similarly, this was why the sensible men of the ancient world made a habit of withdrawing frequently to such places…"

42. Susan Palmer, "From Fields to Gardens: The Management of Lincoln's Inn Fields in the Eighteenth and Nineteenth Centuries," London Gardener 10 (2004-5):11, notes that the garden square was 7.25 acres.

43. For a detailed description and drawings of the progression of Lincoln Inn's Fields see Palmer, "From Fields to Gardens."

44. Soane's RA lecture 1 in Watkin, ed., Sir John Soane: The Royal Academy Lectures (Cambridge: Cambridge University Press, 2000), 629.

45. Ptolemy Dean, Sir John Soane and London (Burlington, VT: Lund Humphries, 2006), 46.

46. Palmer 1997, 1.

47. District Surveyor William Kinnard filed the charge that the façade of no. 12 projected beyond the plane of the terrace block; Soane won the court case. See Darley, 211.

48. Nichols, 6, cites Jefferson, "all the new and good houses are of a single story." This quote is dated after Jefferson's tenure in France and consequently later than the presumed dates for the study plans in question.

49. Book I.XXVIII of Palladio's Four Books of Architecture details stairs configurations. Each of the eight arrangements composed on the two plates are of stairs inscribed within geometric solids.

50. According to Nichols, 6, Jefferson possessed an aversion to grand staircases, "which are expensive and occupy a space which would make a good room in every story."

51. The stairs specifications were for one of Jefferson's other architectural endeavors, probably in Philadelphia, Nichols, 4a.

52. "Of all the cankers of human happiness none corrodes with so silent, yet so baneful an influence as indolence. Body and mind both unemployed, our being becomes a burden, and every object about us loathsome, even the dearest. Idleness begets ennui, ennui the hypochondriac, and that a

diseased body." Jefferson to Martha Jefferson, 1787, E-text 3821; "Determine never to be idle. No person will have occasion to complain of the want of time who never loses any. It is wonderful how much may be done if we are always doing." Jefferson to Martha Jefferson 1787, E-text 3823.

53. Dean, Sir John Soane and London, 46. Drawings from the SJSM show that from July 23, 1792 to August 25, 1792 Soane was drawing different plan arrangements for no. 12. The reorientation of the stair and the design for a starfish-ceiling Breakfast Room later appear in built form.

54. For details on the sequence of Soane's Royal Academy lectures see Watkin 2000, 21.

55. Watkin 2000, 196.

56. Watkin 2000, 197.

57. Howard 2003, 61; Stein, 21.

58. Watkin 2000, 19.

59. For a discussion of the collections and use of natural light at Soane's Museum see Mullen, 14.

60. "Multiply the length, breadth & height together in feet, & extract the square root of their product. This must be the sum of the areas of all the window." Stein, 21 note 4.

61. McLaughlin, 213.

62. The size of the oculus was defined by the largest piece of glass that could be blown at the time; see William L. Beiswanger, Monticello in Measured Drawings (Charlottesville, Thomas Jefferson Memorial Foundation, 1998), 42.

63. Beiswanger, 42.

64. Jencks, Charles. "The Riddles of John SoaneL Deciphering the Enigma Code of Soanic Architecture," Annual Lecture, transcribed (London: Royal College of Surgeons, 1999), 32.

65. Allan M Hing, "Design Lessons from Sir John Soane," Journal of Interior Design 19, no. 1 (1993):, 13.

66. Palmer 1997, 3.

67. Richardson and Stevens, 21-24.

68. Outram, 18. The Enlightenment was one of the first recorded time when silent reading, not in public forum, was recorded as a prolific and even encouraged activity. The idea of introspective, self-guided study will be examined further in the text.

69. Jefferson's letter to James Madison. Paris, 1785. E-text 437.

70. Soane, Royal Academy lecture I in Watkin 2000, 41.

71. Hooked on Books, 6.

72. William Bainter O'Neal, Jefferson's Fine Arts Library: His Selections for the University of Virginia Together with His Own Architectural Books (Charlottesville: University of Virginia Press, 1976), 8. See the 1793 catalogue of books.

73. Wilson 1996, 25-6.

74. Jefferson to Edmund Randolph,1794, E-Text 922.

75. For a succinct description of Jefferson library and classification system see Douglas L. Wilson, Jefferson's Books (Charlottesville: Thomas Jefferson Foundation, 1996). ""The arrangement [of the library at Monticello] is as follows: 1. Ancient History. 2. Modern do. 3. Physics. 4. Nat. Hist. proper. 5. Technical Arts. 6. Ethics. 7. Jurisprudence. 8. Mathematics. 9. Gardening, architecture, sculpture, painting, music, poetry. 10. Oratory. 11. Criticism. 12. Polygraphical" Jefferson to James Ogilvie, 1806, E-Text 4728.

76. Charles B. Sanford, Thomas Jefferson and His Library (Hamden, CN: Archon Book, 1977), 71, n. 278.

77. Hooked on Books: The Library of Sir John Soane Architect 1753- 1837, exh. cat. (Nottingham: Weston College, 2004), 9.

78. A large portion of Jefferson's original books sold to Congress were lost in the fire of 1851 that struck the Capitol. Today visitors to the Library of Congress can view an exhibit recreating Jefferson's original catalogue of books from the 1815 sale comprised of the original texts, books in the Library of Congress's collections that match Jefferson's editions, other books acquired through gifts, and 'place marker' books that represent the remaining titles and editions yet to be acquired in order to complete the exhibit. Unfortunately, many of these remaining texts may never be acquired; Jefferson's catalogue entry for some texts is too vague and many of the remaining items were small pamphlets or privately printed editions. An online exhibit of Jefferson's library at the Library of Congress is available at www.myLOC.gov/exhibitions/jeffersonlibrary.

79. Jefferson to S.H. Smith, 1814, E-Text 4726. Jefferson estimated his shipment of books to Congress in 1815 contained, "seven or eight thousand volumes." See Wilson 1996, 12.

80. Jefferson to John Adams,1815, E-text 915.

81. Jefferson to James Madison, November 15, 1817, E-text.

82. "My Architecture has been so much subordinated to the law of convenience, & affected also by the circumstance of change in the original design, that it is liable to some unfavorable & just criticisms." Jefferson to Benjamin Henry Latrobe 1809, Library of Congress PTJ:RS 1:595.

83. Soane married Elizabeth Smith on August 21, 1784; John Soane junior was born April 29, 1786; the second son born in December 1787 died six months later; George was born on September

28, 1789; Soane's fourth son, born after Jefferson's tenure abroad in October 1790, died one year later. See Palmer 1997 and Palmer's chronology in Richardson and Stevens, 282.

84. In the 1780s Soane began building his architectural practice while renting rooms at 10 Cavendish Street and took on his first, and only live-in, pupil John Sanders in 1781.

85. See Howard 2003, 66-79; McLaughlin, 25.

86. Howard 2003, 68. During an early restoration of the Capitol, an employee of the architectural firm responsible for the work referred to Jefferson and his architect Clérisseau. Adams, 240.

87. A New Description of Sir John Soane's Museum, 31.

88. Howard 2003, 66.

89. Robert Adam Study Centre. Darley, 324, dates a portion of the acquisition to 1818.

90. Elizabeth Cometti, "Maria Cosway's Rediscovered Miniature of Jefferson," The William and Mary Quarterly 9 no. 2 (1952): 152.

91. Cometti, 155.

92. John P. Kaminski, ed., Jefferson in Love: The Love Letters Between Thomas Jefferson & Maria Cosway (Madison, WI: Madison House, 1999), 21.

93. Darley, 41.

94. Sir John Soane Museum. III.C.4.

95. A July 1, 1830 letter states, "great pleasure in conversing with my old friends in England". An August 19, 1830 letter laments the loss of Soane's sight. Sir John Soane Museum. III.C.4.

96. Darley, 123, see note 31.

97. Jefferson to Dr. Ramsay, 1787, E-text 3449.

98. "The Thomas Jefferson Timeline: 1743:1827," Library of Congress, http://memory.loc.gov/ammem/collections/jefferson_papers/mtjtime3a.html

99. Hooked on Books, 6. Soane was attracted to books not only for their context but also their provenance.

100. Soane Library Database. Cited 3 July 2007.

101. Marquis Chastellux, Travels in North America in the Years 1780, 1781, 1782, trans. H.C. Rich, Jr. (Chapel Hill Press: Chapel Hill, 1963), 11.

102. Chastellux, 11.

103. Robert Adam Study Center. Sir John Soane's Museum Foundation, London, http://www.soanefoundation.com/robertadam.html, accessed 11 October 2007.

104. Wilson 1996, 47. In Jefferson's will his retirement library was left to the University of Virginia, duplicates were willed to two of his grandsons, but the majority was put through to the auction.

105. At the time of Jefferson's death, July 4, 1826, the debt was estimated to be over $107,000.

106. Frank Edgar Gizzard Jr., ed., "Three Grand & Interesting Objects: An 1828 Visit to Monticello, the University and Montpelier," Magazine of Albemarle County History 51 (1993), http://etext.virginia.edu/jefferson/grizzard/smith.html.

Thomas Jefferson
Monticello
Charlottesville, VA
1769-1809

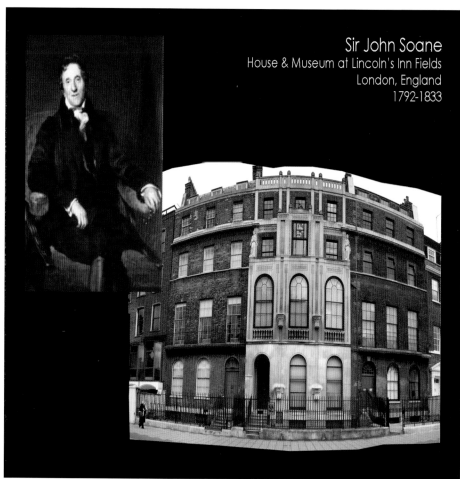

Sir John Soane
House & Museum at Lincoln's Inn Fields
London, England
1792-1833

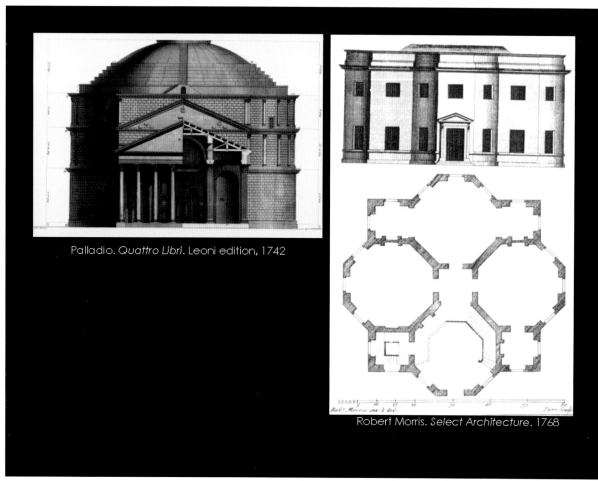

Palladio. *Quattro Libri*. Leoni edition, 1742

Robert Morris. *Select Architecture*. 1768

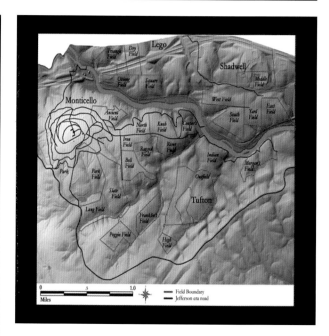

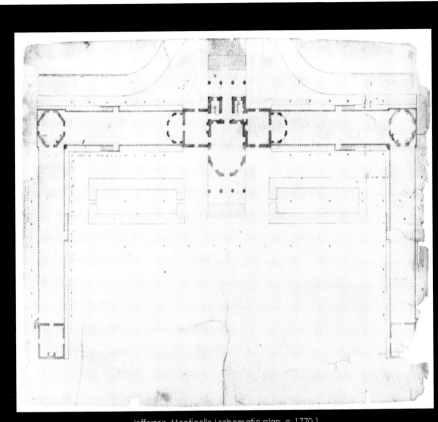

Jefferson. Monticello I schematic plan. c. 1770-1

Here I am gazing whole hours at the Maison quarrée, like a lover at his mistress. This, you will say, was in rule, to fall in love with a female beauty; but with a house! it is out of all precedent. No, madame, it is not without a precedent in my own history. While in Paris I was violently smitten with the Hotel de Salm, and used to go to the Tuileries almost daily, to look at it.
-- Jefferson to Madame La Comtesse De Tesse, 1787 letter

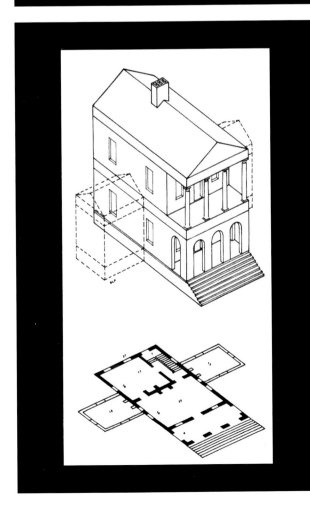

Newton's Cenotaph. Boulee. 1764

Saltworks at Chaux, France. Ledoux. 1775-9

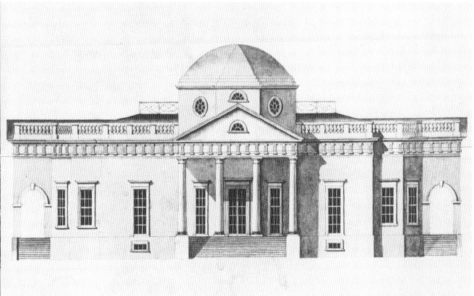

I need not tell you my attention is entirely taken up in the seeing and examining the numerous and inestimable remains of Antiquity, as you are no stranger to the zeal and attachment I have for them and with what impatience I have waited for the scenes I now enjoy…

--Soane to Mr. Wood
August 1, 1778

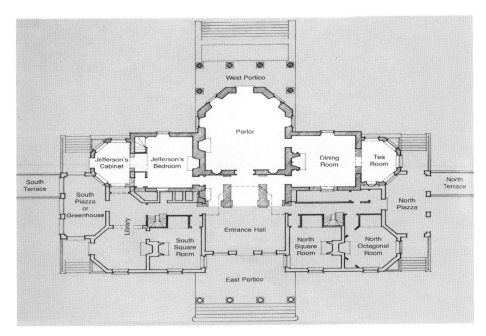

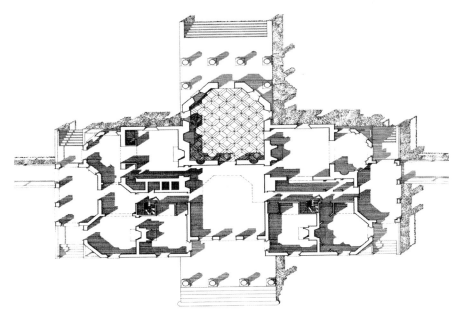

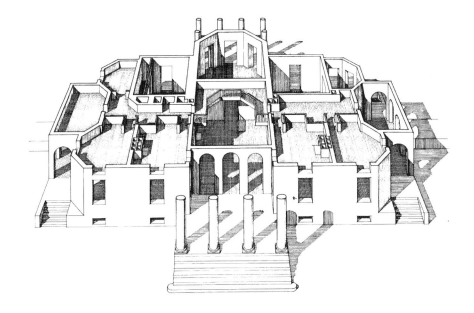

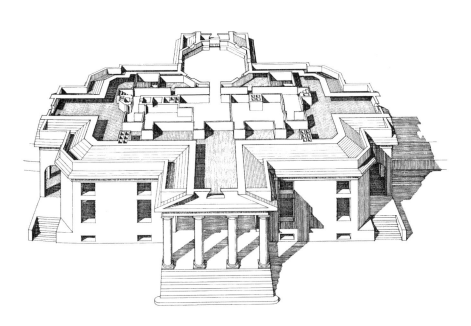

Architecture is a coy mistress, only to be won by constant attention; but when the mind is wedded to her, the imagination is always filled with wonder and delight, and the possessor feels himself well rewarded for the trouble of the pursuit.

--Soane
Professional Life of an Architect, 1835.

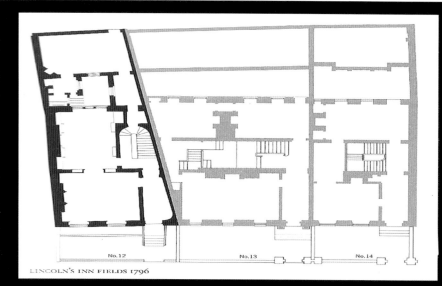

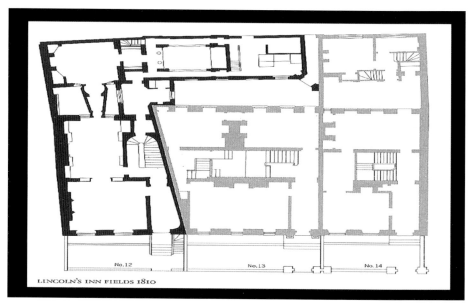

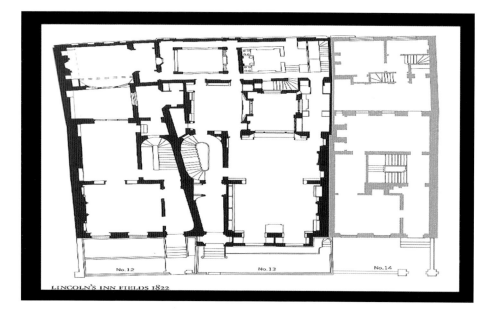

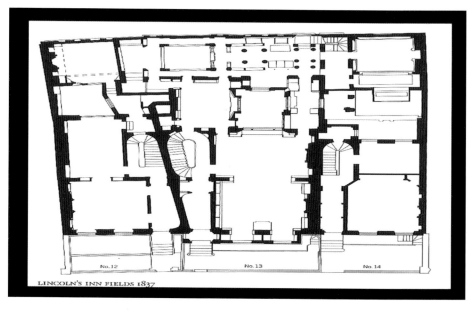

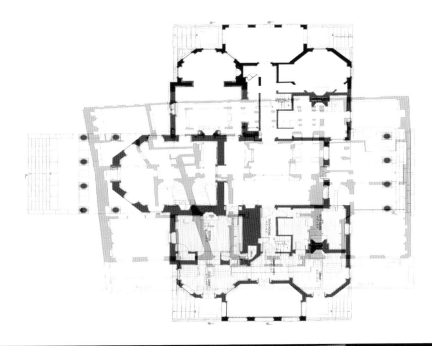

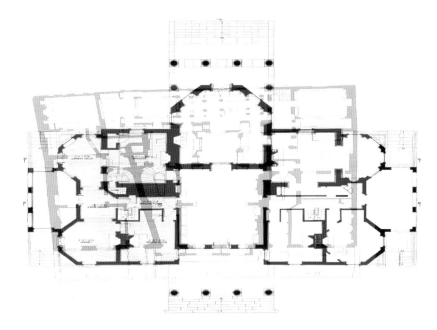

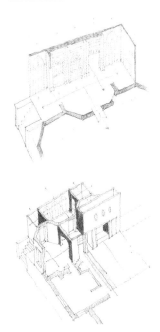

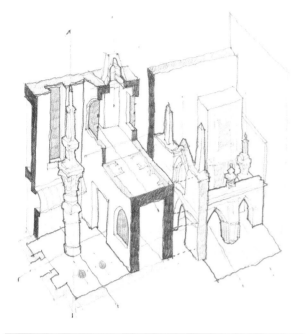

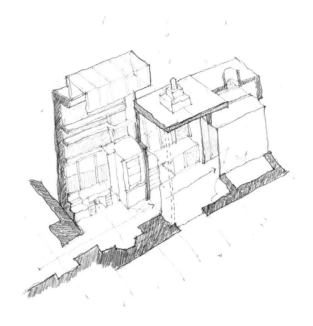

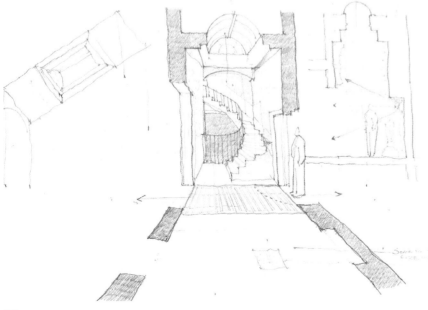

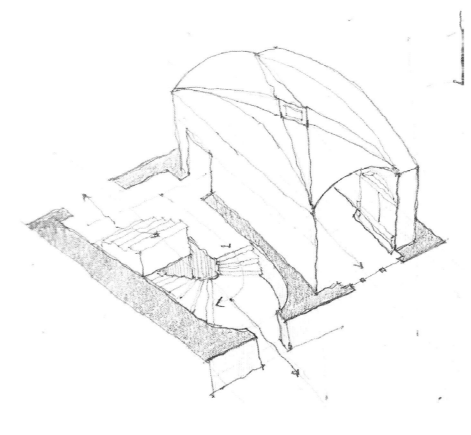

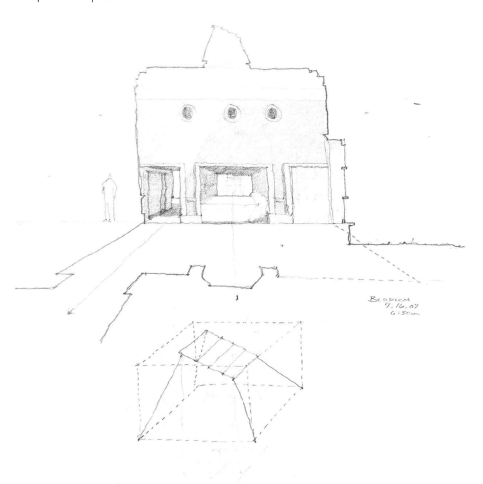

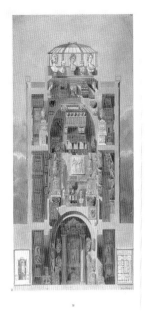

The news of the reopening of Sir John Soane's Museum in Lincoln's Inn Fields, after a rigid black-out lasting over seven years, will be greeted with enthusiasm by students of architecture, sculpture, painting, taste and Egyptology. The building has suffered somewhat from bomb damage, and parts of the galleries will have to be closed from time to time for reconstruction. But the Museum will remain open five days a week throughout the year except for the month of August-for longer... to satisfy a growing appetite for the atmosphere of a picturesque, past age.

--Burlington Magazine, October 1947

On Poplar Forest: A Table of Contents
Paul Golisz

In the clearing of a Poplar Forest in Bedford, Virginia one stumbles upon a table manifested from the wood of a fallen poplar tree. An object, one of event, is the catalyst to orient one's self within the world reconciling the familiar with the unfamiliar.

Poplar Forest is Thomas Jefferson's second home of exacting geometry. A reading of this formal logic will lead to an understanding of how one might begin to situate their role in a world in which they are inextricably bound. Beginning at the origin we discover an interesting proposition.

Situated at the center of a 20' x 20' x 20' void is a table.

If this is to be a reading of architecture, what is the meaning of a table? By placing meaning outside of the object itself and in its capacity for social engagement the potential of understanding of architecture reveals itself It becomes an object for gathering; for feast, for work, for leisure, ultimately it becomes a catalyst for discourse, a place for event.

Jefferson locates the table at the origin of three axes reaching to the distant landscape as well as to the sky. It is not only a spatial origin, but also a temporal and spiritual origin located within the public realm of the house hold. We will read the formal logic as an experiment in how architecture might reveal our origin while allowing us to orient ourselves in the world.

The project became manifest once Jefferson sent his mason to Poplar Forest to survey a plot of land within the forest. The mason proceeded to establish the origin by driving his spade into the earth to begin the foundation of the house. Each shovel full of dirt removed from the ground at Poplar Forest was eventually molded into a squint brick to complete the construction of the octagonal villa.

Earth was continually transformed through the course of construction at Poplar Forest. Jefferson had the ground of the south lawn removed in an area of 100 by 200 feet. The earth that was removed became the two mounds which flank Poplar Forest to the East and West.

The role of architecture is to situate ourselves within the world, by contextualizing our anthropocentricity. Poplar Forest succeeds in this endeavor by placing a space for event at the center of three axes. Using a table, an object of immense social capacity, an origin is established where the familiar is reconciled with the unfamiliar, the visible with the invisible, and the center with the edge through interaction.

An object provides the framework in which to understand how we might orient ourselves through event. At Poplar Forest it happens at the scale of the individual, or perhaps of a few individuals, but through a similar reading of the Academical Village, event at the scale of the Lawn becomes an origin. A place of common ground for students and faculty alike, ultimately citizens in general, to become aware and perhaps self-conscious of the environment in which they are in inextricably bound.

Poplar Forest was intended to be a place for Jefferson to think, to study, and to read. Unlike Monticello, Poplar Forest proved to be a different model for construction. Rather than an exercise in building the unfinished, Poplar Forest was conceived as a whole; a domestic design of beauty and restraint. The first of the three requisites of beauty as stated by Aquinas was made manifest, *Integritas*.

The manor of Poplar Forest is perceived in relation to the rest of the visible pre condition. Prior to 1773 The Council of Virginia granted William Stith to join two tracts of uncleared woodland at the Poplar Forest. Simultaneously, Peter Jefferson was speculating in the western lands of Bedford County where he found to his liking the red soil of the Poplar Forest. Eventually the plat of land that made up Poplar Forest would be bequeathed to Thomas Jefferson and his wife Martha. Prior to Jefferson's acquisition of the tract, the meter of the *Lirioden dron Tulipifera* had been cleared to provide for arable land. Jefferson's first visit allowed him to experience the plantation operations for a tobacco crop that were well underway.

Thomas Jefferson was led to the pin driven in the center of the spot destined for a dwelling house under an autumn full moon, which is known as the 'blood moon'. The silent figures made their way through the forest, moon overhead; they were pale as a corpse with the cold light betraying the creatures of the wood. During the journey in the faint moonlight under the red rock, the image of a constructed swale among the staccato of the remaining Tulip Poplars with the grass singing of the precondition of the site revealed itself.

Jefferson's past was bound up and inseparable from his work at Poplar Forest. His time spent in France, his work at Monticello, the experiments conducted at the President's house, and his infrequent journeys to Poplar Forest all marked the undertaking of his retreat in Bedford County. While serving as President, Jefferson supervised the building of two earthen mounds that became known as The Jefferson Mounds. In addition to being important components of the landscaping these helped screen the environs of the Presidents house and gave them privacy. Such mounds were important elements of pleasure grounds at the time.

A bounding line of an octagon, a Platonic Form, is drawn about the structure; the aesthetic image presented in time and space. The Poplar Forest manor is apprehended as self-bounded and self-contained upon the immeasurable background, yet a further investigation reveals a reflection back into the world. I came in from the wilderness, a creature void of form, only to situate myself at a table when the sun was at its highest point in the sky among the clatter and chatter of the men from Bedford County; where the walls of Poplar Forest hold inexplicable splendor of Ionian white and gold. Once inside, I move from room to room where the formal lines of a Palladian villa are revealed. The rhythm of the octagonal rooms joined at the center by a perfect cube allows for the apprehension of a system that is complex, multiple, divisible, separable; made of brick from the red soil, timber from the fallen Poplars. *Consonantia*.

Finding oneself in the Form of a cube is the pinnacle of experience at Poplar Forest, meaning coalesces. The central dining room is the private precursor to the Lawn of the Academical Village. A place for contemplation, gathering for a meal. A glazed bone china bowl is touched by the suns last rays. After the feast, when the eyes and back turn upwards from the table the human engine waits to see the cosmic performance through the prismatic canopy.

"The instant wherein that supreme quality of beauty, the dear radiance of the aesthetic image, is apprehended luminously by the mind which has been arrested by its wholeness and fascinated by its harmony is the luminous silent stasis of aesthetic pleasure, a spiritual state; enchantment of the heart." Poplar Forest allows one to feel the world and see the world. To touch the heart of the forest, the table; to look into the heart of the sky, the window.

"Art does not reproduce the visible; rather, it makes visible." A table made manifest from the raw lumber of the poplar forest makes visible the relationship between human and nature. One that must be reconciled to situate ourselves within the web of life, one that humankind certainly did not weave.

Construction of Poplar Forest began in September of 1805 when Jefferson sent his builder, Hugh Chisolm, to Bedford. During his first months there, Chisolm most likely, "spent his time preparing the site, assembling stones, excavating for the foundation, digging clay for the bricks, and obtaining sand for mortar." (Chambers, Poplar Forest and Thomas Jefferson, p.32) The octagonal plan required the manufacture of specific bricks from the clay of Bedford County. These bricks, known as "squint bricks", have a special angle at one end to accommodate the forty five degree angles at the eight corners of the house.

Shortly after receiving a letter from Chisolm, around June 16, 1806, Jefferson traveled to Bedford in order to help lay the foundation for the house at Poplar Forest. Although Chisolm was a master builder who had certainly laid foundations before, it appears that the octagonal shape of the house required extensive precision. "As Jefferson's own drawings of octagons indicate, determining the proper angles and wall lengths of a regular octagon was a sophisticated geometric exercise, dependent on arcs, radii, and quadrants." (Chambers, Poplar Forest and Thomas Jefferson, p.36)

Around July 22, 1808 Jefferson's slaves began the digging of the sunken lawn. Presumably the fill that was obtained from the digging was used to construct the two mounds to the East and West of the house. Due to whatever reason, the mounds were misplaced and do not align with the axis of the house as was intended by Jefferson. This misalignment caused additional confusion because the foundations of the two necessaries are neither in line with each other nor with the axis of the house. Jefferson noted, "Plant on each mound four weeping willows on the top in a square 20 (feet) apart. Golden willows in a circle round the middle. 15 (feet) apart. Aspens in a circle round the foot. 15 (feet) apart..." (Chambers, Poplar Forest and Thomas Jefferson). Obviously Jefferson intended the mounds to be covered with dense, thick shade. As was mentioned, George Washington had given his ornamental mounds as Mount Vernon a similar treatment, and had also utilized willows to create the effect he wanted.

In landscape design vocabulary, the term mound generally refers to an artificial hill, a raised feature in natural and constructed landscapes. Mounds have been used across regions throughout time. Native Americans used raised ground for burials, as well as for elite residences and sacred areas in the case of larger mounds. "In Euro pean and American gardens, mounds were used as observation places or as an ornamental variety of surface." (O 'Malley, Keywords in American Landscape Design, p.429) Throughout the world mounds were raised over graves, known as tumuli, with notable tombs including those at Macedonia.

A variety of surfaces and materials were used for ground cover, specifically at Poplar Forest, as noted by O'Malley in Keywords in American Landscape Design: "grass, altheas, gelder roses, lilacs, calycanthus, weeping willows, and aspens were planted on the mounds... Furthermore, symmetrically placed mounds could be used to frame distant views, as at Mount Vernon, or to frame a house, as at Poplar Forest."

Jefferson paid special attention to the design of the two octagonal necessaries which flanked the house. They also provide additional insight into the inspiration Jefferson took from George Washington's Mount Vernon. Chambers notes in Poplar Forest and Thomas Jefferson:

"Other examples of garden 'temples' or ornaments that combine architectural form with utilitarian function can be found throughout European landscapes of the eighteenth and early-nineteenth centuries. While rarer, American examples can be cited as well, among them the two octagonal necessaries which serve as focal points in the gardens at George Washington's Mount Vernon."... Writing James Dinsmore on December 28, he advised: The window frames at Poplar Forest may be of poplar dug out of the solid, with locust sills; tho' I do not know why the sides and the top might not also be of locust dug out of the solid.

Although Poplar Forest appeared to be conceived as a finished product, Jefferson proved to be incapable of living in a completed house. Constant adjustments were made, some requiring larger investments than others which would affect not only the architecture but also the social dynamics of the estate. Jefferson's actions were not limited to the bricks and mortar of the built house but the landscape proved to be within his crosshairs as well. Adjustments made to Poplar Forest reflect the nature of Jefferson as his values were tested in relation to the positions he held and the countries he visited. Poplar Forest exemplifies the capability to engage the world through the act of construction.

Because Jefferson was extremely devoted to his family, it was of utmost importance to Jefferson that his grandson, Francis Eppes, accept the bequeathal of Poplar Forest.

Realizing that Poplar Forest was constructed to serve as a villa, adjustments were necessary in order for Poplar Forest to become a suitable for year-round living. "Sociologically, the addition of the office wing can be seen as a beginning step in the transformation of Poplar For est from a villa to a farmhouse. Until this time, and indeed throughout his ownership, Jefferson enjoyed Poplar Forest in the same manner as the ancients had enjoyed their villas: as occasional retreats. But Jefferson was not building the office wing primarily for himself. It was constructed only after he had determined that Francis Eppes would make Poplar Forest his year-round home, and contained rooms that were far more essential to such use that to a villa retreat." (Chambers p 84)

In 1814, Jefferson laid the foundation for a wing of service rooms, or offices, in a letter to his master carpenter, Hugh Chisolm. Both Monticello and the President's House served as precedent to a certain extent, although both houses were built with two wings flanking the estate. In contrast, Poplar Forest was built with only one wing of offices, situated between the eastern stairwell and the eastern mound.

The construction of only one wing destroyed the intellectual symmetry of Poplar Forest perhaps to the advantage of aesthetic interest. Although Poplar Forest only maintained one wing, the construction of the offices was identical to those built at Monticello and the President's House. "In all three places, the wings were built into the slope of the land. On one front, all a viewer could see was a low wall, extending only a few feet above grade. On the opposite side, the wings were fully above grade, and there a covered walkway protected the passage, with doors opening from it into the individual rooms behind. Above, the roofs were topped with plank, forming a 'terras,' as Jefferson generally termed it, which served as a deck or promenade for walking in good weather." (Chambers p 81) After a substantial dinner was consumed in the central dining room, Jefferson habitually walked with his granddaughters on the terrace above the offices.

Aware that constructing only one wing would put the symmetry of Poplar Forest into question, Jefferson made sure that the appearance of the sole wing remained symmetrical. Four rooms were built, each serving different purposes and each built with different dimensions. To account for the variation in room sizes and still maintain visual symmetry, Jefferson spaced the doors to the four rooms at regular intervals, every twenty-five feet:

"The room closest to the house was almost square, measuring sixteen by fifteen feet, and was unheated, a condition that hints it was intended either as a dairy or simply a storage room. The next room in sequence, moving east, was the largest of the four. It measured twenty-four by fifteen feet, and was the kitchen. Beyond, and sharing the same chimney, was what is thought to have been the cook's room. It was almost square, measuring fifteen feet, two inches, by fifteen feet. The fourth room was a smokehouse, which measured twenty-three by fifteen feet. The eastern wall of this last room was partially built into the eastern mound." (Chambers)

The red rock or "blood moon" which previously led Jefferson through a forest of Poplars to a clearing now... became an ominous reminder of the unpredictability of the weather. Jefferson's original schedule needed adjustment as storms challenged his ability to complete the offices. Jefferson was detained at Poplar Forest longer than he expected so that he could see that the walls were covered with their plates. Chambers notes, "The plates - timbers laid on top of the walls, and thus covering them - would protect the still-damp walls and mortar until they finished settling. Once that was done, the plates could safely receive the heavy joists needed for framing the deck above." The rain which moved across the Piedmont was relentless, simultaneously providing for his highly valued crops while situating his construction within an armature of infrastructure.

The adjustment of Poplar Forest did not stop with the completion of the offices. Jefferson's next endeavor was concerned with the aesthetics of the main house, specifically the addition of a balustrade circumscribing the aperture above the dining room which opened to the sky.

He had in mind a specific height for the balusters, to be in correct proportion to the rest of the house. As the Tuscan order Jefferson used at Poplar Forest had no established rules for balustrades, Jefferson in all likelihood based his proportions on the Doric order. This was the order he had used at Monticello, and the heights of the balusters in the corresponding position there accord well with the dimensions given in his directive to Mr. Atkinson for Poplar Forest. (Chambers)

Jefferson spent a great deal of time engaging in improvements at Poplar Forest that continually adapted to his beliefs. Jefferson's adventures provided scaffolding for his values to be inevitably tested in a realm that is common among all entities and systems.

To live together in the world means essentially that a world of things is between those who have it in common, as a table located between those who sit around it; the world, like every in-between, relates and separates me at the same time. (Arendt, The Human Condition)

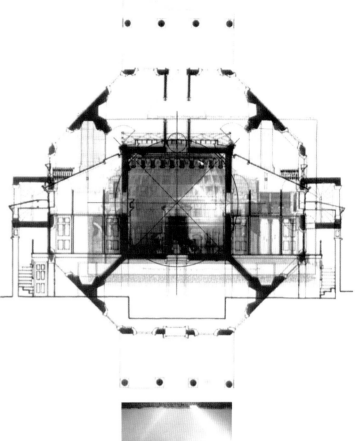

THE TWO HVNDRED INCH TELESCOPE ~

Connective Tissue #4: Un-Private Houses: On Self-Reflective Shelters
Peter Waldman

Two powerful Enlightenment Citizen Architects, Thomas Jefferson (1743-1826) and John Soane (1753-1836), each made a half-century commitment to the evolution of their dwellings as museums of cultural histories: Monticello, in Virginia and the Soane Residence/Museum at Lincoln's Inn Fields, London. During the latter two decades of Jefferson's life, he also devoted himself to the nearby hobby of his old age: The Academical Village, and to yet another dwelling, Poplar Forest in far-away Bedford County. During the same last two decades of his life, Soane envisioned distinctly scaled other hobbies of his old age: first in the Bank of England, and then second and finally a third enlargement of his Lincoln Inn Fields project as it evolved from a dwelling into a National Museum.

The Lessons of the Lawn reveal that Jefferson first conceived of The Academical Village as a 693 feet x 693 feet wide square in Plan with three Pavilions on each of the North/East and West sides as Garden Walls, but transformed the organization because of the topographic irregularities of the site, into the now narrow and directional zone opening to the South of a colonnaded Lawn, with two arcaded Ranges to the East and then again, the West with gardens in between, all opening to the Lewis & Clark expansion to the South. Each of the three zones is 231 feet wide fulfilling the Cabalist sum of 693, which is where Jefferson through Palladio began.

Willkens reveals the Soane Project first as an essay from South to North and then across decades from East to West. Golisz begins on the other side of the Atlantic with a territory deeply concealed in the Forest, where clearings were made first for agricultural programs and finally a dwelling erected as a retreat from Monticello. Giant Poplar trees screen the house from Northern winds, as the Soane proto-modern relief framing façade screen does as well, while a deep cut was made to the south where clay for brick production was excavated and the surplus gathered up to frame the house with two hills, or burial mounds, or beloved colle as coda to Monticello. The sections of both Soane's house and Jefferson's Poplar Forest parallel the deep basement of the Rotunda, as well as rise to evoke the Oculus, where Canopy, Tent and Celestial Soffits are documented in all three projects in section. All three projects are constructed landscapes in plan and section, are essays on dimness if not darkness) as well as the prismatic, in a dual obsession for mirrors, making fractal sectional elevations from frontal to lateral and then oblique light sources, in fireplaces on the oblique in the Rotunda stair landing, in the oblique Poplar Forest dining room, in re-entrant corners in the Soane residence.

These are self-reflective spatial essays with a great sense of the Intimate Interior, Cabinets of Curiosities, while both architects were also preparing their most public of civic theaters.

Soane's father was a master bricklayer, Jefferson's father was a surveyor. Both worked off of the accountability of digits, of the modular with materials transformed from the immediacy of the earth as source. But both were in the world trade of unearthing the past in both the original artifacts and second hand representations of archeological finds. Both gathered busts of heroic voices from antiquity side by side with the contemporary, and framed them both in a spatial model borrowed from Raphael's School of Athens (1510). Soane and Jefferson were both Modern in their self-conscious presence as well as totally engaged with Antiquity if not the Archaic, certainly Primal and not at all Primitive. Mirrors for the

Moon, a 9th Century Japanese epic poem by Saigyo, connecting a Nocturnal Journey between memory and place, inspires a Generative Dialogue between contemporary citizens and a love of perfect strangers. Soane's House is in the dense City of London; Poplar Forest is in a far-removed wilderness at the frontier of Arcadian America. Both projects became museums. A place to muse on here and now. On an island somewhere between Lincoln Inn Fields and Poplar Forest, Shamus Haney wove a tale of a farmer and a city stranger as the dialogue of the Dialect of recurrent dualities between Nature and Artifice which is the ethical agenda and epistemological debate of these Connective Tissues.

Mirrors for the Moon refers to the poem by Saigyo, a 9th Century Japanese monk who saw humanity's primary task is reflection here and now on the accumulation of knowledge from far, far away and long, long ago. This collage as a two-page spread is a reflection on the interiorities of the Rotunda and the exteriorities of the Lawn as Solnit projects in the phrase The Blue of Distance. There are two labyrinths projected here in this spatial college. One attempts to convey two densities in plan and section generated by Jefferson's Rotunda as spatial covenant at the scale of global intentions invoked in Borges' Library of Babel surrounded by his Garden of Forking Paths.

The Academical Village is abstracted into the left side of the two-page spread is derived from Golisz's composite collage of Poplar Forest in plan and section which is in dialogue with Wilkens' collage of Monticello/Lincoln Inn composite plans, elevations and sections. Both essayists stress the intentional complexity of call and response, echoes North to South and East to West in plan and from deep basements, some call Grottoes, and Attics, some call Celestial Soffits. Two landscapes of sequential transformation are depicted: above is Soane's rendering of The Bank of England as a construction site and in ruin, and below is Cole's The Architect's Dream, both haunted by the compression of the temporal agenda. Consequently, the left image of the densification of the Rotunda faces the extent of the Lawn to the South on the right panel. The spatial fields of the Lawn are rendered as both parterres of permutations and combinations of Jefferson's experiments with seed banks and hybrids extending from the center fold to the blurry open-ended mirage of a telescopic vision contemplating Solnit's The Blue of Distance focused on Lewis & Clark's journey along the 38th North Latitude heading West. As in all the Connective Tissue collages, the five pavilions to the East and the correspondent five to the West are articulated by the juxtaposed images from the distinct Kenan essayists above and below.

As in the other collages, the leitmotifs of the telescope and microscope at the scales of the pavilions are inserted to suggest the juxtaposed scales of encyclopedic knowledge both projects represent in the enlightenment project of connective tissues, suggested by Defoe in Robinson Crusoe (and Friday) requiring Schama's Landscape and Memory requisite for topographic and archeological imaginations embedded in Jefferson and Soane as surveyors, nomads, and lunatics. Finally, images of the busts of Jefferson and Soane in their respective reception halls slide through the Poplar Forest inversions with the leitmotif plan of the Rotunda Dome Room in all collages, two talking-heads, visionaries one of the Archaic past in London and the other of the Arcadian future from this Piedmont Condition on a transect across both sides of the Atlantic. The past has a measurable duration for Soane, the future shares the nervous sensibilities of Brodsky's Watermark and/or Berger's The Shape of a Pocket.

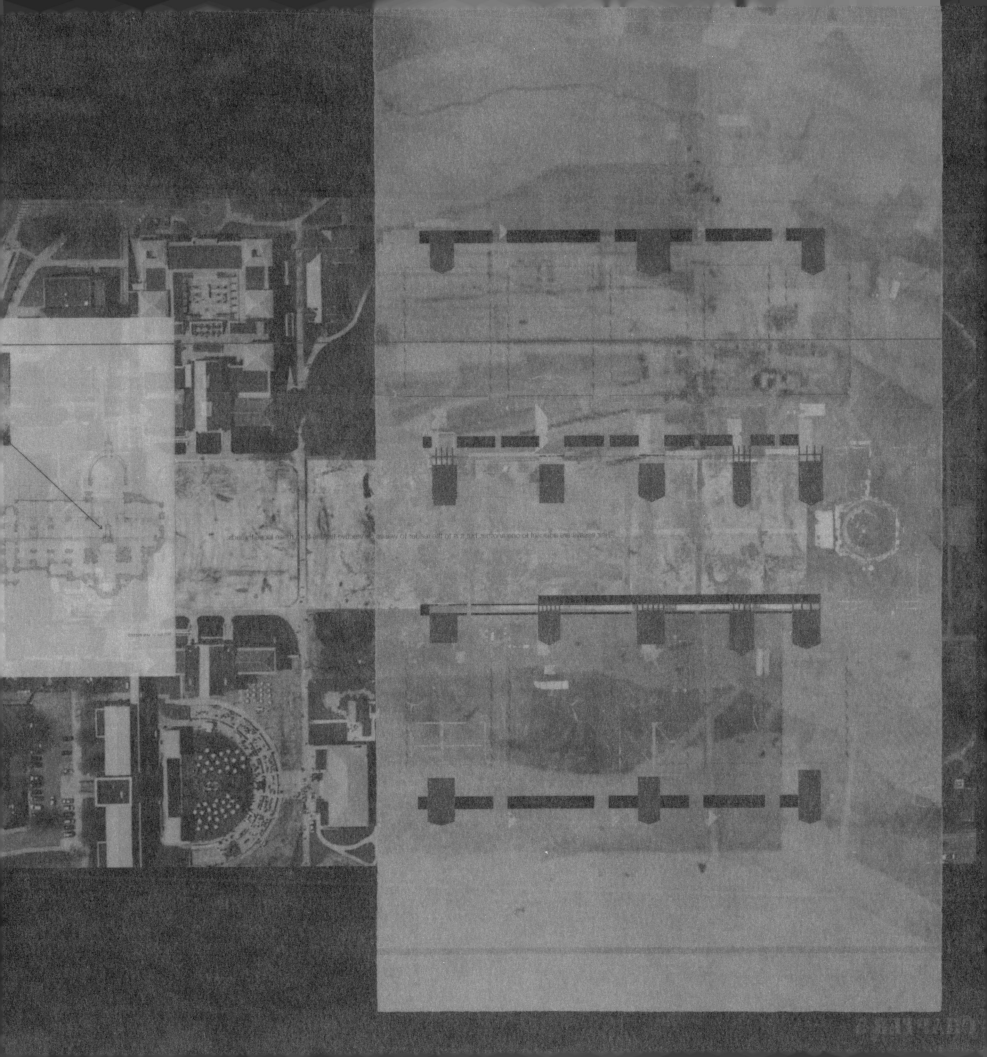

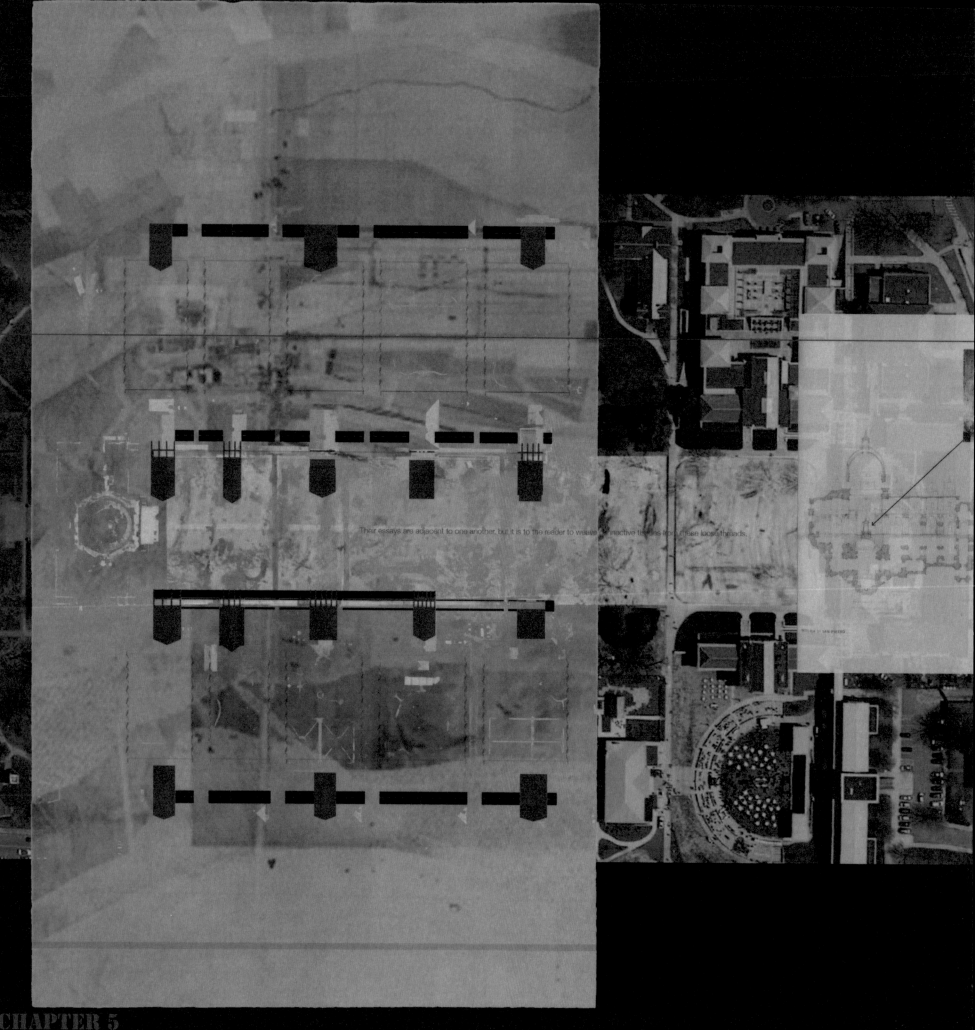

Their essays are adjacent to one another, but it is to the reader to weave connective tissues from these loose threads.

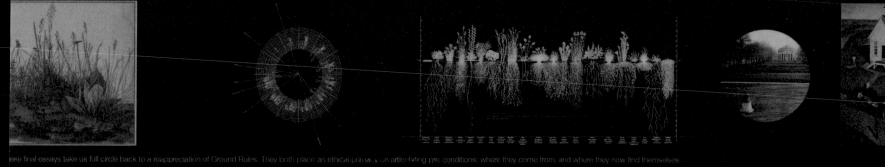

These final essays take us full circle back to a reappreciation of Ground Rules. They both place an ethical primacy on articulating pre-conditions: where they come from, and where they now find themselves.

They both trace histories as heuristic links across time and space reinforcing the utility of incipient dualities. They both appreciate building as a verb, and the construction site to be valued more than an occupancy permit.

They both commit to counter the hubris of urbanism as the pretense of environmental negotiation and advocate the humility of animistic engagement, for bearing witness to systems greater than ourselves as articulated by Walt Whitman in Leaves of Grass.

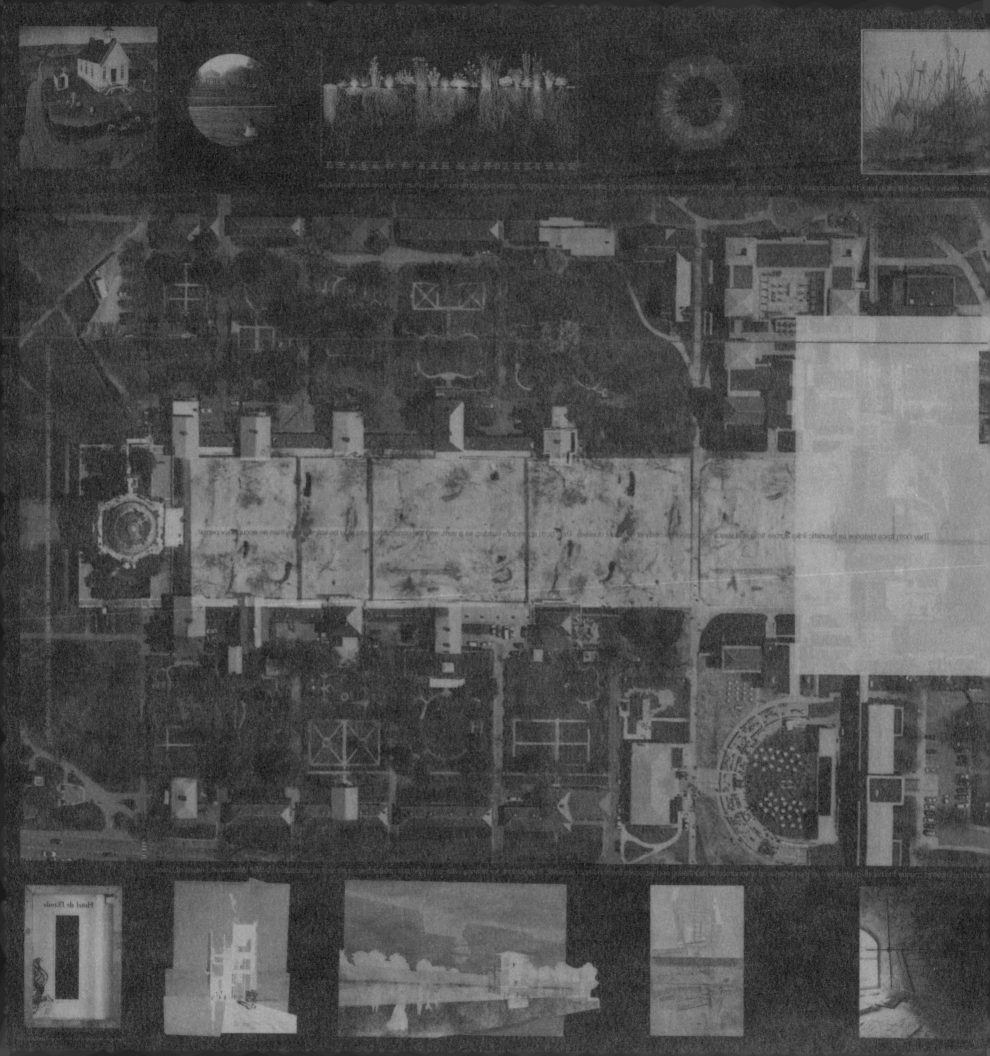

CHAPTER FIVE: FALLOW GROUND

These final essays take us full circle back to a reappreciation of Ground Rules.

They both place an ethical primacy on articulating pre-conditions: where they come from, and where they now find themselves.

They both trace histories as heuristic links across time and space reinforcing the utility of recurrent dualities.

They both appreciate building as a verb, and the construction site is to be valued more than an occupancy permit.

They both commit to counter the hubris of urbanism as the pretense of environmental negotiation and advocate the humility

of animistic engagement, for bearing witness to systems greater than ourselves as articulated by Walt Whitman in Leaves of Grass.

Their essays are adjacent to one another, but it is to the reader to weave connective tissues from these loose threads.

Collage by Count and Weight

Polly Smith Finn

In this lecture, "Collage by Count and Weight," I will discuss ways of reading architecture, illustrated by several of my own projects. By looking at these projects not as individual completed works, but as part of an on-going exploration, education, and interest in collage, I am able to build upon previous ideas and create a richer continuum, rather than starting anew. This is the process Peter has suggested several times for your own es says- beginning with where you come from, and adding each week, never starting with a clean slate.

This is also an essential design process—starting with what is there. As Beth Meyer told us that the ground is never empty, but full of histories, prehistories, and traces of nature's processes- as designers our own experiences and associations are always present.

I will begin with where I came from, then move into understanding semiotics to find meaning in architecture. I will demonstrate recurrent dualities through a semiotic lens in projects of analysis and design. Lastly, I will touch on a design process of material assemblage, as an expression of a continuum through reuse. This essay demonstrates a way of finding connective tissues through my own work and interests.

So first, where I came from?

WG Clark showed us the image on the left, of Byrd Mill in Louisa County, Virginia, the place he is from, and a building that makes its environment more beautiful by giving it a use, in this case manipulating the water for the need of man.

I come from the place on the right, Lake Martin, Alabama. Like WG's tie to water, land, and structure, this series of paintings explores the relationship between space and place by depicting these same key elements.

Through layering a plan view of the lake's shoreline, perspective views, and details of a tactical object, the hammock rope, this series explores memory, experience and mapping through layering ambiguous geometries of varying scales. These elements are visible as symbols that together provide a sense of place.

In these etchings, the discrete pieces—the rope, the landscape (as the blue of distance), the shoreline—are more clearly separated, defining the units of the visual language which are then combined in the paintings, such as the one on the right. We may read the bottom left image of the shoreline of the lake superimposed over the grid of hammock rope as a relationship between nomad and lunatic.

This expression of the shoreline is one way of reading terrain. In the so-called Frenchman's map of Williamsburg, the topographic condition is shown through the waterways and marks indicating slope.

Likewise, we know that the slope of the academical village is distinctively more dramatic on the east range than the west, and that the lawn itself is shaped with terraces stepping down away from the Rotunda, towards the precondition of wilderness.

SEMIOTICS

Now I will turn to a brief discussion of finding meaning in architecture.

This course, Lessons of the Lawn, uses Jefferson's Academical Village here at the University of Virginia, as a primer, to explain how we can read architecture. Our study of the foreground Lawn and the background gardens is used to clarify the importance of applying an analytical system commencing with the preconditions of the site. Jefferson's Enlightenment project, a Village on the edge of Arcadia, teaches the conventional primacy of structure, geometry, inter-relationships, and context, but in this study the preconditions of context comes first.

Relationships are clear among these images, linking various ideas from the course. We start with the Maverick plan of the Academical Village, and the symbol of it, transformed into a simple geometry to convey a spatial idea of our University. The circle within a square is a repeated motif, at the Tempietto, Hadrian's Villa, DaVinci's Vitruvian man, Villa Rotonda, and in a painting by Sol Lewitt, which is further broken down into parts in this study. We compare the Lawn to the ancient Greek Acropolis in its scale and arrangement of forms. At the Acropolis the Temple of Athena Nike, as a cave and tent, displays structural forces as well as references cultural values with the relief sculpture of Nike adjusting her sandal. The Propalaea at the Acropolis is likened to Michael Graves' Benaceraff House which is compared to Peter Eisenman's manipulation of geometry.

Architecture is a form of communication; it is a language framed by gravity and orientation. We can begin to understand architecture as a communicative vehicle by reading architecture as a system made up of signs. We can see the composite image from the front of our syllabus as this system, and on the right the signs separated so that they may be recombined to find new meanings again and again.

Semiotics is the study of relationships between signs, those individual units in a system, and what these signs stand for. This analytical process is pedagogical- the consciousness of exposing signs and their relationships gives the system new meaning. Architecture, when studied through this lens, begins to frame the world around us.

Architecture is made up of frames and planes or structures and walls. We can think of beams and columns as units that transmit meaning. An assemblage of a column and a beam can be read as load and support, weight being distributed, and its structural implications. This structural rationalism is evident in the Temple of Athena Nike and the Kimbell Museum by Louis Kahn.

This wall drawing by conceptual artist Sol Lewitt is analyzed by Sanda Iliescu and her students on the right. The composite is broken down into its parts, and all possible combinations of line types are illustrated. Here we can see the power in a system of signs in its many possible mutations and capacity for creating new ideas.

Mario Gandelsonnas wrote a pivotal essay in 1972 "On Reading Architecture," which describes two branches of Semiotics, as illustrated by two architects we have met in this course, Michael Graves and Peter Eisenman.

Graves' architecture represents the Semantic branch of semiotics, referencing an outside repository of references and ideas from a larger cultural context. The ancient Propylaea, the Greek monumental gateway to the Acropolis is reimagined as an exterior staircase in the addition to the Benacerraf House.

Peter Eisenman's work represents the Syntactic branch, relating signs within a system only to each other. This creates a self-referential architecture that communicates with its own formal system, having infinite permutations.

Graves' drawing on the cover of Progressive Architecture in which Gandelsonnas' article was published illustrates the semantic and syntactic branches.

The exhibition of Wittgenstein's house in the Elmaleh gallery recently reveals these two ways of reading architecture. Wittgenstein himself was a leading philosopher of the 19th-20th century, especially dealing with logic but also visual languages and understandings.

Representing the syntactic branch, the columns and wall planes describe structural qualities.

The addition of the dining scene shows larger cultural values; the curves of the chairs, the folds of the tablecloth, the planter bringing the landscape in- these all work in a dialectic against the orthogonal form of the building, creating interest, context, and dialogue. We've seen this idea before in the wicker basket against the geometry of the window at Vanna Venturi's house.

Here the syntactic/tectonic, and semantic/associative, work together to express an idea of a dwelling.

A goal of semiotics is to expose a system, a relationship, interrelationship, or dialectic. We can relate this to Jefferson's Academical Village, where multiple readings change over time as synthetic ideas are broken down and reassembled with added meaning. The dialectic, conversation, debate, discourse, and discussion is our Lesson of the Lawn.

In this next part of the lecture, I am going to show the syntactic and semantic branches of semiotics, in other words the tectonic and associative, as recurrent dualities. First, we will look at an analytical project using this lens, and then a design project, both in Rome, Italy.

I had the wonderful opportunity to spend last summer in Rome as a Carlo Pelliccia Fellow. But, also the incredible challenge: How can we read this ancient yet contemporary city?

We go back to what we know, the Lawn. Rome provides a similar kit of parts-wavy lines that divide space (serpentine walls and rivers), centers the Rotonda and Colosseum, Pantheon, or Vatican, open spaces for gathering enclosed with architecture, and buildings along streets. We can read the seven hills of Rome as Pavilions, and even see the river as a knot or rope that holds the city together, drawing on my earlier paintings.

We can also look to a repository of references, such as Le Corbusier's The Lesson of Rome.
In this analysis, I've read Rome from city scale to human scale as an expression of dualities-tectonic and associative.

One way to read the city as system of paths connecting monuments or important places. Street building and urban planning initiatives have taken place in Rome across time periods, by leaders as an expression of their values. In Ancient Rome the fora, places of democratic gathering and decision making, were organized along the Via Sacra. Popes in the 18th century created a system of straight streets connecting important Christian pilgrimage sites. In the modern era, from 1886-1935, leaders of unified Italy built roads to connect important sites from previous eras, enabling tourist access and likening Italian power to Imperial Rome.

So, I followed this path of modern streets across the city. Following a path as a cross-section was my method of understanding, of finding the expression of one idea across scales- from the urban scale to materiality.

Benito Mussolini was the fascist leader of Italy from 1922 1944. He built a wide, straight street, Via dei Fori Imperiali, from Piazza Venezia & the Campidoglio, the seat of governmental power, to the Colosseum. This involved leveling a hill and demolishing housing-but enabled access to ruins of Imperial Rome. Citizens and visitors were now able to link modern Italy to the ancient Roman empire which conquered much of the Mediterranean region.

To read this road, this urban planning initiative, I employed semiotics. My drawings seek to identify the tectonic and the associative. The power of the Italian state is expressed across scales through visual and material connections.

We can first read this street, like the lawn as having a straight axis, lined with constructed elements, and culminating at a central-plan structure, the other end is open, to the city, or to the wilderness.

Via dei Fori Imperiali can be read as the lawn, a rhythm of footsteps and columns, ancient fora alongside as gathering spaces like pavilions and gardens. movement is encouraged in the longitudinal direction with secondary transverse access.

This drawing of the same road from a lower position illustrates the importance of trees, natural, against columns, built, as the combination of the nomad and the surveyor. The combination reiterates Venturi's argument for both and the branches in combination with framing make the environment richer.

There is an emphasis on geometry, the framing of a circle in plan, in both the Rotunda and the Colosseum. In Jefferson's Rotunda there is in elevation, a false window on the exterior masking the fireplace on the interior demonstrating the importance of metric continuity on the urban perception of the exterior to Jefferson. Also on the interior of the Colosseum, there is in plan a strong sense of multiple scales of this public theater, but on the exterior, viewed from Via Sacra, there is in elevation a strong vertical hierarchy revealing its political context. Distinct views are framed in both projects on the exterior and the interior, specifically in Jefferson's project read from the interior awn and onto the exterior Range.

Next, I will briefly discuss some projects we have already seen in this course within the lens of my study.

Il Campidoglio by Michelangelo is both axial/ frontal (as the lawn) and twisting. We may recall Eisenman's process sequence of rotating elements. The void at one side of the piazza opens the space to the city/ wilderness, and buildings enclose the other three sides. Geometry is expressed in dynamically juxtaposed paving patterns, as a secondary rhythm to the pounding of footsteps. These drawings show the same place as both measured, in section and plan, and experiential, in the perspective of the accumulation of buildings across time. To make up the full picture, this dialogue is important.

The Pantheon by Hadrian, the primary compositional idea of center and edge is depicted in the geometry of overall form (plan), elements (coffers; circle in a square), and material composition (marble floor) - emphasizing orientation and gravity.

The Tempietto by Bramante is similar to the Pantheon in central plan, dome, connection to the heavens and the deep in the earth, but emphasizes center in a different way—a layering exterior to interior, thickened threshold—steps, columns, niches, which reiterates the sanctity of center as site of St. Peter's crucifixion. This building references larger ideas in Christianity and also the Renaissance proportional ideal.

We can imagine the spatial qualities of the Tempietto and Pantheon by juxtaposing plans at scale with our Rotunda, 72 feet in diameter.

Across the river, approaching St. Peter's Basilica, one travels along the Via Della Conciliazione, also designed by Mussolini- a physical relic of the Italian state harnessing the power of the Vatican by designing access to it, linking the city with the center of the Catholic church. In a semiotics reading, the composite or separated parts can be rearranged to create meaning and understanding.

The Baldachino by Bernini is set within the basilica, again a layered approach from city to object. This is also an associative moment, referencing the place Peter is buried against geometry, and the organic within a frame.

Tectonics and gravity are expressed in the body of Christ in the Pieta and monumental piers and arches - both by Michelangelo. Spatial and religious ideas are combined across scales, subjects, and purposes. The Pieta is, like Il Baldachino, expressing a duality of the organic within a frame. We see a human-scape against architecture, the choreography of gathering and ritual.

In the Piazza before Santa Maria Sopra Minerva, one witnesses the tectonic and associative in the whimsical, baroque, involved obelisk by Bernini against the church's flat Albertian facade. The facade serves as a frame work for street life, while the sculptural fascination of Bernini works as a stabilizing feature. The surveyor is present in the regulating lines, the nomad in the path of the visitor, and the lunatic in the exotic elephant and its Egyptian porphyry passenger reaching to the sky.

DESIGN

This way of reading architecture has served me as a tool for analysis and understanding that allows, leads to, and encourages reconstruction and design.

This project is a culinary institute, located on the Piazza Santa Maria in Trastevere, is integrated into the fabric of the oldest part of Rome. Mara Miller in *The Garden as Art* describes grafting onto the site, an excess of meaning beyond function, and articulating space in the interest of articulating time. By emphasizing both the referential and the tectonic in recurring dualities, the culinary institute aims to realize Miller's ideas.

Here we see the existing condition and proposed plan, expressing ideas of parasitic occupancy, integrated spatiality across scales at site level and in building assembly.

The tectonic and referential are demonstrated in the structure of the building against the human stuff inside, and the choreography of the piazza outside, gatherings around the hearth and fountain as centers. But at the same time the construction is expressed in the form section model with stages of construction assembly. The syntax of structure is most clear in the Rotunda in photographs after the fire of 1895, as the columns stand among ruins.

This image of destruction and rebuilding leads me to the final part of the lecture. We have seen transformation and reuse in the ruins of Rome, diminished and remade and as the Rotunda is burned and built again, now I'll discuss how cities could be purposefully unbuilt and recombined as collage.

This thesis project is entitled "Every Day and Eternal: Designing Enduring Architecture with Recurrent Collage Operations."

It is about finding meaning and giving meaning through materiality, using collage as a method of assemblage that expresses time.

The project exists in two parts, first research then design, like the Roman analytical drawings and culinary institute design. The table of contents of the research gives you an idea of the structure and depth of the project. The physical consequence is a design project in a small city in Spain, existing and proposed plans on the right- which I will describe after briefly going through the research.

This project looks to collage as a design methodology for reassembling previously used building materials as found objects.

Collage as reuse of materials is syntactic and semantic because it's about construction and putting things together physically but also inherently about an outside larger system because the materials are already full of meaning. Finite natural resources are being depleted, and there is much contemporary scholarship on 'urban mining' and future stock reuse. We can look to unbuilding, deconstruction, and mining the city to create a surplus of the very materials we need for future building. There is an embodied energy in these materials available in buildings rather than newly produced.

EDUCATIONAL ENVIRONMENTS

Deconstruction and rebuilding enforces the idea that a changeable environment is a good one. Longevity and new things are mutually reinforcing when placed together. The plurality, of old and new, creates a rich and complex environment, an awareness of the present time within the context of a broader history. People enjoy familiarity but also a changing environment.

Our environment teaches us how to act, by providing security, continuity, and attachment to place, but also change rather than permanence, and constant shifts between old and new. We must design our environment to enable us to discover unexpected relationships, combining the past and present to provide an ever-changing, interesting, exploratory world.

Colin Rowe and Fred Koetter advocate the design of a Collage City. It is a city of fragments from the past, present, and future, juxtaposing and layering small designs into a whole a changeable, not utopian, solution to overly scientific or ad-hoc designs. Collage City provides a solution that sets up a flexible framework to adapt to the future.

This cyclical approach builds upon economic and logistic solutions to reuse. In the future we can pick and choose from the materials marketplace, combining materials from multiple buildings, changing the way elements are put together, reusing elements for an original use or a new use- all with the aim of environmental protection as well as designing interesting, thought provoking, inspiring environments.

This idea of material longevity is not new. St. Peter's Basilica steps were constructed from Colosseum Travertine. Marble has been removed from the Pantheon over thousands of years for use in other Roman building projects.

Architecture has an underlying capacity to reconcile different levels of reality. It has the ability to communicate abstract ideas and concepts in the built environment of everyday life. Architecture is a physical manifestation of our larger culture and communicates the conceptual through its material and forms.

Collage, the putting together of two things not normally associated with each other, can be used in architecture and landscape architecture, not as convenient fragments, but as a link to larger cultural ideas. The reuse of materials in collage creates an accommodating framework that allows for non-formal relationships between parts, a reframing of context, references, history, and memory. Using collage principles that produce multiplicity of meaning, architects are able to frame ethics and sustainability with aesthetically pleasing results. Iliescu uses the example of Duisberg Nord Park by landscape architects Peter and Annelise Latz, as a spatial depiction of collage principles developed by artists such as Braque, Kline, and Kurt Schwitters. We can also see the architecture of Jef7rey Hildner as such an assemblage.

Collage is an art method that can be useful to architects because it investigates three- dimensional space in a two-dimensional medium. For Picasso, Braque, and Juan Gris its existence between painting and sculpture facilitated a new way of thinking about space. As architecture can take abstract ideas in the two-dimensional realm and realize them in the three-dimensional built environment, both collage and architecture are in-betweens or links between the two worlds, and they can inform each other.

Collage simultaneously offers spatial, material, and intellectual content, placing an emphasis on process, which can be compared to architectural design and construction. As collage is a synthesis of unrelated fragments, its construction process remains evident in the finished work. The architectural experience is similar, as buildings are not perceived as a totality but an assemblage of overlapping materials.

Multiplicity exists in the word collage itself: as a verb, to assemble fragments, as a noun, a work of art, a technique, and even a state of mind, according to Rowe and Koetter.

This multivalence extends to the process of collage, which imparts multiple meanings in its final product. Each collage operates on three levels: as its original identity, the new meaning it gains in association with other object, and the meaning it acquires as the result of its change into a new entity.

Collage evokes many dualities, including "representational/abstract, gestural/precise, field/ figure, surface/depth, literal/metaphorical, and as we discussed previously, tectonic and associative.

Rowe and Koetter examine multiplicity in Collage City, stating that collage has "an attitude which encourages the composite." Seemingly opposing ideas pair to provide a more whole understanding as well as an unexpected delight. Picasso's Bull's Head, 1942, a sculpture composed of two found objects, a bicycle seat and handlebars, displays this duality:

"With Picasso's image one asks: what is false and what is true; what is antique and what is of today and it is because of an inability to make a halfway adequate reply to this pleasing difficulty that one finally, is obliged to identify the problem of composite presence in terms or collage."

Collage brings about multiplicity and yet synthesizes spatial and material conditions, making it a process and product appropriate to architecture.

GIVING PURPOSE TO FOUND FRAGMENTS

Collage finds opportunity in excess and waste, transforming trash into a productive material. The trash of the construction industry, building materials which are now wasted, yet have collectively have an enormous value, have inherent qualities for reuse and potential for industry. These items can no doubt be linked to architectural production; the process of collage can be connected to building with discarded items, since collage has a transformational power elevating everyday discarded items to high art. For instance, Kurt Schwitters collected street trash, old posters, and discarded theater tickets, which he reassembled into richly nuanced color compositions.

Collage gives new meaning and value to found fragments. Rowe and Koetter discuss collage's use of bits of low culture in high art as another duality, seemingly opposite pairing which becomes mutually reinforcing:

> For collage, often a method of paying attention to the leftovers of the world, of preserving their integrity and equipping them with dignity, of compounding matter of the ambiguities of fact and fiction as a convention and a breach of convention, necessarily operates unexpectedly. A rough method, a kind of *discordia concors*, a combination of dissimilar images or discovery of occult resemblance in things apparently unlike.

Sanda Iliescu in her course Lessons in Making, writes on how collage imparts much meaning by expanding the boundaries between:

> What makes a collage surprising, but also meaningful, it its open invitation to the presence of worldly, 'unaesthetic' things within the artistic frame... Yet, spanning this difficult divide between art and non-art, between the aesthetic and the worldly, is collage's greatest achievement. When we experience a Latz park or look at a collage by Braque, Kline, or Burri, we sense a kind of transparency, as aesthetic impressions and other more worldly phenomena come forth and then recede. As this happens, one may be touched unexpectedly by emotions as personal and even spiritual as they are aesthetic.

EXPRESSING PAST, PRESENT, AND FUTURE

Time and place are linked in the human mind, that the sense of place greatly contributes to the human sense of time. Collage flattens not only space, but time as well. Collages express the past, present and an implied future by allowing objects to retain their identity from former use, yet adding new meaning by juxtaposing with associated objects. The implied future would be the assumed cyclical deconstruction and reuse of the material. This element of time in collage directly links it to the construction practices of deconstruction, reclamation, and reuse- especially if we continue that process as a cycle, designing for deconstruction and emphasizing the longevity of materials.

The process of designing using reclaimed materials as collage becomes not only environmentally friendly and cost efficient, but also links the new construction to a broader cultural and historical context and situates the occupant in the present, a unique moment within the framework of time.

AN EXPANDED SENSE OF TIME

Collage is inherently non-chronological. In collage, the concept of date is unimportant, and time is free to rearrange itself.

Joseph Cornell's assembled boxes, currently exhibited at the Fralin Museum, confront issues of time and place, urging the viewer to reflect on his or her existence in a larger time and universe.

In my Master's thesis project on the pilgrimage town of Manresa, Spain I focused on an extensive study of existing topographic and archeological preconditions of the site. My analysis of existing site conditions led to the design of a new corridor, connecting the city to a currently inaccessible religious institution as well as natural resources and agricultural practices. A comprehensive index of existing conditions, both physical materials and socio-economic factors, communicates the reading of a project. Construction assemblies were developed as re-assembly of found materials and expressions of unbuilding, rebuilding, and future changeability. These study models are assemblages, attempting to expand time, showing old, new, and implying future reuse. Frameworks that allow for variation insinuate possibilities of being unbuilt and recombined iteratively.

The final plan is a collage in itself of my experiences, analyses, and designs of the past that contribute to the current project. A perspective from the culinary institution is visible, as are a sketch of Corso Emanuele in Rome, and a section of Chiesa Nuova, as a baroque precedent to the existing church in Spain. Rubbings of the ground in Manresa, as well as Rome, imply monumental gatherings, and planted form is expressed as texts from my research. My previous studies are revealed, as garden textures are formed by Richard Diebenkorn paintings—the subject of my undergraduate art history thesis, and my own paintings of Lake Martin describe the wet zone of river and flood plain.

Experiential collages as well as sections and details provide semantic and syntactic viewpoints.

To conclude, I go back to where I came from and look to where I am going.

I have found meaning through the separation and recombining of materials. There are associative and tectonic qualities, water and light within structural frameworks, and expressions, extensions, and manipulations of time through materiality. A layering and making visible of the processes of analysis, design, and construction provides revelations and complexities.

Reflections on where I come from reverberate in the simultaneity of sky and water, reflections mandated by the horizon and negotiated by the figure of Caravaggio's Narcissus.

The importance of two, of dual images, of complementary ways of understanding, of recurrent dualities, of tectonic and associative, is my Lesson of the Lawn.

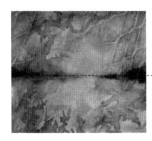

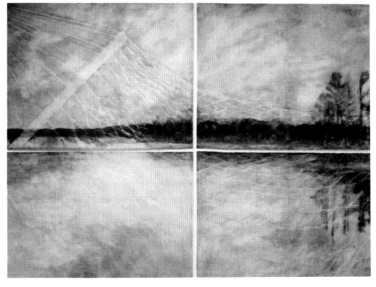

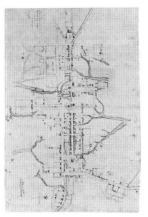

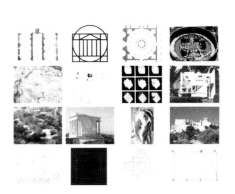

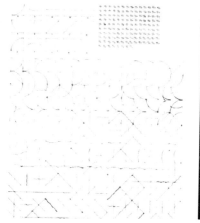

SEMANTIC/ ASSOCIATIVE:

reveals relationships with a
larger context

SYNTACTIC/ TECTONIC:

self-referential, describes its
own forms and structural forces

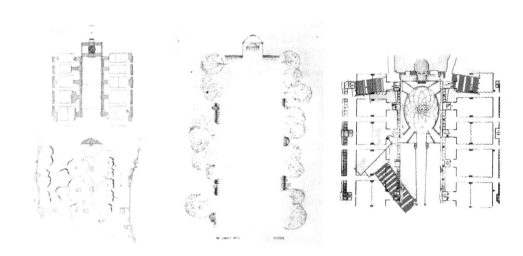

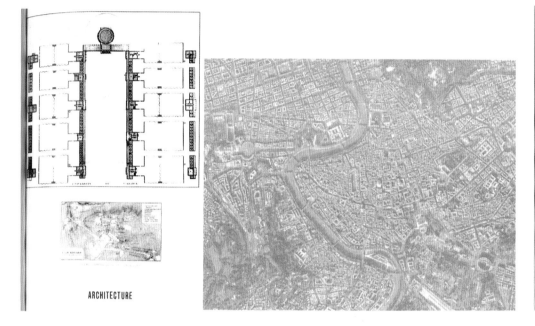

ARCHITECTURE

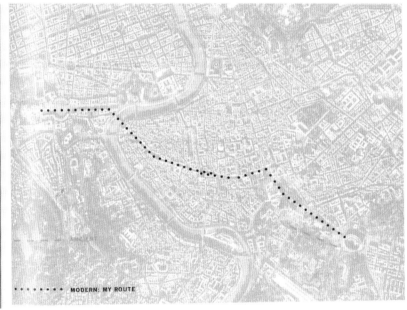

• • • • • • MODERN: MY ROUTE

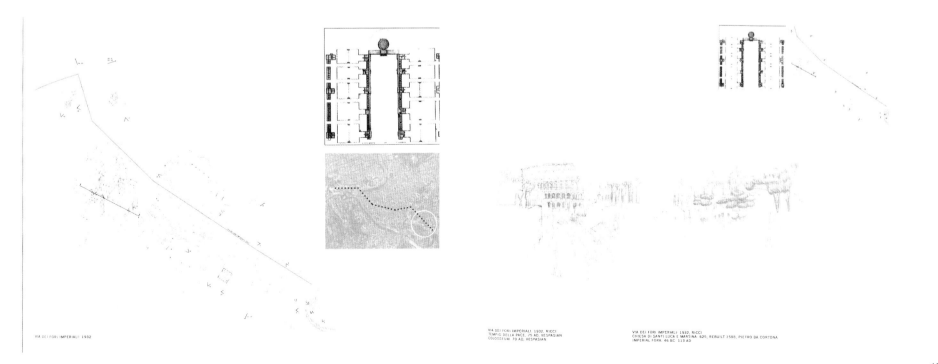

VIA DEI FORI IMPERIALI, 1932

VIA DEI FORI IMPERIALI, 1932, RICCI
TEMPIO DELLA PACE, 75 AD, VESPASIAN
COLOSSEUM, 70 AD, VESPASIAN

VIA DEI FORI IMPERIALI, 1932, RICCI
CHIESA DI SANTI LUCA E MARTINA, 625, REBUILT 1588, PIETRO DA CORTONA
IMPERIAL FORA, 46 BC 113 AD

VIA DEI FORI IMPERIALI: 1932, RICCI
CHIESA DI SANTI LUCA E MARTINA: 625; REBUILT 1588, PIETRO DA CORTONA

COLOSSEUM FROM VIA SACRA

COLOSSEUM: 70 AD, VESPASIAN

COLOSSEUM VIEW TO VIA SACRA & ARCH OF TITUS: 82 AD

PIAZZA DEL CAMPIDOGLIO & PALAZZI FACADES: 1576, MICHELANGELO
PALAZZO DEL SENATORE: 13-14th C

CAMPIDOGLIO PAVING

PIAZZA DEL CAMPIDOGLIO & PALAZZI FACADES: 1576, MICHELANGELO
SANTA MARIA IN ARACOELI: 12th C
MONUMENT TO VITTORIO EMANUELE II: 1885-1925, SACCONI

SANTA MARIA IN ARACOELI MOSAIC FLOOR

CAMPIDOGLIO AND PIAZZA VENEZIA

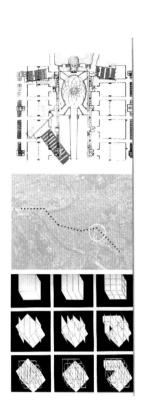

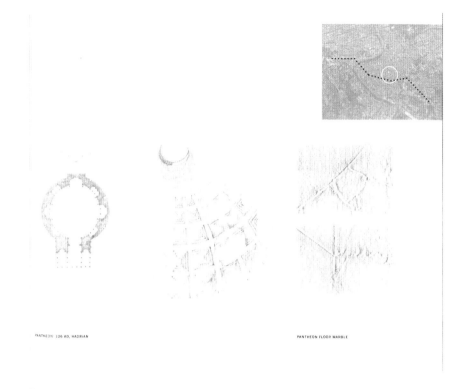

PANTHEON: 126 AD, HADRIAN

PANTHEON FLOOR MARBLE

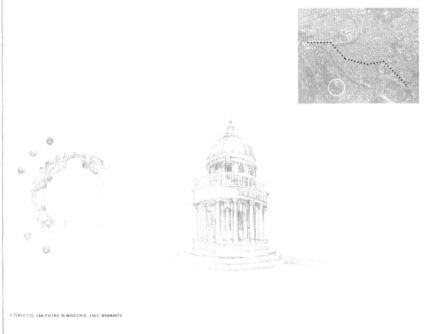

IL TEMPIETTO, SAN PIETRO IN MONTORIO: 1502, BRAMANTE

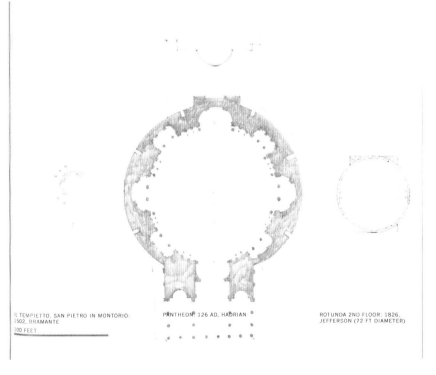

IL TEMPIETTO, SAN PIETRO IN MONTORIO: 1502, BRAMANTE

100 FEET

PANTHEON: 126 AD, HADRIAN

ROTUNDA 2ND FLOOR: 1826, JEFFERSON (72 FT DIAMETER)

162

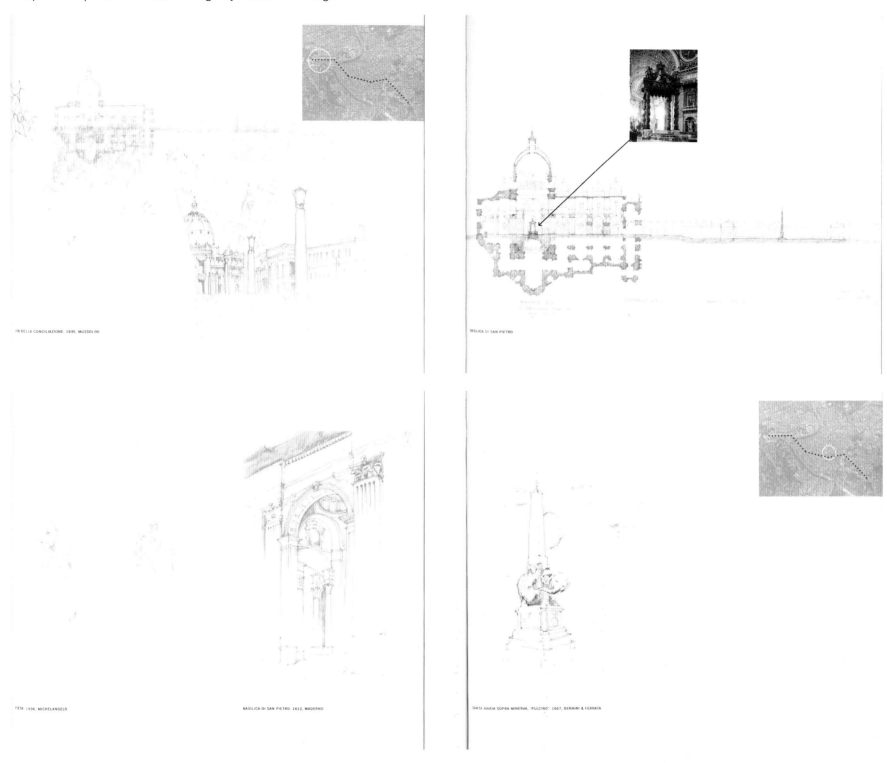

VIA DELLA CONCILIAZIONE, 1935, MUSSOLINI

BASILICA DI SAN PIETRO

PIETA, 1496, MICHELANGELO

BASILICA DI SAN PIETRO, 1612, MADERNO

SANTA MARIA SOPRA MINERVA, 'PULCINO', 1667, BERNINI & FERRATA

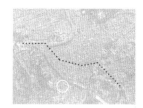
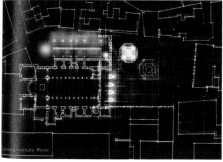

American Academy Institute, Rome

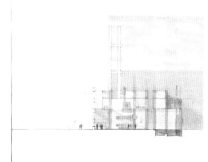

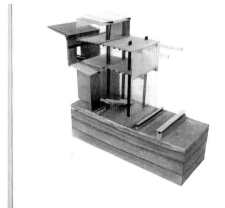

EVERYDAY AND ETERNAL
designing enduring architecture with recurrent collage operations

INTRODUCTION
    Thesis Statement
    Diagram
    Framework

PART 1: DECONSTRUCTION AND REUSE
    The Condition
    Benefits
    Terms
    Turning Difficulties into Benefits
    Case Studies

PART 2: CHANGE IS GOOD
    Educational Environments
    Material Longevity

PART 3: ASSEMBLAGE & ARCHITECTURE
    Collage: A Brief History
    Collage as Architecture, or Architecture as Collage
    Flattening
    Multiple Meanings

PART 4: COLLAGE: A PROCESS FOR REUSE
    Giving Purpose to Found Fragments
    Added Value

PART 5: ENDURING ARCHITECTURE
    Expressing Past, Present, and Future
    An Expanded Sense of Time

PART 6: TESTING GROUND

REFERENCE
    Notes
    Bibliography

The nature of all construction is fundamentally transitory. No building is ever a completed project...Every act of building is only a momentary contribution to a larger whole that in itself is constantly evolving, for every transformation of the extant can, and likely will become the subject of yet another transformation at a later point in time.

"Mine the City," Andreas and Ilka Ruby

Peter and Annelise Latz, *Hafeninsel (Island Park)*, Saarbrucken, Germany, 1985-86.

Pantheon marble plundered for reuse elsewhere; St. Peter's basilica steps are travertine from the Colosseum

COLLAGE AS ARCHITECTURE, OR ARCHITECTURE AS COLLAGE

"Like a collage, revealing evidence of time and its methods of construction, a work of architecture contains accumulated history as it is lived and engaged rather than observed. Just as a work of architecture is only fully created and comprehended through bodily, sensory engagement, collage can serve as a representational analogue, providing the medium to interrogate spatial and material possibilities."

Sanda Iliescu, "Beyond Cut and Paste"

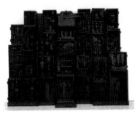

Jeffrey Hildner, *Ithaca: Dante | Telescope House digital collage*, 2010

Peter and Annelise Latz, Hafeninsel (River Island Park), Saarbrucken City Park, Germany, 1985-89.

Pablo Picasso, *Still Life with Chair Caning*. 1912, collage, oil, oilcloth, paper, canvas, rope.

Louise Nevelson, *Untitled*, 1964 and 1985

ON FRAGMENTS

"A city is never seen as a totality, but as an aggregate of experiences, animated by use, by overlapping perspectives, changing light, sounds, and smells. Similarly, a single work of architecture is rarely experienced in its totality but as a series of partial views and synthesized experiences. Questions of meaning and understanding lie between the generating ideas, forms and the nature and quality of perception."

Steven Holl, *Questions of Perception*

Sverre Fehn, Hamar Bispegaard Museum, Hamar, Norway, 1973

"With Picasso's image one asks: what is false and what is true; what is antique and what is of today, and it is because of an inability to make a halfway adequate reply to this pleasing difficulty that one, finally, is obliged to identify the problem of composite presence in terms of *collage*."

Colin Rowe and Fred Koetter, *Collage City*

Picasso, *Bull's Head*, 1942

Carlo Scarpa, Castelvecchio, Verona, 1959-73

3: COLLAGE: A PROCESS FOR REUSE

"You may paint with whatever material you please, with pipes, postage stamps, postcards or playing cards, candelabra, pieces of oil cloth, collars, printed paper, newspapers."

Guillaume Appolinaire, in defense of collage, 1913.[1]

Robert Rauschenberg, *Canyon*, 1959.

Kurt Schwitters, *Untitled (ered)*, 1929, paper on paper

Kurt Schwitters, *Merzbau*, 1933, waste materials, wood

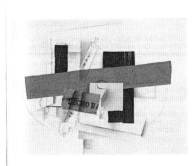

George Braque, *Still Life with Tenora*, 1913, pasted paper, charcoal, chalk, oil on canvas

Franz Kline, *Untitled II*, 1952, ink and tempera on pasted newsprint

A work of architecture retains its ability to prompt interpretations for generations beyond its creation...the ability of a building or structure to move us to see and hear ourselves and our place in the world.

- Sandy Isenstadt, "The Interpretive Imperative."[1]

Matadero, Madrid

Joseph Cornell, *Night Skies: Auriga*, 1954, box; wood; glass; paint; paper.

DESIGNING A PROCESS FOR MATERIAL REUSE AS COLLAGE

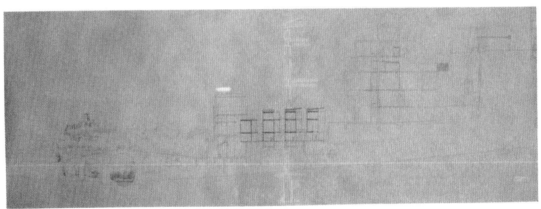

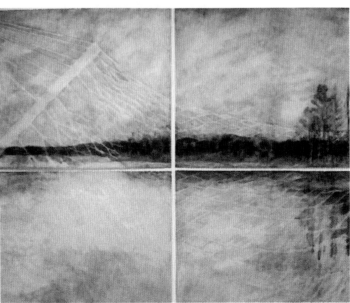

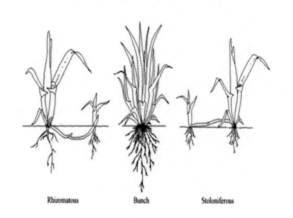

Rhizomatous   Bunch   Stoloniferous

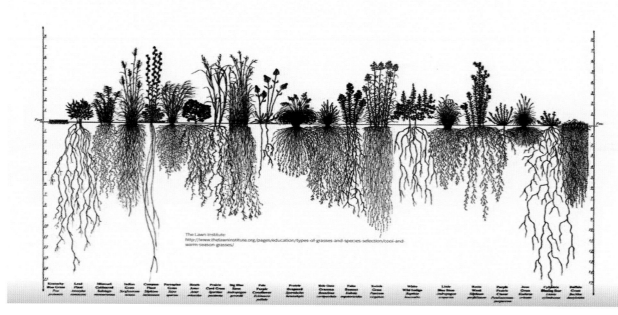

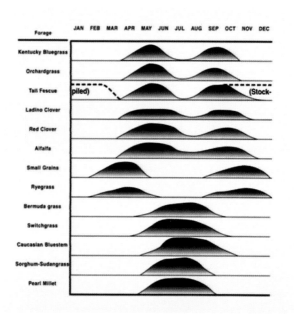

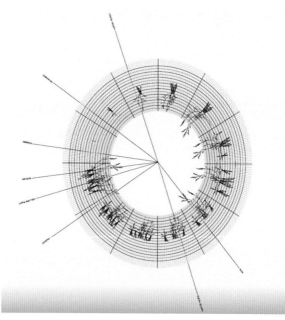

Blades of Grass
Hannah Barefoot

Today I'm going to talk about grass.

Initially from the perspective of a botanist – let's call it a surveyor. What is grass comprised of? How does it operate, what are the parts and joints you could identify – analyze, test, and draw?

Next from the perspective of ecology and cultivation – the farmer (a nomad, a surveyor) – the grower, the person who studies and understands the morphology of the plant enough to know how to use it and encourage its propagation.

Then with a foundational understanding of the biology and presence of grass in the environment and particularly the beloved Lawn – I'll give you the most brief pop-up shop lesson in landscape design and the history of the development of this form – the rolling turf.

Next, I'll dive into an interpretation of our own American lunatic Walt Whitman's Leaves of Grass – something those of you might be familiar with from high school English classes. The specificity of language is critical – as we've begun to see throughout this course. Through the lens of a familiar poem – *Song of Myself* by Walt Whitman we'll glance at contemporary images by painters and think about how to vacillate between individual blades of grass to the great whole. How a citizen can exist within a civilization. This is fluid-romantic poetry with the invention of free verse Whitman blasts open the field of poetry and the way people understand thought, language, space and ground.

Then we'll do another close reading of the displaced Catholic Northern Irish nomad Seamus Heaney and his conclusion to *Strand at Lough Beg* while looking at his chronologic contemporaries. Then through our examination of visual media artists Agnes Denes and Ana Mendieta, we will explore how bodies and the ground interact both in remote Mexico and in Battery Park, New York City. Again, what is it to use the formal, multiple leaves of grass to express the individual existence within the larger context of the proverbial city.

Finally, we will return to the Lawn, with our new, nuanced understanding of groundcover to rediscover the simplicity and possibility of complexity.

Let's do a warm-up on ground. Is it everything below us? Is it that right angle where the ground meets things that move vertically? What happens in cracks, drops, pockets of soil. What does it mean to look at the earth – back up to the sky – all the things in between what is right below your feet and distantly above one's head?

Ground cover types

What is grass? Let's get right into it. Morphology: a branch of biology studying the structure and form of organisms is an initial means of understanding this seemingly humble class of plants. Defined by their root systems important to draw plants with their roots defines them and lends specificity to any section

Rhizomatic spreads as a mat through rhizome root systems extending and then growing above ground when they've sought out water or better conditions away from the mother plant.

Bunch stays in one place and reproduces through scattering seeds more distance, but less control. More genetically diverse, and dependent on wind pollination, *Stoloniferous* spreads through tilling blades, taking advantage of leaves as a means to spread and forming roots similar to the rhizome but above ground.

These are the roots (stolon, rhizome root) which are all fibrous in the grass family. Other component parts of grass are the blade (leaf), the panicle (group of flowers and seeds), the node (joint), and the culm (a monocotyledonous stem as of a grass or sedge). Because it is a monocot, meaning it grows in one direction developing laterally rather than weaving and overlapping, botanists clarify for us the names for grasses.

Turf salesmen indicate we are in the Piedmont condition of Virginia in a zone of transition between warm weather grasses native to our area and cool weather grasses which are traditionally European imports. This zone of dramatic ground conditions liminally between freeze and thaw creates this opportunity to speculate on what is the significance of a lawn of grass. This may raise the necessity to discuss hybridity in this new millennium. This is a growth cycle of non-native cool season grasses, and our political condition as well.

These are our native bunching grasses one can see in early stages of succession meadows. They populate ground that is bare after fires, or clearing in forests after the falling of trees or flooding. They are pioneers for the ground. Short-lived but perennial, these grasses are herbaceous, though visibly dying seasonally, these roots remain dormant in order to produce more photosynthesizing parts during the next growing season. The root systems of the two types vary wildly in composition and depth. There are lawn systems dependent upon seasonal re-sodding and others which are perennial meadows such as our Lawn.

The maintenance of this rhizomatic body of individual plants and matting ground cover requires skill and mastery. There is a turf manager here at UVA, and his name is Chris Ward. He oversees the aeration, installation, complex choreography of the ground material, a responsibility significantly more expensive in upkeep than the constructed brick walks crossing the Lawn. Herein lies the major fallacy of green space being inherently natural as a ground cover. This maintenance requires unnatural, human generated aspirations of artificial continuities of permanence. Rather, nature's expectation is for nutrient cycling, pioneering, successional native grasses which are then allowed to be taken over by small woody plants and eventually the hardwood forest. There is no way grass is sustainable.

Management forms

When the turf at UVA got patchy in 2012 there was a full replacement made using sod from New Jersey and North Carolina—splitting the climatic difference and using "Turf Type Tall Fescue," a blend of multiple, consistently green grass seeds. The lawn is fertilized twice in the fall and once in the spring depending on soil tests patched by sod from Virginia and aerated and seeded twice a year while other areas require more attention.

Our ideals of this pristine enduring surface condition in reality is filled with implications of a failed assumption of humans' control over natural processes expressed in Jefferson's Enlightenment vision for the Lawn.

What are the cultural, historic precedents for green, low turf grass?
-Virgil, 29 BC "Georgics"
the first written account of the agrarian utopia and its maintenance.
-Hitchmough and Woudstra's medieval, "Enameled Mead, or Flowering Meadow"
tracking the trajectory of diversity in grassy swards
-Durer 1503, "Unicorn in Captivity"
an idealization of human control over flora and fauna
-Jethro Tull 16th century, "Drill Husbandry" a treatise on tillage radical
reconsideration of the construction of ground.
-Switzer 1715, "Forest", rural garden treatise with the agency of a garden boy
-Hawksmoor 1725, Castle Howard, Yorkshire, ferme ornee "ornamental farm"
-Vanbrugh 1725, Blenheim Palace, Oxfordshire, grazing sheep as mowers.
Nobility of agriculture, reference Thomas Cole's "Arcadian Empire"

The word "lawn" dates back to the 16th century prior to Tull and Switzer's treatises and is derived from the Old English *launde* denoting an open space or glade. Thomas Cole's image in the "Pastoral Setting" portrays a shepherd and sheep with the sheep grazing a lawn as the first step toward civilization.

Walt Whitman

Whitman was born on May 31, 1819 in Long Island near New York City. His father was initially a farmer there but moved the family, a wife and nine children to Brooklyn four years later where he became a carpenter. Whitman was apprenticed to a printer at the age of eleven, and spent the next decade as journeyman, an editor, type compositor, and eventually a writer. During this apprenticeship in New England, there appeared Ralph Waldo Emerson's essay "The Poet" published in 1844. Emerson calls for a great American muse to step forward and celebrate the emerging nation. Arising from the Transcendentalist movement in New England was the philosophical and spiritual belief that all people are inherently good—a tricky word, but one which infected Whitman's rebellious spirit.

Whitman responds

He self-published, set the type, sold the first edition of "Leaves of Grass" on July 4th, 1855. For the next four decades, "Leaves of Grass" is Whitman's life work. We are reading from the "Deathbed Edition" rather than the first. Our version of "Song of Myself" is at the start of a body of 200 poems. In the initial edition, one of 12 editions of book this poem occurs much later. This relocation points to the value and importance of his role as a typesetter. Whitman was able to relocate this specific poem as it emerged over time as in a compost heap. Leaves drop and fall regenerating and cycling providing nutrients to the soil. Performing a function, mulching, shading, a singular leaf in its lifetime, and plural leaves as noun and verb are extensions of a plant. Plants grow as self awareness from buds or the rhizome extending for a season or a lifetime. Plants, as well as human Whitman's self-conscious poetic being, seek to photosynthesize and gain nutrients from the sun. Whitman is responsible for unshackling the English language and extending it not only new to America but the world.

William Carlos Williams, a 20th century doctor, turned poet wrote of Whitman's first edition on 1855:

> Certainly, we are in our day dismissive now of Whitman's loose freedom as he employed in his verses in the blind belief that it was all going to come out right in the end. A new order had hit the world, a relative order, a new measure with which no one was familiar, offering a new language.

The surveyor referenced in this course together with the sensibilities of a nomad and lunatic would be unfamiliar with Whitman's language as it is unmeasured, transitional, fluid and new still today. Finding a way into the text is always the hardest. Let us be lunatics and nomads roaming through "Song of Myself" with confidence and depth. Ignoring conventional rules for meter and rhyme we will have to make up our own narrative of oases and mirrors for the moon by which to measure this poetic work of external nature and inner self.

While I talk through some lines of the poem, we will gaze at paintings by Martin Heade produced in the decades after the first edition of "Leaves of Grass," representing four decades of rewriting in multiple editions. These paintings of harvesting hay from the brackish marshes of Newbury Meadows are from the early realist movement of glorifying specific particular scenes of work and labor. Great attention is given to both the native flora and fauna and the transitional maintenance of these species which provide for the people of the region.

Heade's depiction of Newbury Meadows occurred at the same time Jefferson's Lawn was written about by students with a capital "L" describing it is an improved condition in 1870: "By the aid of Nature, and under the protection of the surrounding wires, the Lawn is assuming a very improved appearance…"

Now, let's turn to Section Six of "Leaves of Grass": "A child said What is the grass? Fetching it to me with full hands, how could I answer the child? I do not know what it is any more than he."

We know what grass is now, correct? We've had our crash course on botany, the relevance of species, region, and specificity when observing a blade of grass demands our engaged thoughts. We understand grass as a mat or a clump spreading by tiller leaves, rhizome roots, and or seeds.

But what Whitman wants to answer is more along the lines of essence; the leaves in the child's "full hands" make up a group a whole. The edges, ribs, pieces form a unit. You could count them measure them like a surveyor. By extending and abstracting, Whitman is able to imagine a reality though, where a singular leaf is a "flag out of hopeful green stuff woven" understanding it as a material woven, linked and formed through the interaction of fiber, but also a symbol, a flag representing his disposition his circumstance and mood. This is about assigning power to a seemingly insignificant thing returning to transcendentalism reading all people and things as significant and inherently good.

This empathy carries throughout Whitman's poems. He is making "guesses". The fact of this curious child holding out a clump of grass our factual understanding of the morphology of grass enables the creation of fiction we stretch and pull away from the idea that physical stuff and meaning are separate.

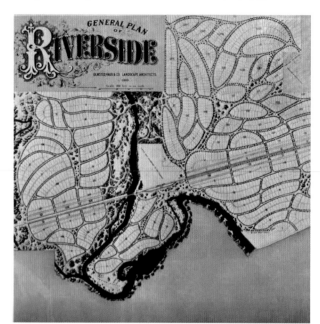

His guesses are grasps at meaning or significance he is floating through ideas designing a landing pad for the meaning of grass. His guess that grass is "itself a child, the produced babe of the vegetation," reflects back at the holder of the grass informed by his understanding of cultivation and plant growth.

His guess of a "uniform hieroglyphic" makes the leaves of grass itself not only his topic but a language which with we can read meaning. He understands grass as an indiscriminate grower speaking through symbolic language about the democracy of the whole the equality of soils or citizens.

Whitman lands on the idea, within this section that grass is "the beautiful uncut hair of graves."

It is critical that we understand the ground as a body that grows things out of its hair, trimmed or wild, as grass is a comparison we'll return to again in Heaney and Mendieta's work. It is also critical that we examine the beginning of this line.

"And now it seems to me the beautiful uncut hair of graves."

Whitman starts this realization by pulling from the past he threads this conclusion to his past musings with the word "and".

This freedom with the English language is still only reserved for poems and prose writers with gumption and skill. By beginning with the word "and" there is an implication that his work is continuous. It is fluid and representative of thought. He can and does start anywhere he draws out of his experiences and invents definitions for grass that imply a greater nuance to the subject through abstraction.

We will return to this obsession with grass as related to death in Heaney's poems and the understanding that grass is a ground cover that is commonly found in graveyards is not lost on anyone who studies lawns. The work of grass is to grow from the soil and "breasts of young men."

Even in the botanical book "How to Know the Grasses" by Richard Pohl the scientist waxes poetically on the grass: "they hold the hills, plains and mountains against the destructive erosive forces of wind and water. In the end, they form the sod that covers the sleeping dead."

This concept that the leaves of grass not only return nutrients gained from sunlight but draw nutrients from our decomposing bodies hints at the deep implications of ground and our place above it or below.

As Whitman points out: "the smallest sprout shows there is really no death."

And so, leaves extend not only the length of a table but the length of our existence. Our nutrients live on the leaves of grass.

This expansiveness and expression of a new freedom in language and form are seen in the 45th section of *Song of Myself* Whitman is ecstatic in declaring by releasing his body from his lovers who "suffocate" him he opens his window and sees the night sky all the "far sprinkled systems."

"Wider and wider they spread, expanding, always expanding, Outward and outward and forever outward....There is no stoppage and never can be stoppage."

If we are pushed down beneath or upon surfaces of the world, we will stand again… "And surely go as much farther, and then farther and farther" Whitman insists that to measure the distances between us and this infiniteness is useless "They are but parts, anything is but a part" reminding us of easy pieces and the difficult whole, measuring the distances for us the architects of surveyed space is not useless. We are rigorous and confused by the whole, the difficulty in comprehending that extended terrace of the Lawn falling away to the southwest.

This optimism of the whole and the extension that the impossible to comprehend the infinitely measurable are related to how we permit grass to exist within a civilization.

Okay we'll take a quick break and rendezvous with some work after Whitman.

With the advent of the lawn mower in the 1860s, a democratization and slow development of the American lawn, now a suburban standard, became visible in the work of Frederick Law Olmsted who designed the first streetcar suburb of Riverside in Illinois nine miles outside of Chicago. The concept of trees and turf borrowed from wealthy landowners and previously English estates translates to public space under a canopy with ground cover cool and green to "loafe" on. Olmsted was the pioneer of the American lawn along with the rapid invention of domestic lawn maintenance equipment in the period just after the Civil War.

Grant Wood's paintings made about four decades after Whitman's death in 1892 are exposing the flatness of a surface covered in grass and the historic implications of grassy lawns. This first image is interesting, Jefferson and Washington were actually some of the first Americans to have grass lawns having traveled to Europe and wealthy enough to transfer that tradition at both Monticello and Mount Vernon as both the rolling arcadian, Georgic, Switzer lawn from the 1740s and English country estates as well as the structured, formal, contained grass parterres of French formal gardens Versailles or Vaux de Vicomte.

This work leads us toward what Peter will walk us through next week with the formal and significant connections to Modern American landscape architecture in the Miller House and Garden by Kiley and Saarinen. The green is distinct, specific and for Kiley almost purely formal that element of drawing in two dimensions to create a three-dimensional space precluded turf to the role of mute surface, trimmed to emphasize and measure the ground.

The hedges are specific and trimmed after they grow the rigor of form is lost in this image of Pavilion IV from 1960, contemporary to the Miller House and Garden development. The wild nature of both the hedge and surrounding grasses imply some of that limitless optimism that meadows imply and Whitman expounds upon.

Or a walk-through it in a student publication in 1884: "The long-matted grass entangles the feet and seriously incommodes one's progress in the daytime, but when night has settled down over this wilderness, the Lawn possesses all the intricacies and difficulties of an Indian.

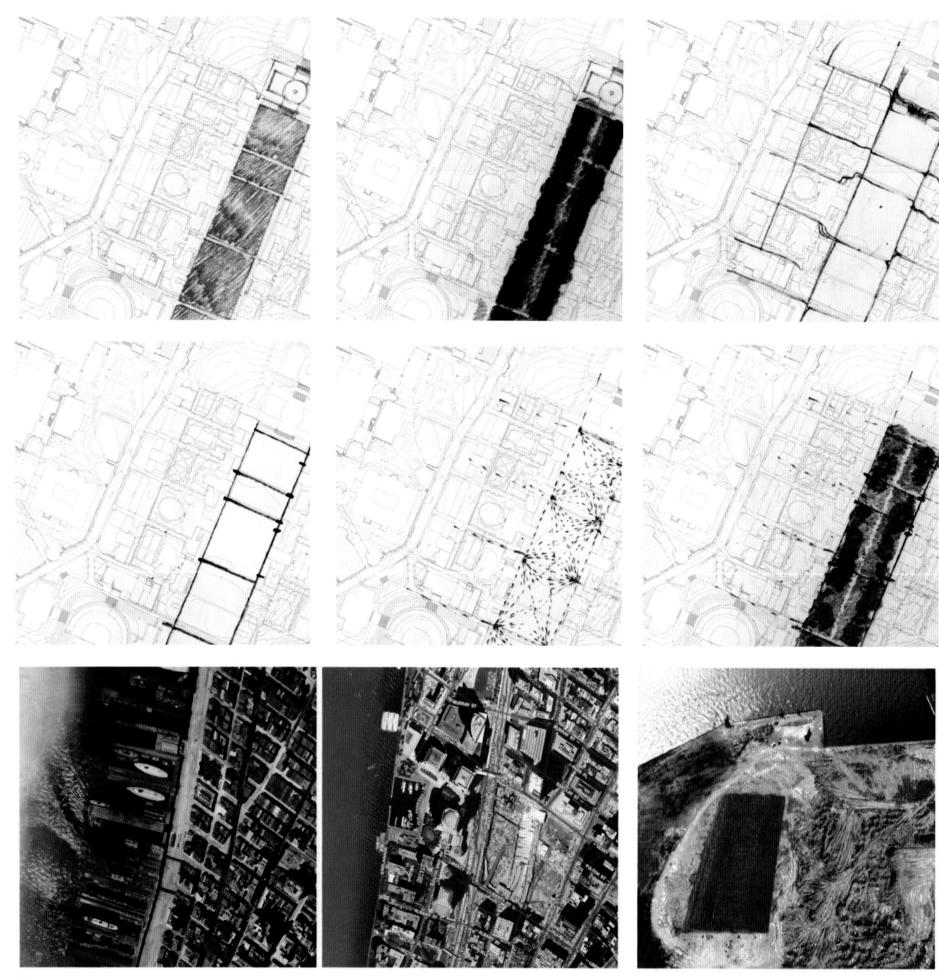

Now we turn from these precise and flat renderings of grass to a complex optimism from Agnes Denes through her installation (propagation) of amber waves of wheat on the Battery Park City landfill. Prior to the construction of Manhattan's western edge called Battery Park City, Agnes Denes used two acres to grow and then harvest wheat. A gesture of American ambivalence, the occupation of space, and the harvesting of a cereal grain a humble rough gesture within a neat rectangle on a mess of constructed ground complex and global in its make-up worth 4.2 billion dollars. Agriculture serves as a postage stamp of false reality or historic reminders.

Her work with agriculture extends to installation of rice fields in upstate New York and sheep in the American Academy of Rome in 1995.

Now we'll take this energy of expansion and free verse from Whitman's text and complicate our reading of ground cover through a close reading of Heaney's poetry.

It is essential that we now look at the work of Ana Mendieta, a conceptual and land artist from the 1970s. Her work is contemporary to that of Heaney's and similar in both the use of the land, ground cover, and earth. They both examine landscapes of aggression, violence and rawness within forms that are foreign but part of a complex whole.

Following her work, we'll glance at my work from my not–so–distant past in the studio art world working on similar issues through the medium of video.

They are both individuals with political agendas deciphered from the ground. The sectarian violence of Northern Ireland that Heaney splices open through his specific renderings of landscape reminds me of the violence towards women and the rifts and strife of Mendieta's home in Cuba. In her "Silueta" series that take form in both Mexico and Iowa, Mendieta exposes through a construction of her form by lying on the ground, burning, piling, and then fertilizing. Through the two mediums of poetry and landscape art, please search for how each person deals with grief, violence and that concept of the "uncut hair of graves" that Whitman initiated.

Famous Seamus, as he's known in Ireland was born April 13th 1939 and died in 2013. Heaney was a Catholic, but grew up in Protestant Northern Ireland, as part of a family of poor farmers. His language is terse, but thick with the sounds and meanings of Irish languages.

In the introduction to the section of the Norton Anthology for Contemporary Poetry Jahan Ramazani, a phenomenal professor here at UVA and the editor of the anthology says about Heaney's poetry.

"It is earthy and matter of fact, saturated with the physical textures, sights, smells, and sounds of farm life. Yet it is also visionary, enacting spiritual pilgrimages and tentatively crediting miracles. Heaney, as we see in the poem, represents his poetic quest as digging, a grim archaeological process of recovery from dark and unknowable depths. Yet he also moves upward into the open and the glimmering light of hope, spirit, and unbridled imaginings."

I hope you gathered this from reading the texts are critical that we again remember language as the medium of the poet; material, drawing, diagramming, growing and building is ours as well. The construction of work from unknown depths is the construction of ground our digging goes into the preconditions of the site reading site and understanding the way that both the land fluctuates, succeeds, fails, reveals, and changes.

"Heaney saw the peat bog as a kind of 'memory bank' or unconscious, of the landscape."

"The Strand at Lough Beg" is an elegy from his book *Field Work* (apt title) dedicated to his cousin Colum, killed by sectarian violence of Northern Ireland in 1975. The context is right after hearing about the murder of his cousin. This poem is the initial response to an imagined return to the beach (strand) at a lake west of Belfast, NI, UK.

In the description of the final walk where Seamus turns to find his ghosted cousin Colum, one sees everything is about the ground cover: "squeaking sedge, drowning in dew, brimming grass, and rushes that shoot green."

The three types of ground cover we know from the rhyme: sedges have edges, rushes are round, grass has knees wherever it is found all take part in this final imagined moment of Colum's life. Seamus cleans his brow with "handfuls of the dew" and washes his bloodied cousin in water accumulated in the ground cover during the cool night and morning "haze" accumulating over Lough Beg.

The dew makes the grasses seem like a vehicle for this final bath. Heaney's specificity in description and knowledge in the site this distant lake's edge manipulates the way we understand the place.

Grass is a dew collector and the walker's movement through is like a "dull blade" as is the lake "honed bright." You see what Heaney has done here, both the walkers and the lake are dull blades: both the individual and the difficult whole of a societal ether relate through action and form of Colums's death and nature's persistence. Ground cover is born again out of the traumatic, constructed ground grass is the "uncut hair of graves" that "shoot green" again.

After laying his cousin flat, this is the final step, the spatial circumstance of death, Heaney plaits "green scapulars to wear over your shroud." This is critical where the vehicle for brimming dew and articulating movement becomes the spiritual and symbolic material of Catholicism. Material collected, as a harvest which has power to be woven into a rosary. The rushes plaits can be counted meditated upon, surveyed by our surveyor. The resourcefulness of gathering materials at hand belongs to the skills of the nomad.

MAKE
DEATH
LEGIBLE

In the end we are using these materials – in my case and perhaps in yours – shrub, hedge, rushes, sedge and grass along with trees. But what are we trying to say with them? The syntactic language of architecture is often reduced to points, lines, planes, and volumes. However the semantic language of architecture is expanded with the engagement of the ground and the sky, with grass and trees, with the fluidities of dew and ocean, and with the passage of the sun and the moon. Heaney and Whitman both wield language about these spatial qualities – and demand interpretation.

What can the lawn be?

We've gathered language to describe and abstract grass we've looked at examples of different morphology. How can we question constantly the material and space in a site? Consider leaves and their ability to expand, grow, die, regenerate, and fertilize.

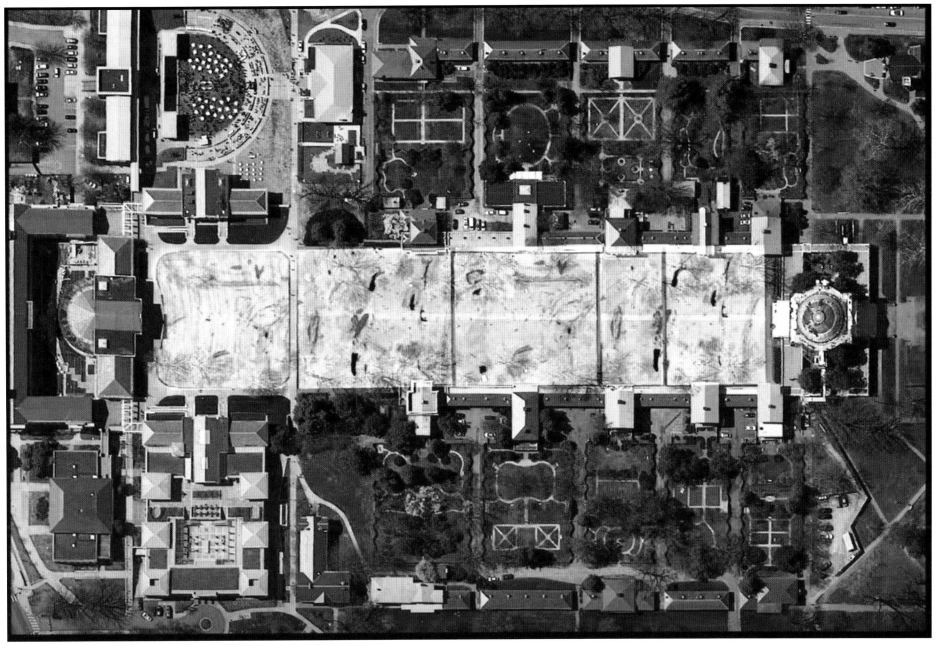

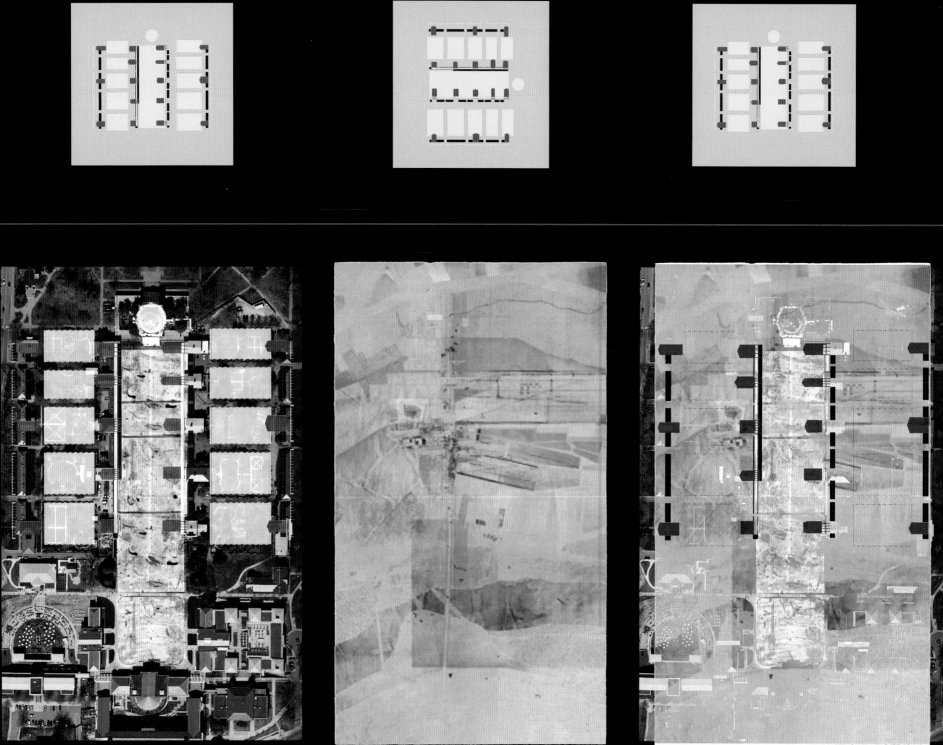

Connective Tissue #5: The End is Now The Beginning
Peter Waldman

Polly Smith Finn, M. ARCH, (2015) and Hannah Barefoot, MLAR, (2016) were among the final Kenan Fellows at the University of Virginia. They represent in their singularities the specific strengths of this surrogate *School of Athens*, now-here, not no-where in Virginia's Piedmont.

Their essays place an ethical primacy on articulating preconditions: where they come from, and where they now find themselves.

They both trace histories as heuristic links across time and space reinforcing the utility of recurrent dualities.

They both appreciate building as a verb, and the construction site is to be valued more than an occupancy permit.

They both commit to counter the hubris of urbanism as the pretense of environmental negotiation and advocate the humility of animistic engagement, for bearing witness to systems greater than ourselves as articulated by Walt Whitman in *Leaves of Grass*.

Their essays are adjacent to one another, but it is to the reader to weave connective tissues from these loose threads.

That is the pedagogic intent of interrogating why we are here, first dialectically as students and faculty, simultaneously citizens and strangers, engineers and gardeners, but also now perhaps tripartite in our complex character amalgamation of the surveyor, nomad and lunatic. Perhaps at this point in connective tissues the nomadic condition is pivotal as a ligament, no, rather catalytic as a chemical agent.

Now, we all find ourselves as participants in the larger world, in simultaneities James Joyce would appreciate. However, Walter Lippmann in *Preface to Morals* reminds us that we, here and now, should remain stained by the soil upon which our ancestors toiled daily under the forces of the sun and the moon. He makes a case for an endurant sense of origin, some call preconditions, as we seemingly move out of our contexts and in the process move away from our cultures. Perhaps, the connective tissues resonate in the haunted lyric "Four strong winds, they blow lonely, seven seas they run dry." (Ian and Sylvia ,1961)

These two final essays take us full circle back to the posture of a spatial tale of origin in Catharine Killien's essay Two Hands and Ten Digits, as well as an expanded understanding of the ground rules of collage at the scales of both telescopic continental imaginations as well as the microscopic scale of a blade of grass.

Both came to Virginia from the Piedmont condition of the South with studio art and cultural history backgrounds as contemporary students in Architecture and Landscape architecture respectfully.

Both presented their lectures at the end of the foundation course *Lessons of the Lawn*. The Lawn at the end of the semester had evolved from a superficial expanse of grass terraces, merely a green feature, a residual space serving as a common ground between academic pavilions, student rooms and a monumental library.

Then, Smith Finn's/Barefoot's microscopic and telescopic dialogues herein, back and forth in intensity, exemplified "The Word Made Flesh" in these texts and collages, and were at first awesome, then inspiring and finally exemplary of how deeply the students at Mr. Jefferson's university were expected to read into the profound stage sets offered for their architectural education. Serlio would smile in approval, if not exuberant delight.

Polly Smith Finn provided a rare capacity to trace the critical context of her speculations grounded in 20th Century art and architectural histories and theory. As a good Surveyor, she traced the epistemology of the 20th century evolution of Semiotics from Cubism, to Purism, to Collage, to Cornell's Boxes, to Schwitters, and to Latz's postindustrial landscapes. As a good Nomad, she took us home to her early place of amusement—Lake Martin—touchingly parallel to WG Clark's oasis in a humble Mill Pond in Louisa VA evoking the Obligation of Replacement. And as a good Lunatic, she revealed astonishing reflectivity in Alabama's humid luminosity painted onto water and wind, to be encountered again in the dusty iridescence of the sunburnt urban landscapes of her thesis project Every day and Eternal: Designing Enduring Architecture with Recurrent Collage Operations, projected for Manresa, Spain.

Hannah Barefoot sees, as a landscape architect, that a spatial tale of origin commences with the seed and the ground. Into this setting, water and sun sustain growth, and develop though maturity onto death. With this new appetite for resilience, an eschatological new beginning is also maintained in Wislawa Szymborska's two generative poems "The End and The Beginning" and "Water," serving as connective tissues. Barefoot is a masterful designer of conceptual consequences in this final essay with this admonition: Make Death Visible.

> Let us talk about grass from the perspective of a botanist; next from the perspective of ecology and cultivation; then with a foundational understanding of biology and the presence of grass in the environment and particularly our beloved Lawn as an evolution of rolling turf; expanding into literary parallels in Walt Whitman's "Leaves of Grass", and Shamus Haeney's "Strand at Lough Bog;" onto artists Agnes Denes and Ana Mendieta, with a final return to the Lawn with an expanded understanding of the complexities of ground cover.

Anyone named Smith, in my book, is obliged to be a maker, employing base metals and fire and human force to forge magical connections. Anyone who bears the name Barefoot possess a soul in dialog with the ground. Two sensibilities of agency and communication are again haunted by Semper's admonition: "The first architectural act is to break the Ground."

EPILOGUE

LABYRINTH R.U.N., by Jef7rey Hildner

"THE ARTIST'S FUNCTION IS THE MYTHOLOGIZATION OF THE ENVIRONMENT AND THE WORLD,"
said Joseph Campbell, the renowned 20th-century scholar of comparative religion and comparative mythology.
Thomas Jefferson gave 19th-century expression to Campbell's ideal through the University of Virginia's
Academical Village.

JEFFERSON MADE THE LABYRINTH LEGIBLE

The golden threads of memory, art, and myth connect us through the ages and stages of recorded time . . . respun by every generation,
these threads lead us safely into and out of the Labyrinth . . .

L A B Y R I N T H   R . U . N .

"Architecture is the stage set for the drama of life and death." —Michelangelo A. Roland Slate

THE ANCIENT GREEKS DIDN'T FEAR DEATH.

BUT THEY DID FEAR THE ONE THING THAT DOOMS US TO A FATE WORSE THAN DEATH.

AND THEY KNEW THAT EVEN IF WE SUMMON ALL OF OUR RESOURCES TO HEAD OFF THAT FATE AT THE GUARDIAN GATE, VICTORY DOESN'T REST ENTIRELY, IF VERY MUCH AT ALL, IN OUR POWER.

AND POWER MIGHT PROVE LESS IMPORTANT THAN LUCK.

THE ANCIENT GREEKS KNEW THAT TO SLAY THE MINOTAUR, THE TERRIFYING MONSTER THAT PROWLS THE LABYRINTH— WE MUST ENLIST THE HELP OF A SUPERNATURAL AIDE.

A GOD.

J E F 7 R E Y H I L D N E R
FLIGHT MASTER. 2010. OIL ON CANVAS. 62 X 93 IN.

ACT 1: D E P A R T U R E

"HE FEARED YOU MIGHT FOLLOW OLD OBI-WAN ON SOME DAMNED-FOOL IDEALISTIC CRUSADE LIKE YOUR FATHER DID." —*STAR WARS: EPISODE IV - A NEW HOPE*

THE STRANGE WAY

I'll always remember that summer in 2001 when my Columbia University screenwriting teacher, David McKenna, opened my eyes to the underlying architecture of the human condition.

There I was, mid-40s, in a classroom of young twenty-somethings. I had stepped over the threshold from my familiar, ordinary world into an unfamiliar, special world. But I felt right at home. I felt like an astronaut who struck water on Mars.

When I entered that screenwriting class, I was well versed in principles of the architecture of Form. Even taught them. I'd written many essays on the theory and practice of art. I'd become a painter. Braque, Picasso, and Diebenkorn had shaped my search, via my canvases, for the aesthetic and symbolic space-making language of my architecture. I'd earned my architecture license and been lucky enough to do a few buildings. But when it came to age-old principles of the architecture of Story, principles that story architects typically trace back to Aristotle's *Poetics*, I was like the movie: *Clueless*.

But Dante|Telescope House (1991–1996) paved the way to my encounter with those story design principles. The house expresses my view that architecture is a complex chess game of Move & Meaning. I lean toward architecture that trades in both sides of the coin of art—architecture that presents not only a compelling Abstract Aesthetic System ("Moves") but also a compelling Symbolic Image System ("Meanings"). Buildings that reflect not only pleasing aesthetic Control but also possess a deep symbolic Soul. For Dante|Telescope House, that was my goal.

And when it comes to Control and Soul, could there be a more iconic example than Jefferson's Academical Village? Or Le Corbusier's 1953 masterwork in Chandigarh, India, the Palace of Assembly?

In my first design studio, as a second-year undergrad at Princeton, Peter Waldman assigned every student a landmark 20th-century building to analyze. Professor Waldman waved his magic wand, and Corb's Palace of Assembly landed on my desk. That was my lucky day. I'd never laid eyes on a building like that and fell immediately under its spell. Ever since, this great work of art has been my Move & Meaning North Star.

Years later, my North Star got a sidekick: Antoni Gaudi's 1910 Casa Milà aka La Pedrera, in Barcelona, Spain. It wasn't until after Dante|Telescope House was built that I got a chance to go to Barcelona and see La Pedrera and wander through it. And as I stood atop that damned-fool building and looked to the Mediterranean Sea, as I strolled through Gaudi's enchanted roof garden dotted with his stone chess-piece sentinels, well, it was unforgettable.

Those two grand masterworks continually mentor me and breathe into me the aspiration and courage to chart the same artistic course. Dante|Telescope House gave me my first chance. Like Corb and Gaudi, I wanted to architect a building you don't expect . . .
—a building that lifts you out of your ordinary world into a special world . . . because **THE PURPOSE OF ART IS TO WAKE US UP**: rip the blindfold from our eyes. As Georges Braque said, "The purpose of art is to disturb." But he means disturb in a positive sense: disturb us out of our slumber, disturb us out of our prison cell of limited ways of seeing, false assumptions and fears, disturb artists creatively into a bolder desire to risk everything, go on a crazy idealist crusade and make something the likes of which nobody's ever seen before. In 1907, when Braque first laid eyes on his buddy Picasso's go-for-broke *Les Demoiselles d'Avignon*, Braque felt like a bomb exploded, and the impact disturbed him right into the invention of Cubism.

Picasso and Braque's paintings and Le Corbusier's and Gaudi's buildings show me that what Russian Formalist Viktor Shklovsky said rings true: "Precisely because it is the familiar way, it is not the artistic way." The artistic way is the *defamiliar* way —the strange way.

CAVE

38° NORTH LATITUDE | GSM

ITHACA

THE PROBLEM IS TO EVOKE TH SIMULTANEOUS PRESENCE OF PAINTING AND ARCHITECTURE. —Theo van Doesburg | 1917

The steel-beam telescope sights the North Star | .

"Precisely because it is the familiar way, it is not the artistic way." —Viktor Shklovsky, "Art as Device" | 1917

IN A WORK OF ART, EVERYTHING MUST BE *FORMED*, BUT THE PURPOSE OF ART GOES BEYOND FORM:

"to make perceptible the texture of the world in all aspects" —Boris Mikhailovich Eikhenbaum

DANTE | TELESCOPE HOUSE

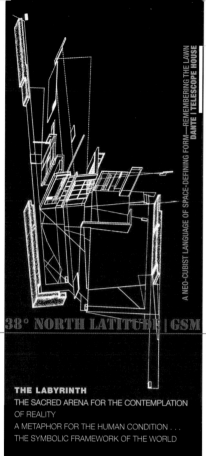

A NEO-CUBIST LANGUAGE OF SPACE-DEFINING FORM—REMEMBERING THE LAWN
DANTE | TELESCOPE HOUSE

38° NORTH LATITUDE | GSM

THE LABYRINTH
THE SACRED ARENA FOR THE CONTEMPLATION
OF REALITY
A METAPHOR FOR THE HUMAN CONDITION . . .
THE SYMBOLIC FRAMEWORK OF THE WORLD

The artist is the wild card, a disruptor, seeking to upend our ordinary world and defy what we expect to see. And read. In the hope of setting us free.

ARCHITECTURE IS A VISION QUEST

But Corb and Gaudi's buildings, and Jefferson's campus for UVA, resonate with the spirit of antiquity as well as the spirit of the brave. Like ancient architecture, Palace of Assembly, Casa Milà, and the Academical Village resonate with meaning. They taught me something very important: Architecture is metaphor. And they set me on a path—a vision quest—to find more answers, compelling answers, to the question, What is architecture?

Viktor Shklovsky and other early 20th-century literary theorists known as the Russian Formalists validated my question, my quest. These art theorists concluded, rather rationally, I believe, that before we can achieve mastery of an art form, we must first know what it is. "What is architecture?"

For the more direct fountainhead of Dante|Telescope House, I point you to a fourth Move & Meaning building: Giuseppe Terragni's 1937 unbuilt Danteum—a project that twinkles in the night sky of my mind as a sister North Star. Through the Danteum, Terragni tells the story of Dante's *Divine Comedy*, an early 14th-century Italian epic poem in which Dante describes his travels, led by the ancient Roman poet Virgil, through Hell, Purgatory, and Heaven. Terragni's Danteum helped me eventually see, Architecture is a story told through a building.

The Danteum evokes the original link between architecture and literature. The first books were buildings, and the first buildings were books. Think, for example, of the Egyptians, who wrote their histories and scientific ideas, recorded their concepts of life and cultural memories, on the walls and columns of their temples. (I hope that as you read this "column of text" you'll feel your pulse quicken as you consider the deep and significant connection between the arts of writing and building.)

As to the Telescope? The steel beam that angles up through the "Dante|Telescope Monolith" and points to the North Star? The original connections between architecture and astronomy floor me. As they surely floored Jefferson, who created a poetic simulacrum of the world, a domed tower, a pantheon, for his University of Virginia library—which, for all who study and dream within the sacred arena of its encirclement, filters wisdom into their hearts and minds from the books on the shelves and from the celestial light above. Jefferson's Rotunda faces south to The Lawn, but, today at least, we enter the Rotunda, his figurative representation of the cosmos, from the north.

If you look up the word *temple* in the *Oxford English Dictionary*, you'll find that a temple, the archetypal first building, was laid out by an architect cast in a surprising role.

Temple: "the sacred space marked out by astronomer-priests for the observation of reality." Yes, through Move & Meaning, architecture presents the sacred arena for the contemplation (the con-*temple*-ation) of reality. Through Move & Meaning, architecture makes perceptible the symbolic framework of the world. These deep-seated origin concepts infuse the four architectural works that North Star my path.

Add to the mix that the word *building* comes from an ancient Indo-European word that means "to be." And you get an idea what Dante|Telescope House is about. I thread through the project Move & Meaning themes about literature and astronomy, painting and architecture, seeing and being. I hope you get some sense of how much I owe to these four architect poet-philosophers—Le Corbusier, Gaudi, Terragni, and Jefferson—how I remember them as I blaze my trail. They coach me along the west, east, south, and north sidelines of The Lawn of my work.

THE LABYRINTH PATH

More about The Lawn and its Space Master later. But first, to go back to my learning curve about story. Until I read McKenna's course syllabus, I had somehow managed to walk this planet for over 40 years without ever hearing about, let alone reading, Joseph Campbell's book *The Hero With A Thousand Faces*.

Hero is gender neutral, like pilot, chef, and architect. The word *hero* comes from the Greek, meaning "to serve and protect" and refers to someone motivated by values other than self-interest, someone who gives their life to a purpose bigger than themselves in the service of others—for example, an age-old purpose that flows from the desire to inspire others through one's work.

Campbell's book woke me up. Like Cesare in the classic 1920 German-Expressionist silent film *The Cabinet of Dr. Caligari*, I had been sleepwalking . . . sleepwalking through the maze of life. I was blind to the connective ground between architects today and Daedalus—the mythical ancient Greek architect of the Labyrinth.

For the ancient Greeks, the labyrinth was a metaphor for life, for the human condition, a metaphor for how the human spirit inspires us to crusade idealistically forward through ongoing overlapping cycles of Departure, Transformation, and Return. The ancient Greeks conveyed this archetypal three-act pattern (which shapes everyone's multi-layered story arc) through the metaphor of the labyrinth and the stories they wove about it. Those ancient storytellers dreamed up the story of Daedalus and his architectural invention to illustrate the architecture of the human journey. Daedalus made the path through his building (the labyrinth) hard because the path through life is hard.

The myth of Daedalus made me double down on my desire to make an architecture less like a Move & Meaning *collage* (Palace of Assembly, Casa Milà, the Academical Village, and Dante|Telescope House) and more like a Move & Meaning *narrative* (the Danteum). My desire landed me on another way to describe the two sides of the coin of architecture—the two iconic costars in the war of art: Form & Story.

I signed up for that college class to learn about the architecture of a screenplay for a movie. I didn't expect to learn about the architecture of the screenplay of life, about the archetypal patterns and principles of the Form & Story of the human condition. Or to learn about the architecture of a building. But as Virgil says in his own epic poem, *The Aeneid*, "Your path to safety will open first from where you least expect it."

WHERE AM I? The steel-beam Telescope (a shard of ambient suns) cuts through the Dante Monolith and sights the North Star.

IN A WORK OF ART, EVERYTHING MUST BE *FORMED*, BUT THE PURPOSE OF ART GOES BEYOND FORM:
DANTE | TELESCOPE HOUSE

"to make perceptible the texture of the world in all aspects" —Boris Mikhailovich Eikhenbaum

The Aeneid tells the story of the epic hero Aeneas, including the tragic story of his star-crossed love affair with the queen of Carthage, Dido. Aeneas was the demigod son of an immortal mother, Venus, and a mortal father, Anchises, who Aeneas carried on his back to safety when the Greeks burned down the city of Troy. The gods impelled the Trojan refugee Aeneas to move forward bravely along his legendary journey toward his ultimate destination, his destiny, which he could not foresee: Italy, where his descendants Romulus and Remus would found the city of Rome. Like heroes past and present, Aeneas's journey took twists and turns. Adversity tested him along his quest. Aeneas waged war against inner and outer resistance. He enlisted allies and battled enemies. He experienced epic triumph and epic fail . . . love and heartbreak. To fulfill his purpose in the service of others— to no less than lay the foundation for a new world—Aeneas was forced to sacrifice everything.

Even his heart.

DAEDALUS 9

THE LAWN. THOMAS JEFFERSON, 1817.

Engraving of the University of Virginia, From the South, J. Serz, 1856

ACADEMICAL VILLAGE | VIEW LOOKING NORTH

LABYRINTH ARENA: TOWER, MAZE, AND LAWN—STAGE SET FOR THE DRAMA OF LIFE AND DEATH

DAY AND NIGHT, MEMBERS OF THE UNIVERSITY COMMUNITY SLAY THE MINOTAUR OF IGNORANCE, CONFUSION, AND FEAR BY WIELDING THE SWORD OF ENLIGHTENMENT, CREATIVITY, AND COURAGE.

improv 1.0

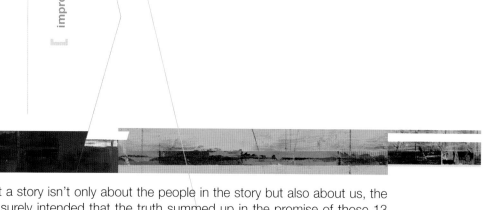

RIFF ON THE BOOK COVER FOR DAEDALUS 9, FEATURING SPACE MORE EMPTY THAN FULL

All good storytellers know that a story isn't only about the people in the story but also about us, the people in the audience. Virgil surely intended that the truth summed up in the promise of those 13 words—about how the path ahead might twist safely through the mortal maze in ways we can't expect— applies not only to the mythical Aeneas but to everyone, from those of us part of invisible history to Thomas Jefferson.

38° NORTH LATITUDE | GSM

A LAWN IS PART OF EVERY LABYRINTH. THE LAWN IS THE *SIGNIFICANT SPACE* AT THE LABYRINTH'S HEART. THE LAWN IS THE ARENA FOR THE EPIC SHOWDOWN.

Jefferson, in the service of others—through his Declaration of Independence and establishment of a university, which he made forever tangible through his construction of the Academical Village—battled adversity, persevering to fulfill his Aeneas-like vision and lay the foundation for a new world.

No journey unfolds without elements of serendipity. Surprise. Turning points. Tests. Adversity. Change. That's how the journey through the labyrinth of life works—how the design of the universal story unfolds. How, to one degree or another, our journey through the labyrinth of a significant architecture unfolds.

Whether a building or a life, Virgil's heads-up applies. On the journey through the labyrinth, fraught with peril and laced with promise, "Your path to safety will open first from where you least expect it."

LABYRINTH ii | TOWER, MAZE, AND LAWN. JEFFREY HILDNER. 1998. OIL AND PENCIL ON CANVAS. 32 X 48 IN.

VISUAL EFFECTS
VISUAL EFFECTS
ARCHITECTURE AND THE CHESS GAME OF FORM & STORY

38

ARCHITECTURE IS A CHESS GAME OF FORM & STORY WAGED ON THE BATTLEFIELD OF A BUILDING AND ITS SITE.

THE ARMIES OF FORM & STORY FIGHT THE **WAR OF ART.**
THEY FIGHT FOR OUR **MIND** AND **SOUL** AND **HEART.**

NORTH

"[DAEDALUS] IS THE HERO OF THE WAY OF THOUGHT — SINGLEHEARTED, COURAGEOUS, AND FULL OF FAITH THAT THE TRUTH, AS HE FINDS IT, SHALL MAKE US FREE. AND SO NOW WE MAY TURN TO HIM, AS DID ARIADNE. THE FLAX FOR THE LINEN OF HIS THREAD HE HAS GATHERED FROM THE FIELDS OF THE HUMAN IMAGINATION."

—JOSEPH CAMPBELL, *THE HERO WITH A THOUSAND FACES*

DAEDALUS | THE SILVER KNIGHT

DAEDALUS

Photography by Apple Hill Co

SILVER KNIGHT ARCHITECTURE

THE ARCHITECT PAINTER | Knight Head Quarters

SACRAMENTO, CALIFORNIA

THE ARCHITECT PAINTER PRESS

ARCHITECT, PAINTER, AND WRITER
JEF7REY HILDNER

I.AM.DAEDALUS.

Legendary first architect, descendent of Greek myth, inventor of the labyrinth and wings.

38° NORTH LATITUDE | GSM

One of countless reincarnations of Daedalus since time began.

FORM & STORY

Trapped in a labyrinth that I myself devised.

"All art tends towards structuring the contradiction between that which appears and that which signifies, between form and meaning."
—Robert Slutzky, "Re-Reading Phenomenal Transparency"

Summoning, as best I can, escape capacity through wings of serendipity and creativity . . .

My name is DAEDALUS.

And I am a Workaholic.

Architecture is a vision quest. A rite of passage from the ordinary to the extraordinary— a brave reimagination of the world.

A member of WA: Workaholics Anonymous.

More lucky in work than love.

My work does not betray me.

Reject me.

Leave me.

Cause me heartbreak and grief.

Die.

My work lifts me up.

Will never hurt me.

Or desert me.

I.AM.DAEDALUS.

D |
DANTE |
DAEDALUS |
HILDNER |

And I am Theseus, Daedalus's alter-ego, an ancient-medieval-modern Silver Knight—

JEF7REY HILDNER

ARCHITECTURE AND THE CHESS GAM OF FORM & STORY

[

ARCHITECTURE IS A SILVER COIN

somehow shielding and swording my way through the labyrinth to the light.

"I DRAW NO DISTINCTION BETWEEN THE CONSTRUCTION OF A BOOK AND THE CONSTRUCTION OF A PAINTING."
—HENRI MATISSE

Inscribed on one side,

while also soaring like Daedalus above the labyrinth to worlds beyond the horizon of this earthly plight.

& MEANING

"WE BRING TO OUR PROJECTS THE ARCHITECTURE OF OURSELVES."
—MIKHAIL BAKHTIN

I hope.

FORM

ARCHITECTURE IS THE STAGE SET FOR THE DRAMA OF LIFE.

"GREAT MUSICIANS ARE LIKE GREAT FIGHTERS. THEY HAVE A HIGHER SENSE OF THEORY GOING ON IN THEIR HEADS."
—MILES DAVIS

LIVE BRAVE.

"THE THING IS, DON'T BE AFRAID."
—Laura Middleton

Inscribed on the other side,

9. FORM & STORY

STORY

ARCHITECTURE IS A STORY TOLD THROUGH A BUILDING.

VISUAL EF9ECTS

VE9

STAR-CROSSED LOVE

In his book *How to Write Great Characters: The Key to Your Hero's Growth and Transformation*, David Wisehart shares his favorite definition of a story: "Someone wants something and has a hard time getting it."

I want something that I will likely have a hard time getting. Like Dido who lost Aeneas. Like Ariadne who lost Theseus. Like Karen Blixen who lost Denys Finch Hatten (*Out of Africa*). Like all star-crossed lovers—from Romeo and Juliette to *Casablanca*'s Rick and Ilsa. Like anyone who has lost someone they love, like anyone trekking as best they can through the labyrinth of grief, I want my truelove to come back.

But I can only get her back through art.

Fortunately, art is one of the ways to save someone from the fate worse than death.

MNEMONIC DEVICE

A fate worse than death? Really? What could be worse than death?

Well, first. Let's identify the god, according to ancient Greek mythology, that intervenes on our behalf to spare us that fate worse than death. The god that keeps us from falling into the abyss. The void. From being erased as if we never existed. The god that vanquishes the Minotaur waiting to devour us.

The ancient Greeks gave this special god the name Mnemosyne (ni-MA-zi-nee), which means "Memory." Memory is the great rock that withstands the relentless erosion of the most terrifying villain of all: Oblivion. If we forget those we love, they are doomed. And if people forget us, we too are doomed. As they observed and contemplated the architecture of reality, the ancient Greeks figured and feared that the greatest curse is to be forgotten. But they also calculated that the god of Memory equips human beings with the capacity to avoid being forgotten through the transforming and safeguarding power of art—the supernatural aid of art.

In the Greek cosmology, Memory had nine daughters: the Muses—the sisterhood of supernatural help that inspire in us the creative spirit of the arts . . . Memory's way of saying to the howling winds and violent waves of forgetfulness, "No. Go away. I am here to stay." Remember me.

The arts, daughters of Memory, muse in us resistance to amnesia, which comes from the Greek word *amnēsia* ("forgetfulness, not remembered"). The words *remember*, *memorial*, *memory*, and *Mnemosyne* spring from the word that's right there in the word *remind*: *mind*. The word *mnemonic* derives from Greek *mnēmōn* ("mindful"), which itself comes from the Greek word meaning to remember. Only with the aid of the Mnemonic Device of Mind—the Mindful Device of Memory—can we slay the Demonic Device of Oblivion.

For the ancient Greeks, to be forgotten is a fate worse than even the post-death nightmare that awaits some earthlings in the underworld. The Disney/Pixar movie *Coco* echoes this. There's only one real Hell: Memory Lost. In the Master Labyrinth, the light goes out forever if we are Remembered Ultimately Never.

THREAD & SWORD | ARIADNE RISING

Jefferson knew that oblivion awaits those who don't push back. We see clues of his awareness everywhere—for example, by the gravestone obelisk that stands today in the graveyard of Monticello almost 200 years after his death. By Monticello itself. By the establishment of UVA and construction of the Academical Village. By his letter to James Bowdoin III, thanking him for the sculpture of Ariadne reclining. Jefferson told Bowdoin, "It shall be deposited [at Monticello] with the memorials of those worthies whose remembrance I feel a pride and comfort in consecrating there."

In Greek mythology, Ariadne (ar-ee-AD-nee) was the daughter of King Minos of Crete, the site of Daedalus's Labyrinth. When she caught sight of Theseus, the future king of Athens who sailed from Greece to slay the Minotaur, Ariadne fell instantly in love. Fearing that even if he were to slay the Minotaur, Theseus might never find his way out of the labyrinth, Ariadne turned to Daedalus, the only one who knew the labyrinth's secret blueprint. He spun a spool of yarn and gave it to Ariadne, instructing her to tell Theseus to unspool the yarn as he wandered through the labyrinth. Daedalus's idea worked. Theseus found his way to the center of the labyrinth, slayed the Minotaur, then wound his way back through the labyrinth, following the thread to safety.

Ariadne not only gave Theseus the yarn that Daedalus spun to aid Theseus's labyrinth run. To slay the Minotaur, she also gave Theseus a sword. Picture Ariadne forever rising to offer brave souls the special gifts of thread & sword. Daedalus's thread and Ariadne's sword are metaphors for the hero's path and the hero's power. Sadly, thread & sword proved not enough to save Theseus and Ariadne from the agony of star-crossed love.

Thomas Jefferson Grave Marker. Photo courtesy littlery

Thomas Jefferson Foundation

Our Rock on Bihler Point, The Sea Ranch, CA

LIVE BRAVE
THE MIDDLETON MEMORIAL
N
11.29.17

Plan of the memorial at Masonic Lawn

The plan of The Middleton Memorial conceals the sacred "Chamber of Memory for the Muse and The Silver Knight."

< Ariadne reclined on the rocks of Naxos, where Theseus had just abandoned her because the gods crossed the lovers' stars—making Theseus fulfill his mission without his truelove.

CENTURIES BEFORE JEFFERSON'S ACADEMICAL VILLAGE, THE INCAS, IN THEIR 15TH-CENTURY MOUNTAINTOP CITADEL,
MADE THE LABYRINTH PERCEPTIBLE/LEGIBLE.

TOWER (MOUNTAIN)
MAZE (THE COMPLEX NETWORK OF BUILDINGS)
LAWN (THE CRANKY ECCENTRIC PRISTINE STEPPING ERODED-RECTANGULAR FIGURAL VOID:
THE MAIN ORGANIZING SPATIAL-DEVICE OF THE INCA KINGDOM)

MACHU PICCHU

DAEDALUS'S LABYRINTH

ARCHITECTURE IS THE STAGE SET FOR THE DRAMA OF LIFE AND DEATH.
ARCHITECTURE IS A STORY TOLD THROUGH A BUILDING.

38° NORTH LATITUDE (38°)

TRANSIT ROOM: LATITUDE 38° NORTH | THE LAWN OF THE INTERIOR

*We hoped
someday we
would build
our Dream
House.
Where
we would
stay young
together and
live for the
rest of our
lives.*

Photo by Laura Middleton

LABYRINTH : LAWN, MAZE, AND, TOWER (CAVE)

MACHU PICCHU

MAUSOLEUM

FORM & STORY

"SOMETIMES THE ONLY WAY TO HEAL OUR WOUNDS IS TO MAKE PEACE WITH THE DEMONS WHO CREATED THEM." —*GODZILLA: KING OF THE MONSTERS*

"THE ARTIST'S FUNCTION IS THE MYTHOLOGIZATION OF THE ENVIRONMENT AND THE WORLD." —JOSEPH CAMPBELL

THE DAEDALUS OF CHARLOTTESVILLE

"[Daedalus]," Campbell says in *The Hero with a Thousand Faces*, "is the hero of the way of thought—singlehearted, courageous, and full of faith that the truth, as he knows it, shall set us free."

"And so now we may turn to him as did Ariadne. The flax for the linen of his thread he has gathered from the fields of the human imagination. Centuries of husbandry, decades of diligent culling, the work of numerous hearts and hands, have gone into the hackling, sorting, and spinning of this tightly twisted yarn."

Campbell paints a portrait of Daedalus as an idealistic crusader, a storyteller—a spinner of yarns—who sprung from the imagination of ancient Greek story architects.

Campbell adds, "Furthermore, we have not even to risk the adventure alone: for the heroes of all time have gone before us; the labyrinth is thoroughly known; we have only to follow the thread of the hero-path."

Remember those 13 words, Virgil's labyrinth anthem—his prophecy— in *The Aeneid*? "Your path to safety will open first from where you least expect it"? Guess what the end of that sentence says. Here's the whole sentence: "Your road to safety will open first from where you least expect it—a city built by Greeks!"

For Aeneas, indeed, the path to safety opened in a way he could never imagine: from the same Greek culture who sponsored the Odysseus-led army that sacked and burned Aeneas's hometown to the ground—namely, from his enemies.

I least expected that the opportunity to create my first building since the completion of Dante|Telescope House over 20 years ago would be a tomb. I didn't expect that the path to the next stage of my creative journey would open first from the enemy that invaded my universe: death.

Our never-ending labyrinth runs change us, and we either get more fully lined up with our given name. Or our run-in with truth shakes us so deeply that we undergo irreversible change—and we change our name. In which case: To our ordinary lives, we choose to R.U.N.—Return Under (a new) Name. Charles-Édouard Jeanneret-Gris became Le Corbusier. Karen Blixen became Isak Dinesen. Cassius Clay became Muhammad Ali. Reginald Dwight became Elton John. Walter White became Heisenberg. Carol Danvers became Captain Marvel.

Thomas Jefferson didn't change his name, but the flawed hero, The Daedalus of Charlottesville, made the Labyrinth legible: Tower, Maze, and Lawn. Which changed me so much that I changed his name for him. Marvel Comic Superhero: LABYRINTH M.A.N.

TOWER AND WINGS

King Minos punished Daedalus for helping Ariadne and Theseus slay the Minotaur. The King locked up Daedalus and his son, Icarus, in a prison that Minos forced Daedalus to design and build. Foresighted Daedalus built a tower.

The tower rose from the heart of the labyrinth. And in that tower, Daedalus invented the device for their escape: wings.

But Icarus ignored his father's warning and flew too close to the sun. Icarus's wax wings melted. He fell to his death in the sea. Daedalus was heartbroken, but he didn't give up. On wings of defeat, he flew to the island of Sicily—38° North Latitude. Where he created major works of architecture.

Then where did Daedalus go? To what new lands beyond the horizon did he fly? Egypt? Maybe. Did he ever return to Athens? *Where he once ruled as king?* Until chaos invaded his universe . . .

We don't know. What King Daedalus did along the storyline of his later years in life—well, the ancient weavers of Greek myth leave that to our imagination. But we do know that Daedalus dodged a fate worse than death.

Because we remember him.

And not only for his work. We remember the architect of the Labyrinth and wings because he threaded through the labyrinth of the human condition on wings of resilience and boundless brave creativity. Every misstep of the way, summoning his inner Theseus—seizing Ariadne's sword and slaying Minotaurs of Adversity. Inspiring us to feel maybe we can slay likewise. Maybe if we heed Virgil's advice and "never bow to suffering, go and face it, all the bolder, wherever Fortune clears the way"— maybe like Daedalus, we too can Rise Undaunted Now.

By the architecture of our art and life, in the service of others, maybe we too can meet the same enduring fate.

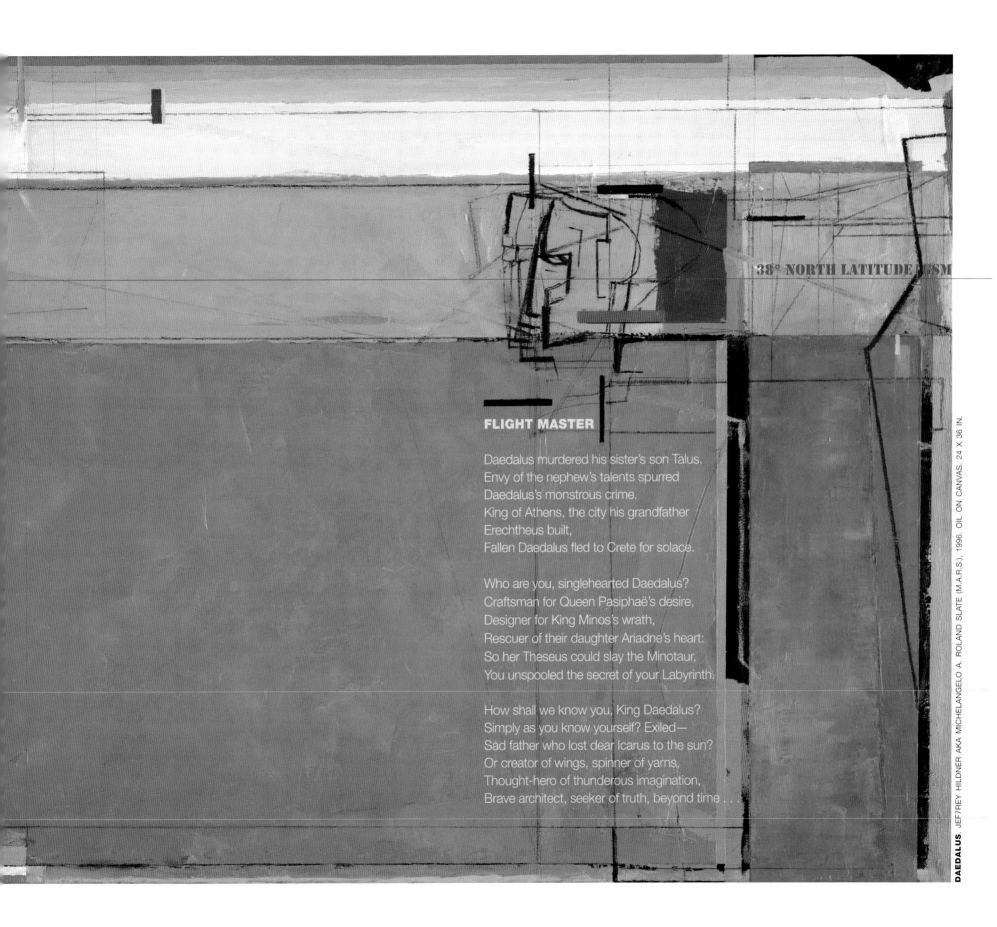

FLIGHT MASTER

Daedalus murdered his sister's son Talus.
Envy of the nephew's talents spurred
Daedalus's monstrous crime.
King of Athens, the city his grandfather
Erechtheus built,
Fallen Daedalus fled to Crete for solace.

Who are you, singlehearted Daedalus?
Craftsman for Queen Pasiphaë's desire,
Designer for King Minos's wrath,
Rescuer of their daughter Ariadne's heart:
So her Theseus could slay the Minotaur,
You unspooled the secret of your Labyrinth.

How shall we know you, King Daedalus?
Simply as you know yourself? Exiled—
Sad father who lost dear Icarus to the sun?
Or creator of wings, spinner of yarns,
Thought-hero of thunderous imagination,
Brave architect, seeker of truth, beyond time . . .

DAEDALUS. JEFFREY HILDNER AKA MICHELANGELO A. ROLAND SLATE (M.A.R.S.), 1996. OIL ON CANVAS. 24 X 36 IN.

"Never bow to suffering, go and face it, all the bolder, wherever Fortune clears the way. Your road to safety will open first from where you least expect it—a city built by Greeks!"
—Virgil, *The Aeneid*

RETURN OF THE KENAN 12

The classic pattern of the Hero's Journey requires that the hero return home and tell the story of their adventures. To share what they learned. How they changed. How following the hero-path of the yellow brick road, lined with danger and inner and outer resistance, awakened in the hero enhanced capacities: brains, guts, and heart. Only then, by way of the hero's Return, does the tale come full circle. Members of the hero's home tribe—having experienced vicariously, psychologically, through the power of storytelling, the epic cycle of Departure, Transformation, and Return—these members return to their lives re-membered, redesigned . . . the yarn inspiring them to move forward with renewed wisdom, courage, and character . . . along their own damned-fool idealistic labyrinth run.

Architect-Storyteller Peter Waldman, for the flax of the linen of his thread, has gathered from the fields of the human imagination the lessons of 12 Kenan Fellows, remembering them for us, returning with them through this book to his home-tribe, regaling us with tales of this band of explorers and tales of the hard-won insights that have shaped his own brave journey.

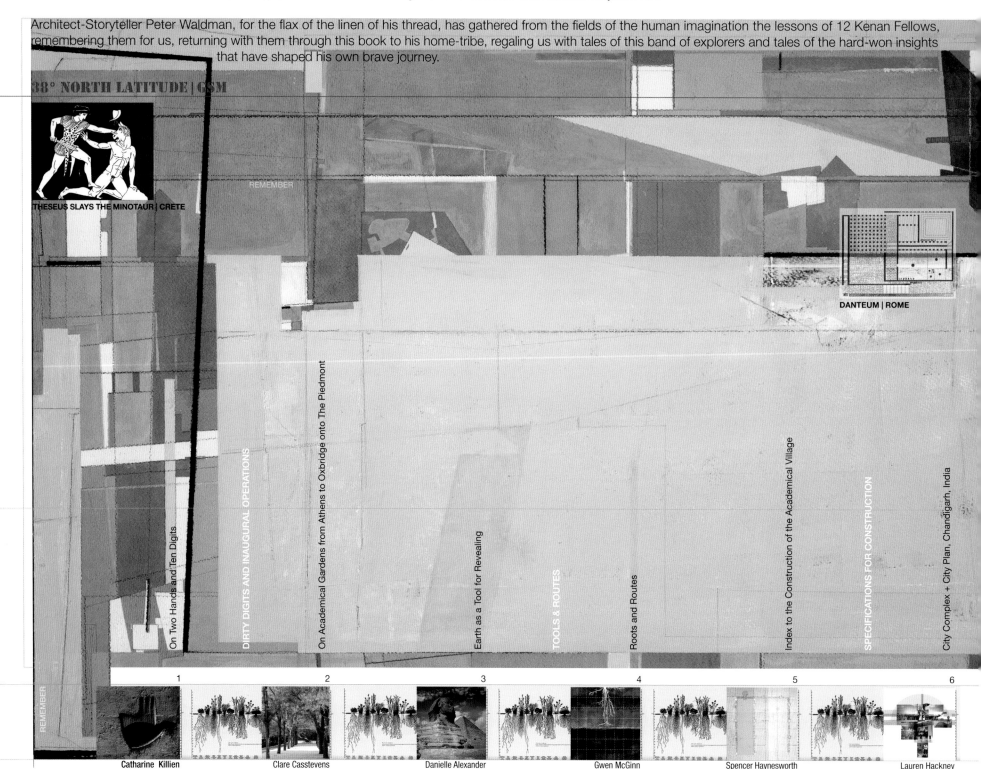

38° NORTH LATITUDE | GSM

REMEMBER

THESEUS SLAYS THE MINOTAUR | CRETE

DANTEUM | ROME

On Two Hands and Ten Digits

DIRTY DIGITS AND INAUGURAL OPERATIONS

On Academical Gardens from Athens to Oxbridge onto The Piedmont

Earth as a Tool for Revealing

TOOLS & ROUTES

Roots and Routes

Index to the Construction of the Academical Village

SPECIFICATIONS FOR CONSTRUCTION

City Complex + City Plan, Chandigarh, India

REMEMBER

1	2	3	4	5	6
Catharine Killien	Clare Casstevens	Danielle Alexander	Gwen McGinn	Spencer Haynesworth	Lauren Hackney

RE-MEMBER THE WORLD

The art of architecture plays a unique role. Architecture is Memory—the god, Mnemosyne: Mother of the Muses, Mother of the Arts, the connective influence that threads through time, heralding us to remember the world. *Re-member the world*. Reorganize it. Rediscover, reenvision, and rebuild it. And every time architects do, they present anew, to one degree or another, the archetypal stage set for the drama of life and death: Daedalus's Labyrinth. Through unending expressions of Forms & Stories, Moves & Meanings—Spaces & Symbols—the Labyrinth springs to life, continually reminding us, "The path through life runs like this. But we can slay the Minotaur. We can keep Oblivion at bay." Imagine future buildings that reverberate with this truth.

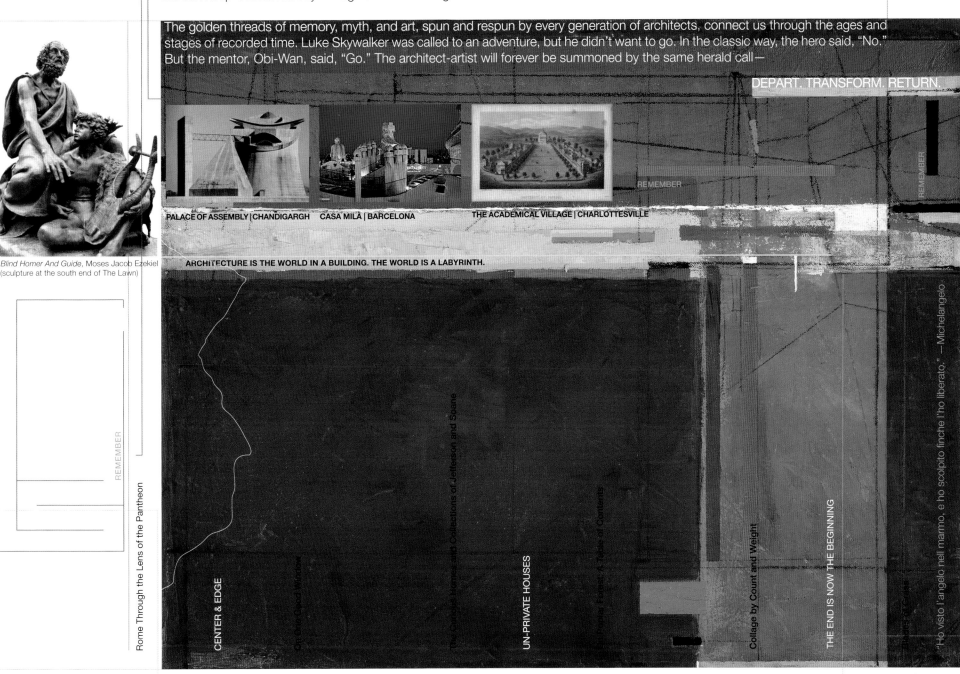

The golden threads of memory, myth, and art, spun and respun by every generation of architects, connect us through the ages and stages of recorded time. Luke Skywalker was called to an adventure, but he didn't want to go. In the classic way, the hero said, "No." But the mentor, Obi-Wan, said, "Go." The architect-artist will forever be summoned by the same herald call—

DEPART. TRANSFORM. RETURN.

REMEMBER

REMEMBER

PALACE OF ASSEMBLY | CHANDIGARGH   CASA MILÀ | BARCELONA   THE ACADEMICAL VILLAGE | CHARLOTTESVILLE

ARCHITECTURE IS THE WORLD IN A BUILDING. THE WORLD IS A LABYRINTH.

Blind Homer And Guide, Moses Jacob Ezekiel
(sculpture at the south end of The Lawn)

REMEMBER

Rome Through the Lens of the Pantheon

CENTER & EDGE

UN-PRIVATE HOUSES

Collage by Count and Weight

THE END IS NOW THE BEGINNING

"Ho visto l'angelo nel marmo, e ho scolpito finché l'ho liberato." —Michelangelo

7   8   9   10   11   12

Jim Richardson

Maria Bninski

Danielle Willkens

Paul Golisz

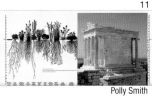
Polly Smith

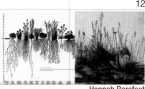
Hannah Barefoot

ACKNOWLEDGMENTS

ON COLLABORATION - A TWO-PART PROJECT

First, Kenan Research,
Then the Design of this book of Spatial Transformations of the Lawn as Labyrinth

This book was at first conceived to give voice to Kenan Fellows, my most recent graduate students who prepared lectures for our foundation course Architecture 1010: Lessons of the Lawn from 2001-2016 at the University of Virginia. These resultant essays, now curated as dialogues, were prepared as stand-alone contributions to an evolving curriculum from distinct years and were never intended to be juxtaposed or sequential. As in the exercise of The Exquisite Corpse, an exercise in unpredictability and the immediate consequences of circumstantial invention, I have selected to link distinct lectures, now essays to yield connective tissues between intentionally juxtaposed spatial components. New insights were revealed to instill an appetite for interpretation.

We commenced with the prefacing intimate scale of Two Hands and Ten Digits and then situated ourselves in the trans-chronological primacy of Academical Gardens commenced pretentiously in Eden, certifiably in Plato's Sacred Grove, reconstructed in medieval Padova and Oxbridge. Five more pairings of essays, we now call chapters, later we end in the art of collage, or back to fingerprints in the act of making, now juxtaposed as an odyssey through Whitman's *Leaves of Grass*, with the final admonition to Make Death Legible. Each inaugural pairing then required me to write scripts and to collage connective tissues, spaces of systems within systems, narratives within the narratives derived from each juxtaposed essay.

However, in the Spring of 2019 on our journey to Sea Ranch as the last oasis at the edge of the world, the idea of the book expanded with my invitation to Jef7rey Hildner, one of my first students at Princeton four decades ago, to write the Epilogue: Labyrinth R.U.N. The space of the book then came full circle from recent students in dialogue with an ancient professor, to include now this well-seasoned student collaborating with if not interrogating his once adolescent and ever-curious thesis advisor. His epilogue initial draft, responding then to Barefoot's mantra: "Make Death Visible", suggested an alternative spatial dimension to the heretofore didactically juxtaposed collages. We now focused on the role of the center-fold of the book, its spine, not as a hidden seam but the marrow of inquisitive labyrinthine space akin to De Chirico's "Enigma of the Oracle." The didactic collage vellum plates were extended beyond the juxtaposed pairs to investigate the spatial extensions of Jefferson's plan as Borges' "Garden of Forking Paths," now as two-page spreads reinforcing the over-riding theme of The Word Made Flesh. Hildner's work on the Epilogue spurred me initially, and recently InDesign collaborators subsequently to transform the juxtaposed pages of these vellum collages now into spatial labyrinths contained herein as a result of this collaboration. Herein, the design of this book now as labyrinth is another reconsideration coming out of collaboration of the contemporary relevance of the Academical Village which is the on-going agenda of the Kenan Foundation research agenda for the University of Virginia.

This recent example of a collaboration between students and teacher I realize now has always been the consistent posture I place in work as life, in explorations never alone, but inspired by Rebecca Solnit, a perfect stranger in *A Field Guide for Getting Lost*. Jef7rey Hildner reminded me last spring that coincidentally we dwell across this nation on 38 N Latitude. I dwell simultaneously on the 38th degree Latitude North on both the West Coast in Mill Valley, a short journey across the Golden Gate Bridge from Solnit's' locus of sojourns in San Francisco, and while heading East one coincides with Hildner's cinematic world in Sacramento, to confirm covenants with mythic ground rules. Continuing on, I journey on; it seems to pause frequently in a long-term encampment in North Garden. Virginia down the road from the Jefferson projects, and then propelled in mind and memory if not self-guided, I find myself extrapolated with good luck onto the 38th Latitude in Athens, Greece also by coincidence in the vicinity of the coordinates of Daedalus' labyrinth. I have recently discovered *Traveling the 38th Parallel*, a book extending to a unique line of cultural fecundity around the globe all too recently revealed in footsteps across the DMZ spatial zone of pause dividing the Korean peninsula. There is the trace of the 38th degree latitude presented on the title page and then intermittently inscribed in this book serving as a reminder of the role of topological and archeological imaginations requisite for epistemology, some call the foundation of education. Be warned, this fascination of new coordinates never ends, as 38 degrees South Latitude nurtures Borges' capacity for magical realism as now another necessary anchor to these myopic northern hemispheric oases.

Obviously, all my Kenan Fellows have been essential collaborators across generations, for decades while only 12 appear herein this initial proposition. Other immediate collaborators in the past two years, and certainly in the past two months have been other graduate students. Recently, Michael Peterson whose magic eyes, serving as camera lens attached to his essential drone made possible first the diurnal front and nocturnal back cover collages. This initial offering then yielded the first passes on the didactic collages, expanded conceptually as a template of the Jefferson plan by Hildner, then more recently advanced substantially with delicacy and intelligent wit as Lawn/Labyrinth Vellums by Andres Soria as he prepared the comprehensive digital files, fonts, and links. Andres is the most essential link as Yunni Dan had been to LESSONS. Michael Peterson returned to this final team effort to remap the world as he first introduced me to "Traveling the 38th Parallel: A Water line Around the World" by the collaborative forest rangers and cultural historians, David, and Janet Carle. Peterson then critically and pragmatically set out to quarry our vast archive of Kenan Research image files for the highest quality of dpi resolution. I am grateful to them all for this recent advancement on the design of this project of spatial simultaneities, by which James Joyce, William Saroyan, and Peter Carl might be amused.

Over the three-year span of LESSONS and then CONNECTIVE TISSUES, David Turnbull has been consistently and constructively essential to this book project from his world-wise perspectives, his amazing observations of the power of myth across cultures and generations, and whose prefacing remarks herein I value tremendously. The five contributors to this book have been essential witnesses as colleagues to my life and work for which I am profoundly grateful: first, Robin Dripps, Fitzgibbons Professor of Architecture, whom I have admired since our Princeton days in 1961, onto William Sherman, Lewis Professor of Architecture, one of my earliest Princeton students, and even then professional collaborator, and gratefully forever-colleague at Rice and now Virginia; onto Shiqiao Li, Weedon Professor of Architectural History and Architecture, a recent colleague from another world, whom I value tremendously as demonstrably grounded through history in mind and spirit, and Michael Lee, Reuben Rainey Professor of Landscape Architecture, my most youthful colleague and now collaborator, closest perhaps as he is my academic neighbor who is attractive to me as one encounters the wisdom of strangers, though we both share a common admiration of the enduring cultures sun-burnt into the extensive horizons of Texas.

Finally, in terms of duration and curatorship, I acknowledge in tremendous gratitude two fine Sons of the South, Matson Roberts and Todd Stovall, students who have suffered six-year tenures with me, who have labored with me, unthwarted by my evolving intentions, and for the past intense two years as my prime research and teaching assistants working on the course, Arch 1010 as well as this book CONNECTIVE TISSUES. We have immense files for this effort, assembled from 2001-2016 which they gathered fragments of texts and lecture images, a labyrinth of sorts, making it possible to frame the potential of this focused research. I have been fortunate to take joy in the fecundity of frictions and alignments with all these collaborators. Obviously, all my Kenan Fellows and these recent explorers with telescopes and microscopes have been essential collaborators across generations.

In the end, Jake Anderson as my patient editor of LESSONS and now managing editor of CONNECTIONS recently with Alejandro Guzman-Avila's most comprehensive editing, together with the consistent faith of Gordon Goff, have provided the realization of these book projects.

My last words are In gratitude to the first words of this effort, in gratitude to yet another pivotal student, Alex DeMott for introducing me to the contemporary Polish poets herein as his advisor for his thesis project for Krakow. The introductory poems: "The End and the Beginning" gives me hope to continue these journeys onto terra incognita, "And Yet The Books", to interrogate the space between Genesis and Exodus, all five responsive texts, and finally, "Water", sweet and salty of 38 degree North Latitude nourishing the latest collaborators of Carle and Carle, both forest rangers and cultural historians, prolonging the sunset.

Bruegel, *Harversters*

Bruegel, *The Fall of Icarus*

CONTRIBUTOR BIOGRAPHIES

INTRODUCTION

David Turnbull

David Turnbull is a Director of ATOPIA Innovation, and Design Director of ATOPIA Research / PITCHAfrica, an award winning 501(c)3 tax exempt organization registered in New Jersey, USA, with a specific focus on the development and construction of building types that address global ecological and social challenges. He is also a Professor of Architecture with 30 years of experience in Design Education Internationally. His academic career started in 1989 at The Architectural Association in London while he was working in the office of James Stirling, Michael Wilford and Associates, leading major projects in Spain, Japan and Singapore. His academic appointments since 1990 include the Eero Saarinen Visiting Professorship in Architecture at Yale University, and Visiting Professorships at the University of Toronto, Canada (sponsored by CITY-TV), Columbia University's GSAPP in New York and Cornell University. He was Professor of Architecture at the University of Bath in the UK from 2000-2005 and from 2012 -13, Visiting Professor of Design & Innovation at The African University of Science & Technology, a Nelson Mandela Institution, in Abuja, Nigeria. He was a Professor of Architecture at The Cooper Union in New York from 2006 to 2017. He is a Senior Research Fellow in the Cluster for Sustainable Cities, in the Faculty of Creative and Cultural Industries at the University of Portsmouth, a member of the Advisory Board for the 'Padiglione Italia - Biennale Di Venezia 2020' and a Visiting Expert at ARUP, working on resilience.

GROUND RULES

Catharine Killien

Catharine Killien is an architect at The Miller Hull Partnership in Seattle, Washington, an award-winning architecture and planning firm that creates dynamic and environmentally-responsible buildings for public and private clients across multiple typologies and scales. She has primarily focused on developing spaces that support diverse learning environments for higher education clients, including recently completed projects at the University of Washington and the University of Arizona.

Catharine received a Bachelor of Arts in Architecture from the University of Washington in 2010, followed by a Master of Architecture from the University of Virginia in 2013. In 2011, she was the AIA Committee on the Environment Research Fellow and published research on strategies for deep green renovations of existing buildings. Catharine earned the Kenan Fellowship in 2012 and 2013 as a graduate student. Closely tied to her work as a Kenan Fellow, her master's thesis examined material and tectonic strategies for the adaptations of buildings over time.

A native to the Pacific Northwest, Catharine spends her free time rock climbing and mountaineering. She is an instructor and climb leader with The Mountaineers and after summiting the highest peaks in Washington state, has now set her sights on high-altitude expeditions in Alaska and Canada.

Claire Casstevens

Claire Casstevens is a landscape designer at OLIN. She graduated with her Master of Landscape Architecture from the University of Virginia and received her Bachelor of Arts from Vassar College, where she studied Art History and Anthropology. Her undergraduate thesis on early 19th-century imagery of Oxford and Cambridge universities initiated the broader inquiry into landscapes and education that underpins her lecture in this book.

Whether working on farms, mapping the trees of Monticello, or assisting with the Los Angeles River Master Plan, Claire is invested in strengthening personal and collective relationships to land. A recipient of the Benjamin C. Howland Traveling Fellowship in 2017, she worked in partnership with four colleagues to conduct fieldwork along the Dakota Access Pipeline. The group drew upon situated knowledge—site reading and conversations with oil rig workers, water protectors, and farmers—to create an exhibit of large, synthetic drawings expressing the pipeline's physical and cultural implications across the American heartland. Claire currently lives in Philadelphia, PA, where she casually experiments with soils and microclimates in her backyard garden of potted plants.

CHAPTER 1

Dani Alexander

Dani Alexander is a passionate designer working to transform the public realm to be more equitable, resilient, and compelling. She is Founding Principal of Studio AKA, a landscape architecture and urban design practice based in Washington, DC, which focuses on design solutions that are ecologically sensitive and foster connections between people and place. Through volunteering, teaching, and writing, she is committed to communicating the impacts of design, climate change, and resilience efforts on people's lives and their relationship with their environment. Recently, she was the Urban Wild Writer in Residence for Freshkills Park, and her essay on the former landfill's transformation appeared in Urban Omnibus, a publication of The Architectural League of New York. She is currently at work as an editor with Craig Verzone and Cristina Woods on Food Urbanism, which examines how urban agriculture can have measurable impacts on urban quality.

Before founding her firm, Dani worked at Reed Hilderbrand Landscape Architects, Verzone Woods Architects, and Michael Van Valkenburgh Associates. She additionally served as adjunct faculty at the Boston Architectural College, teaching in the Architecture and Practice Departments, and continually serves on juries at many design programs. Dani earned her Bachelor of Arts in East Asian Studies and Visual and Environmental Studies at Harvard University and her Master of Landscape Architecture from the University of Virginia. She lives in Capitol Hill with her husband, Nick Knodt, and their dog and cat.

Gwendolyn Dora McGinn

Gwendolyn Dora McGinn is an Associate at Studio Outside Landscape Architecture in Dallas, Texas. She graduated from the University of Virginia with a Master Degree in Landscape Architecture and holds a Bachelor of Fine Arts from the Rhode Island School of Design. Recently she co-taught The Prairie's Yield, a graduate studio at the University of Texas Arlington, and served as an Artist-in-Residence at the University of Oregon's Overlook Field School.

Her work often considers scientific theory and thoughtful moments of joyful whimsy. She is fascinated by novel ecologies in urban spaces, and strives to always bring an interest in the vernacular to her design work. She is an explorer of places hidden in plain sight, and of places just out of sight. As a graduate student, her design thesis described tree roots as entities that transform and create the spaces that surround them. By synthesizing research from the fields of botany, horticulture, forestry, and arboriculture, she considered ways the morphology of root systems can become a tool for landscape architects to design from the ground to the canopy.

CHAPTER 2

Spencer Haynsworth Woodcock

Spencer Haynsworth Woodcock is the Director of Marketing and Business Development at Chiang | O'Brien Architects, a woman- and minority-owned firm in Ithaca, NY. Before her work at Chiang | O'Brien, Spencer was the Director of the Ithaca Sustainability Center, a community-based non-profit organization established to promote sustainability efforts across Tompkins County. In her free time, Spencer works for Cornell Cooperative Extension's Master Gardener program to expand garden-based educational outreach throughout the community. She is also the mother of two active and inquisitive boys.

Spencer is a member of the fifth class of the Enterprise Rose Fellowship. After completing her fellowship work in 2008 with the Housing Trust in Santa Fe, NM, she continued to manage the organization's Housing Development Program, including the design and construction of a 60-unit multifamily development for people transitioning out of homelessness and a rehab/acquisition project that converted a Route 66 motor inn into multifamily rental for low-income families. Prior to, Spencer worked at the GreenBlue Institute in Charlottesville, VA to develop a green building database for affordable housing developers and at the Charlottesville Community Design Center to co-develop an influential and acclaimed international design competition with Habitat for Humanity. Spencer holds a bachelor of arts degree in classical literature and the history of math and science from St. John's College in Annapolis, MD and a master of architecture and landscape architecture from the University of Virginia. She was a Pelliccia and Kennan Fellow in 2005 and 2006 respectively.

Lauren Hackney

Lauren Hackney is a landscape architect whose design work focuses on urban and cultural landscapes and their dynamic issues of place: community, culture, temporality, and ecology. She is a Senior Associate at CMG Landscape Architecture in San Francisco, and previously was a designer at PWP Landscape Architecture in Berkeley and William Rawn Associates in Boston. At CMG, she leads large-scale planning and design projects, including the Civic Center Public Realm Plan in San Francisco, the Headlands Center for the Arts in Sausalito, the Sunnylands Administration Campus in Rancho Mirage, and the Irishtown Bend Vision Plan in Cleveland. At PWP, she worked on the Glenstone Museum in Potomac, MD and the winning competition entry for Constitution Gardens on the National Mall, and led the firm's internship program.

Lauren received a Bachelor of Science in Architecture, a Master of Landscape Architecture, and a Master of Architecture from the University of Virginia, where she was awarded the Carlo Pelliccia Drawing Fellowship, the Kenan Teaching Fellowship, the Lori Ann Pristo Award, and was selected as a National Olmsted Scholar Finalist. Her graduate thesis, which explored the ecological systems and material exchanges of the Kanawha River Valley in West Virginia, received an honor award in the 2011 AIA-DC Unbuilt Competition.

CONTRIBUTOR BIOGRAPHIES

CHAPTER 3

Jim Richardson

Perceptive. Opportunistic. Inspired. Jim Richardson is a licensed architect and Senior Associate at VMDO Architects, where he enjoys working on a diverse set of projects that are carefully made and valued in the communities where he works. We all experience architecture every day. Fundamental to architecture's mission is a core understanding that where we are influences who we are in ways both small and profound. Jim believes that it is possible to bring together form, material, and use into a coherent architecture that offers not just a place to be, but a way to be. He brings insight to each project in depth and breadth alike, striving for continuity of strong conceptual thinking with an ethic of craftsmanship. Jim searches for architecture of impactful allegiance with its place that fits seamlessly and performs brilliantly, allowing it to last and be loved. His designs are rooted in how he works: motivated by a deep creative urge and a type of modest confidence, he listens actively, engages thoughtfully, and advances collaboration through a shared sense of purpose that resonates throughout the resulting architecture.

The growing body of work that Jim leads has been awarded for architectural excellence at the local, state, and national levels. Parallel to his practice, he strives to maintain an active academic career. He has taught architectural design at the University of Virginia School of Architecture in 2007, 2008, 2011, and most recently in 2016. Jim earned a Master in Architecture in 2007 and a Bachelor of Science in Architecture in 2002 from the University of Virginia, where he was awarded the Lori Ann Pristo Award, the AIA Henry Adams Medal, and the UVA Faculty Award for Design Excellence. He is a William R. Kenan Fellow for teaching and research, and a Carlo Pelliccia Fellow for travel and graphic representation. In 2010 Jim was named as an Emerging Leader in Architecture by the Virginia Society American Institute of Architects. He lives in Charlottesville, Virginia, with his loving wife, two energetic children, and elderly dog. Jim looks forward to a professional sabbatical next summer in Portugal to research creativity in architectural practice, to surf, and ultimately, to make better architecture.

Maria Bninski

Maria L. Bninski is a practicing architect specializing in the design of learning environments. She continues to be inspired by Peter Waldman's call to imagine acts of construction that leave behind a place for citizens and strangers to meet between ground and sky. She seeks to realize environments for emerging citizens that communicate the richness of the world Here and Beyond, speaking at the scale of the planet, the watershed, the fingertip, the synapse.

Maria graduated from the University of Virginia's M.Arch program in 2010, receiving the AIA Henry Adams Certificate of Merit. She completed her B.A. with Distinction also at UVa, receiving degrees in Italian Studies and Religious Studies and earning the 2006 Kyle Award for Excellence in Religious Studies. Before arriving at Thomas Jefferson's Academical Village she lived the nomadic life of a military child, learning the meaning of "school" in landscapes from post-industrial New Jersey to a Sicilian orange grove in the shadow of a volcano. She is the recipient of UVa's Pellica Travelling Fellowship, the Kohn Pedersen Fox Travelling Fellowship, and most recently the VMDO Travel Fellowship. She is an associate at VMDO Architects and lives in Charlottesville, Virginia with her husband and three young daughters.

CHAPTER 4

Danielle S. Willkens

Dr Danielle S. Willkens, PhD, is an Assistant Professor at the School of Architecture at Georgia Institute of Technology. Prior to joining the faculty at Georgia Tech, she was an Assistant Professor of Architecture at Auburn University and received a 2017-2018 Association of Collegiate Schools of Architecture, AIAS New Faculty Teaching Award for her service. She was the 2015 recipient of the Society of Architectural Historians' H. Allen Brooks Travelling Fellowship and from June 2016 to May 2017, she traveled to Iceland, the Faroe Island, Cuba, and Japan to the study the impact of mass tourism on cultural heritage sites. She holds a BS in Architecture and a Master of Architecture from the University of Virginia, a M.Phil in Architectural History & Theory with a concentration in Italian Renaissance Art and Architecture from Cambridge University, a Graduate Certificate in Historic Preservation from the Savannah College of Art and Design, and a PhD in Architectural History & Theory from the Bartlett School of Architecture, University College London. Following her M.Arch, Willkens was the Project Manager for the Learning Barge, the University of Virginia's innovative design/build project for a floating classroom and sustainable field station on the Elizabeth River. Building on time as a historical interpreter at Monticello, a Sir John Soane Museum Travelling Fellow, and her PhD research, her manuscript is in development with the University of Virginia Press: The Transatlantic Design Network: Jefferson, Soane, and agents of architectural exchange, 1768-1838. Her research has been supported by the International Center for Jefferson Studies, the Society of Architectural Historians of Great Britain, and an American Philosophical Society Franklin Research Grant.

Paul Golisz

Depending on which direction the breeze blows across the East River, Paul Golisz is pleasantly greeted with the smell of Greek food grilling on the corner truck when he opens the windows in his New York City apartment. If he is lucky, the humid air of summer will cling to him like a blanket as he walks to the subway, transporting him to the Piedmont where he studied architecture at the University of Virginia. The stacks of Alderman, his first true experience of the Library of Babel, and The Lawn, where form was made manifest from the merits of the known and the unknown, become palpable in his memory. While listening to the radio at work, specific songs will take him back to the brick sidewalks of Benefit Street, to the dust filled wood shop overlooking the Providence River, where he received an education from Rhode Island School of Design. Lessons that taught of combining intuitive interpretation with a profound knowledge of a discipline and exercises that instilled a responsibility for every inch of a composition, all while being covered in charcoal and sawdust, can be precisely recalled. It has been said that you can happen upon a sentence, a phrase, a lyric, that touches you so deeply that you have no choice but to believe it was penned for you. This is possible with place too, that your individual experience of a place is so profound that you carry it with you for a lifetime. Place does matter. Paul Golisz does not live far from the park where he first questioned if there is a difference between architecture and nature. It was a burning question he could not shake. And speculations on this question can be excavated from Poplar Forest. Paul Golisz sees equivalence when he studies the octagon constructed in a forest clearing. He sees symmetry, set up in a way that suggests all things are more similar than different. It is a project that employed natural and artificial means alike to establish order and logic. And most importantly, the methods of composition were used to reaffirm the notion that the rather primitive act of gathering at a table, with friends and strangers, to share a meal under the stars, is uniquely important.

CHAPTER 5

Polly Smith Finn

Polly Smith Finn pursues an interest in the intermingling of art and architecture. She holds a Bachelor's of Art in Art History and Studio Art from Washington and Lee University, where she presented a painting thesis of layered elements and scales to depict a sense of place. Working as a Development Associate at the National Gallery of Art, she was influenced by the seminal artists of minimalism and space-making. Polly received a Master's of Architecture from the University of Virginia. Drawings done in Rome as a Carlo Pelliccia Fellow while at UVa sparked an interest in adaptive reuse as means to create meaning through architectural collage. She continues to combine architectural and natural elements to create meaning of place in two dimensional media.

Polly is a Project Manager at Pursley Dixon Architecture in Charlotte, North Carolina. She leads residential projects focused on elemental materiality, structural expression, and environmental connectivity. Polly lives with her husband, daughter, and dogs in Greensboro, North Carolina.

Hannah Barefoot

Hannah Barefoot received a Bachelor of Arts from UVA in English and Studio Art with a concentration in printmaking she spent a year as an Anspaugh Fellow at UVA. Hannah was drawn to landscape architecture when she realized the field could encompass her study of craft in sculpture and printmaking and her obsession with plants and ecosystems. She pursued her Masters in Landscape Architecture at UVA. Her landscape architecture thesis work was on flowers, decay and landscape management.

Hannah is particularly interested in how the design, stewardship and cultivation of landscapes can manifest cultural and social values. With specific interests in site analysis, research, and plants, Hannah enjoys working on projects at Surface 678 in Durham, NC as a project manager and designer with an emphasis on creating intimate spaces at a human scale. A native North Carolinian, Hannah particularly enjoys being a part of designing landscapes in the Southeast and working with her knowledge of the ecosystems and vernacular aesthetics

EPILOGUE

Jef7ery Hildner

ARCHITECT, PAINTER, AND WRITER JEF7REY HILDNER launched The Architect Painter Press in 2005 under the banner, "Live Brave." The Architect Painter Press presents Hildner's buildings, paintings, and insights—work that reflects his focus on the visible and invisible architecture of art and life. The Architect Painter Press also seeks to present the work of other artists. Current titles range from Hildner's books Visual Ef9ects, Daedalus 9, Henry Trucks — Painter, Picasso Lessons, and Garches 1234 to his books Metaphysical Warrior and Live Brave. His work also appears in a wide array of other venues—for example, Architectural Record, Journal of Architectural Education, ANY, Oz, The Christian Science Monitor, IMDb, and Global Architecture Houses. The book Architectural Formalism, by Hakan Anay, features Hildner's essay "Formalism: Move|Meaning" alongside essays by theorists Rosalind Krauss, Peggy Deamer, Robert Slutzky, and Colin Rowe.

Hildner's project Dante|Telescope House won the New Jersey Chapter of The American Institute of Architects "Blue Ribbon Award for Excellence in Design." He also received an Association of Collegiate Schools of Architecture award for excellence in teaching. He paints under the name Henry Trucks. He writes under the names Madison Gray, Eliot Plum, and Michelangelo A. Roland Slate. Hildner's one-word life theme—architecture—shapes his quest, his outlook, and his output, including his work as screenwriter and story architect. He earned his undergraduate and graduate degrees from Princeton University.